US, THEM, AND C

MW01104976

Pluralism and National ideniuy iii Divei.. ....

How do countries come to view themselves as being 'multicultural'? *Us, Them, and Others* presents a dynamic new model for understanding pluralism based on the triangular relationship between three groups – the national majority, historically recognized minorities, and diverse immigrant bodies. Elke Winter's research illustrates how compromise between unequal groups takes on meaning through confrontation with real or imagined outsiders.

Us, Them, and Others sheds new light on the resilience of Canadian multiculturalism in the late 1990s, when multicultural policies in other countries had already come under heavy attack. Winter draws on analyses of English-language newspaper discourses and a sociological framework to connect discourses of pan-Canadian multicultural identity to representations of Québécois nationalism, immigrant groups, First Nations, and the United States. Taking inspiration from the Canadian experience, *Us, Them, and Others* is a timely examination of national identity and pluralist group formation in diverse societies.

ELKE WINTER is an associate professor in the Department of Sociology and Anthropology at the University of Ottawa.

ELKE WINTER

Us, Them, and Others

Pluralism and National Identity in Diverse Societies

UNIVERSITY OF TORONTO PRESS
Toronto Buffalo London

© University of Toronto Press Incorporated 2011
Toronto Buffalo London
www.utppublishing.com
Printed in Canada

ISBN 978-0-8020-9692-0 (cloth)
ISBN 978-0-8020-9639-5 (paper)

Printed on acid-free, 100% post-consumer recycled paper with
vegetable-based inks.

Library and Archives Canada Cataloguing in Publication

Winter, Elke, 1971–
Us, them, and others : pluralism and national identities in diverse societies /
Elke Winter.

Includes bibliographical references and index.
ISBN 978-0-8020-9692-0 (bound).   ISBN 978-0-8020-9639-5 (pbk.)

1. Multiculturalism – Canada.   2. Cultural pluralism – Canada.   3. Québec
(Province) – History – Autonomy and independence movements.   I. Title.

FC105.M8W55 2011   305.800971   C2011-903042-X

This book has been published with the help of a grant from the Canadian
Federation for the Humanities and Social Sciences, through the Aid to
Scholarly Publications Program, using funds provided by the Social
Sciences and Humanities Research Council of Canada.

University of Toronto Press acknowledges the financial assistance to its
publishing program of the Canada Council for the Arts and the Ontario
Arts Council.

University of Toronto Press acknowledges the financial support of the
Government of Canada through the Canada Book Fund for its publishing
activities.

To my parents

Contents

Acknowledgments

The arguments in this book have been developed over several years. During this time, my project benefited from the intellectual and practical support of many friends and colleagues. I am particularly indebted to Veit Bader, Klaus Eder, Ratiba Hadj-Moussa, Will Kymlicka, Alan Simmons, and Brian Singer, whose generous comments and suggestions have helped to improve the manuscript substantially. Special thanks also to Engin Isin, Marcel Martel, David Miller, Rinus Penninx, Melisa Salazar, and Daiva Stasiulis for many questions, ideas, and critical observations. Eamonn Callan, Marguerite Cognet, Thomas Faist, Blanca Garces-Mascareñas, Tariq Modood, Oliver Schmidtke, and Hans-Olaf Schultze have commented extensively on earlier versions of individual chapters. I am grateful for thoughtful comments by members of the SIAS Summer Institutes on Migration and Citizenship 2007–2008 (Wissenschaftskolleg zu Berlin & Stanford University). In addition, UTP's anonymous reviewers, who engaged closely with my work, provided valuable suggestions. I thank all these colleagues for their criticism and encouragement. Both helped me to frame my arguments better. The usual disclaimer applies: I remain solely responsible for all errors of fact or interpretation.

Over the past years, the manuscript travelled with me to many places including Montreal, Toronto, Amsterdam, Berlin, and Palo Alto, California. Being able to present and discuss my work in various research and teaching settings has been an extremely valuable experience! Institutional support was provided by the Canadian Metropolis Project (IM Montréal and CERIS Toronto), the Institute for Migration and Ethnic Studies (IMES) at the University of Amsterdam, the Institute for Social Sciences at the Humboldt University in Berlin, the MCRI Ethnic and Democratic Governance at Queen's University, and the Europe Centre at the FSI at Stanford University. Many thanks for hosting me!

I gratefully acknowledge financial assistance from the German National Merit Foundation (*Studienstiftung des deutschen Volkes*), the Social Science and Humanities Research Council of Canada (SSHRC), the German Academic Exchange Service (DAAD), the International Council for Canadian Studies (ICCS), York University, the University of Ottawa, and the Canadian Federation of the Humanities and Social Sciences. This project would not have been possible without their generous support.

Portions of this book build on arguments that were previously published in the following journal articles: 'How Does the Nation Become Pluralist?', *Ethnicities*, 7 (4), 2007, 483-515, 'Neither "America" nor "Québec": Constructing the Canadian Multicultural Nation,' *Nations and Nationalism*, 13 (3), 2007, 481-503, 'The Dialectics of Multicultural Identity: Learning from Canada,' *World Political Science Review* 5 (1), 2009, Article 9 (translated from German and republished by nomination from the *Swiss Political Science Review* after receiving the journal's 2009 best paper award)), '"Immigrants Don't Ask for Self-government": How Multiculturalism is (De)legitimized in Multi-national Societies', *Ethnopolitics*, 10 (1), 2011 (in press). I would like to express my gratitude to the publishing houses Sage, Wiley-Blackwell, Berkeley Electronic Press, and Taylor & Francis for permission to use this material.

Finally, I want to thank my friends and family, whom I have often neglected in the process of researching and writing this book. Your presence, patience, and affection means so much to me! I am particularly thankful to Benjamin Zyla for his love, companionship, and support on so many levels. I dedicate this book to Peter and Irmgard Winter, my parents, who have accompanied me on my path sometimes in awe, sometimes in bewilderment – but always with wisdom, encouragement, and love.

PART I

Introduction

1 How Do 'We' Become Pluralist?

The modern polity, as Wimmer succinctly reminds us, comprises three notions of peoplehood: 'The people as a sovereign entity, which exercises power by means of some sort of democratic procedure; the people as citizens of a state, holding equal rights before the law; and the people as an ethnic community undifferentiated by distinctions of honour and prestige' (2002: 2). Although analytically distinct, these three notions of peoplehood are intrinsically related and inform each other mutually. The 'indivisible trinity' of popular sovereignty, democratic citizenship, and shared ethnic features (ibid.) confronts scholars and political decision-makers with the question of how it is possible – in an age of globalization, immigration, and increasing ethnic diversity – to secure the stability of the first two pillars of contemporary polities, while redefining the third one, the idea of an ethnically integrated nation.

National identities defined in narrow 'ethnic' or cultural terms are obviously problematic because they tend to be homogenizing and thereby preclude ethnic minorities from full participation in the polity. Strictly 'civic' definitions of citizenship, however, have been deconstructed as illusory (Bauböck, 1998, 2002). Bureaucratic structures and rules can never be entirely neutral; otherwise they would not provide citizens with a sense of loyalty and cohesion (Taylor, 1995, 2001). Thus, a new type of national self-understanding is needed. It must promote both collective authenticity – which provides national polities with legitimacy – and ethnocultural pluralism – which allows for the expression of diverse types of identities within the public space without reinforcing ethnic segregation and inequality.

This book argues that rendering the idea of the nation compatible with ethnic diversity is primarily achieved through the paradigm of pluralism, that is, an approach that encourages the recognition of ethnic diversity and its expression within the public space. It uses a neo-Weberian framework to theorize both the construction of ethnic identities in unequal power relations and ethnocultural diversity's normative incorporation within representations of the nation. An empirical study then examines how an overarching pluralist identity is constituted within a particular type of majority discourse. In short, the book asks the following question: How does the national majority come to represent itself as normatively pluralist?

Taking its inspiration from the Canadian case, the book concentrates on a particular type of pluralism, namely, the *multicultural* transformation of national identity. Multiculturalism is usually understood as addressing a country's ethocultural diversity produced through immigration. It is not the only type of pluralism, as there are also multinationally, regionally, religiously, or linguistically driven regimes of accommodating ethnocultural diversity within the modern polity. Nonetheless, in recent years, multiculturalism has become one of the most contested forms of pluralism. The Canadian case is interesting in this regard. In 1971, Canada was the first country in the world to adopt multiculturalism not only as a policy towards minorities but also, in principle, as a basic feature of shared identity. It therefore serves as a model to multiculturalism in many other immigrant-receiving societies. Second, even today, at the time of an international retreat from pluralist policies, multiculturalism as an *idea* of societal integration and national identity continues to hold much currency in public debates and policies (Kymlicka, 2009). What makes Canadian multiculturalism so resilient?

Canada has been spared neither from tensions arising from ethnic diversity nor from the explosive debates on pluralist accommodation. Attacks on multiculturalism were particularly strong in the early 1990s. Only a couple of years later, in 1995, Québécois nationalism brought the country to the brink of a break-up. Surprisingly, the political tensions between the country's so-called founding nations, did not bring about another wave of criticism of multiculturalism. On the contrary, by the late 1990s, commentators observed the consolidation of multiculturalism in dominant discourses about national identity (Karim, 2002). This provides the Canadian case with a particular twist: Did Québécois nationalism during the 1990s serve as a counter-image facilitating the conditional inclusion of ethnically diverse immigrants into a multicultural Canadian 'we' (Winter, 2001)?

Incorporating empirical findings from an analysis of Central Canadian English-language newspaper discourses during the 1990s into a theoretical framework inspired by Weberian sociology, this book develops a theory of pluralist group formation. In particular, it argues that pluralism is best understood as a dynamic set of triangular relations where the compromise between two, often unequal, groups – 'us' and 'others' – becomes meaningful only through the presence of (real or constructed) outsiders ('them'). This model of pluralism is used to examine the transformation of Canadian national identity into a 'multicultural we.' This process is observed from three different angles. First, the model of pluralism as a triangular relation is used to study the constitution of Canadian multicultural identity *in relation* to newspaper representations of diversity management in the United States and Quebec. Second, it is used to investigate how multinationalism – in particular representations of Québécois minority nationalism – have an impact on the legitimization and delegitimization of pan-Canadian multiculturalism. Third, the model of pluralism as a set of triangular relations also leads us to identify three competing discourses within the mainstream press. These discourses articulate different views of *who* exactly constitutes the Canadian 'multicultural we.' Canadians of British background? English and French Canadians together? Aboriginal peoples and recent immigrants? All of the above?

Through the analysis of Canadian English-language mainstream newspaper discourses, this book aims to provide a window through which we can view and better understand the complex group representations and proliferations of meaning involved in the consolidation of multiculturalism as a dominant discourse of pan-Canadian identity in the second half of the 1990s. Furthermore, theorizing the results of the newspaper analysis, it strives to develop a sociological understanding of the multicultural transformation of national identity.

The remainder of this introduction lays out the thesis of this book. It then provides a short overview of the agenda and the structure of the book.

Thesis: Pluralism as a Triangular Relationship

This book examines how a pluralist 'national we' is bounded by opposition to a real or imagined 'Others' with a capital O. These Others are constructed as 'them.' It also traces whether and how this 'national we' includes references to 'others' (lower case) in our midst, that is, alongside of 'us.' The perspective chosen is that of the national majority as it is represented within two mainstream English-language newspapers, the Toronto edition of the *Globe and Mail* and the *Toronto Star* during the 1990s. During that last decade of the 'differentialist turn' – which had been on the rise since decolonization and the human rights movement in the United States – a unifying multicultural pan-Canadianism has taken root mostly in the rest of Canada, and there mainly in urban contexts. Despite its quantitative and qualitative limitations,[1] the selected sample of newspaper texts provides a window through which we can observe a variety of relations that are constructed within public discourse between those viewed as insiders to the multicultural nation and those projected, at certain times and for specific purposes, to the outside of the collectively imagined 'we.'[2]

The empirical study confirms and expands our understanding of pluralism as a negotiated compromise. It reveals that the 'multicultural we' is, in fact, constructed as a triangular relation where the compromise between two, often unequal, groups becomes meaningful only through the presence of third persons. Pluralism is thus best understood as overlapping and dynamic sets of triangular relations, where the conditional association between 'us' and 'others' is rendered possible through the exclusion of 'them.' Put differently, two or more groups come together – that is, enter in negotiation processes about pluralist collaboration – not because they are equal in terms of power or similar in terms of 'culture,' but because they are confronted with a (real or imagined) third group that forces the national majority to give concessions to minority groups – or to attempt their co-optation, as the glass is always either half full or half empty. The triangular relation is a minimum requirement that allows for a theoretically easy and empirically applicable model. Obviously, reality is more complex. The notion of 'overlapping sets of triangular relations' speaks to this complexity.

The conducted newspaper analysis traces a multitude of these triangular relations with numerous 'players' (such as francophones, immigrants, English Canadians) with changing attributes (such as, for francophones: Québécois 'de souche', separatists, nationalists, members of a linguistic minority, etc.) in various positions (e.g., included as 'others' within the Canadian imaginary or excluded as 'them' outside the multicultural nation).

Within these triangular relations, in the Canadian case, national minorities play an important role. The rights granted to and/or claimed by the francophones of Quebec serve as points of reference within both legitimizations and delegitimizations of pan-Canadian multicul-turalism. In public discourse, the separation between national minor-ities and ethnic groups of immigrant origin is thus not as strict and static as political theorists make us believe. The abominable absence of Aboriginal peoples from the newspaper sample draws the attention to Canada's two *dominant* projects of nationhood: the Canadian 'multi-cultural we' is primarily negotiated in relation to dualism or 'bination-alism' rather than trinationalism. Nevertheless, within the examined discourses, Quebec is univocally situated neither inside nor outside the Canadian multicultural nation. This volatile situation appears to be beneficial for turning multiculturalism into an integral part of pan-Canadian identity, as it allows one to draw a sharp line between the country's 'tradition' of group accommodation and what are deemed the limits of legitimate diversity claims. Similarly, images of an extra-national 'player,' the United States, are highly relevant for the multi-culturalization of Canadian national identity. Imagined Americanness interferes with the representation of internal social group relations in that it forces the national majority to accept its particularity and to view itself as one group that shares society with others.

The model of pluralism as a constantly renegotiated triangular re-lation accounts for a diversity of views. In the examined newspaper texts, three majority perspectives on multiculturalism have been identi-fied. Although unable to agree upon who constitutes the multicultural nation, these perspectives converge in their rejection of 'ethnic nation-alism.' The book argues that in Canada, during the 1990s, multicultural-ism acquired a different meaning, from a seemingly group-rights based approach to a much stronger and openly acknowledged emphasis on individual choice. This reduced multiculturalism's imputed divisive-ness and rendered it socially acceptable, even to the critics. Constituted in opposition to – rather than in extension of – French/English 'dualism' and its seemingly obsolete communitarian underpinnings, multicultur-alism became invested with legitimacy and moved from a discourse at the margins to a social imaginary at the centre.

As such, this book provides us with a better understanding of how multiculturalism became consolidated as a dominant discourse at a time of multinational conflict. It also helps to explain why public sup-port for multiculturalism merely 'dipped' in the early 1990s. Gaining insights into the causes for the rising acceptance of multiculturalism as a source of pride and identification, in the second half of the 1990s, helps us to better explain the Canadian exceptionalism at a time of an international retreat from multiculturalism as a normative framework for the transformation of national identity and the integration of immigrants. It also allows us to adopt a position from where we can adequately identify and tackle the new challenges to Canadian multiculturalism that have come to the fore in the aftermath of the terrorist attacks on 11 September 2001 (Roach, 2003), and the securitization of immigration and ethno-religious difference (Labelle et al., 2009).

Agenda and Structure of the Book

This book aims to develop a sociology of pluralist group formation. It asks the question: 'how do "we" become pluralist?' This book's approach is 'optimistic' in so far as it views the development of pluralist group identity as difficult but feasible. It is critical in so far as it situates the development of pluralist group identities within a framework of unequal power relations. It rejects both overly optimistic approaches where benevolent majorities voluntarily give concessions to minority groups and 'pessimistic' views of power and ideology where minorities are thought of as lacking the agency to improve their destinies. In other words, this book does not embrace the view that pluralism primarily aims to 'contain' minorities. Rather, pluralism is viewed as a negotiated compromise between admittedly unequal groups.

The empirical focus of the book is Central Canada during the 1990s. Particular attention is paid to the impact of Québécois nationalism on multiculturalism, or better of representations thereof. The question 'how do "we" become pluralist?' is examined by means of analysis of opinion pieces from the Toronto-based newspapers the *Globe and Mail* and the *Toronto Star*. The main agenda of this book is nonetheless theoretical in nature. I first develop both a theory and method that render justice to the study's focus and its limitations. Second, I draw upon the results from the empirical case study to advance the aforementioned critically optimistic sociology of pluralist group formation. Third, I extrapolate from the newspaper findings and the theoretical model – which defines pluralism as a triangular relation between unequal groups and (real or imagined) others – to better understand the consolidation of multiculturalism as an essential element of pan-Canadian identity in dominant discourses.

While the relevance of the newspaper analysis will become evident in later chapters, I briefly want to list its most obvious limitations (for details on methodology and content, see Chapter 6). First, the focus lies on dominant discourses in Central Canada. This is a very 'Upper

Canadian' sample, which excludes any representations for other English-speaking regions. Representations in the ethnic press and French-language media are also not covered here. Second, the empirical study operates on the level of discourse, and while the latter can serve as a proxy for concrete group relations, the overlap between discourse and praxis cannot always be taken for granted. As such, this study concentrates on representations of pluralist identity formation, and mainly those that lead towards the multicultural transformation of pan-Canadian 'national' identity.

Chapter 2 situates the question that drives this book – 'how does the "national we" become pluralist?' – within the Canadian context. It shows why, in comparison with other countries, Canada is an interesting case to study with respect to the multiculturalization of national identity. The chapter explains what circumstances provide the multicultural transformation of a Canadian 'national we' with a particular twist: namely, the presence of two competing projects of nationhood within the same state. As such, even the term Canadian 'national' identity is controversial and therefore, within this book, often replaced by 'pan-Canadian' identity.

Chapter 3 approaches the topic of this book – the multicultural transformation of national identity – and its particular Canadian twist – the interrelation between different types of ethnonational diversity and diversity accommodation – from a theoretical perspective. The chapter explores the theoretical trajectory of pluralism studies from the post – Second World War era to the crisis of multiculturalism in the 1990s, and the end of the 'differentialist turn,' which received its death blow on 11 September 2001. It then reveals gaps in the current literature on multicultural nationhood and identifies two theoretical 'puzzles.' The remainder of the book aims to solve these puzzles, first by putting forth some theoretical considerations (Chapters 4 and 5) and second by conducting an empirical case study (Chapters 6–9).

Revisiting Max Weber's concept of social closure, Chapters 4 and 5 locate the constitution of ethnic groups and nations within inter- and intranational relations of power and alterity. Chapter 4 is a 'supporting chapter' (as in the category of 'supporting actor' in the American Oscar awards). Taking its starting point in Weber's reformulation of the *Gemeinschaft/Gesellschaft* dichotomy (Tönnies), it develops a sociology of ethnic relations whose theoretical underpinnings inform the notion of pluralism used in this book. The chapter concludes by explaining why and how we can appreciate minority efforts to constitute themselves as 'different but equal' without essentializing their ethnic, cultural, or religious difference.

Chapter 5 uses the theoretical insights gained from the discussion of ethnic groups for the development of a sociology of pluralist nationalism. Locating the construction of national identities within a context of unequal power relations allows us to deconstruct the civic/ethnic dichotomy without abandoning the theoretical value that is inherent to these concepts. The chapter traces the emergence of distinct types of pluralism within different types of nations. Chapter 5 provides a partial answer to the theoretical puzzles identified in Chapter 3. Pluralism is here defined as being produced through conflict and struggle between the dominant group and various minorities; it is neither concession nor containment but a permanently renegotiated middle ground that will never be entirely free from power relations. The chapter concludes by formulating four hypotheses about possible relations between multi-nationalism and multiculturalism.

Chapter 6 outlines the research design and methodology of an empirical investigation on the discursive construction of multicultural nationhood. Its goal is to examine to what extent a 'multicultural we' is constructed in a particular segment of Canadian English-language majority discourses during the 1990s, and to identify the representations of ethnic and/or national groups and their relations that sustain this construction. From a larger corpus of academic texts and newspaper articles, 123 op-ed pieces from the *Globe and Mail* and the *Toronto Star* have been submitted to in-depth examination. The chapter first outlines the contours of the newspaper sample. It then develops a method of discourse analysis whose emphasis on differential inclusion replaces Critical Discourse Analysis's traditional focus on 'othering.' Concentrating on (at least) triangular relations between constructed categories, this approach is able to account for pluralist integration and coalition making. Different angles of this approach will be explored in Chapters 7, 8, and 9.

Based upon a detailed analysis of selected opinion discourses in the Canadian mainstream newspapers the *Globe and Mail* and the *Toronto Star*, Chapters 7, 8, and 9 propose a new interpretation of how changing group relations, and their respective representations in discourse have catalysed the multiculturalization of Canadian national identity. Chapter 7 traces the boundaries of Canada as a multicultural nation vis-à-vis the attitudes towards ethnocultural minorities that are attributed to the United States and Quebec. It contends that Canada/U.S.

and English Canada/Quebec comparisons are essential elements for constructing a unique Canadian identity, particularly one that wants to be both unified 'national' and heterogeneous 'multicultural.' The chapter pays special attention to the particularization of Canada's national majority, the ambiguities of recognizing minorities within the nation, and the consequences of projecting conflict and otherness outside the boundaries of Canadianness.

Chapter 8 examines the shifting relations between binationalism and multiculturalism. The chapter argues that the concept of the 'dual majority' comprises two dimensions: One dimension refers to *relative agreement,* which in the Canadian case has led to a discourse that presents multiculturalism as a logical extension of French/English dualism, without, however, proposing either to racialized and ethnic minorities or to Aboriginal peoples the same structural rights that are enjoyed by the two 'founding nations.' The second dimension refers to *relative conflict* between the two dominant players. Interestingly, in the 1990s, it is conflict not compromise that allows immigrants and ethnic minorities to be portrayed – and to portray themselves – as multicultural unifiers of the pan-Canadian nation.

In Chapter 9, the variety of perspectives within the newspaper sample becomes central. Concentrating on the internal dimension of the group boundary, the chapter examines representations of 'us' vis-à-vis multiculturalism. A strict examination of the prevailing triangular relations within the textual material leads to the identification of three diverging majority perspectives on Canadian multicultural nationhood: republican, liberal-pluralist, and liberal-multiculturalist. For each perspective, the chapter identifies an ideal-type and strategic variations. It also discusses how these perspectives contradict and reinforce each other.

The general conclusion of the book is divided into two chapters. Chapter 10 first revisits the pluralism model. It then extrapolates from the study's findings to discuss the consolidation of multiculturalism as a dominant discourse in Canada during the 1990s. Chapter 11 situates the Canadian case in a comparative perspective and draws lessons for the analysis of current trends in citizenship and immigrant integration and in diverse societies.

2   A Canadian Paradox

This chapter locates this book's research question within the Canadian context. It first illustrates why, in comparison with other countries, Canada is an interesting case to study. It then shows in what way the general question addressed in this book – 'how does the "national we" become pluralist?' – gets transformed in the Canadian context. In fact, the presence of two competing projects of nationhood within the same state provides the multicultural transformation of Canadian 'national we' with a particular twist. As we will see below, even the term Canadian 'national' identity is controversial. Within this book, it is often replaced by 'pan-Canadian' identity.

The chapter is divided in three sections. The first reviews the success and failures of Canadian multiculturalism. The second defines the dimension of multiculturalism that is under investigation in this book. The third section adds a new twist to this dimension, namely, the relationship between Canadian multiculturalism in response to immigration and Canada's other forms of recognized ethnonational diversity.

A Multicultural Success Story

At the beginning of the twenty-first century, Canada is one of the few remaining countries that adheres to multiculturalism as a normative framework of immigrant integration. An official policy of multiculturalism was first enacted in 1971, followed by the Multiculturalism Act in 1988. Affirming both individual and collective rights, section 27 of the Constitution, the Canadian Charter of Rights and Freedoms, adopted in 1982, provides that the Charter 'shall be interpreted in a manner consistent with the preservation of and enhancement of the multicultural heritage of Canadians' (Canada, 1982). Today, the Government of Canada entertains a Program of Multiculturalism, which operates within the Department of Citizenship and Immigration Canada. The success of Canadian multiculturalism is attested to by higher levels of public support for immigration and for multiculturalism in Canada compared with other countries (Adams, 2007; Ward and Masgoreth, 2008), the virtual non-existence of a far-right backlash against immigration (Hiebert et al., 2003), the high naturalization rates of immigrants (Bloemraad, 2006, chapter 1), the absence of ethnically motivated violent conflict, and the emergence of Canada's largest city – Toronto – as seemingly 'the most multicultural city in the world' (Doucet, 2001).

The success of Canadian multiculturalism is surprising at a time of strong backlashes against multicultural policies in almost all countries where they had previously been implemented. The turnaround has been particularly dramatic and complete in the Netherlands. Previously celebrated, in the 1970s and 1980s, along with Sweden, Canada, Australia, and New Zealand, as a model for ethnocultural tolerance, the Netherlands have now become a forerunner in restrictive immigration and integration policies.[1] There are now stricter criteria for asylum and family reunification, policies of zero labour immigration in combination with a new guest worker regime for highly skilled professionals, mandatory integration courses, and sharpened naturalization requirements (Entzinger, 2003). A similar rhetoric and policies can be observed in other European countries, such as Denmark, Italy, and Norway (Bird, 2005; Lithman, 2005). Initiated in the 1990s and gaining strength in the new century, 'the return of assimilation' (Brubaker, 2001) quickly supersedes a previously assumed convergence in favour of multiculturalism among scholars and policy-makers in immigrant-receiving societies (Kymlicka, 2001). Today, Nathan Glazer's (1997) book title *We Are All Multiculturalists Now* seems almost like a reminiscence from another time (for more optimistic views, see Faist, 2009; Kymlicka, 2009).

Admittedly, even in Canada, the success of multiculturalism is not undisputed. Canadian researchers have for a long time been critiquing the dismantling of Canadian multiculturalism in both ideological and institutional-financial terms. Reacting to a wave of national and international criticism and fears of 'balkanization' – the same wave that hit the Netherlands and other Western democracies in the aftermath of the Kosovo war, the genocide in Rwanda, etc. – the Government of Canada reduced multiculturalism from prominence (in 1993) and adopted a new mandate (in 1997–98), namely, 'to foster an inclusive society in which people of all backgrounds, whose identities are respected and recognized as vital to an evolving Canadian identity, feel a sense of belonging and an attachment to this country, and participate fully in Canadian society' (Canadian Heritage, 1997–98). Funding for multiculturalism programs was cut from about $27 million annually in the early 1990s to $18.7 million in 1996–97 and has been on very low levels since (Abu-Laban and Gabriel, 2002: 115). Scholars also show that the type of initiatives that received support under the Multiculturalism Program were linked to multiethnic organizations serving a Canadian 'mainstream society' rather than to mono-ethnic organizations, which would be necessary for a vibrant culturally and institutionally pluralist society (McAndrew et al., 2005). The success of multiculturalism is also called into question by the fact that recent immigrants to Canada – mostly racialized or 'visible' minorities – are doing less well economically than previous generations of immigrants, who mainly came from European countries. Not only do they find it difficult to get their foreign credentials recognized on the Canadian market, even if they find jobs, their incomes are significantly lower than those of Canadians with comparable skills (Ornstein, 2006). The second generation of 'visible minority' Canadians, in particular, seems to experience feelings of alienation and disenfranchisement (Reitz and Banerjee, 2007). Official multiculturalism has therefore been reproached for being merely a lip service, a political strategy motivated by the neo-liberal agenda of 'selling diversity' and/or attracting votes from minorities (Abu-Laban and Gabriel, 2002). In sum, for commentators from the political left, multiculturalism in Canada lacks substance.

By contrast, critics from the political right blame multiculturalism for the failures of immigrant integration. While multiculturalism may have worked for European immigrants to Canada, they argue, today's countries of emigration and diasporic connections no longer allow such an approach. Immigrants are increasingly coming from non-Western countries, and they have very different cultural backgrounds and little or no experience with democratic institutions. Technology allows them to stay in close contact with their homelands, and they may not learn the English (or French) language properly, may work in ethnic enterprises, and increasingly, may live in segregated neighbourhoods. Multiculturalism is encouraging them, so the argument goes, to care more about their home countries and/or their segregated ethnic communities than about Canadian civil society (Bissoondath, 1994). According to these critics, multiculturalism also suggests that cultural traditions and group rights are more important than individual rights and principles of gender equality and respect for sexual orientation (Stoffman, 2002; Collacott, 2002).

In order to qualify the success of multiculturalism in Canada, it has been suggested to distinguish between three levels of multiculturalism: as a social fact, as a policy, and as a normative framework for society-building and national identity (Kymlicka, 2004). First, in a widely cited article, Leslie Laczko (1994) shows that when it comes to the breadth of ethnic, linguistic, and religious diversity, Canada is a 'statistical outlier' among Western democracies. In 1901, for example, people who reported Aboriginal, British, or French origins comprised the lion's share of the population. By contrast, in the 2006 Census, more than 200 ethnic origins are reported (up from 25 in 1901).[2] The census shows that 83.9% of the immigrants who arrived between 2001 and 2006 were born in regions other than Europe. More than 5 million individuals identified themselves as a member of the 'visible minority' population (16.2% of the total population; Statistics Canada, 2006).[3] Thus, it can be said that in Canada ethnocultural diversity is a demographic fact. In that sense, Canada is a 'multicultural' society and is becoming more so by the day.[4]

Second, in contrast to other countries which chose to deny ethnic diversity (like Germany over long periods of time) or encourage assimilation (like France), Canada has been the first country (in 1971) to adopt a policy aiming at the egalitarian integration of immigrants by recognizing and accommodating ethnocultural diversity within public institutions and supporting immigrant organizations and the expression of 'heritage cultures' for purposes of emancipation. Two points are noteworthy: (1) History has known many cases where ethnocultural diversity was translated into a vertical order of segregation (the United States), apartheid (South Africa), or even extinction (Nazi Germany). Canada, by contrast, aims for an egalitarian incorporation strategy. (2) While Canadian multiculturalism recognizes the importance of cultural communities, its legal framework neither subdues the individual to the group, nor supports cultural conservatism or religious orthodoxy (Kymlicka, 1998). On the contrary, in past years, multiculturalism's second dimension, the support of mono-ethnic organizations, has lost importance both financially and ideologically.

Third, although laws and policies have an impact on social action and may promote a certain kind of ethos among citizens, they do not emerge out of nowhere. Rather, they are part and parcel of a normative project for society building, *un projet de société*. As such, multiculturalism policy is integrated into a larger legal and discursive framework about what it means to be Canadian, and what Canadians want their society to be. Thus, multiculturalism as an approach to immigrant integration is closely connected to the idea of national identity and its pluralist transformation. This dimension of multiculturalism, namely, multiculturalism as collective identity and normative project of society building, is the object of this book. In fact, I will argue that, in Canada, the success of multiculturalism as a normative approach to immigrant integration – which guides multiculturalism policy – can only be understood because it is, at the same time, an essential part of the country's nation-building ideology.

It is mainly this third dimension of Canadian multiculturalism – multiculturalism as a societal project or ethos – that can be celebrated unequivocally as a 'success.' To put it with Rainer Bauböck: 'No other Western country has gone as far as Canada in adopting multiculturalism not only as a policy towards minorities but also as a basic feature of shared identity' (2005: 93). Multiculturalism enjoys indeed widespread support among Canadians. Opinion poll after opinion poll shows that Canadians accept multiculturalism as a 'cornerstone of Canadian culture' (66% in 2002; Jedwab, 2005: 96), and that they agree that 'people from different racial and cultural groups are enriching the cultural life of Canada' (83% in 2002; ibid.). While there are, as Jedwab shows, variations and sometimes inconsistencies depending on the exact question, the country seems to be even more easily coping with the challenges of its postmodern 'multicultural' phase than it did with its premodern (bi- or tri-cultural) phase (Soroka et al., 2007: 586). To paraphrase yet another eminent Canadian scholar: 'Canadians today are proudly multicultural. Along with publicly funded health care, multiculturalism has become part of the sticky stuff of Canadian identity' (Stein, 2007: 1).

The Contours of Multiculturalism

Where does the resilience of Canadian multiculturalism come from? In a recent article, Will Kymlicka (2004) links the success of Canadian multiculturalism to two contingent factors: timing and geography. With respect to timing, Kymlicka points out that, initially, the multiculturalism policy in Canada was neither demanded by nor designed for non-European immigrants. Rather, ethnic groups of predominantly

European origin (particularly Ukrainians, Germans, Poles, Finns, Dutch people, and Jews) asked a question that has preoccupied Canadians since: 'if it is valuable for French Canadians to maintain their distinctive culture and identity, why is it not so for other groups' (Palmer, 1975: 516)? In 1971, Prime Minister Pierre Trudeau addressed this question by implementing 'multiculturalism within a bilingual framework' as an official state policy and 'the very essence of Canadian identity' (House of Commons, 1971: 8580). 'For although there are two official languages, there is no official culture, nor does any ethnic group take precedence over any other' (ibid.: 8545).

Non-European immigrants to Canada became gradually involved in the multiculturalism debate. By the late 1980s, 'visible minorities' displaced the original white ethnic groups as principal actors. Their demands of anti-racism and inclusion were retorted by commentators from the political right, with questions about 'balkanization,' stark cultural differences, and the 'limits of tolerance' (Abu-Laban and Stasiulis, 1992). With the increased intake of immigrants from non-traditional sources, diversity became ethnically and 'racially' more pronounced. This led to a rise in xenophobia and racism (Stasiulis and Jhappan, 1995). In addition, fears arose that immigrant groups would invoke the ideology of multiculturalism to demand legal protection of illiberal practices such as forced marriages, female genital mutilation, and honour killings. Rightly or wrongly these practices are often associated with Islam. Indeed, in Canada, as in other countries throughout the West, in recent years, Muslims have come to be seen likely to be culturally and religiously committed to illiberal practices and to be supporters of undemocratic political movements (Modood, 2007). The fears about a 'clash of civilizations' became first highlighted in the 1989 Rushdie Affair, and are paramount since 9/11, 2001 (Schmitt and Winter, 2009). As a consequence of these developments, almost everywhere in the Western world, public support for multiculturalism soured in the 1990s. In Canada, if we track public support for the multiculturalism policy over the past twenty-five years, support was lowest in the early 1990s (see Figure 2.1).[5] Interestingly, while this wave of criticism had devastating effects in other countries such as Australia and the Netherlands, in Canada public support for multiculturalism merely 'dipped' temporarily. Support for multiculturalism rose again in the second half of the 1990s, and this not only to its original levels. Rather, support for multiculturalism reached historic highs in 2002–03 (*Globe and Mail*, 2003; Kymlicka, 2004: 843) and was still strong in 2006 (Karim, 2008).

Figure 2.1: Importance of multiculturalism to Canadian identity (1985–2003)

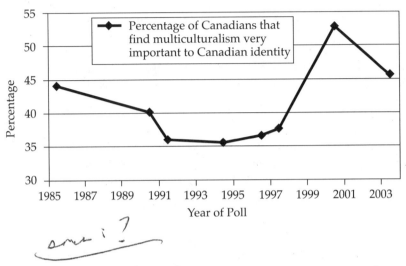

Kymlicka offers three explanations for the continued – or better, renewed – success of multiculturalism in Canada: First, the multiculturalism policy had been in place for twenty years before the issue of cultural relativism and the 'limits of tolerance' emerged; it had been institutionally embedded, not just in a particular federal government department but also in mainstream institutions and, since 1982, in the Canadian Constitution. Second, fear-mongering about immigrant illiberalism was proven wrong in practice: no major immigrant organization had demanded the right to maintain illiberal practices. Third, contrary to most of Western Europe, where Muslims often constitute the largest group of non-Western immigrants – up to 80 per cent or 90 per cent in countries like France, Spain, Italy, Germany, and the Netherlands – Canada's Muslim population is very small (less than 2% of the total) and forms only a small fraction of recent non-white immigration (non-Muslim Caribbean Blacks and Chinese being far more numerous and 'visible'). If it is true that, as it seems, public support for multiculturalism has declined as Muslims have come to be seen as the main proponents or beneficiaries of the policy (Liddle, 2004), these three reasons may indeed help to explain why the public backlash against multiculturalism was less profound in Canada than elsewhere.

Canada has also geographical advantages over its European counterparts. Most importantly, 'it is virtually impossible for people from poor or unstable countries to get to Canada without government authorization' (Kymlicka, 2004: 847). Canada has only one land border, and very few people who manage to enter the (richer) United States have any desire to move to (poorer) Canada. In other words, geography reduces the fear about 'being swamped.'[6] It limits also the strong moral objections that often arise in native populations vis-à-vis illegal immigrants. Canada has neither colonial obligations with respect to immigration (apart from those towards its colonized Aboriginal peoples, in which it fails miserably) nor responsibilities derived from a former guest-worker regime. On the contrary, by selecting the type of immigrants that it finds most suitable (whether, in earlier times on the basis of 'race' or religion, or, currently, on the basis of education, income, and professional qualifications) and the time of arrival, the Canadian government reduces the risk of creating an ethnic underclass, avoids the massive intake of those immigrants who are (perceived to be) an economic burden. By balancing out the composition of its immigrant population (no single immigrant group forms more than 15% of the total immigrant intake) Canada also escapes the prospect of one particular immigrant group challenging the hegemony of the national languages and institutions. We may thus conclude that 'the distinction between traditional immigration countries and European nation-states has not lost all its importance' (Bader, 2005a: 10). Settler countries traditionally facilitated the integration and naturalization of migrants. European states, by contrast, for historical and geographical reasons, long resisted the prospect of any cultural pluralization.

Timing and geography are undoubtedly important for the successful adoption and implementation of multiculturalism as policy and normative framework for society building, but they only partially explain the success of multiculturalism in Canada. The United States is in a similar situation with respect to timing and geography as Canada,[7] yet it never subscribed to multiculturalism as an ethos or normative approach to society building. On the contrary, the United States, famously, has always insisted on the unity of its national identity, *e pluribus unum*, and the American melting pot.[8] Australia was the second country after Canada to adopt, in 1973, a policy of multiculturalism. It is only surrounded by oceans and does not even have a single land border to control. Nevertheless, in Australia, multiculturalism suffered extreme backlashes in recent years (Hage, 1998; Jakubowicz, 2005).

Scholars have, therefore, pointed to another characteristic of multiculturalism in Canada, namely, that it is part of a wider set of pluralist arrangements within Canadian society (Helly, 2001; Juteau, 1997b; Laczko, 1994; Winter, 2007a). David Cameron, for example, maintains that 'the experience of a country with a profound ethnocultural division [...] equipped Canadians with the capacity to accommodate the [factual] multiculturalism that is the product of postwar immigration' (Cameron, 2007: 80). Indeed, the coexistence of three different types of minority groups and their distinct accommodations is said to have become an essential element of Canadian citizenship and identity (Kymlicka, 1995, 2003). Aboriginal peoples and francophone Québécois demand (and have been partially granted) recognition as 'nations'; ethnic groups of immigrant origin, by contrast, are accommodated through multiculturalism. This book is interested in the interrelations between these different types of diversity and their accommodations.

A brief reminder of Canadian history is necessary. Canada is a country built on two distinct processes of conquest and colonization followed by a steady flow of immigrants. French settlers first acted as colonizers and subordinated Aboriginal peoples (in the seventeenth century). Later, the French settlers became colonized themselves. When the British gained the upper hand in politics after their victory on the Plains of Abraham in 1759, *Canadiens* (of French origin) and Aboriginals were turned into British subjects with the expectation that they would either assimilate or vanish. For reasons of demography and 'institutional completeness' (Breton, 1964) French Canadians were able to negotiate a relatively high degree of autonomy alongside their British conquerors. Aboriginals, by contrast, were placed under tutelage. In the subsequent, never-ending process of nation building 'the colonizers called themselves the founding peoples, the founding peoples were called Indians and Natives, and all others were called immigrants and/or "ethnics"' (Juteau, 1997b: 102).

The 1867 British North America Act created a structure that allowed English and French Canadians to be masters of their own destinies – interpreted as provincial pluralism by the former and as national dualism by the latter. As a result of their different positions within the system of power relations, their strategies differed. English Canadians situated the Dominion of Canada within the larger project of British imperialism. They developed a national model similar to the French *Staatsnation* where the state actively pursued its goal of nation building by imposing Anglo-conformity, assimilation, and relegating the French fact to Quebec. French Canadian elites, by contrast, favoured a more narrowly defined 'organicist' nationalism based on culture, language, and religion. Shared ancestry and history (the Conquest) also became central elements of defining the boundaries of the nation.

After the Second World War, three simultaneous yet autonomous factors changed this version of Canadian French/English dualism dramatically: the rise of Québécois nationalism, the increasing rate of immigration, and the political emergence of Aboriginal peoples as Canada's First Nations. The modernization of Quebec's society and state during the Quiet Revolution led to an identity shift from a French Canadian 'we' to a Québécois 'we.' The new identity transformed the former dualism of linguistically defined French and English Canadians into a territorial opposition between Quebec and the rest of Canada. It had a direct impact on the forms of rights and recognition demanded in the political sphere, such as renewed federalism, binationalism, and special status. As a consequence, in 1963, the Royal Commission on Bilingualism and Biculturalism was established on the assumption that Canadian society was composed of two linguistic and cultural groups whose fundamental relationship needed clarifying.

As mentioned above, the subsequent shift from factual French/English dualism to a normative pluralism combining bilingualism and multiculturalism has been catalyzed by the increasing number of Canadians who did not belong to one of the two 'founding peoples.' Having become a 'third force' in Canadian politics,[9] immigrants of predominantly European origin questioned the legitimacy of granting cultural and linguistic rights only to French Canadians and thereby provoked the commission to 'take into account the contribution made by the other ethnic groups to the cultural enrichment of Canada' (Royal Commission on Bilingualism and Biculturalism, 1969, vol. IV). The late 1960s saw a series of important policy changes. In 1967, Canada replaced its immigration system based on 'national preference' with a supposedly 'race blind' universal points system.[10] In 1969, the Official Languages Act recognized the equality of French and English as Canada's official languages. In the same year, the Statement of the Government of Canada on Indian Policy (the White Paper) proposed the elimination of all government arrangements addressing Aboriginal rights.[11] Finally, in 1971, 'multiculturalism within a bilingual framework' became an official state policy and was declared 'the very essence of Canadian national identity' (House of Commons, 1971: 8580).

Despite the rhetoric of its being for all Canadians, multiculturalism was directed chiefly to 'ethnic minorities,' whereas official bilingualism was implemented to meet the demands of French Canadians (Kobayashi, 1993). While official bilingualism provoked much contention in Western Canada, the francophones of Quebec and Aboriginal peoples, seeing themselves as separate nations and not as immigrant-type ethnic groups, rejected multiculturalism as a political strategy aiming at the co-optation of immigrants (Bouthillier, 1997; Corbo, 1996; Schwimmer, 1995). In fact, the motivations underlying the institutionalization of the multiculturalism policy by Prime Minister Trudeau in 1971 (and its consequences) remain hotly debated even today (McRoberts, 1997; Winter, 2009). Overall, it seems fair to say that Québécois nationalism has, at the very least, functioned as a catalyst for the implementation of multiculturalism as a policy and government-promoted dimension of Canadian identity. Being politically, economically, and demographically stronger than Aboriginal nationalism, the alienation of French Canadians in Canada, particularly of those who formed a majority within the province of Quebec, could not be ignored. In the postwar period, the accommodation of the new Quebec was one of the major political challenges for Canada. The other was immigration. Aboriginal peoples, by contrast, only entered the political stage in the 1980s (Cairns, 2000).

The success of Canadian multiculturalism is, in fact, often associated with the notion that it is an 'extension' of previously institutionalized French/English dualism. The question 'What does multiculturalism owe to dualism?' (Cameron, 2007: 80) has been raised repeatedly, and answered in many different ways, mainly with respect to Canadian history (Cameron, 1990; McRoberts, 1997; Lacombe, 2002). These accounts do not deny Aboriginal peoples' past and present struggle for recognition and self-government. Rather, they draw attention to the two *dominant* projects of nationhood in Canada under the impact of immigration.

Dualism versus Multiculturalism?

A country's historical experience with the accommodation of ethnocultural diversity can certainly provide an ideological and institutional matrix sustaining multiculturalism as both ethos and policy. Nevertheless, Canada's history of dualism can only partially explain multiculturalism's success today. The Netherlands also look back upon a history of pluralism and 'corporate identities.' The system of pillarization (*verzuiling*) formed around groups that shared a common religion or a philosophy of life. These 'pillars' were more or less closed communities that had their own institutions, including hospitals, newspapers, schools, housing associations, trade unions, and political parties. For a long time, it was argued that multiculturalism in the Netherlands worked well because it 'extended "pillarization" (*verzuiling*) and the Dutch commitment to equality to new groups' (Guiraudon et al., 2005: 75). However, the arrival of postwar Turkish and Moroccan 'guest workers' and the successive advancement of Islam came at a time when pillarization was already in decline (Rath, 2005). The first signs of uneasiness with multiculturalism began to surface in the early 1990s (Penninx, 1996). The events on 9/11 in New York City and Washington accelerated the backlash against multiculturalism, and the criticism has still not ceased (Sniderman and Hagendoorn, 2007).

The history of pluralism alone is thus not sufficient to sustain multicultural immigrant integration in the present. Rather, there seems to be a missing contemporary component. The Dutch case suggests that the multicultural transformation of national identity is an ongoing process of group relations. Once the power equation has altered definitely in favour of one (set of) group(s) rather than another, it seems difficult for the latter group(s) to make their claims heard within the public arena (Winter, 2010). Thus, in the Dutch case, as the dominant narrative moves away from pluralism as a national 'tradition,' newcomers find it increasingly difficult to demand their 'pillar' and multicultural accommodation. Drawing upon these observations, this book addresses the question 'What does Canadian multiculturalism owe to dualism?' in yet another way. It is interested in the often overlooked 'coincidence' that multiculturalism became a publicly endorsed dominant discourse (Karim, 2002) at the very time when Canada was also characterized by a profound conflict between its two linguistically defined 'founding nations,' a conflict that was highlighted by the Quebec referendum on sovereignty in 1995. Once again, a brief reminder of Canadian history is necessary.

The Constitution Act of 1867, a law passed by the British Parliament as the British North America Act, along with numerous amendments, served as Canada's Constitution until 1982. The discussion of constitutional renewal was first launched in the 1960s but quickly entered into an impasse because of concerns over Quebec's status within Canada. The vision of a pan-Canadian bilingual and bicultural nation, promoted by the federal government, conflicted with Quebec's own nationalist aspirations. In 1980, the Parti Québécois government under Réné Lévesque called the first Quebec referendum on sovereignty-association, which was defeated by 60 per cent of the voters. Shortly after the referendum, the federal government under Pierre Trudeau relaunched the constitutional rounds. In 1982, they led to the successful patriation of the Constitution Act. Multiculturalism and equality rights were enshrined in the Constitution Act as part of an extensive bill of rights, the Canadian Charter of Rights and Freedoms. The Charter is usually considered as one of the most progressive in the world in terms of liberal rights.[12] However, it also caused intense contention francophone Québécois. In fact, the Quebec government did not sign the Constitution, in part because it enabled the Supreme Court of Canada to invalidate Quebec's laws and regulations in the name of individual rights (Bourque and Duchastel, 1995). This left Canada with an important anomaly which dominated the political debates in the years to come.

The Meech Lake Accord, drafted in 1987, was the first attempt to bring Quebec into the patriated Canadian Constitution. The centerpiece of the Meech Lake Accord was the recognition of Quebec as a 'distinct society.' Leaders of ethnic groups and Aboriginal peoples criticized the accord for giving special status to one group, French Canadians, while not ensuring the equality of all others. The Meech Lake Accord failed to be ratified by the provincial parliaments of Newfoundland and Manitoba. It collapsed on 23 June 1990 as a result of the procedural obstruction of Elijah Harper, an Aboriginal member of the Manitoba Legislature. Harper's refusal to approve Meech Lake challenged the notion of Canadian French/English 'national' dualism and forcefully underlined the arrival of Canada's 'First Nations' on the political stage (Jhappan, 1993; Laczko, 1997).

Two years later, the Charlottetown Accord was designed to build on the earlier efforts and add protection for the Aboriginal way of life. However, a majority of Canadians were still not satisfied with proposed constitutional reforms. The rejection of the accord in a pan-Canadian referendum on 26 October 1992 left the federal government without a project of constitutional renewal: yet another struggle to constitutionally accommodate a multiplicity of often mutually exclusive claims – raised not only by Quebec and First Nations, but also by the federal government, the remaining provinces, and various 'special interest groups' (women, ethnic groups, the disabled, etc.) – had ended in vain (Cook, 1994; Bourque and Duchastel, 1996; Rocher, 1992).

The failure of five successive rounds of constitutional negotiations since the 1960s and minority groups' vocal claims for political and also cultural recognition left many Canadians of British extraction (and those who identified with this group) wondering about the future of their own 'national community' (Resnick, 1994). As Raymond Breton maintains, 'being Canadian historically meant being defined as speaking English within a British-type institutional system' (Breton, 1984: 129). As a consequence, as Québécois nationalists, Aboriginal peoples, and immigration-derived 'ethnic groups' slowly acquired a larger voice in political, economic, and cultural affairs, their accommodation through the Canadian state was greeted with scepticism or outright hostility on the part of many English Canadians. The latter felt that their way of imagining their country with reference to clearly recognizable British symbols had come under attack (Ayres, 1995).

In addition to fears of binationalism and multiculturalism, many English Canadians also felt threatened through 'encroaching Americanization' (Ayres, 1995: 189). Opposition to the Canada – United States Free Trade Agreement in 1988 (later, in 1993, the North American Free Trade Agreement) was strong in English Canada, whereas in Quebec, federalists and sovereigntists 'were alike in thinking that free trade with the United States would be a very good thing for Québec' (Longstaff, 1992: 35). As a consequence, many Canadians in the rest of Canada viewed Quebec's 'market nationalism' (Courchene, 1986) as an act of treachery. They felt that francophones lacked loyalty at a point when English Canadian identity was thought to be jeopardized by the cultural and economic supremacy of its dominant neighbour to the south.

For many francophone Quebeckers, the ratification of the Free Trade Agreement and the failure of the Charlottetown Accord were indeed incentives to continue with the project of building a Québécois nation. Since the Quiet Revolution, Quebec has striven to build a nation based on French Canadian culture and language within a territorial state. The government slowly started to adapt a proactive role with respect to immigration and integration (Piché, 2003). In 1975, it adopted a bill of rights, the *Charte des droits et libertés*, which also recognized the rights of ethnic minorities within Quebec. Two years later, in 1977, the hotly debated Charter of the French Language (Bill 101) settled the question of which of the province's language groups – 'allophone' immigrants (whose mother tongue was neither French nor English) – should integrate (McAndrew, 2003). 'Interculturalism,' a policy of normative pluralism similar to multiculturalism, was implemented in the early 1980s (McAndrew, 1996; see also Labelle et al., 2007)[13] to slowly foster a better integration of ethnic minorities into Québécois society. However, as *communautés culturelles*, they remained at the margins of the French-Canadian nation (Fontaine and Shiose, 1991), and few of them identified with the project of national sovereignty. In the 1995 Quebec referendum on sovereignty-partnership, 95 per cent of non-French Quebeckers voted against the prospect of independence whereas 60 per cent of francophone Quebeckers voted for separation (Drouilly, 1997; Helly and Van Schendel, 2001).[14]

The referendum on 30 October was defeated by the extremely narrow margin of 50.6 per cent No votes to 49.4 per cent Yes votes.[15] This prompted the federal government to increase its efforts to redefine national belonging in Canada through the promotion of Canadian symbols and celebrations – such as declaring 15 February as National Flag of Canada Day only three months after the referendum[16] – and the review of its multiculturalism policy (1995–97), which was already mentioned in the beginning of this chapter.[17] With respect to Quebec, three measures were taken after the referendum: First, a resolution in parliament that recognized Quebec as a 'distinct society' within Canada. Second, the 1997 Calgary declaration in which the provinces recognized the 'unique' character of Quebec while affirming the equality of all provinces (the declaration was not ratified by Quebec). Third, a call to the Supreme Court of Canada to rule on the legality of a unilateral declaration of independence.[18]

Although the conflict between nationalists in Quebec and English Canada might have caused another wave of criticism against multiculturalism, the opposite was the case: support for multiculturalism, lowest in 1995, rebounded quickly in the following years. In fact, in the years leading up to the referendum, critics often condemned all types of 'groupism,' whether they involved multicultural group rights for immigrants or recognition and self-government rights for national minorities (Beiner, 1995; Schnapper, 1994; Schlesinger, 1998). In both cases, it was feared that 'identity politics' would lead to societal fragmentation (in the republican view) or curtail individual freedom (from the point of view of liberalism). Even commentators who were in favour of multicultural accommodation of immigrants made sure to balance their position by drawing a line between multicultural accommodations, on the one hand, and 'ethnic nationalism' and separation, on the other (Glazer, 1997; Young, 1997).

By contrast, in the period that followed the referendum, hostility was almost solely directed against francophone Québécois and far less against immigrants and ethnic minorities. On the contrary, minorities living in the province of Quebec were seen as victims of Québécois nationalism (Elmer and Abramson, 1997; Webber, 1999). To paraphrase Kymlicka: Otherwise sensible and intelligent people invoked apocalyptic scenarios of segregation and violence. It was not uncommon to hear commentators point ominously to Bosnia or South Africa, as if Canadians were on some slippery slope to civil war or apartheid (1998: 4). Scholarship in media analysis finds that 'ethnicizing, even racializing "slips" about Quebec, Quebeckers, Lucien Bouchard, and the sovereignist government' – which had previously been limited to a number of extremist prejudices – intensified in the post-referendum years (Potvin, 2000b: 2). Maryse Potvin argues that 'by exposing the myth of the Canadian nation, the results of the 1995 referendum have activated an identity crisis among English Canadians, a breakdown of universalist ideas, and a desire for revenge' (2000b: 19). In the Canadian English-language media, francophone Quebec is identified as an inferior 'Other,' its difference is naturalized, and its population seem vulnerable to the conspiracy and irrational appeals of political agitators (who themselves are highly emotional and/or greedy for power and wealth).

English Canadians' 'self-defence,' by contrast, was legitimized by their superior (rational and universalist) institutions and their self-satisfied image of having 'the best country in the world' (Lacombe, 1998: 278). While the quality of these institutions used to be attributed to their genuinely 'British' character, 'flexible federalism' is now considered a 'Canadian' invention, which is carefully disconnected from any particular cultural connotation (Lacombe, 1998, 1997). According to Lacombe (2007), ten years after the referendum, the tone of the debate had even become harder. These observations provoke the question to what extent the 'ethnicization of Québécois nationalism' (Winter, 2001) plays a role for the successful multiculturalization of Canadian 'national' identity. In other words, did Québécois nationalism during the 1990s serve as a counter-image ('them') facilitating the conditional inclusion of ethnically diverse immigrants ('others') into a multicultural Canadian 'we'?

This question, which emerges from my interpretation of the Canadian context in the 1990s, adds a particular twist to the main research question of this book. In the Canadian context, the question 'how do "we" become pluralist?' must not only be translated into 'how do "we" become multicultural?' It also must address to what extent expressions of multinationalism are accounted for. Formulated this way, the notion of Québécois nationalism as a counter-image facilitating multiculturalism provides a focus and working hypothesis for both the theoretical considerations in the following chapters and the empirical study that will be presented further below.

Conclusion

In this chapter, I have developed this book's research question and situated it within the Canadian context. I have argued that the presence of two competing projects of nationhood within the same state provide the multicultural transformation of Canadian 'national we' with a particular twist. The notion of Québécois nationalism as a counter-image to Canadian multicultural inclusion of ethnic groups touches on a number of theoretical debates that will be discussed in the next chapter. Two issues are particularly relevant: first, the question whether the multiculturalization of national identity should be interpreted as concession to or containment of minority groups and nations. The second question that needs to be explored is whether and to what extent previous forms of minority accommodations – such as multinational arrangements – have an impact on the multicultural rights and recognition granted to newcomers.

PART II

Theoretical Considerations

3 Theoretical Puzzles

The multicultural transformation of national identity is a complex process. Reacting to increasing claims made by minority populations, in the 1960s, governments started to introduce policies and legislations related to the concrete, practical aspects of 'managing' ethnocultural diversity caused by immigration. In Canada, examples are the 1971 multiculturalism policy, the 1982 Charter of Rights and Freedoms, and the 1988 Multiculturalism Act, all of which were meant to have an important impact on the Canadian national self-understanding. In the 1980s and 1990s, political philosophers started to 'ratify and explain' these changes (Kymlicka, 1995: 127). The Canadian school of multiculturalism was particularly active and influential in this field (Kernerman, 2005).[1] On the one hand, these theories have convinced both scholars and policy makers that societies *should* be normatively pluralist and why this *should* be so. In fact, towards the end the 1990s, experts predicated a converging consensus of 'liberal culturalism' within Western immigrant-receiving societies (Kymlicka, 2001, chapter 2). Steps towards multicultural immigrant integration policies were taken in many countries (Vertovec and Wessendorf, 2009). For some, Canada served as a role model in this regard (Fontaine, 1995).

On the other hand, the theories of the Canadian school of multiculturalism also promote a very specific reading of ethnocultural diversity and minority accommodation, namely, a highly normative one that is based in political theory and in which ethnic and national minorities are treated separately and are each granted particular rights. While many of these theories bridge the gap between liberalism and communitarianism, they are also grounded in 'liberal culturalism.' As implied by this term, ethnicity and nationality are here not primarily viewed as the outcome of unequal power relations, but treated as relatively static collective identities that provide the background against which individual choices obtain meaning.

During the 1990s, liberal-culturalist theories have come under serious attack by anti-foundationalists for whom state-promoted and philosophical approaches to multiculturalism are merely 'old wine in new bottles,' namely, nationalism and white supremacy in disguise. Critics argue that the apparent concessions of 'multicultural recognition' and 'minority rights' camouflage a politics of containment practised by the dominant group. Indeed, several years into the new century, it has become evident that liberal culturalism did not establish itself as a widely shared consensus. However, critical theory and anti-foundationalism have not taken the upper hand either. On the contrary, the current situation is characterized, as Brubaker (2001) famously put it, by the 'return of assimilation' and the overwhelming assumption that multiculturalism implies far too many concessions (Fulford, 2006; Granatstein, 2007; Gwyn, 1995; Kaplan, 2006; Kent, 2008; Stoffman, 2002). How did we get here, and how can we apprehend the current trend?

This chapter explores the theoretical trajectory of pluralism studies from the post – Second World War era to the crisis of multiculturalism in the 1990s, and the end of the 'differentialist turn,' which received its final death blow on 11 September 2001. The chapter first traces the historical, sociological, and anthropological debates on ethnic diversity and pluralism. The review of these debates shows that there was no 'absence of theory' (as some political theorists suggest; see, e.g., Kymlicka, 1995: 127). On the contrary, recalling some of these older anthropological and sociological debates and concepts can help us to overcome some of the impasses that we are experiencing today.

The chapter then identifies two theoretical puzzles and examines them in detail. The first puzzle has already been mentioned: it relates to the concession/containment dichotomy. The second theoretical puzzle also derives from Canadian scholarship in political theory. It deals with a disciplinary split between theories of nationalism and nation building, on the one hand, and theories on multiculturalism and/or immigration-derived diversity and accommodation, on the other. In the remainder of the book, these two puzzles will be addressed both theoretically (Chapters 4, 5, and 6) and empirically (Chapters 6–9). Solving them, I will argue, is crucial for a better understanding of the pluralist transformation of national identity.

Historical Perspectives

National Minorities and Ethnic Relations

Historically, there have been different ways of dealing with ethnic diversity and cultural rights. In the Old World, at the beginning of the twentieth century, the presence of national minorities ('nationalities') within the geographical territories of newly created political entities ('nations') was considered problematic. This was the golden age of the nation-state. The dominant view that the optimal political unit was the mono-cultural 'one-nation-state' created an environment that was far more hostile to the political expression of ethnic diversity than what we experience today. The challenge was great, indeed, because the disaffected nationalities referred to the same principle that was used to legitimize the nation-state: popular self-determination. In Imperial Austria, Marxist scholars like Otto Bauer and Karl Renner criticized the homogenizing nation-state. They proposed, instead, the incorporation of minorities based on the principles of personality and territoriality (Bauer, 2000; cf. Nimni, 1999). Similar questions concerning cultural minority rights, discussed during the Russian Revolution of 1905–07, caused Max Weber to reflect on the possibilities of cultural autonomy for minority groups in the multinational state (Weber, 1994; Winter, 2004, Ch. 3).

By contrast, what was at stake in New World settler societies were not so much the historical memories and claims for autonomy of minority groups viewing themselves as 'nations,' but rather the incorporation of immigrants into the male-dominated white Anglo-Saxon and Protestant fabric of society (widely known as WASP). In the United States, the model immigration country par excellence, the debate was led in terms of assimilationism versus pluralism (Kivisto and Faist, 2010, chapter 4). Despite the protest of scholars like Horace Kallen (1915) and Randolph Bourne (1977), assimilationism came to be the dominant American ideology. In 1909, the idea of creating a 'new man' through 'melting' found its expression in Israel Zangwill's famous play *The Melting-Pot.* The studies of the Chicago School in the 1930s followed this tradition. Robert Park's (1950) well-known 'race relations circle,' for example, described the sequence of four stages from the initial social contact (which often resulted in conflict) to competition, accommodation, and, finally, assimilation of ideas, cultures, or populations. For Park, the long-term assimilation process of immigrants in the

United States was an inevitable and desirable outcome. By contrast, Louis Wirth (1945), writing in the aftermath of the Second World War, portrayed minorities as groups produced by social and economic inequalities as well as by the atrocities of war rather than by cultural differences. By describing the recognition of their cultural and economic rights as a potential alternative to assimilationism and secessionism Wirth was one of the first defenders of normative pluralism.

From Ethnic Plurality to Normative Pluralism

Following the work of John S. Furnivall (1939, 1945, 1948),[2] in the 1960s, a group of social anthropologists, primarily trained in Britain, started to draw conclusions from their studies of post-colonial societies and to challenge the functional 'equilibrium' model of pluralism in Western societies as being too optimistic.[3] In the old model, individuals were viewed as free to move among different collectivities and associations without being bound by or discriminated against because of ethnicity or culture. By contrast, the young critics argued that the relations between different cultural and 'racial' groups 'are generally characterized by inequality' which is created, to a large degree, through unequal conditions in the market place (Kuper, 1997: 220). They reproached researchers in North America for having 'neglected the major cleavage within their society, that is, the system of racial stratification which reduces Afro-Americans and other people of color to the status of second class citizens' (Van den Berghe, 1967: 69, my translation). In sum, North American society was not 'pluralist' as the old model wanted to have it, but 'plural' because there was a lack of egalitarian integration. The ongoing discrimination against African Americans made it, indeed, increasingly difficult to defend an optimistic view of 'integrative pluralism.' Soon, sociologists scrutinizing ethnic inequalities in the settler societies joined the critics. Their work criticized, for example, the persisting 'color line' in the United States (Glazer and Moyinhan, 1963) and the 'vertical mosaic' in Canada (Porter, 1965).

In 1970, Richard A. Schermerhorn (1970: 122–5) distinguished between four components of pluralism: Cultural pluralism describes 'factual' ethnic, 'racial,' or religious diversity. Political pluralism implies the existence of multiple social and political 'interest groups' and associations (which are operating at an intermediate level between the individual and the state and which are generally associated with civil society). Structural pluralism presupposes the division of society and its institutional structure into multiple segments. Cultural, political, and structural pluralism are merely descriptive. In Schermerhorn's model, only the fourth component, normative pluralism, contains an ideological dimension. It responds to the questions of what kind of society is desirable; whether and how minority groups should be incorporated; and what role the state should take to foster the realization of this vision. Historically, there have been many different answers to these questions.[4]

Denial and assimilation of ethnocultural diversity (in cases where diversity is viewed as a handicap for individual integration and social cohesion) are usually not considered 'pluralist' approaches. By contrast, institutionalized racism and apartheid are, strictly speaking, 'pluralist' state responses to ethnocultural diversity. Some scholars therefore discredit the concept of pluralism altogether (Jenkins, 1997, chapter 3). Schermerhorn (1970: 122) avoids this type of criticism by defining normative pluralism not from the point of view of the dominant society but citing Louis Wirth: 'a pluralistic minority is one which seeks toleration for its differences on the part of the dominant group' (1945: 354). Defined in this way, pluralism cannot be interpreted as an instrument of ethnic oppression. (No minority would ask to be oppressed by the dominant group.) Rather, pluralism encourages the expression of group cultures and identities within society, promotes equality, and condemns discrimination. Further elaborated as 'democratic institutional pluralism' (DIP), pluralism provides resources and opportunities for minorities to be able to redress inequalities and power asymmetries (Bader, 2003: 132).[5] In sum, the normatively pluralist society does not want to be a 'plural' one (Rex, 1997).

Pluralism as a framework for society building remains, nevertheless, highly controversial. While Schermerhorn's definition of normative pluralism suggests an egalitarian incorporation of ethnic minorities (as affirmed in the slogan 'different but equal'), it does not provide an answer as to how much institutional variety and group-differentiated rights this idea implies. In fact, for the sociologist, this decision is left open to constant renegotiation. In Schermerhorn's theory, the translation of factual cultural diversity into other forms of pluralism depends to a large degree on (1) the dynamics of power (in demographic, economic, and political terms) between dominant and subordinate groups, and (2) the historical relationship that brought these groups into contact in the first place (i.e., slavery, migration, conquest, or colonization). Depending on their access to power and resources, minority groups have a smaller or greater capacity to pressure for modes of social, cultural, economic, and political integration, on the one hand, or autonomy, self-government, and separation, on the other. To concur with Raymond Breton (1964), they are characterized by different degrees of 'institutional complete-ness.' In Canada, this difference is particularly evident when comparing the francophones of Quebec with immigrant associations.

Rethinking Citizenship

In the 1970s and 1980s, the debate about ethnic pluralism became grad-ually translated into a controversy about multiculturalism. The term is inherently linked to the Canadian experience with ethnic diversity. According to the *Longer Oxford English Dictionary* (quoted in Stratton and Ang, 1998: 138), multiculturalism was first used to describe Montreal as a 'multicultural' city (in the Montreal *Times,* June 1959), and was then employed (in 1965), in the *Preliminary Report of the Royal Commission on Bilingualism and Biculturalism.* In the 1990s, the term became associated with the idea of citizenship – a concept that had been largely absent from public and academic debates for several decades (Kymlicka and Norman, 1994).

In 1949, T.H. Marshall had argued that citizenship is a system of equality that developed alongside and in relationship to capitalism. Within this logic, class inequality is balanced, to a certain extent, by citizenship equality (Turner, 1990). Citizenship assures that all mem-bers of a given collectivity are equal in terms of rights and obligations, and this not only in terms of legal status but also in a factual sense. According to Marshall, citizenship can only be integrative when a minimum of equality is achieved: 'the right of freedom of speech has little real substance if, from lack of education, you have nothing to say that is worth saying, and no means of making yourself heard if you say it' (1973: 97). In the 1990s, this 'thick' conception of citizenship-as-practice (as opposed to a 'thin' conception of citizenship-as-status) became the general perspective adopted by theorists (Kymlicka and Norman, 1994: 354).

Marshall further divided citizenship rights into three categories which he saw as having been institutionalized (in England) in the rough historical sequence of three centuries: civil rights were developed in the eighteenth century, political rights in the nineteenth, and social rights in the twentieth.[6] Although this sequence has been criticized for suggesting a linear, quasi 'natural' evolution of citizenship rights

(Birnbaum, 1996; Isin and Wood, 1999), commentators have also predicted that negotiations over the implementation of cultural citizenship rights (as a fourth component) will play an important role in the social and political history of the twenty-first century (Rocher, 2000: 41; Stevenson, 1997).

Like many scholars writing on social differentiation (such as Parsons, Bourdieu, or Luhmann), Marshall failed to acknowledge the link between the increasing internal inclusiveness of citizenship and the reinforcement of the nation's external borders. In fact, the extension of modern citizenship develops alongside and in close relationship with the external closure of the political community along ethnic or national lines. Recent scholarship has confirmed that citizenship practices are deeply informed by the dominant national culture – which is not only class-based, as Marshall would have it, but also marked by gender, 'race,' language, and ethnicity.

Although Marshall's account of citizenship is concerned very little with the inclusion of minority populations (Dietz, 1992; Hirschman, 1991; Mann, 1996), his definition of citizenship as an evolving ideal of equality (Marshall, 1973: 92) foreshadows Talcott Parsons' (1967) understanding of the actualization of equality as a double process of inclusion: The horizontal extension of citizenship implies the progressive extension of citizenship status to new populations (slaves, women, non-property-owners, immigrants, etc.). The vertical extension of citizenship rights requires the passage from equality as a value and status to de facto equality which, in increasingly ethnically diverse societies, relies upon the institutionalization of legal, political, social and eventually, cultural rights and practices (Juteau, 1993, 1997a).

In his 1964 essay 'Full Citizenship for the Negro American?' Parsons maintained that 'by being included in larger community structures, the individual need not cease to be a member of the smaller ones' (Parsons, 1969: 280). He explicitly distinguished between inclusion and assimilation (ibid.: 258) and emphasized the task of the larger society to eliminate status-inferiority based on 'race,' creed, or colour (ibid.: 280). On the one hand, Parsons' concern was more with anti-discrimination, or 'laissez-faire pluralism' in Milton Gordon's (1981) terms, than normative pluralism: The 'American Negro' had to be transformed into a 'Negro American.' Therefore, the basic demand of Black Americans could not be 'for domination or for equality on a basis of separateness [as is the case with Orthodox Jews or the French-speaking minority in Canada]' (Parsons, 1969: 280).

On the other hand, Parsons' discussion of culture and identity claims for the achievement of 'full citizenship' points to the heated debates about multiculturalism and citizenship in the 1990s (Birnbaum, 1996: 75). In fact, T.H. Marshall already cautioned that under certain circumstances citizenship equality may also become 'an instrument of social stratification' (1973: 121, cf. 77).[7] This argument has been elaborated by Iris Marion Young (2000), one of the most influential proponents of group-differentiated citizenship rights.

The idea of universal citizenship in Western political thought relies heavily upon the distinction between the public sphere (defined as the realm of generality in which all particularities are left behind) and the private sphere (defined as the particular, the realm of affectivity, affiliation, need, and the body). In this model, we all participate in the public sphere as equal citizens. Members of groups characterized by 'particular' features can only be accommodated by assimilation or by practising their culture within the private realm, where it does not interfere with the functioning of the common institutions.[8]

Challenging this separation, feminists have argued that the public realm of politics, citizenship, equality, and inclusion relies heavily upon 'private' material, biological, emotional, cultural, and symbolic reproduction and nurturing. As Young puts it: 'As guardians of the private realm of need, desire, and affectivity, women must ensure that men's impulses do not subvert the universality of Reason' (1989: 254). The so-called virtues of modern citizenship – defined as universal humanity – derive thus from specifically masculine and bourgeois experiences and norms. Women 'who are responsible for tending to that private realm, and who lack the dispassionate rationality and independence required of good citizens' are excluded from this view (ibid.). The logic of exclusion qua 'difference' has been extended from women to the working classes and ethnic minorities, all associated with subjectivity, irrationality, and partisanship (Pateman, 1988; Phillips, 1993).

Thus, rather than being neutral and all-inclusive, universal citizenship based on representation in the public realm speaks to the particular interests, values, and hegemonic culture of the dominant group. Blind to power differences, Young claims, universal citizenship merely privileges the dominant group and reproduces 'inequality in practice.' Differentiating between five different types of oppression – exploitation, marginalization, powerlessness, cultural imperialism, and random violence and/or group hatred (Young, 1989: 261) – she advocates a concept of citizenship that promotes group-differentiated representation.

As a critical theory of multiculturalism 'from below,' Young's theory challenges dominant conceptions of citizenship. It constitutes, to paraphrase Christian Joppke (1998: 286), a challenge to the nation as the premier cultural community of the modern world, a quest for recognition and compensatory treatment of historically disadvantaged and discriminated-against groups in society, and a generalized form of anti-colonial discourse and struggle. As such, it does not lend itself easily to sociopolitical operationalization and policy making (Barry, 2001; Joppke, 2002; Baumeister, 1999).

Other commentators have chosen a different path. Their apprehension of group-differentiated citizenship operates within a state-supported logic of multiculturalism which implies 'an official recognition of the existence of different ethnic groups within the state's borders [and] concerns about disadvantage and equity which the state recognizes as its responsibility to address' (Stratton and Ang, 1998: 138). In these cases, theory 'merely ratifies and explains [political] changes that have taken place in the absence of theory' (Kymlicka, 1995: 239). It 'does not create a mandate for a vast change' (ibid.). Two of the most influential scholars in this respect have been Charles Taylor and Will Kymlicka. Strongly inspired by the Canadian context, they have overcome the cleavages between liberals (Rawls, 1971) and communitarians (Sandel, 1982), and introduced Canadian pluralist politics to an international audience. In the next section, I will lay out these authors' important theories, the opposition they triggered, and the theoretical puzzles that we are grappling with today.

The Multiculturalization of National Identity: Concession or Containment?

Justified Concession

In his seminal essay 'The Politics of Recognition,' Charles Taylor argues that achieving the recognition of difference and preserving Canadian multinational society[9] implies that the orthodox model of liberalism, with its assumption of neutrality and application of 'difference-blind' procedures, has to be abandoned. His argument in favour of multiculturalism is based on the idea that identity is a vital human need: identity 'is who we are, "where we're coming from." As such it is the background against which our tastes and desires and opinions and aspirations make sense' (Taylor, 1994: 33–4). Since identity is dialogical not monological 'we can flourish only to the extent that we are recognized' (ibid.: 50). According to Taylor, the *misrecognition* of Québécois and Aboriginal identities is harmful or even detrimental to the well-being of their bearers. They deserve the recognition of their difference and the necessary means to preserve their collective goals and culture.

Taylor's argument is in line with communitarian and feminist scholarship. He argues that societal rules and institutions are not neutral but deeply informed by culture. For him, the politics of non-discrimination are therefore profoundly discriminatory. Citing the example of Quebec Aboriginals in Canada, Taylor argues that these groups' collective goal of securing the survival of their cultures outweighs some less important individual rights (such as commercial signs in English or sending one's children to schools conducted in English). In place of 'procedural liberalism,' Taylor offers a recognition-based theory of pluralism which guarantees certain rights to all, but distinguishes 'these fundamental rights from the broad range of immunities and presumptions of uniform treatment that have sprung up in modern cultures of judicial review' (1994: 61). In other words, his 'politics of recognition' does not replace the liberal 'politics of equal dignity' – which is based on the idea that all human beings are equally worthy of respect – but supplements it with a 'politics of difference' – that, roughly speaking, extends this view to the realm of cultures. According to Taylor, we do not owe equal appreciation to all cultures (ibid.: 66). However, because cultures which 'animated whole societies over some considerable stretch of time have something important to say to all human beings' (ibid.), we owe these cultures equal respect – and, consequently, the necessary institutional means to assure their 'survival.'

A problem arises, nevertheless, when the survival needs of one cultural group conflict with those of another. In practice, a certain hierarchy of cultural worthiness seems thus unavoidable. Elsewhere, Taylor consequently differentiates between 'first level diversity' – that is, a relative homogenizing expression of individual-based belonging to the Canadian nation shared by ethnic minorities and English-speaking Canadians – and 'second level diversity' or 'deep diversity' – that is, the expression of community-based belonging to Canada formulated by many French Canadians, (French-speaking) Quebeckers, and Aboriginal peoples. According to Taylor, Québécois, Cree, or Déné can thus be Canadian by virtue of being members of their national communities (Taylor, 1993: 183).

Will Kymlicka builds upon this proposition in his influential book *Multicultural Citizenship*. Placing more emphasis on liberalism than Taylor, Kymlicka argues that some group-differentiated minority rights are consistent with freedom and justice, as well as with the long-term requirements of a stable liberal democracy and shared civic identity (1995: 173).[10] Similar to Taylor, Kymlicka starts by abandoning the assumption of state neutrality. He argues that modern states invariably develop, consolidate, and rely upon a 'societal culture,' that is, a set of common (educational, political, and legal) institutions, covering both public and private life, and a common language (2001: 53). Both freedom of choice and equality of opportunity are made available to the individual through membership in a societal culture which provides individuals with equal opportunities to participate in common institutions and allows them to make free and informed decisions about how to lead their lives. Societal group membership becomes thus a crucial feature for individual autonomy, freedom, and equality. Because most individuals have a strong bond to their own native culture, ethnic and national minorities can and should enjoy certain collective rights in liberal democracies, on the condition that these do not limit the liberty of the group's own members in the name of group solidarity ('internal restrictions'), but rather ensure that the resources and institutions on which the minority depends are not vulnerable to majority decisions ('external restrictions').

Kymlicka distinguishes between three types of rights: (1) polyethnic rights (or accommodation rights), for example, financial support and legal protection for certain practices associated with particular ethnic or religious groups; (2) special representation rights, for example, guaranteed seats for ethnic or national groups within the central institutions of the larger state; and (3) self-government rights, for example, the delegation of powers to national minorities through some form of federalism. According to Kymlicka, polyethnic and representation rights are consistent with – or may even be beneficial for – the integration of immigrants and ethnic groups into the mainstream societal culture. By contrast, self-government rights 'pose a serious threat to social unity, since they encourage the national minority to view itself as a separate people with inherent rights to govern itself' (1995: 9).

Like Taylor, Kymlicka uses a historical, culturalist justification to differentiate between different types of cultural diversity and the rights associated with them. First, in multinational states, he argues, 'cultural diversity arises from the incorporation of previously self-governing, territorially concentrated cultures into a larger state' (1995: 6). National minorities have developed a societal culture and should therefore be entitled to polyethnic representation, and even a certain amount of self-government rights – because 'denying self-government rights can also threaten social unity, by encouraging secession' (ibid.: 9). Second, in polyethnic (or multicultural) states, 'cultural diversity arises from individual and familial immigration' (ibid.: 6). According to Kymlicka, ethnic groups derived from immigration no longer possess a vibrant societal culture and/or have 'relinquished' their right to it by immigration (ibid.: 96). They nevertheless deserve polyethnic and representation rights which are viewed as fostering their integration into the mainstream culture.

In Kymlicka's view, Canada is characterized by two or even three (if a distinction is made between the Québécois and Aboriginal peoples; Kymlicka, 2003) types of diversity. Canada contains 'national minorities' like the Québécois and Aboriginal peoples, as well as 'ethnic groups' composed of 'immigrants who have left their national community to enter another society' (1995: 19).[11] Kymlicka's vision of Canada also contains, as Richard Day reminds us, a 'majority' (ibid.: 121), 'a "we" that would have done the "incorporation" of cultures and immigrants, and would now "need to supplement traditional human rights principles with a theory of minority rights"' (ibid.: 5, quoted in Day, 2000: 211–12). Who exactly this dominant Canadian 'we' is remains unspecified. We may assume that it refers to the anglophone majority composed by those of British ancestry and, presumably, those white (Protestant) Europeans who have assimilated to it.

Taylor's and Kymlicka's contributions have helped to transform multiculturalism from a discourse of resistance to a mainstream theoretical approach. Multicultural rights appear here as *justified concessions* which are granted to individuals on the basis of their ethnocultural identity. While both authors argue in favour of Québécois and Aboriginal peoples' recognition as national minorities and some sort of asymmetrical federalism within the Canadian state, they specifically insist on interpreting immigration-derived ethnic groups' demands for multiculturalism as the quest for integration rather than separation. Over several years, their theories have provided a normative rationale for decision makers in charge of designing integration policies for immigrants. Nevertheless, as we will see in the next section, these authors' normative theories have also raised much contention. Furthermore, as I will briefly describe below, liberal culturalism has not become an uncontested 'consensus' as some had predicted it would (Kymlicka, 2001, chapter 2).

Containment

Liberal culturalism has come under sharp criticism by a series of new theoretical perspectives ranging from reflexive feminism and social psychoanalysis to post-modernism, post-structuralism, or post-Marxism. Although inherently diverse, these 'anti-foundationalist' approaches (Malesevic, 2004: 143) are united in their objection against universalism, positivism, and the totalizing objectives of 'conventional' sociology and other disciplines. They criticize – from various theoretical points of view and, thus, with various outcomes – political philosophy's naive or even Eurocentric preoccupation with culture. Multiculturalism 'from above' (Bannerji, 2000: 44–5) is here viewed as an ideology of 'containment' which promotes the ethniciziation and racialization of non-white, non-Western immigrants and Aboriginal peoples and thus reifies – rather than changes or challenges – these groups' subordinate place within the existing social order and the national imaginary (for the Canadian context, see Bannerji, 2000; Day, 2000; Mackey, 1999; McFarlane, 1995; Moodley, 1982; Razack, 2002; Thobani, 2007).

On the one hand, the notion of group-based 'multicultural' rights is contradicted by the fluidity of identity formation. As Edward Said puts it: 'No one today is purely *one* thing. Labels like Indian, or woman, or Muslim, or American are not more than starting-points, which, if followed into actual experience for only a moment, are quickly left behind' (1994a: 336). In post-modernist approaches, identities are here manipulable and may thus be used for resistance to fixed and imposed categories of culture (Waters, 1990).[12] On the other hand, opportunities of hybridity and fluid identity formation are not distributed equally among social actors. Post-colonial theorists insist that members of minority groups often find themselves deeply constrained by socio-economic inequality and racism. To concur with Bannerji, multiculturalism 'obscure[s] deeper/structural relations of power' and 'reduces the question of social justice into questions of curry and turban' (Bannerji, 2000: 38). Multiculturalism ('recognition') is here viewed as neglecting and camouflaging material inequalities ('redistribution') and even as (re)producing them through the ethnicization and racialization of groups (Fraser, 1998).[13]

In Canada, Eva Mackey and Richard Day have advanced sharp critiques of multiculturalism. Mackey's *House of Difference* (1999) is an anthropological study of the construction of Canadian national identity. She combines a macro-analysis of the historical evolution of Canadian nationalist discourse with micro-case studies of the 1992 celebrations of Canada's 125th anniversary in rural Ontario. Mackey argues that Canada, rather than seeking to erase or homogenize ethnocultural diversity, has tended to appropriate it, pressing it into the service of a national project defined by 'white and most often British settlers' (ibid.: 89). Within multicultural nationalism, Mackey contends, Aboriginal, French Canadian, and immigrant cultures are framed as colourful marginal additions to Canada's (Anglo-Saxon) dominant culture. The latter remains unmarked and invisible, a non-hyphenated de-ethnicized 'Canadian-Canadian' norm in comparison with which all other practices and identities are constructed as 'multicultural.'

In *Multiculturalism and the History of Canadian Diversity*, Day extends this argument. Linking present-day multicultural policy to the history of colonialism and the management of populations in Canada, he traces the changing and proliferating categories of otherness from the early twentieth century to the development of official multiculturalism in the 1960s and 1970s (2000: 122–6). Day argues that Aboriginal peoples, French Canadians, European immigrants, and non-white populations became gradually incorporated into the rational bureaucratic project that has come to represent 'the Canadian Way' (ibid.: 113) of dealing with ethnocultural diversity. Like Mackey, Day admits that Canada has taken a different route from the traditional modern nation-state, which '*simulated a unity and dissimulated its multiplicity.*' By contrast, a postmodern nation-state like Canada, Day argues, '*dissimulates its unity and simulates a multiplicity*' (ibid.: 205, original emphasis). State-produced multiculturalism disciplines officially constructed (ethnic) identities to control and 'manage' them. At the same time, 'the perennially problematic and excluded Other is in fact *required* to create a simulation of wholeness for the [national] Self' (ibid.: 34, original emphasis). According to Day, full multicultural inclusion is thus unachievable.

The 'simulation' of assimilation of Self to Other also seems to inhibit some of Canadian scholarship (Day, 2000: 6, 27). According to Day, there is an implicit normative 'we' in Taylor's and Kymlicka's much-cited works on multiculturalism. These theories fail to question the legitimacy of a 'silent, Invisible Self group that chooses to give, or not to give, gifts of recognition and self-government to noisy, Visible Others' (ibid.: 216). This 'invisible self group' corresponds to the group of 'Canadian-Canadians' identified by Mackey. It is this group that enjoys (majority) rights in an unquestioned fashion without requiring a theory of 'multicultural' justification (ibid.: 212).

To a certain extent, these critiques of multiculturalism are very convincing. In fact, the approaches discussed in this section challenge the undertheorization of power inequalities in philosophical approaches as naive or even deliberate. For them, multiculturalism is a political tool that caters to the national majority (or majorities – as in the Canadian case) through ethnicization, racialization, and incorporation of others into a fixed structure of material and symbolic ethnosocial stratification.

Unfortunately, the approaches discussed in this section fail to provide us with alternatives. If ethnocultural pluralism is not an option, what then? This flaw seems to be systemic in the epistemological program of critical and anti-foundationalist theories. A Foucauldian perspective, for example, is very good at showing how ethical-political ideas are constructed through a history of disciplinary practices. But if all construction is 'power,' and all power is necessarily problematic, it becomes difficult to articulate whether some constructs – such as the multicultural one – may be preferable to others. Furthermore, within these theories, culture and ethnicity seem to be primarily a concern of the dominant group, if not ultimately produced by it. Very little is said about minority agency and why minorities often voice their claims for recognition and inclusion in terms of culture and ethnic identity.[14] As Ian Angus puts it: 'It is commonplace at conferences, and at universities, to hear the claim that multiculturalism was, or is, a strategy of the federal government for maintaining its control. This account requires that one ignore all the places in the history of multiculturalism where ethnic groups entered into the fray and affected the outcome' (2002b: 78).[15]

These discussions show that we need a relational approach to multiculturalism which theorizes both dominant constructions of ethnic categories and ethnic and national minorities' agency in subverting these constructions. Regrettably, in recent years, yet another perspective has taken the upper hand. We are experiencing an extended backlash against multiculturalism, in which the use of culturalism plays an important role. As Anne Phillips (2007) eloquently shows: While critics misrepresent culture as the explanation of everything that individuals from minority and non-Western groups do, advocates of multiculturalism fail to reject the reified concept of culture on which their arguments often rely.

Too Much Concession

The theoretical stand-off – located, roughly speaking, at the political left – between multiculturalism as justified concession, on the one hand, and as illegitimate containment, on the other – has invigorated yet another critique of multiculturalism, which originates further right on the political spectrum. This critique posits that Western liberal democracies have gone 'too far' in their accommodation of increasingly non-Western immigrant minorities. Critics argue that state-supported multiculturalism fails to encourage immigrants' integration and adherence to liberal values. As such, it entails *too much concession*. Critiques are voiced from two separate but interrelated perspectives: orthodox liberalism and civic republicanism.

In liberal theory, individuals are considered to be more important than the political community they belong to. Based on the Enlightenment idea of universal Reason, liberalism defines the boundaries of political communities not in terms of culture or tradition but as the agreement on supposedly 'neutral' procedures. They are justified in utilitarian or functional terms which are necessary to assure individual freedom from constraints. Consequently, from a liberal point of view, differentiated multicultural group rights are neither necessary (because no culture prevails over the other, and all citizens agree upon neutral, universal procedures) nor desirable (because they undermine the principle of individual equality). Most recently, Brian Barry (2001) has revived this point of view.[16] Commentators are particularly concerned about the tensions between individual freedom and the often traditional and sometimes openly anti-liberal practices of minority groups. They maintain that multicultural 'group rights strengthen dominant subgroups within each culture and privilege conservative interpretations of culture over reformative and innovative ones' (Tamir, 1999: 47). Instead of contributing to the promotion of 'human well-being' and a just social order, multiculturalism fails to protect the most vulnerable individuals, that is, cultural minorities and women within minority groups (Okin, 2002).[17]

(Illiberal) restrictions imposed on minority members are a serious problem that should not be discarded easily (Shachar, 2001). Nevertheless, many commentators overstate the 'anti-liberal' characteristics of minority groups. They overlook that illiberal features such as economic protectionism and racism are also widespread within the mainstream society (Parekh, 1995; Bauböck, 2002), and that economic, cultural, and political marginalization impacts minority intragroup relations and often dramatically diminishes the status of women (Yuval-Davis, 1993; Arat-Koc, 1999). To put it with Bhikhu Parekh: 'fundamentalism is often provoked by liberal intolerance' (Parekh, 1995: 204). In sum, liberal approaches fail to question why certain groups may indeed be(come) factually more 'illiberal' than others, and what causes some groups rather than others to stress cultural homogeneity and 'tradition.'

Liberalism's concern with minority anti-liberalism finds its counterpart in civic republicanism's fear of social fragmentation. Republican citizenship rejects both the 'natural' cohesion implied by ethnic ties and the agglomeration of 'egoistic' individual interests within liberalism. It requires an active commitment on the part of the individual to cherish a common cause and asserts the need for strong civic institutions, national cohesion, and shared identity to create a durable allegiance between the citizens of the nation.[18] As a consequence, civic republicans are thus deeply concerned that group identities displayed in the public space may lead to 'ghettoization' (Beiner, 1995: 6–8; Schlesinger, 1998; for a critique, see Ryan, 2010). They accuse multiculturalism of encouraging groups to look inward and focus on their 'difference,' thereby leading to the politicization of ethnicity and the creation of a spiral of competition, mistrust, and antagonism which erodes the citizens' ability and/or will to communicate and interact in solidarity across group differences.

While civic republicans are correct in arguing that a societal project requires a certain amount of shared values, they tend to overlook the conflicts, inequalities, and differences inherent in social relations (Mouffe, 1992b; Guérard de Latour, 2009). To paraphrase Ernest Renan's memorable lecture about national myth making, they 'have forgotten many things' (1991: 34, my translation). As a consequence, civic republicans tend to construct a false equation between social cohesion and ethnic homogeneity (Bernard, 1999; Helly, 1999; Jenson, 2002; Juteau, 2003).[19] Furthermore, civic republicanism bears the tendency to equate dominant nationalism with civic values. Historically *ethnos* and *demos* have never been completely disentangled (Nimni, 2006). Wherever and whenever this disentanglement existed, very much of the reasoning in favour of *civisme* was done on behalf of the dominant group (Birch, 1989; Billig, 1995; Gagnon et al., 2007).

In recent years, orthodox liberalism has been increasingly supplanted by civic republicanism. First, liberalism only provides a weak and instrumental notion of collective identity and solidarity, which does not seem sufficient to hold together national societies that – as a result of the pressures of globalization – are increasingly diverse in ethnic, cultural, religious, and professional and lifestyle terms (Bader, 2005b; Bauböck, 1998, 2002; Taylor, 1995, 2001). Second, the assumed 'civic' dimension of republicanism has been intensely deconstructed both in theory and practice (Giesen and Junge, 1998; Nielsen, 1998; Nimni, 2006; Seymour et al., 1998; Stolcke, 1997). This leads to the question of to what extent current immigration, integration, and citizenship policies are indeed mainly 'civic' (Joppke, 2008a) or increasingly 'renationalized' (Jacobs and Rea, 2007; see also Chapter 11).

We have seen that two of the most influential normative theorizations of multiculturalism distinguish between national and ethnic minorities. Taking their inspiration from the Canadian case, Charles Taylor and Will Kymlicka distinguish between Québécois and Aboriginal peoples as 'minority nations' and immigration-derived 'ethnic groups.' While the distinction between various types of minority categories is crucial for these influential theories, the relations between different types of national and ethnic struggles for rights and recognition have remained unexplored. As argued above, for the sociologist, this normative prescription of rights and duties based upon culturalist group characteristics is problematic because it fails to understand these groups' mutually constitutive relations. In the next section, I will, therefore, explore the relations between different types of diversity and their accommodations.

Different Types of Diversity Accommodation: With or without Relations?

National minorities have often been described as previously self-governing peoples who – through colonization, conquest, or treaties of federation – have become incorporated into states in which they do not constitute the majority. They are territorially concentrated and usually characterized by a great degree of institutional completeness (Breton, 1964). The members of immigration-derived ethnic groups, by contrast, are said to have become members of society 'individually' through more or less 'voluntary' immigration (Kymlicka, 1995: 96). They are geographically dispersed and lack the capacity to create fully functional social, political, and economic institutions of their own. These sociological differences create demands for different kinds of pluralist accommodations (Juteau, 1999a). National minorities, typically, ask for rights that enable them to pursue their own cultural values, religious beliefs, language, and lifestyle. They want to create or maintain separate societal institutions. By contrast, members of ethnic groups usually strive for integration into the dominant society.[20] Members of ethnic groups also ask for group-specific accommodation and the right to express their cultural particularity. However, they seldom demand the right to form 'parallel societies.'[21]

In responding to these different demands, states have typically aimed at introducing clear-cut policies, partly accommodating these groups' claims, partly curtailing them. In the Canadian case, for example, different rights were granted to Aboriginal peoples, the francophones (of Quebec), and 'ethnic groups.' But these rights did neither emerge from a deep normative foundation, nor did the layering of federal policies and laws over time lead to one integrated framework (Kymlicka, 2007: 41).

In sorting through the diverse sets of state policies and normatively grounding them (Kymlicka, 1995: 127), Canadian scholars reinstated the sociological categories, linked them to a 'Canadian way' of dealing with ethnocultural diversity (Kymlicka, 1998), and provided them with normative foundations of universal validity. Thereby, they produced internationally accepted differentiations between national and ethnic minorities. As we have seen, Charles Taylor's (1993) concept of Québécois and Aboriginal peoples' 'deep diversity' (versus other Canadians' 'first level' membership in the polity) translates into Will Kymlicka's (1995) liberal theory of minority rights, which grants more substantial autonomy rights to Québécois and Aboriginal peoples (both viewed as 'minority nations' with distinct 'societal cultures') than to immigration-derived 'ethnic groups.'

It is not my aim here to challenge the normative reasoning behind these theories, even though, from a sociological point of view, it is doubtful whether one can durably associate one type of minority with a particular set of rights that is unattainable for another group. This is because the empirical differences between national minorities and immigration-derived ethnic groups are not as clear-cut as normative theorizing may want to have it. I do not intend to challenge sociological categories here either, but let us briefly consider the following examples: In some cases, second- and third-generation immigrants are not integrated on equal terms with the mainstream population. In Canada, this has recently been demonstrated for second-generation 'visible minorities' (Reitz and Banerjee, 2007). Long-term (voluntary or involuntary) geographical concentration or 'ghettoization' of immigrants can also lead to a situation where immigration-derived 'ethnic groups' take on many of the characteristics that are typically associated with national minorities. In other cases, the distinctiveness of national minorities may slowly become eroded, and this even without much contestation by the groups' members. How do we justify fixed differential rights attributed to the status of 'national minority' versus 'ethnic group' in these situations? These difficulties within Taylor's and Kymlicka's theories have received much scholarly attention (Baumeister, 1999; Choudhry, 2002; Parekh, 1997; Pogge, 2003; Stasiulis, 1995; Walker, 1997).

My focus here is yet another one. As argued above, here I do not challenge the distinction between the different categories of minorities and minority accommodations, on which these influential theories so heavily rely. Rather, I contend that the relations between the different types of national and ethnic struggles for rights and recognition have remained unexplored, and this not only in Taylor's and Kymlicka's work but also in much of the subsequent scholarly literature.

Indeed, in the contemporary literature, the relationship between national minorities and their accommodations and those of immigrants is either absent or treated as a historical phenomenon, which shaped the implementation of multiculturalism policies in countries like Canada and the Netherlands before the latter developed a dynamic of their own (Lijphart, 1968; McRoberts, 1997). Connections between multinationalism and multiculturalism can be traced in some approaches to pluralism (Bourque and Duchastel, 1996; Fennema and Tillie, 2001), but recently a division of labour along disciplinary lines has become manifest.

On the one hand, many political theorists, roughly speaking, focus on nationalism, federalism, and the conditions of diversity in 'multinational' democracies (Gagnon and Tully, 2001; Gagnon et al., 2003). Recently, for example, English Canada's nationalism has been conceptualized as 'dominant' as it manifests itself primarily through laws and institutions while integrating certain expressions of diversity, such as official bilingualism, liberal multiculturalism, and the Canadian Charter of the Rights and Freedoms (Bickerton, 2007). In Chapter 7, I will argue that these studies can help us to better understand Canadian nationalism but fail to theorize its inherent multicultural character.

On the other hand, sociologists tend to examine group relations and immigrant integration in increasingly 'multicultural' cities (Anisef and Lanphier, 2003; Renaud, 2001). What tends to be missing here is the problematization of the relations between immigrants and historic minorities. More specifically, Québécois and/or francophones are rarely at the centre of attention (for an exception, see Maddibo, 2006). As a consequence, within contemporary scholarship, theories of nationalism and theories of multiculturalism seldom cross-fertilize.

The gap in the literature is by no means limited to the Canadian case. In Europe, too, scholars deplore 'the radical analytical split between the demand of two kinds of cultural pluralism movements: minority nations, on the one hand, and ethnic groups, on the other' (Máiz and Requejo, 2005: 2). This is even more astonishing as many European states (Belgium, Spain, the United Kingdom, Sweden, and others) need to accommodate both national minorities and immigration-derived ethnic groups (Guibernau, 2006; Harzig, 2004; Hussain, 2006; Martiniello, 1996, 1998). Do these accommodations operate entirely separately from each other (as suggested by Kymlicka, 2007), or does the accommodation of historically established groups in some way 'guide' the integration of newcomers?

In Canada, the sharp separation between minority nations and ethnic groups is a fundamental departure from the way multiculturalism was debated in the years before and after its original implementation in 1971 (Rocher, 1971). As outlined in Chapter 2, the rights of immigrants and their descendants – defined as 'other ethnic groups' by the Royal Commission on Bilingualism and Biculturalism (1963–70) – were very much associated with those of French Canadians. According to some commentators, it is precisely through this comparison that ethnic groups in Canada gained rights as a 'third force' (Lütsch, 2004). Others insist that the shift from overt racial distinctions between the French and the English (as the 'two founding races') to the terrain of language and culture weakened the demands of Aboriginal peoples and non-white Canadians as racially excluded groups (Haque, 2005). In other words, while the parallel between European ethnic groups (established by themselves and others) and the French-Canadian 'national' minority allowed all ethnic groups in Canada to gain cultural rights, it undermined Aboriginal peoples' and non-European immigrants' contestation of ongoing racial discrimination. Has the relationship between Canadian dualism and multiculturalism become a matter of the past? Or does the presence of Canada's historically established national minorities still inform the debates on immigrant integration and multiculturalism?

At this point, we can merely conclude that explicit multinationalism (or similar arrangements between a country's national groups) and multiculturalism as a recent response to immigration-derived diversity do not seem to exist parallel to each other without interrelations. On the one hand, being incorporated as 'traditions' within the organization of the nation-state (its system of laws, institutions, norms, symbols, etc.), the relations between national groups and their explicitly or implicitly 'multinational' accommodations impact the framing and scope of multicultural rights for immigration-derived ethnic groups. On the other hand, learning from and comparing themselves with pre-existing national minorities, immigration-derived ethnic groups exploit pre-existing discourses and structures in the hope to achieve similar social, cultural, and political rights and recognition.

In order to understand the multiculturalization of national identity, it is therefore not sufficient to concentrate merely on the relation that a seemingly unified 'host society' entertains with its ethnic group of immigrant origin and to evacuate questions of multinationalism and other pluralist compromises from our analysis. Rather, this relationship is mediated by other pluralist arrangements within a society in question. It is therefore important to elaborate a theoretical framework that overcomes the analytical split between minority nationalism and its accommodation, on the one hand, and multiculturalism as a response to immigration-related diversity, on the other.

Conclusion

In this chapter, the multicultural transformation of national identity and its particular Canadian twist – the interrelation between different types of ethnonational diversity and diversity accommodation have been approached from a theoretical perspective. The chapter has first explored the trajectory of pluralism studies from the post – Second World War era to the crisis of multiculturalism in the 1990s. It then identified two theoretical puzzles in the current literature on multicultural nationhood. First, the chapter revealed a dichotomy between approaches that theorize multiculturalism as concession to minorities and those theorizing multiculturalism as a strategy of containing and essentializing minorities. Second, the chapter described a disciplinary split between theories of nationalism and nation building, on the one hand, and theories on multiculturalism- and/or immigration-derived diversity and accommodation, on the other.

From a sociological perspective, these particularities in the current literature appear as gaps and shortcomings. In the following chapter, I will therefore develop the theoretical foundations that are necessary to overcome these shortcomings. Chapter 4 proposes a theory of ethnicity that views majority and minority categories as being constituted in relation to each other within processes of social closure. Emphasizing the interdependence between the constructions and the claims of dominant groups and minorities is not only crucial for rejecting culturalism, it also helps us to discern potential relations between national and ethnic groups.

In Chapter 5, the theoretical premises established in Chapter 4 are transposed upon the level of national identities and nationalism. The chapter deconstructs the civic/ethnic dichotomy that is often used in relation to Canadian and Québécois forms of national identity (Ignatieff, 1994; Rodal, 1991) and provides partial answers to the two theoretical puzzles identified above. First, pluralism becomes here defined as neither concession nor containment but a permanently renegotiated middle ground that will never be entirely free from power relations. Second, the chapter concludes by formulating hypotheses about the relations between multinationalism and multiculturalism. These hypotheses will later be examined empirically (Chapter 8).

Finally, the theoretical premises developed in Chapter 4 will inform the model of pluralism as a triangular relation that will be developed in Chapter 6 which describes a transition from the theoretical considerations in this part of the book to their operationalization in the next part of the book, namely, an empirical case study on newspaper representations.

4 Social Relations and Processes of Ethnicization

Unsatisfied with the current approaches to multiculturalism as a theoretical framework of national identity and society building (see Chapter 3), in this and the following chapter I propose an alternative theory of ethnic relations and the integration of pluralism within conceptions of the nation. The present chapter lays the groundwork for this theory, and the following chapter will take the argument one step further and address the issue of multicultural nation building. In particular, I develop a Weberian sociology of ethnic relations and nation building. My argument follows an established tradition in the theorization of ethnic relations and draws upon the work of many scholars in the field (e.g., Banton, 2007, 2008; Hechter, 1975, 1987; Jenkins, 1997; Juteau-Lee, 1979; Juteau, 1999a; Malesevic, 2004; McAll, 1990; Rex, 1986; Simon, 1983).

In my book *Max Weber et les relations ethniques* (2004), I engage with these contributions in detail and show how my own understanding of Weber's theorization of ethnic relations and the multinational state evolves from this earlier scholarship. I do not have the space to elaborate on this here. I will merely draw upon individual contributions whenever they are salient. In Chapter 6, the Weberian framework of ethnic and/or national group relations will be translated into the concept of a 'multicultural we' and further explored in the empirical chapters of the book.

Before introducing the notion of pluralist we-group formation, it seems useful to clarify some issues related to the construction of ethnic categories and group relations. Revisiting Max Weber's theory of social closure and majority/minority relations, in this chapter, I show that (1) processes of ethnicization are at the heart of social relations, and

(2) we can appreciate minority efforts to constitute themselves as 'different but equal' without essentializing their ethnic, cultural, or religious 'difference.'

I start my discussion with an excursus into the history of sociology. In particular, I will review two important terms that have not yet lost much of their currency: the ideas of community and society. These terms, even though they are not always explicitly mentioned, still inform contemporary debates on national identity and multiculturalism, where immigrant cultures and 'communities' are sometimes constructed in opposition to the values and conventions of the 'host society.'

The terms community and society are also frequently implied in the debates about national dualism and French/English relations in Canada. As such, they are at the heart of this investigation. For example, in a recent book, the distinguished Canadian political scientist John Meisel borrows Ferdinand Tönnies' *Gemeinschaft/Gesellschaft* dichotomy to describe the difference in societal organization and self-understanding between francophone Quebec and English-speaking Canada. In *As I Recall: Si je me souviens bien*, Meisel writes:

> In reviewing [the Quebec vs. rest of Canada debate], I am vividly reminded of the insightful analysis of social structure developed during the 19th century by Ferdinand Tönnies. He made a fundamental distinction between *Gemeinschaft* (communal society) and *Gesellschaft* (associational society). In the former, people feel that they belong together because they are of the same kind; ties are warm, informal and self-evident. In the latter, bonds are voluntary and largely based on the rational pursuit of self-interest.
>
> While the analogy is not perfect, to my mind, francophone Quebec still exhibits many of the characteristics of *Gemeinschaft*, despite the fact that it is now a much more heterogeneous and textured society than it once was. The history of Quebec has left a vestigial sense of shared community. The rest of the country is held together less by emotional ties (although these cannot be dismissed altogether) and more by rational pursuit of self-interest. (Meisel, 1999: 113)

The quotation from Meisel illustrates how the difference between Quebec and the rest of Canada is often framed by domestic and international commentators. Even distinguished academics have extended the community/society analogy and argued that Québécois nationalism – in contrast to Canadian nationalism – has an 'ethnic heart' (Ignatieff, 2000: 132) and hosts the dangers of 'ethnic cleansing' (Cook, 1995: 245;

see also Chapter 7).[1] Given the implications of these representations for the transformation of national identity in pluralist terms, it is important to gain a better understanding of the community/society dichotomy and its underlying connotations.

In this chapter, I attempt to overcome both a perspective that presumes a modernizing evolution from *Gemeinschaft* to *Gesellschaft* and a perspective that views these two social formations as opposing poles unrelated to each other. In contrast, I argue that both terms are intrinsically related and that the unacknowledged foundations of *Gemeinschaft* within *Gesellschaft* enhance tendencies of communalization within neighbouring and marginalized collectivities. The first two sections of the chapter review Max Weber's reformulation of the community/society opposition as dynamic processes. The last two sections locate these processes within unequal power relations and thereby show how we can conceptualize ethnic minorities without essentializing their cultural difference.

Community versus Society?

In the 1970s and 1980s, when scholars in North America and Europe began to grapple with the 'ethnic revival' of both migrant communities and minority nations, they could gain little from the tradition of sociology. Whereas the notion of ethnicity had become increasingly crucial for anthropologists in the 1960s, a period marked by the process of decolonization and the creation of numerous new nation-states in Africa and Asia, it was suspiciously absent from theories of modernity and modernization in the Western world. Within this literature, *ethnies* were viewed as atavisms of pre-modern times, which were still to be found in the underdeveloped regions of the world but which had been replaced by rationally motivated relationships in modern societies. Similarly, as a traditional, communitarian, ascriptive, bourgeois or pre-rational phenomenon, ethnically motivated nationalism was said to precede the modern, rationalized, and individualized class society. In sum, 'most of classical grand theory was constructed as a series of socio-structural types: from feudalism through capitalism to communism, from *Gemeinschaft* to *Gesellschaft*, organic to mechanical solidarity, traditional to modern society, etc.' (Wimmer, 2002: 43; cf. Bader, 1995b; Delanty, 2003; Eder et al., 2002; Esser, 1988; Knöbl, 2003).

The conceptual contrast formed by the communal and the noncommunal is indeed a vivid and articulated element in the sociological tradition from Comte to Weber. It can be traced back to thinkers of antiquity (Simon, 1997: 63–72), and has shaped social thought ever since. What changed, however, were its value implications. To the philosophers of the Enlightenment (from Kant to Rousseau), the communal relationships of feudalism were not only repugnant on moral and political grounds, they also lacked the sanction of natural law and reason. The hostility towards the ethos of traditional community became radicalized by nineteenth-century utilitarianism (from Jeremy Bentham to Herbert Spencer). Industrialization and the inherent isolation and insecurity within the new social order did not remain without intellectual consequences. The realization that 'modern society acknowledges no neighbour' provoked a sharp reaction against the 'community of purpose that constitutes society' (Thomas Carlyle, quoted in Nisbet, 1966: 52). Robert Nisbet argues that the idea of community 'holds the same pivotal importance in the 19th century that the idea of the contract had held in the Age of Reason' (1966: 47). Then, the rationale of contract was used to give legitimacy to social relationships. It provided the model of all that was good and defensible in society. In the nineteenth century, however, the idea of the contract was waning before the rediscovered symbolism of community. 'In many spheres of thought, the ties of community – real or imagined, traditional or contrived – come to form the image of the good society' (ibid.).

In 1887, Ferdinand Tönnies (1991) gave the real or imagined antithesis of communal versus non-communal relations its lasting terminology: *Gemeinschaft* and *Gesellschaft*. The evolution from traditional and/or irrational order of kinship ties to the rational, impersonal, and contractual relations of modern society was a widely accepted theme among European scholars. Nevertheless, Tönnies provided the dualism with a particularly German twist, namely, 'a connection between historicism and rationalization, i.e., [the elaboration of] a historical-sociological dimension *(Dimensionierung)* of what has become known, since Tönnies, as the theme of rationalization' (Breuer, 1996: 227, my translation). Following the tradition of romanticism, the term 'German' refers here to a positively connoted organic culture and a particular *Geist* (spirit) or *Wesen* (character) of the people. In sum, it is profoundly marked by the attributes of *Gemeinschaft*.[2] At the beginning of the twenty-first century, this phenomenon is still an important dimension of German national identity, which has come to be recognized as the prototype of the 'ethnic nation.'

Émile Durkheim's criticism of the 'German' perspective is symbolized by an exact reversal of Tönnies' terminology of organic and mechanical solidarity. In Durkheim's *De la division du travail social*, published in 1893, the increasing differentiation of societies replaces the negatively connoted mechanical solidarity of traditional societies by a positively connoted organic solidarity in modern societies. However, even Durkheim does not manage to conceive cohesion in modern society without the characteristics of community, that is, by being based on (irrational) 'beliefs and sentiments held in common.' But these communal relations are not *natürlich* (natural) and *ursprünglich* (original), as they tend to be portrayed in romanticist thought. They are social in the sense that the individual assimilates the values, norms, culture, and social ties of the group into which he or she is born. Although the nuance may be small, it reveals a stronger trust in the creative capacities of 'the social' within Durkheimian/French social thought, in contrast to German romanticism's resort to 'the natural.' Admittedly, since the relations Durkheim describes are certainly not rational, nor based on contract, Robert Nisbet points to a continuing paradox: 'For Durkheim, society is simply *community* written large' (Nisbet, 1966: 84). This paradox is still at the heart of French republicanism and the idea of the 'civic nation.'

Vergemeinschaftung and *Vergesellschaftung*

Stefan Breuer has argued that Max Weber breaks with the tradition of early German sociology by rejecting to trade in the ideal of bourgeois society for the nostalgia of *Gemeinschaft*.[3] For Weber, 'community' cannot durably replace the general social order based on the rational, interest-motivated exchange of goods and services. He thus never suggests that *Gemeinschaft* could or should replace *Gesellschaft* (Breuer, 1996: 241). On the contrary, Weber avoids both concepts altogether (Salomon, 1935; Kalberg, 1989). Indeed, by proposing to replace the 'strictly conventional' term 'society' by 'societal relations and societal institutions' (Weber, 1969a: 153, my translation), Weber 'offers a "view of society" as constituted from an array of moving, even dynamically interacting "parts"' (Kalberg, 2000: 178). It thereby dissolves the difference between *Gesellschaft* and *Gemeinschaft*.

On the one hand, writing at a time when the division of humanity into biologically different 'races' was widely accepted and even social inequalities within society were interpreted as divergences in individuals' 'natural dispositions,' Weber makes a considerable intellectual effort to dismantle these doctrines and to limit their ideological grip on sociological investigation (Coutu et al., 2001: 20–36; Winter, 2004: 31–56,

139–56). On the other hand, Weber's 'sociology without society' (Tyrell, 1994) allows us to think of society as non-essentialist, open, fluid, and 'global,' because neither Weber's notion of the social nor his sociology end at the boundaries of the nation-state (Holton, 2003: 31).

In particular, Weber suggests four ideal-types of meaningful social action: value-rational, means-end rational, affectual, and traditional (Weber, 1978: 24–5; 1980: 12–13).[4] Stephen Kalberg (1994) shows that these types of action constitute the centre of Weber's multicausal mode of sociological analysis. They can be found in all epochs and civilizations, and they are, ultimately, at the core of every possible type of social formation. Following closely the theoretical framework outlined by Tönnies (whose main concepts *Gemeinschaft* and *Gesellschaft* are each divided into two sub-categories) Weber's four causes for action-orientation give rise to two basic forms of social relationships.[5] Weber does thus not break with the dualism. However, he translates the static opposition suggested by Tönnies' terminology[6] into two dynamic social relations. First, affectual and tradition-motivated social action give raise to *Vergemeinschaftung,* a communal relation in the (re)making. Second, means-end rational and value-rational motivated social action translate into *Vergesellschaftung,* an associative relation in the (re)making (Weber, 1978: 40–1; 1980: 21–2).[7] Redefining the distinction between types of solidarity and cohesion into dynamic social relations has important consequences because it dislocates the place of the dichotomy: the latter is no longer associated with two antithetical types of human collectivity but refers to two analytically distinguishable types of social relations that are inherent to all types of group formations and institution building (Patez, 1998).

Like Tönnies, Weber uses these two concepts as ideal-types. They describe the two extremes of a continuum where *Vergemeinschaftung* designates traditionally and affectively motivated social action oriented primarily towards peaceful exchange, whereas *Vergesellschaftung* denotes rationally (value-end and means-end) motivated social action oriented towards 'violent conflict,' that is, limited and purely rationally motivated collaboration among competitors (Weber, 1978: 47, cf. 38; 1980: 25, cf. 20). Designed as ideal-types, these two basic types of relations are not mutually exclusive, as modernization theory falsely assumed. On the contrary, in practice, one type of relation tends to engender the other (Weber, 1978: 41; 1980: 22). Weber assumes that processes of *Vergemeinschaftung* also take place in modern, rational institutions, and that associative relations exist even within the traditional family, the archetype of *Gemeinschaft*. In other words, even when social action seems highly bonded to a social structure, within a Weberian approach, it can be deconstructed into a multiplicity of heterogeneous motivations at its foundation (Bader, 1991, Chapters 4–5). A great array of motives within a single 'external form' is then not only analytically and empirically possible but also sociologically significant: it determines the success and durability of social structures. Weber is convinced that in the absence of individual and subjectively motivated action-orientations – towards, for example, the nation – these structures would cease to exist (Weber, 1978: 13; 1980: 7).

Both *Vergemeinschaftung* and *Vergesellschaftung* can be 'open' or 'closed' towards outsiders who wish to join the social relation (Weber, 1978: 43; 1980: 23). The process of social closure is at the heart of Weber's theory of group formation. It provides a sociological explanation for the constitution of majority/minority relations and thereby allows us to locate the processes of *Vergemeinschaftung* and *Vergesellschaftung* within power relations. Understanding this dynamic will help us not only to theorize the emergence of ethnic boundaries. It will also shed new light on the concept of 'ethnic' nationalism.

Social Closure and Majority/Minority Relations

For Weber, group formations are based on the necessary condition of a confrontation with outsiders. This is because common characteristics (like language, culture, memories, and 'ethnicity') may facilitate 'communalization,' but they do not constitute it in themselves. Rather, a commonality must be recognized subjectively as a shared situation, and this symbolic dimension – the constitution of identity – is necessarily relational: We know who we are only by reference to who we are not. Whether group formations are primarily motivated for affective or traditional reasons (for the belief in the superiority of the group's customs and religion, for example, or by distrust of the unknown Other) or whether they involve the conscious attempt by social actors to secure collective interests – which can be material (such as employment opportunities, resources, and customers) or ideal (the appropriation or restriction of social honour, the will to uphold the quality of religious practices or the 'purity' of the 'race') – depends on the concrete situation and must be examined empirically. In general, however, the social relations *Vergemeinschaftung* and *Vergesellschaftung* are both involved in the process of group formation. Communal and associative motives are closely interwoven since different (material and ideal) interests are pursued by different members of the collectivity or even by a single actor. Weber observes that even 'communities [and not only associations] are very often economically conditioned by the competition for economic opportunities' (Weber, 1978: 341, translation altered; 1980: 201).

A similar dialectic between communal and associative dimensions, ideas, and interests is at stake in the process of 'monopolistic closure.'[8] Formally, the closure of social relations can be motivated traditionally, affectually, or rationally (in terms of value or means-ends). Its principle motives are: '(a) the maintenance of quality [of the real or imagined characteristics of the group], which is often combined with the interest in prestige and the consequent opportunities to enjoy honour, and even profit [...] (b) the contraction of advantages in relations to consumption needs [...] (c) the growing scarcity of opportunities for acquisition.' Weber concludes: 'Usually motive (a) is combined with (b) or (c)' (1978: 46; 1980: 24–5). Monopolistic closure is therefore most likely to occur when a social relation provides the participating individuals with opportunities for the satisfaction of spiritual *and* material interests. To restrict the access to social and economic opportunities, individuals have an interest in acting collectively to curb competition. Weber describes the process of (economically motivated) group closure in the following way: 'Usually one group of competitors takes some externally identifiable characteristic of another group of (actual or potential) competitors – race, language, religion, local or social origin, descent, residence, etc. – as a pretext for attempting their exclusion. It does not matter which characteristic is chosen in the individual case: whatever suggests itself most easily is seized upon. Such group action (*Gemeinschaftshandeln*) may provoke reaction on the part of those against whom it is directed' (Weber, 1978: 342; 1980: 201).

This quotation contains a series of important insights regarding the ethnicization of social relations. It situates the process of attaching meaning to ethnicity in a social relation of (economic) conflict and exclusion/marginalization, it shows that the boundaries between 'us' and 'them' are chosen (relatively) arbitrarily within unequal power relations, and it indicates that the differences are attributed to those excluded/marginalized (the minority or minorities). Weber's statement, furthermore, indicates that the closure of the dominant group (majority) is achieved through (temporary) 'group action' and that it may provoke the counter-reaction by those excluded (the minority). Several of these elements have been theorized in recent scholarship (Winter,

2004). In the remainder of this section, I will first discuss the constitution of majority and minority groups within power relations and then address the emergence of ethnic communalizations.

Expanding Weber's interpretation of groups as constituted within social relationships, we can define a group that successfully effectuates social closure as a 'majority.' Groups that become 'excluded' in this process are 'minorities.' A minority is defined 'as a group of people who, because of their physical or cultural features are *singled out from others* in the society in which they live for *differential and unequal treatment,* and therefore consider themselves as objects of collective discrimination' (Wirth, 1945: 347, my emphasis). It is thus not 'the specific characteristics [...] whether racial or ethnic, that mark a people as a minority but *the relationship of their group to some other group* in the society in which they live' (ibid.: 352, my emphasis). Furthermore, majority/minority relations do not refer to numbers or population size. Rather, they describe a particular type of social relations which imply different forms and degrees of social inequality such as domination, exploitation, discrimination, and exclusion (Bader, 1995b) or physical appropriation such as slavery and 'sexage' (Guillaumin, 1995).

The social stratification based on majority/minority relations differs from the vision of a 'purely economically determined "class situation"' (Weber, 1978: 932; 1980: 534) in so far as it involves social interaction between *Stände* (status groups) which are defined by the attribution of 'a specific, positive or negative, social estimation of *honour*' (Weber, 1978: 932, original emphasis; 1980: 534) which is not monopolized merely by individuals, but rather operates collectively, that is, it generates unequal treatment not of individuals but of groups. While stratification based on majority/minority relations – or in Weber's terminology, status – is generally merely conventional, 'the road to legal privilege, positive or negative, is easily traveled as soon as a certain stratification of the social order has in fact been "lived in" and has achieved stability by virtue of a stable distribution of economic power' (Weber, 1978: 933; 1980: 535–6).[9]

As Weber observes, in the process of social closure the dominant group identifies others' 'differences' and not its own 'commonalities.' Given the inherent heterogeneity of all collectivities, it is much easier to define Other in necessarily arbitrary and reductionist ways than to account for the multiple facets and internal differences of one's own group. Majority group members therefore remain imagined as 'individuals': as neither determined nor even marked by 'race,' sex/gender, culture, ethnicity, or – in Guillaumin's terms – 'nature.' At most, they are characterized by 'civilization.' Indeed, the cultural specificity of the dominant group is masked, as it is conceived as incarnating the social norm. It is, therefore, represented in universal terms (Guillaumin, 1972; Juteau, 1999a).

The perception of universalism, however, does not mean that majority groups are constituted beyond cultural particularity. On the contrary, Weber describes that even the economically motivated group closure of an associative relationship is produced through 'group action'[10] on the part of the participants. While, in theory, there may be entirely rational reasons for social closure, and competitive associative relations within, the boundaries of even the most 'rational' associations like the state, for example, are always based on circumstantial moments of communalization, 'identity,' and an 'irrational' separation between 'us' and 'them.' Although these boundaries may later become rationalized and perpetuated by laws, conventions, and ideology, it is important to remember that, at the source, all social formations – majorities and minorities – are constructed through both types of social relations, universalizing *Vergesellschaftung* and particularizing *Vergemeinschaftung*. It is merely through projection and comparison that majorities appear as *Gesellschaft* while minorities are often perceived (and perceive themselves) as *Gemeinschaft*.

Majority and minority categories are constituted in an antagonistic, dialectic social relationship where 'dominants and dominated can neither empirically nor intellectually (neither in concrete nor in symbolic terms) conceive of themselves without the respective other' (Pietrantonio, 1999: 41, my translation). The 'supposedly "natural" groups only exist by virtue of the fact that they are so interrelated that effectively each of the groups is a function of the other' (Guillaumin, 1995: 135): no proletarians without bourgeoisie, no colonized without colonialists, no slaves without masters, no women without men, no immigrants without non-immigrants, no 'ethnic communities' without 'non-ethnic society.'

As a consequence, what all minority groups have in common – beyond the 'differences' between them – is that they are located within an asymmetrical relation with respect to power, social honour, and the social norm. They are 'always "more" or "less," [and] never the term of reference' (Guillaumin, 1995: 222). They are constituted in a social relation where they are socially constructed as 'different' with respect to a referent, a dominant category that remains unmarked or is vaguely defined by the positive equivalent of each of the marks that draw the boundaries of minority groups (Pietrantonio, 1999: 43–4). The attributes that are imputed onto the minority are generally particularized and devalued in comparison with the social norm. They can even be laudatory at times, but they are always associated with a particular 'nature' that is said to animate and internally program the group in question.

Weber observes that minority categories sometimes accept and internalize ideologies that justify their subordination. The example that impresses him most is that of the Indian caste system. Weber locates the origins of the caste system in the conquest of the dark-skinned Dravidians by the light-skinned Aryans, and the exclusion of the former from all occupations associated with a superior status and social honour.[11] Although most probably pre-dating conquest, the *karma* doctrine was subsequently transformed into a powerful religious tool that was accepted by the members of all social strata and thus sanctioned the ethnocultural division of labour and the superior status of the Brahmans (Weber, 1978: 468–518; 1980: 285–314). Weber observes that the 'sense of dignity' (identity) that characterizes positively privileged status groups is 'related to their "being" which does not transcend itself, that is, it is related to their "beauty and excellence"' (Weber 1978: 934; 1980: 536). Members of the majority category in society 'live for the present and by exploiting their great past' (ibid.), whereas the identity of the negatively privileged strata 'must be nurtured by the belief in a providential mission and a belief in a specific honour before God' (ibid.). In sum, their hopes must concentrate on a better life after death.[12] A negatively privileged or 'minoritarian' status thus limits and circumscribes the volatility of minority groups' collective identities and the horizon of possible shapes that the latter may take. In other words, 'the self-construction of ethnic and national groups as homogeneous and timeless entities results from the fact that they were originally perceived as static by others' (Juteau, 1996: 57).[13]

In sum, treating groups and their cultural expressions as isolated phenomena outside their constitutive social relations hides the fact that the association between a social group and its signifier(s) is born in the context of specific power relations. It camouflages the processes through which individuals, by virtue of their classification as members of certain groups, are allocated specific positions within the social hierarchy, and it occludes the appropriation of their labour (Juteau, 1999a, chapters 1, 8). Most importantly, it contributes to the perpetuation of inequality, the intensification of closed boundaries, and the rise of fundamentalism. Revisiting Weber's concept of monopolistic closure allows us to locate processes of ethnicization within the context of majority/minority relations and thereby to overcome some of the flaws inherent to culturalist approaches. However, a word of caution is necessary: The dualism of the sociological categories majority/ minority does not suggest that the social is organized in binary terms. A nuanced analysis must take into account that different modes of differentiation and subordination produce different majority and minority statuses that impact each other mutually (Bader, 1995b: 58–60; Juteau, 1999a: 137–9).

Emerging Ethnic Boundaries

The previous discussion implies that ethnicizations are inherently imbedded in processes of social closure and in the resulting majority/ minority relations. However, Weber specifies that 'ethnic relations' are most likely to occur within situations of 'peaceful or warlike migrations' (Weber, 1978: 388; 1980: 236) such as conquest, colonization, and (forced or 'voluntary') immigration, that is, past or present situations that generally involve profoundly unequal social relations between different collectivities. Without the movement of people, Weber argues, sharp somatic, phenotypic, and even cultural/religious contrasts between populations rarely exist due to intermarriage and 'imitation' (ibid.). And while even the most superficial features of historically accidental differences of customs (e.g., food preparation, worship), conventions (e.g., eating habits, the division of labour between the sexes), and other 'visible' distinctions (e.g., beard and hairdo, clothing, physical characteristics) can lead to 'repulsion and contempt' of others and to 'a specific sense of honour or dignity in their practitioners' (ibid.), only 'differences' produced over generations tend to be viewed as 'ethnic.'

Weber, as mentioned earlier, rejects objectivist definitions of groups. Minority categories do not 'naturally' form a group just because they share certain characteristics or have been classified through social marks imposed by the dominant group. On the very first pages of *Economy and Society*, Weber argues that persons classified by race, ethnicity, sex/gender, and so on may individually internalize stigmata, feel resentment, and may even react in a similar way against oppression. However, it is only when mental representations of commonality (*Gemeinsamkeit*)[14] lead to the mutual orientation of their behaviour that a process of group formation begins:

> By restrictions on social intercourse and on marriage [racialized] persons
> may find themselves in [. . .] a situation of isolation from the environment

which imposes these distinctions. But even if they all react to this situation in the same way, this does not constitute a communal relationship.
The latter does not even exist if they have a common 'feeling' about this
situation and its consequences. It is only when this feeling leads to a mutual orientation of their behaviour to each other that a social relationship
arises between them rather than of each [of them] to the environment.
Furthermore, it is only [in] so far as this relationship involves feelings of
belonging together that it is a 'communal' relationship. (Weber, 1978: 42;
1980: 22)

In order to become conducive to the establishment of social relationships, ethnic communalities must be subjectively recognized as such
and informed with *meaning*. The emergence of a 'feeling of commonality' (*Gemeinsamkeitsgefühl*) – the mental representation of a collective
'we' through the encounter with (real or imagined) third parties (Weber,
1978: 43; 1980: 23) – is mandatory for the mutual orientation of individuals' actions towards each other, and thus for the formation of a social relation (Bader, 1991, chapter 4). Defined in this way, 'identity' – or
better, the relational, contextual, and temporarily limited 'identification' with perceived commonality (shared situation, common interests,
common ideas and/or values, common memories, common future,
etc.) – is intrinsically political. Identity is political not merely because
once it arises, it can be mobilized, negotiated, represented, reinvented,
distorted, etc., but foremost because without 'identity' – without the
emergence of a mental representation, a more or less irrational 'feeling
of commonality' – there would be no (meaningfully oriented) collective
action. In other words, while shared identity does not necessarily lead
to collective action, it is the only way for the latter to emerge. Identity
is a means of empowerment. It allows individuals to realize their will
even against resistance by associating themselves with other individuals. This collective action generally intends the appropriation of (material or ideal) opportunities and thus engenders an increase in power
(immediately aimed at or as a byproduct of successful 'group action').

Furthermore, what constitutes ethnic identity and marks the group's
boundaries are not merely empty signifiers. Danielle Juteau (1996,
1999a) theorizes ethnicity as a boundary possessing two sides that are
analytically distinct but empirically intertwined, as the external dimension of the boundary impacts on the internal one. Contrary to the
mark constituted by skin colour, which does not have a sense of its
own outside the relationship of slavery, colonialism, and other forms

of racial subordination, criteria that are chosen to draw ethnic boundaries from without (the external dimension of ethnic boundary) often involve elements that have been produced and invested with meaning (by the minority) long before the establishment of the new relationship: these include language, religion, food, material elements of culture, etc. The external markers of the boundary can never account for the totality of elements comprised within the internal dimension of the boundary – the collectivity's 'cultural container,' as Joane Nagel (1994) puts it. There are also pre-existing histories, forged memories, economic situations, non-material elements of culture, etc. – elements that the excluding/marginalizing majority may not be aware of, and that are constantly (re)constructed and informed with meaning from within the minority group. These elements can be mobilized during the process of 'ethnic communalizations,' or the construction of ethnic boundaries from within. They must be interpreted sociologically by taking into account the 'intergroup sequence' which constituted the collectivity and provided its existence with meaning (Schermerhorn, 1970, chapter 3).

If some minorities may fight for equality in terms of 'sameness,' others reject assimilation or the status of included minorities. They want to be (part of) the referent, and not merely define themselves in relation to the referent. By claiming the recognition of their 'difference,' these minority groups also demand the opportunity to shed their necessarily reductionist and limiting 'racial' and 'ethnic' identities, to obtain the 'symbolically open status' of the dominant category (Guillaumin, 1972: 88), to explore/(re)invent their histories in new ways rather then merely targeting them to fit into a hegemonic discourse, and to finally turn (back) into individuals rather than remaining social categories.

Conclusion

In this chapter, I have revisited Weber's concepts of *Vergesellschaftung* and *Vermeinschaftung*. For Weber, these ideal-types of social relations, even though analytically distinct, engender each other mutually. They are thus at the heart of all types of social formations, from the most rational ones – like the state – to the highly emotionally charged and subjective ones – such as the nation. Thinking of social formations in terms of *Vergesellschaftung* and *Vergemeinschaftung* helps us to deconstruct essentialist differences between different groups and cultures. In particular, it allows us to appreciate that all social formations are inherently informed by civic and ethnic dimensions.

However, deconstructing the civic/ethnic dichotomy with respect to ethnic groups or nations should not prevent us from appreciating the analytical nuances that these indicators have to offer. I argue that Weber's concept of social closure reconstructs a *relative difference* between majority and minority categories. Taken as an ideal-type, *Vergesellschaftung* is best understood as a predominant signifier of majority groups, while *Vergemeinschaftung* is likely to be an attributed and/ or often self-inflicted characteristic of minority groups. In the following chapter, these insights will be applied to the realm of nation building and pluralism.

In addition, the present chapter has taught us that supposedly 'civic' and 'ethnic' types of group formation must always be analysed before the background of power relations. Constructed as relations, predominantly civic or ethnic social formations cannot be identified one without the other: there are no civic nations without ethnic nations, no society without ethnicized communities, no liberal values without seemingly anti-liberal cultures. Constructing a contrast with the Other ('them') is a crucial element of collective identity formation. This consideration will be further nuanced in Chapter 6, when we explore the idea of a pluralist we-group formation.

5 Nationalist Exclusion
and Its Remedies

In the previous chapter, I have deconstructed the dichotomy between civic/ethnic forms of identity with respect to ethnic groups. Instead, I have argued that Weber's concept of social closure reconstructs a *relative difference* between majority and minority categories. Taken as ideal-types, a 'civic' form of self-understanding is best understood as a predominant signifier of majority groups, while an 'ethnic' identity is likely to be an attributed and/or often self-inflicted characteristic of minority groups.

In this chapter, I will draw upon these theoretical insights and apply the theory of majority/minority group formation to the realm of nation building and pluralism. This will allow me to locate pluralist nation building within inter- and intranational power relations, and to circumscribe the conditions for the emergence of integrating pluralism into the understanding of who 'we' are/want to be as a nation.

This chapter is divided in four sections. I start by linking Max Weber's discussion of ethnicity and nationhood to that of Benedict Anderson's (1991) conceptualization of nations as 'imagined communities' that are reproduced, among other things, through print media representations. I thereby introduce the idea that nations and national identities are constituted through discourse. This idea will be further explored in Chapter 6, where the rationale and design of an empirical analysis of Central Canadian newspaper discourses will be explained. The remainder of this chapter, however, does not specifically focus on discourse.

In the first section, I concentrate on redefining the dichotomy between so-called civic and ethnic nations, which shaped the debates on citizenship and multiculturalism for much of the 1990s. I will then explore the emergence of ethnic plurality and pluralism within the nation. Third, I will discuss the relationship between different national imaginations and particular types of pluralism. In the last section of the chapter, I investigate the relationship between different types of pluralism, such as multinationalism and multiculturalism. This section offers a partial answer to the theoretical puzzles identified in Chapter 3 as it defines pluralism as a negotiated compromise and develops four hypotheses that will guide parts of the empirical analysis further below (Chapter 8). By exploring different national imaginations, this chapter circumscribes the conditions for the pluralist transformation of group identities. In Chapter 6, these considerations will be translated into a formula that will allow us to examine the constitution of a 'multicultural we' in Canadian newspaper discourses.

Locating Nation Building within Power Relations

The 'concept of the "ethnic group," which dissolves if we define our terms exactly, corresponds [. . .] to one of the most vexing, since emotionally charged concepts: the "nation"' (Weber, 1978: 395, translation altered; 1980: 242). For Weber, the nation cannot be defined unambiguously. Rather, it implies the vague normative assumption 'that it is *proper* to expect from certain groups a specific sentiment of solidarity in the face of other groups [. . .] Yet, there is no agreement on how these groups should be delimited or about what group action (*Gemeinschaftshandeln*) should result from such solidarity' (Weber, 1978: 922, original emphasis; 1980: 528). Weber's statement is intriguing as it reveals an understanding of the nation that is both relational ('it is proper . . . in the face of other groups') and pluralist ('expect from certain groups a specific sentiment of solidarity').

Even though the nation as a state-organized plurality of communities does not appeal to Weber as particularly desirable and/or feasible, he openly acknowledges the possibility of pluralism.[1] In this sense, Weber's perspective differs from that of Benedict Anderson (1991), who famously defined the nation as imagined horizontal comradeship among individuals, an 'imagined community.' In all other aspects, however, the approaches of both authors are highly compatible. On the one hand, both Weber and Anderson are practical materialists who take into account the technological conditions at the basis of new social constellations and the material interests of actors. On the other hand, both authors emphasize the importance of world views and study how ideas, once constructed, develop their own dynamic and impact on the world.[2] It is thus not by accident that both underline the importance of language, print capitalism, and newspapers within the process of nation building (e.g., Weber, 1946: 178; 1969b: 485). In his book *Imagined Communities: Reflections on the Origin and Spread of Nationalism,* Anderson traces the evolution of the idea of the nation as a cognitive frame. Originally promoted through powerful state bureaucracy, the nation as an idea then gains power over people's minds and reshapes the cultures, traditions, and organizational structures that originally contributed to its development. Anderson's work spearheaded a large and diverse body of literature on the symbolic, ideological, and narrative dimensions of nation building (Bhabha, 1990a; Hall, 1997; Räthzel, 1997; Wodak et al., 1998). Within these approaches, the nation is viewed as being socially constructed.

For Stuart Hall (1996b), for example, the idea of the nation is a discourse, a way of constructing meaning that influences and organizes our actions and our conception of ourselves. By producing meaning about 'the nation' with which we can identify, this discourse constructs identities. These identities and representations of belonging are contained in the stories that are told about the nation, the memories that connect the nation's present to its past, and the images that are constructed in literatures, the media, and popular culture of the nation. The narrative of the nation creates thus a connection between 'stories, images, landscapes, scenarios, historical events, national symbols, and rituals which represent shared experiences and concerns, triumphs and destructive defeats' (Hall, 1996b: 613). In other words, narratives of the nation are reflections of – historical and contemporary – group struggles and power relations. Victories and defeat, power and submission are deeply ingrained within the images that are constructed of different types of nations. Thus, nations are imagined, but they are not imaginary. Nations have concrete histories, and these histories can be quite distinct (Smith, 1986). The boundaries of nations, like those of ethnic groups, reflect these histories and material conditions, and they allude to the nation's position within inter- and intranational power relations. Furthermore, the boundaries of the nation are deeply relational: they are created through discursive struggles that can neither abstract from outside perceptions and images (external dimension of the nation's boundary) nor evacuate internal controversies over group representations and interpretations of who 'we' are (internal dimension of the nation's boundary).

Nations are thus imagined differently. Providing the state with legitimacy, these different imaginations impact on the ways in which the nation is enacted through bureaucratic structures and laws. This has been forcefully demonstrated by Rogers Brubaker in his path-breaking work *Citizenship and Nationhood in France and Germany* (1992). Brubaker's work reaffirmed the classic opposition between nations defined predominantly as political or 'civic' associations and those defined in terms of the 'ethnic' or cultural identity of a 'people.' It also reinstituted the *locus classicus* of this opposition, that is, the distinction between the French *Staatsnation* and the German *Kulturnation* (Meinecke, 1922). The distinction between France as a civic nation and Germany as an ethnic nation was subsequently criticized and deconstructed in an endless stream of literature (Giesen and Junge, 1998; Nielsen, 1998; Seymour et al., 1998; Schnapper, 1998). In general, commentators tend either to adhere to the distinction and to take the dualism literally or to fail to appreciate the theoretical value of these concepts by deconstructing their difference. Obviously, I agree that both civic and ethnic dimensions are inherent to all types of nations. However, losing sight of the analytical difference embedded within the ideal-types of civic and ethnic nation building is unfortunate. It prevents us from capturing the underlying motivations and legitimizations for different state responses to immigration and citizenship, as well as from a nuanced understanding of different attitudes towards pluralism and ethnic relations within the nation. On the following pages, I will use the insights gained from the discussion of majority/minority relations to rethink the characteristics of different types of national imaginations.

Civic nations are said to be artificial, universalist, and individualist. Based, in principle, on the political will of belonging without relevance of social determinations such as ethnicity, gender, class, descent, or status, they are, to use Ernest Renan's (1991) famous metaphor a 'daily plebiscite.' Civic nations are, as Brian Singer (1996: 310–11) lays out, artificial because they are the result of rational deliberations among free individuals; they are universalist in so far as, in principle, anyone who agrees to the basic contract can become a citizen; they are individualist in two respects: because individuals are perceived as the primary unit (which chronologically and ontologically precedes the nation), and because the collectivity's goal is often defined in terms of protecting and maximizing individual liberty.

By contrast, ethnic nations are said to emphasize shared culture, religion, language, memory, kinship, and/or descent. Insisting on the notion of being a distinct 'people,' they tend to be viewed as particularist, collectivist, and organicist. They are particularist in that each nation is considered to be (culturally and 'ethnically') unique, and to have its own distinct character which is worthy of being cherished and protected; they are collectivist in that they give priority to the collectivity and view the individual (and his or her identity) as submitted to and dependent on the nation; they are organicist in that the nation and the individual's attachment to it are not rationally or artificially produced but are determined by 'natural laws' beyond human control and ratio. The overlap of these concepts with the conceptual dualism between *Gesellschaft* and *Gemeinschaft* cannot be overlooked. The affinity of civic nationhood with society and ethnic nationhood with community becomes particularly evident when Louis Dumont claims, with respect to the French/German distinction: 'For the French [. . .] the nation is simply the vastest empirical approximation of humanity that is accessible at the level of real life experience. [. . .] For Germans, the need for individual emancipation is not as strongly felt as the need for embeddedness and communion' (Dumont, 1979: 247–8, my translation).

Locating the emergence of civic and ethnic nations within historical time, Singer argues that 'the contractual nation is traced back to the rise of modern democracy, while the origins of the cultural nation are seen to lie in the mists of time, though scholars point to the beginning of the last century and the rise of romanticism' (1996: 10). He thereby reveals an interesting contradiction with respect to the genealogy of the two models. At first sight, ethnic nationhood appears indeed as an irrational atavism from pre-modern times, whereas its civic counterpart seems undoubtedly rational, civilized, and modern. The first is often associated with barbaric 'tearing-asunder nationalism' (Beiner, 1995: 23), the second with integration, democracy, and citizenship. A closer look, however, reverses this spontaneously assumed chronology. At least in the empirical cases that have lent their names to the model, French 'civic' nation building predates the emergence of German 'ethnic' nationhood.

It is beyond the scope of this chapter to provide a detailed discussion of the French and German concepts of nationhood. Quite diverse accounts can be found in Brubaker (1992), Kanstroom (1993), Bommes and Halfman (1994), Stolcke (1997), and Woehrling (2000). Taken together, these studies confirm that German ethnocentrism can be interpreted, in part, as a 'response' to French sociocentrism (Dumont, 1979). Germany's trajectory from a cultural nation – described in the philosophy of Herder

(1968) and the historicist, romanticist tradition – to an explicitly ethnic one – as in Fichte's (1978) concept of the German nation as linguistically defined *Urvolk* – cannot be understood without taking into account the historical context – and here, in particular, Napoleonic occupation and French claims of hegemony. German nationhood was ideologically conceptualized and later politically implemented in reaction to what was (rightfully or not) perceived as a French particularism with complacent 'universalist' pretensions. Indeed, 'while the French consciously postulated only the superiority of the universalist culture [they] identified with it so naively that they looked on themselves as the educators of mankind' (Dumont, 1986: 131). The Germans, by contrast, came to see 'themselves as superior qua Germans' (ibid.).

This interpretation does not deny that German 'ethnic' nationalism was a politically driven attempt of group closure and state formation rather than a 'spontaneous' expression of ethnonational sentiments. Nor does being in a minority position excuse the horrors that are often committed by nations defining themselves in ethnic terms – as the German example sadly and notoriously demonstrates. However, it does reject culturalist approaches that view civic and ethnic nationalism as being rooted within particular cultures, religions, or civilizations. Only by situating groups and nations – as well as the ideas, cultures, and values they have come to stand for – within their constitutive social relations can we avoid the reductionist essentialism implied in propositions such as Huntington's (1996) 'clash of civilizations,' the redefinition of the 'war on terrorism' as a 'war of ideas' (Ward, 2004), and the more subtle assumption – implicit in many academic and political discussions of multiculturalism – of the seemingly intrinsic 'illiberalism' of particular cultures and religions. To repeat, civic and ethnic principles, relations of *Vergesellschaftung* and *Vergemeinschaftung,* operate in all types of group formations – ethnic groups and nations. However, depending on the collectivity's location within past and present power relations, they are emphasized discriminately, thereby producing a tendency to a slightly more civic or ethnic definition of selfhood that only becomes meaningful through comparison with the other. In particular, the image of today's valorized Western *Gesellschaft* can only be upheld through projection of communitarian 'tribalism' upon oriental bodies inside and outside of society (Said, 1994b).

Interpreted as an ongoing process, Weber's concept of social closure and the constitution of groups in majority/minority relations provide us with an analytical framework to examine the relations between nations and their collective identities. Transposed to the realm of nations, Weber's theory implies that national identities, like other group identities, are constructed in relation to others. In the process of external social closure, (at least) two collectivities are created: a majoritarian entity that achieves group closure and establishes itself as an association first and a minoritarian category of those who do not belong but who may eventually also achieve group closure at a later stage. Within this process, dominant nations tend to define themselves in universal terms while particularity is attributed to those deemed 'less civilized.' At one moment or another, however, late nations will attempt group closure on their own. With the claim to embody universality being appropriated by the powerful established nations, less powerful or 'latecomer' nations are obliged to emphasize their cultural 'particularity' to justify their independent existence and to mobilize large segments of their population in favour of the 'national cause.'

From this perspective, the distinction between 'Western' and 'Eastern' forms of nationalism (Kohn, 1955) appears in a different light. The difference between earlier forms of civic nationalism in Western Europe (England, France, the Netherlands, Switzerland) and the United States and late nations' ethnic nationalism in Eastern Europe and other regions of the world (Germany, Italy, Central and Eastern Europe, Asia) should be associated less with culture, ideology, and moral superiority than with power, historical sequence, and the international hierarchy of nations. Brubaker therefore suggests that 'a less ambiguous distinction than between civic and ethnic nationalism can be drawn between *state-framed* and *counter-state* understandings of nationhood' (1999: 67, original emphasis). This reformulation of the civic/ethnic distinction captures the fundamental power imbalance that operates between state-framed nations and counter-state nations. Indeed, counter-state nations are usually deprived of the 'civic' means to reinforce closure, and they are in the unfortunate situation of having to legitimize their quest for independent nationhood. While I agree with Brubaker that not all nations without a state engage in strictly 'ethnic' forms of nation building[3] but also make claims on the basis of territory or region, in a world organized in nation-states, all 'minority nations' – as Will Kymlicka (1995) calls them – are ultimately obliged to formulate their demands in the name of a (more or less 'ethnically') united 'people' to demand independent statehood.

Weber's concept of group closure also allows us to view Liah Greenfeld's (1992) work on the spread of nationalism from a less psychological perspective. Greenfeld observes that England's universal nationalism (the nation as the potentially global collection of autonomous individual citizens) was imitated with *ressentiment*, that is, suppressed envy and hatred of 'the West' as a result of a factual or perceived impossibility of being able to compete with advanced liberal nations. Rather than explaining subsequent definitions of national identity in increasingly collectivist terms by reference to an elite 'identity crisis,' we now understand that minority categories are almost always facing the need to specify their particularity in terms of traditional culture and achievements to achieve group closure and to avoid assimilation.[4] This latter interpretation also explains why, as Greenfeld observes, the idea of the nation was adopted without much variation within another majoritarian nation, the United States. Having demonstrated its superiority over the motherland through a successful revolution, the United States was in the fortunate position to be able to define its national identity in ideological rather than cultural terms. National identity in Australia, by contrast, fared quite differently (Stratton and Ang, 1998). The same holds true for Canada (Lipset, 1990).

Although power relations and status within the world hierarchy of nations change over time, the initial 'intergroup sequence' that historically constitutes a collectivity by rendering its existence socially meaningful has a lasting impact on its collective identity (Schermerhorn, 1970, chapter 3). The historically grounded traditions of nationhood and identity provide the mental 'tracks' along which the legal-rational structures of state and citizenship regimes are built (Brubaker, 1992).[5] In the case of France, for example, it has been pointed out that the republican model of *citoyenneté*, rather than being a political-legal concept, relies on cultural and linguistic assimilation (Giesen and Junge, 1998; Silverman, 1996). It therefore also involves a particular form of social closure. Neither civic nor ethnic nations promote integration on the basis of full equality. Nevertheless, their legitimization and institutionalization of group closure operate on different levels. In France's *politique d'intégration* immigrants may be more easily granted legal citizenship than in Germany, but they must, in exchange, renounce their cultural difference. Until very recently, the German *Ausländerpolitik*, by contrast, prevented long-term foreigners from becoming legal citizens, but immigrants in Germany have stronger rights and possibilities to express themselves because it is seen as normal that they demonstrate their own identity (Woehrling, 2000: 131). Thus, different national imaginaries generate different opportunity structures for minority agency

(Bloemraad, 2006; Koopmans and Statham, 2003; Landolt et al., 2009; Wayland, 1995).

In sum, the distinction between predominantly civic or ethnic forms of nationhood remains useful. But it should never be understood as alluding to a fundamental essence of a particular culture or group. Similarly, we should be careful with the moral connotations that tend to be attributed to these concepts.[6] Rather, a predominantly civic or ethnic interpretation of membership in the nation describes a tendency towards group identity which is best understood in reference to this group's position of power within a particular set of social relations. Furthermore, as I will discuss in the next section, the subtle tendencies towards different forms of national self-understanding also influence the type of ethnic relations and normative pluralism that will most likely prevail within the nation.

How Does the Nation Become Pluralist?

Nations – whether civic or ethnic – usually overemphasize homogeneity. The impression of harmoniously shared culture or values emerges from the dual process of constructing internal sameness and external distinction. Narratives of the nation tend to place emphasis on origins, continuity, tradition, and timelessness. At the inside, national identity is often symbolically grounded on the idea of a pure, original people either with a shared *volonté politique* or a particular *Volksgeist*. Towards the outside, the nation tends to be characterized by its positively connoted 'uniqueness.' Thereby, 'the governing representatives of a political system mostly conceal their forcible act of "homogenization" and erasure of differences which is manifested in the epithet "national"' (Wodak et al., 1999: 27).

There are, however, nations that thrive upon 'diversity.' In recent years, Canada, for example, has made a name for itself by emphasizing the cultural and linguistic heterogeneity of its population. Canada was also the first country in which normative pluralism as an essential dimension of Canadian nationhood became officially implemented through policy (1971) and law (1988). But Canadian nationhood has not always been normatively pluralist, and even now critical voices claim that this goal is far from being achieved (Mackey, 1999; Day, 2000). While there is much discussion about whether or not nations, such as Canada, *are* pluralist or *should be* pluralist, relatively few authors have tackled the questions of (1) how the nation becomes normatively pluralist, and

(2) why particular types of pluralism seem to be favoured in one country rather than in another. Following the line of argument adopted so far, in the last section of this chapter, I will attempt an answer to these questions.

As a first step, it is important to ask why some nations are (perceived as) ethnically 'plural' or, put differently, why they never became homogenized in the first place. Andreas Wimmer's work on ethnic conflict is helpful in this regard. Wimmer (2002, chapter 3) distinguishes between the nationalization and the ethnicization of politics within the nation-state. In some nation-states, he argues, the expansion of state power enables (or violently enforces) the participation of all inhabitants of the territory. National identity is then framed in a way that gives expression to the interests of a wide variety of groups. In addition to uniting elites and 'masses,' the idea of nationhood as an inclusive horizontal comradeship of individuals also depoliticizes and 'nationalizes' the identities of ethnic minority groups. This is the reason why, according to Wimmer, even a linguistically divided country like Switzerland has achieved a united sense of nationhood.[7]

In other nation-states, by contrast, the exchange of political loyalty for (social, political, and economic) participation, security and freedom fails, because the state elite practices ethnic, regional, or religious favouritism by granting privileges and equality only to the members of its own ethnic group. This variant leads to the 'ethnicization of bureaucracy' and the politicization of ethnic differences (Wimmer, 2002: 66). Wimmer identifies two reasons for the ethnicization of national politics. First, state elites may not have sufficient political, legal, and economic resources at their disposal to allow for the non-discriminatory integration of the entire population. This is often the case in states located at the periphery of the world system. Second, state formation precedes the establishment of a democratic civil society, so that state elites are obliged to rely on existing political groupings and networks which are often structured along ethnic lines (2002: 67). Thus, in both cases, the dominant group is suffering from a lack of power. Referring to the ethnicized politics in Ethiopia, Sudan, Rwanda, and the former Yugoslavia, Wimmer provides examples of the 'plural society' (Furnivall, 1939) where different ethnic groups live side by side – usually controlled by an external colonial power – but without substantial interaction other than occasional encounters in the marketplace.

Expanding Wimmer's argument, I want to argue that achieving a homogeneous 'nationalization of politics' is always more difficult for weak nations, or nations that were initially constituted as latecomers, 'imitators,' or are still at the stage of counter-state nationalism. As argued earlier, with the 'road to universalism' blocked by advanced or state-framed majoritarian nations, latecomers and 'imitators' must, at least, address their ethnocultural particularity to affirm their right to independent existence within a world of nation-states. This need not necessarily lead to an 'ethnic' identity in a biological or racial sense, but shared culture and tradition are important means to construct national uniqueness and to reject assimilation to dominant neighbouring nations. This type of national self-understanding, in turn, is likely to offend internal minorities, such as pre-existing 'minority nations' as well as immigrants with different cultural backgrounds. The 'nationalization' or homogenization of politics becomes thus increasingly difficult. To give an example: as a minority nation aspiring to independence, Canada's francophone province of Quebec finds itself in such a dilemma. Explicit minority nationalism aiming at community closure does simply not sit well with Aboriginal peoples and culturally diverse immigrants (Elmer and Abramson, 1997; Juteau, 2002).

The politicization of ethnic identities must, however, not necessarily result in ethnic exclusion or violent conflict. In democratic nation-states, a balance of power between ethnic groups can also lead to the transformation of national identities in pluralist terms. To a certain extent, normative pluralism can indeed be understood as a consequence of the failure of the modern project of the nation-state. While the traditional and successful nation-state emphasizes unity and sameness over difference and diversity, pluralism reverses the value of these ideological assumptions. Without abandoning the idea of 'national' (or even multinational) unity, normative pluralism cherishes diversity where the nation valorizes homogeneity.

In continuity with the perspective outlined earlier, I want to argue that normative pluralism is unlikely to occur in what can be called the ideal-type of the powerful majoritarian 'civic nation' where identity is expressed in culturally 'neutral' ideological and 'universal' terms.[8] By contrast, the ideal-type of a narrowly defined 'ethnic nation' does not provide an adequate framework for equality between ethnic groups either. Rather, a necessary condition for the emergence of normative pluralism seems to be the national majority's awareness of its particularity. In other words, the dominant group must come to accept that it is one particular ethnic group among others, and that it shares society with other groups. As Christian Joppke puts it sarcastically: 'Multiculturalism reflects the West's reduced epistemological status after being confronted with its rebellious oriental Other' (1998: 289). Pluralism as a normative approach to society building is thus most likely to be supported within a hybrid type of nation, that is, a collectivity that is neither dominant nor oppressed, and that emphasizes a collective belonging without defining the nation in ethnic terms.

The pluralist transformation of the nation is then 'civic' in so far as it presupposes an institutional framework that guarantees individual rights – which remains a key component for the interaction between equal citizens of different ethnic backgrounds. It is 'ethnic' or 'particular' in so far as it presents this framework not as (ethnically, culturally, religiously, linguistically) neutral, but as evolving from historically specific processes of group relations.[9]

Furthermore, pluralism must also involve the dominant group. In other words, 'cultural citizenship' – as an addition to T.H. Marshall's (1973) three-layered model of citizenship rights – refers as much to the recognition of minority cultural identities and practices as to the recognition of the majority's cultural identity and practices (Rocher, 2000: 37). This requires a critical review of the cultural and social premises of the nation where numerous forms of majoritarian 'banal nationalism' are inscribed in seemingly 'neutral' institutions (Billig, 1995). Indeed, to such an extent is the nation modernity's dominant system of meaning and moral authority that cultural rights enjoyed by the national majority are usually taken for granted. Cultural rights for minorities, by contrast, are usually not automatically granted. Rather, they must be claimed: 'It is quite rare that a majority automatically grants total equality of status to its minorities. Rather, the latter must advance their cause, by unceasingly claiming their rights, defending and protecting their assets, and especially by taking advantage of the occasions and opportunities that are favourable to them in the balance or imbalance of forces' (Rocher, 2000: 41, my translation).

Within the Weberian perspective presented here, without pressure from national or ethnic groups within the nation-state, normative pluralism is unlikely to occur. Pluralism is not simply 'given' by an altruistic majority. Rather, to be heard and taken seriously, minorities claiming pluralism must have sufficient power, political clout, and/or legitimacy, so that they can neither be assimilated nor expelled. By contrast, without the majority taking an – however motivated – *interest* in sharing its power (Weber, 1988a: 128),[10] pluralism is unlikely to evolve into a normative framework that – although not free from conflict and power relations – allows negotiating national representations of who 'we' are. In sum, pluralism is best described as an ongoing tension, a *Spannungsfeld*, between granted concessions and attempted containment.

Different Types of Pluralism within Different Types of Nations

The multiple layers of majority/minority relations within the framework of the nation-state can be comprehended analytically with Weber's concept of internal closure of social relations. Weber observes that there are 'various ways in which it is possible for [an externally] closed relation to guarantee its monopolized advantages to the participants. (a) Such advantages may be left free to competitive struggle within the group, (b) they may be regulated or rationed in amount and kind, or (c) they may appropriated by individuals or sub-groups on a permanent basis and become more or less inalienable. The last is a case of "closure within"' (Weber, 1978: 43–6, translation altered; 1980: 23–5). Openness and closure may be motivated by traditional, emotional, or purely calculative reasons. 'If the participants of a social relation expect that the admission of others will lead to an improvement of their situation [. . .] their interest will be in keeping the relation open. If, on the other hand, their expectations are of improving their position by monopolistic tactics, their interest is in a closed relation' (ibid.). Weber admits that once a relationship becomes associative – that is, the product of interest or volition rather than tradition or kinship – it becomes difficult to enforce the criteria of closure on a formal basis. However, he observes that internal group closure is usually not formal and explicit (sanctioned by laws or religious beliefs), but rather produced through informal conventions and (systemic or individual) practices of discrimination.

In modern democratic societies, all residents of the national territory are submitted to the law. In exchange, they are formally endowed with equal civic, political, and social citizenship rights. In principle, social and economic advantages are left free to (minimally regulated) competitive struggle among them. Nevertheless, 'scholarship on citizenship has exploded the assumption that once suffrage was achieved for women, blacks, and other minorities, all citizens became automatically equal subjects of the political community' (Werbner and Yuval-Davis, 1999: 4). Indeed, informal types of exclusion (such as economic exploitation and legal and political discrimination) of formally equal citizens on the basis of their 'ethnic difference' have become the typical form of internal closure within nation-states. By responding to these informal and unauthorized mechanisms, normative pluralism aims to redress the above-mentioned types of exclusion. It does not propose the return to the plural society, but suggests modest ways of countering the inherent forms of ethnic exclusion produced by the modern nation-state's cultural closure.

The type of normative pluralism that is implemented depends on complex negotiations and power relations between the national majority and minority groups. Two major forms of normative pluralism can be distinguished: multiculturalism and multinationalism. First, in recent years, increasing numbers of immigrants in almost all Western industrialized states have led to the emergence of 'multiculturalism' as a particular form of normative pluralism aiming at the integration and accommodation of ethnic immigrant minorities. Some nations have explicitly reconstructed their national identities in multicultural terms, others have made arrangements to accommodate 'diversity claims' without the latter having to be 'written on the forehead of the state' (Joppke, 2002: 250). According to Joppke, there are two sub-types of multiculturalism. 'Implicit multiculturalism' describes discretionary legal concessions granted to (some) minorities by a majority group whose cultural citizenship rights are taken for granted. We may conclude that this form of pluralism prevails in nations that are characterized by a strong nationalization of politics. It matters thereby little whether a nation that implements 'implicit multiculturalism' is defined in predominantly civic or ethnic terms. In both cases, ideology (civic nation) or mono-culture (ethnic nation) is valorized more than multiculture; this makes it difficult to consider 'implicit multiculturalism' as a truly 'pluralist' approach as defined by Schermerhorn (1970; see Chapter 3).[11] The two examples that come to mind are the United States and Germany. Although located on opposing levels upon the civic – ethnic continuum with regards to national identity, both have recently implemented – at the national and the local level – a variety of policies and practices aiming at the 'multicultural' accommodation of ethnic minorities (Joppke, 1998). However, the emphasis on the majority's historically grown and intergenerationally sustained national 'ideology' (civic nation) or 'culture' (ethnic nation) entails that immigrant cultures and identities remain excluded from the national imaginary. A multiculturalization of national identity does not take place (Bauder and Semmelroggen, 2009).

Joppke's second sub-type, 'explicit multiculturalism,' at least in principle, implies a more transparent negotiation process. While it may not necessarily be more just or egalitarian, 'explicit multiculturalism' implies a concept of citizenship where cultural particularity is recognized as mediating everyone's access to civic, social, and political rights. Once rendered explicit, cultural rights are open for negotiation by all actors involved. These negotiation processes, however, will never be free from factual inequalities. Which compromises are reached, and what rights the recognition of minority identities and interests ultimately involves depends on the collectivities involved, their constitution in past and present power relations, and their collective goals and objectives.

Similarly, multinationalism, as the second major form of normative pluralism, cannot be legitimized outside the realm described by these relations – but neither can the continuity of the mono-cultural nation-state. Differentiating between multiculturalism and multinationalism is particularly important in countries where structural pluralism has been granted to historically recognized linguistic, regional, or religious groups (such as the Walloons and the Flemish in Belgium, Christian religious groups in the Netherlands, the four language groups in Switzerland, or anglophones, francophones, and Aboriginal peoples in Canada). None of these countries has automatically extended to immigrants the full amount of structural and institutional pluralism granted to national minorities.

In sum, while 'implicit multiculturalism' implies less official recognition to ethnic minorities than 'explicit multiculturalism,' multinationalism involves a greater autonomy for those ethnic minorities that have become recognized as 'minority nations.' Given the fact that all these pluralist arrangements are the outcome of complex negotiations between groups, it seems plausible to assume that the compromise reached by one group affects the balance of power, as well as the horizon of normatively accepted possibilities. It thus impacts on the pluralist rights claimed and demanded by other groups (Bader, 2003). In the last section of this chapter, I will briefly outline four scenarios describing potential interactions between multinationalism and 'explicit multiculturalism.' 'Implicit multiculturalism,' as it does not translate into the pluralization of national identity, is not regarded here.

Intersections of Pluralism: Four Scenarios

*Multinational Compromise and the Multicultural
Accommodation of Newcomers*

Wimmer (2002) cautions that a historically achieved 'cultural compromise' between pre-existing groups entails a particular power effect.

Constituted as a set of collective norms, classifications, and generally binding world-view patterns, a cultural compromise circumscribes the field of collectively accepted representations and 'limits the horizon of possibilities within which individuals can argue in their search for power and recognition' (2002: 35). Stabilizing the status quo, it privileges those individuals and groups that have participated in its creation. Groups entering the political arena at a later stage face a double disadvantage. Not only is there no space for them within the pre-established logic of membership, but to enforce the validity and legitimacy of their claims, they must also articulate their concerns within the terms of widely accepted collective representations: 'Any way that does not at least connect to the prevailing cultural compromise is not understood and quickly marginalized in public debates' (ibid.: 37).

Wimmer's argument reminds us that social change always runs along pre-established 'tracks' that consist of mental frames and/or bureaucratic structures. Both entail particular power effects.[12] Being forced to operate within the logic of a particular cultural and institutional compromise, social change never replaces pre-established entities with anything truly 'unheard of.' Rather, it transforms visions and divisions gradually. A national identity, whether pluralist or not, is such a historically achieved cultural compromise. Previously negotiated by the nation's constitutive members it defines the legitimate vision of the social world (and of its divisions) and imposes it upon all individuals within the realm of social relations. Its content must thus be taken into account when analysing the pluralization of the nation. But what happens if the previously negotiated compromise involves the normative integration of structural pluralism along ethnonational lines within dominant representations of the nation? How can we theorize the relation between multinationalism and multiculturalism?

Following the logic of Wimmer's 'cultural compromise' there are two possible answers to this question. First, a national identity that is firmly rooted in historically achieved compromise poses a serious problem for the inclusion of newcomers. Whether the definition of the nation's legitimate divisions involves the recognition of ethnic/national identities is unimportant as it will not be extended to newcomer groups. In other words, pre-established multinationalism is at best indifferent and at worst detrimental for the establishment of multiculturalism. Examples can be given from countries where rights and recognition granted to national minorities have not been extended to ethnic minorities. Switzerland, for example, proudly presents itself as a country with four officially recognized cultures and language groups. Nevertheless, not in any way has the recognition of these identities and their official inclusion within representations of the nation had a positive impact on the recognition of the ethnic identities of immigration-induced minorities (Pfaff-Czarnecka, 2004). Here, a categorical distinction is introduced to separate minority nations and immigrant groups. Because the established groups are in agreement with each other, ethnic minorities cannot make their voices heard.

Second, a national identity that is firmly rooted in historically achieved compromise does not necessarily pose a problem for the inclusion of newcomers; rather it may also encourage pluralism. This is the case when a similarity is recognized between established types of ethnic/national differentiation that have already acquired legitimacy and new forms of minority groups and identities. The implementation of multiculturalism in the Netherlands can here serve as an example. It has often been argued that the original pillarization of Dutch society has facilitated the extension of this system to ethnic minorities. The logic here is to represent multiculturalism as an extension of citizenship rights that barely changes the 'typically pluralist' character of the nation. The established groups realize the similarity between their group claims and those of the newcomers, and therefore they do not want to undermine the basis for their own particularist identities, and thus agree to the extension of cultural citizenship rights to new minorities.

Multinational Conflict and the Multicultural Accommodation of Newcomers

In *The Established and the Outsiders*, Norbert Elias and John Scotson notice that 'an established group tends to attribute to its outsider group as a whole the "bad" characteristics of the group's "worst" section – of its anomic minority' (1994: xix). They also discern that, 'the self-image of the established group tends to be modeled on its exemplary, most "nomic" or norm-setting section, on the minority of its "best" members (ibid.). Elias and Scotson's observation strengthens the idea that a particular cultural compromise determines the logic of newcomer inclusion/exclusion and the pluralist transformation of the nation. It shows that the naming and classifying of newcomers takes place within limited representations and articulations of same/other. In order to make cognitive sense of newcomers, they are associated with 'something known' – the despised characteristics of the group's 'anomic minority' – and situated within a traditional hierarchy of social relations. In this sense, social change runs along pre-established sociocultural lines. However, Elias and Scotson's observation also reveals that there are cleavages between the group's 'nomic or norm-setting section' and its 'anomic minority.' In fact, the degree of unity and agreement between the pre-established groups is often overestimated. What happens when conflict, not compromise, characterizes the relationship between the pre-established groups? How does this have an impact upon the relation between multinationalism and multiculturalism?

Following the rationale implied by Elias and Scotson, two hypotheses emerge in response to this question. On the one hand, the attempt to impute to newcomers the 'bad' characteristics of internal ethnic/national minorities may not only be a cognitive necessity. It can also be interpreted as a strategy, employed by the dominant group, to distance itself from groups associated with lower human value, stabilize the status quo, and secure its social superiority. Conflict between the nation's pre-established groups is thus not necessarily beneficial for the recognition of newcomer rights and identities. In a situation of polarization, they may, rather, become stigmatized. This has often been observed with regards to the United States: 'once immigrants arrived in the country, whatever their national origin or race, they were ideologically positioned within the hegemonic bipolar white-black model of American society' (Ong, 1996: 742).

On the other hand, that newcomers are characterized by attributes traditionally reserved for internal minorities also demonstrates that the boundaries between insiders and outsiders are fluid. In a situation of conflict within, the boundaries of the nation become more porous and newcomers may be able to negotiate their way in. With respect to the American case, Aihwa Ong points to the differential positioning of light-skinned and dark-skinned Asians between the poles 'white/wealthy' and 'Black/poor' in American society. In this case, (some) immigrant minorities may become 'contingent insiders' as their identities and claims are perceived as less threatening than those of some older groups within society (Cohen, 1999; Back, 1999). Thus, unstable compromises or ongoing struggles about collective self-understandings among established groups may, in fact, be advantageous to newcomers. For example, it has been argued that in Canada 'integration without assimilation' (1964: 204) benefits from a situation that is characterized by 'a considerable amount of competition' between two dominant majorities with their 'virtually separate social systems [and] their own economic, educational, social, and cultural institutions' (Ossenberg, 1964: 205).[13] According to Pierre Anctil, in Quebec, 'the political and legal confrontation between old stock francophones and anglophones freed in Quebec a well-defined sociocultural space that allophones [of immigrant origin] had been able to occupy alone' (1984: 450, my translation).

In sum, national identities – pre-established cultural compromises – are a necessary starting point for pluralist transformations of the nation. Nevertheless, the compromises between established groups can be characterized either by relative harmony/agreement or by relative conflict/struggle. Neither situation predetermines the relationship between multinationalism and multiculturalism. In this section, four hypotheses have been developed: Agreement over the recognition of structural pluralism along ethnic or national lines within public representations can (1) be meaningless or even detrimental to the recognition of newcomers, or (2) lead to an extension of pluralist rights. Conflict over the recognition of structural pluralism along ethnic or national lines within public representations can (3) render the recognition of newcomers extremely difficult, or (4) favour their integration as 'contingent insiders.' We can theorize the conditions and opportunity structures that may facilitate the emergence of multiculturalism in a given situation, but we should also study the actual outcome of group negotiations empirically. In the empirical world, the relation between multinationalism and multiculturalism is still more complex than suggested in the four hypotheses. It involves dynamic relations and shifts over time, as well as a multiplicity of groups and relations, which produce a net of diverse and overlapping situations of integration.

Conclusion

In this chapter, I have applied the theory of majority/minority relations to the realm of nation building and pluralism. Viewing nations and their boundaries as being constructed in inter- and intranational power relations helps us to apprehend differences in national identities and imaginations. It also introduces nuances with respect to the construction of ethnic categories and approaches of pluralist accommodations of minority groups. Depending on national self-understandings, ethnic relations within society take slightly different shapes and, consequently, produce diverse approaches to pluralism. Two major types of pluralism have been identified: multinationalism and multiculturalism.

I have further differentiated between explicit and implicit multiculturalism. Implicit multiculturalism, which can nowadays be found in almost all Western immigrant-receiving societies, merely describes a situation where minority rights are granted on a discretionary level to ethnic minorities. It does not translate into a pluralist transformation of national identity. Multinationalism and explicit multiculturalism, by contrast, describe more transparent forms of pluralist negotiations between the dominant group and ethnic/national minorities. The latter types of pluralism involve a transformation of the national imaginary in pluralist terms.

If the theoretical developments in this chapter are correct, this pluralist transformation of national identity is likely to happen neither in nations that tend to define membership in strictly 'civic' terms, nor in nations whose boundaries are defined in terms of mono-culturalism. Rather, both multinationalism and multiculturalism rely on the national majority's awareness of its own particularity as a group that shares society with others.

The chapter concludes that there is reason to believe that different types of pluralism – such as multinationalism and multiculturalism – impact each other. In the last section of this chapter, I presented four hypotheses as to how these interactions may play out. Although historical examples can be used to support any one of these hypotheses, we must not forget that the underlying relations change over time, and with them also the logics of who is considered to be part of 'us' or 'them.' Furthermore, our research must examine how, at a particular moment in time, the inclusion/exclusion of a particular ethnic or national group within representations of who 'we' are impacts on the legitimization or delegitimization of pluralist accommodations for other minorities within society. In the remainder of this book, I will address this question empirically by taking the constitution of a Canadian 'multicultural we' as a case in point. As mentioned before, I am particularly interested in how representations of Québécois nationalism influence or interfere with those of Canadian multiculturalism (see Chapter 2).

PART III

Empirical Analysis

6 How Do 'We' Become Multicultural?

In the preceding chapter, four scenarios were developed about the potential impacts of multinationalism on the legitimization or delegitimization of multiculturalism in response to immigration. It was suggested that agreement over the recognition of historically established ethnic or 'national' groups can (1) be meaningless or even detrimental to the recognition of newcomers, or (2) lead to an extension of pluralist rights. Furthermore, it was suggested that conflict over the recognition of historically established ethnic or 'national' groups can (3) render the recognition of newcomers extremely difficult, or (4) favour their integration as 'contingent insiders.'

These four hypotheses about potential interrelations between the two types of diversity and diversity accommodation are a first step to overcome the analytical split between multinationalism and multiculturalism that has been identified as a second theoretical puzzle in Chapter 3. However, the established relations between these two types of diversity and their accommodations remain highly abstract and theoretical. In this and the following three chapters, the study of the pluralization of national identity will be pursued on an empirical level. Taking my inspiration from the Canadian case, I will address the two research questions that motivate this book. The first question is a general inquiry, which asks: How does the pluralist transformation of national identity take place? Formulated in relation to the Canadian case: How does the expression of a Canadian 'we' become 'multicultural'? The main reason for asking this question in relation to the Canadian case is the observation that, at the beginning of the twenty-first century, Canada is persistently described as a multicultural country in dominant discourses (see Chapter 2). Numerous studies confirm this trend (Abu-Laban and

Gabriel, 2002; Stein et al., 2007; Jedwab, 2005). Thus, the concern here is not so much *whether* Canadians 'imagine' their country as multicultural, but *how* Canada is constructed as multicultural nation in public discourse.

The rationale for the second, more specific question, has been developed in Chapter 2. It is based on the observation that the 1990s were also marked by various failed attempts to include Quebec into the Constitution, that warnings about Québécois 'ethnic' nationalism were widespread, and that the narrow vote in the referendum on Quebec's sovereignty in 1995 sent shock waves through the rest of Canada. Rather than causing a backlash against any type of pluralist accommodation, Canadians' support for multiculturalism rose to unprecedented heights in the second part of the 1990s. Consequently, the more specific question asks: Did Québécois nationalism during the 1990s serve as a counter-image (them), or Other (in upper case) that facilitated the conditional inclusion of ethnically diverse immigrants (others) into a multicultural Canadian 'we'?

When designing the case study by which I was aiming to find answers to these questions, I encountered two major difficulties. My solutions to these problems have very much shaped the form and content of the empirical analysis in this book. The first difficulty concerns precisely the analytical split between multinationalism and multiculturalism and its translation into the political realm. Solving this problem has shaped the data selection and the sampling context. The second difficulty relates to the fact that some of the inherent presumptions of traditional Critical Discourse Analysis (CDA) by means of which I was going to analyse my material were contradicted by my empirical findings. My solution to this problem has shaped the methodological analysis.

In this chapter, I will first describe the difficulty of sampling discourses about multinationalism and multiculturalism. This leads me to describe the rationale for the selected case study, its methodology, and the contours of the newspaper sample that I decided to collect. This section contextualizes the findings in Chapters 7, 8, and 9. It also reminds us of the limits and specifications of the discourses that the upcoming analysis is drawing from.

In the second part of this chapter, I will address my difficulty in analysing the empirical material by means of CDA's common focus on 'othering.' In response, I develop the model of pluralism as a set of triangular relations. This model is both one of the most important 'findings' of the empirical analysis and an outgrowth of the theoretical framework presented earlier in this book. To be more precise, the analytical model of pluralism sits at the intersection of the Weberian sociology of pluralism developed in Chapters 4 and 5, and the empirical study of Central Canadian newspaper discourses that provides the basis for Chapters 7, 8, and 9. Rather than being preconceived theoretically, the notion of triangular relations between 'us,' 'others,' and 'them' emerged from the empirical material, which, in a way, 'refused' to be studied in binary terms of us/them, and demanded the elaboration of a more creative analysis. Although I am now in the position to deduce the new model of pluralism entirely from theoretical considerations, I gladly acknowledge that this is only the case *after* being prompted to do so by this study's empirical findings. Further below, it will become evident that my approach to discourse analysis continues to build upon insights inherent in CDA. However, the model of pluralism as triangular relations allows me to take the analysis beyond the binaries of us/them, and to identify instances of 'conditional inclusion.'

Contours of the Newspaper Sample

Defining a Sampling Context

The long history of diversity in Canada has been interpreted as a 'palimpsest' (Green, 2005; cited in Kymlicka, 2007: 39) of federal laws and policies, where new layers are continually added on top of the old ones. Within the logic of this image, recent multiculturalism policies for ethnic groups of immigrant origin overlie earlier religious, legal, linguistic, and territorial agreements between English and French Canadians, which were preceded by historic settlements and treaties between the two colonizers and Aboriginal peoples.

While the notion of a palimpsest certainly resonates with the development of pluralism in Canada, a competing image emerges if we examine the current legal arrangements pertaining to Canada's three different types of minorities, Aboriginal peoples, the francophones (of Quebec), and 'ethnic groups' of immigrant origin. What we see then is 'not so much three horizontal layers as three vertical silos' (Kymlicka, 2007: 39). As Kymlicka points out the policies pertaining to these groups have very different historical origins and are disconnected from each other legally and administratively. They are incorporated in different pieces of legislation, administered by different federal departments, enshrined in different sections of Canada's Constitution, and legitimized with reference to different normative principles. 'As a re-. sult, each forms its own discrete silo, and there is very little interaction between them' (ibid.: 40). In other words, the analytical split between national and ethnic minorities finds its pendant in the political and administrative realm.

The striking separateness of the policies pertaining to the different recognized types of minorities in the Canadian political system constitutes a challenge to the design of a case study that aims to analyse how the reference to Québécois minority nationalism impacts upon the (de) legitimization of multiculturalism in dominant discourses. Dominant discourses are in the first instance enunciations that we find in legislations, government publications, and speeches by state officials. Indeed, my first intention had been to examine this type of discourse. In this way I had planned to show, in a classical 'Weberian' manner, how ideas and representations impact upon social structures. However, the legal separation between multiculturalism, bilingualism, and the pluralist rights granted to Quebec under (asymmetrical) federalism rendered policy texts unsuitable for the type of research I had aimed to conduct. I reviewed the possibilities to examine policies, government publications, official speeches, and parliamentary debates but later rejected these options for similar reasons.

Instead, on the basis of daily experiences, I became interested in other types of highly influential discourses, where accommodations of minority nations and immigrant groups are often blurred, intertwined, and articulated in relation to each other: the mainstream media. The newspapers I read echoed the articulations that I was hearing on the streets of Toronto, in conversations with friends and colleagues, and even at academic conferences on multiculturalism. Or should I say, these articulations reflected what was enunciated in the mass media? Mainstream newspapers are both producers and reproducers of public discourse. They are part of a society's dominant discourses, and are thus suitable for research that is interested in the ways in which a national majority represents itself as 'multicultural.' Newspapers are also highly influential because they are widely distributed. In the city, they are also visible at kiosks and newspaper stands.

Being interested in English-language discourses – because it is primarily in the rest of Canada rather than in Quebec that a unifying multicultural pan-Canadianism has taken root[1] – I first included newspapers from several English-speaking provinces in Canada (e.g., from the Prairies and the Maritimes). For reasons of time and resources, I later reduced my sampling context to the Toronto-produced edition of the *Globe and Mail* and the *Toronto Star*. Indeed, in a city like Toronto, where more than 50 per cent of the population is not born and schooled in Canada, newspapers are a very important source of information about Canadian society. Furthermore, reflections from and on a city as ethnically diverse as Toronto are well suited for a study that aims to examine *how* a 'multicultural we' is constructed. Let me briefly elaborate on the various dimensions on which the rationale for this case study is based.

First, Canadians now live in a complex media environment where newspapers are no longer the stand-alone medium that they once were. Nonetheless, 'at present, no other mass medium offers the same combined possibilities for accessibility, in-depth analysis, potential diversity of view-points, and sustained reflection on important political and economic issues' (Hacket and Gruneau, 2000: 11–12). As institutionalized (re)producers of dominant representations, mainstream newspapers are a segment of public discourse, which, in turn, they also help to shape by transmitting central cultural images, ideas, and symbols, and in (re)defining societal 'core values' and national myths (Davis, 1985). Directly or indirectly, newspaper discourses impact a society's understanding of who 'we' are, what kind of nation 'we' live in, want to live in, or should live in (Milner, 2001; *Toronto Star,* 2001). As such, they also continue to have an important impact on political decision making.[2] Finally, although following to a large extent a corporate agenda, mainstream newspapers should not be interpreted as monolithic institutions. Rather, they are a contested site of meaning making, 'truth,' and opinion, where different interests struggle for control over legitimate world views.

Second, once a predominantly white Anglo-Saxon Protestant town, Toronto is now often heralded as 'one of the most multicultural cities in the world' (City of Toronto, 2006; but see Doucet, 2001). With more than 40 per cent 'visible minorities' and almost 50 per cent of its population not being born within the country, Toronto is indeed an extremely diverse place (Anisef and Lanphier, 2003) which distances itself not only from the rest of the country, but also from the other two Canadian immigrant-receiving cities, Montreal and Vancouver. Among the approximately four million people that live in the Greater Toronto Area (GTA) are an estimated 450,000 of Chinese, 400,000 of Italian, and 250,000 of African background. There are almost 200,000 Jews and substantial populations from the Indian subcontinent, Greece, Portugal, Poland, Vietnam, Latin America, and Central and Eastern Europe (Troper, 2003).

As a consequence, media discourses about Canadianness for and from this city are likely to reflect (upon) this multicultural diversity.[3]

Third, based in Toronto, the *Globe and Mail* and the *Toronto Star* cover a spectrum of opinion that is best described as socially majoritarian, urban, and Central Canadian, as well as politically centre and left of centre. The *Globe and Mail* is a liberal, slightly right-of-centre daily with a readership of approximately one million individuals per day. Until 1998, it was Canada's only 'national' newspaper, a status that it now shares with the *National Post*. While the *Globe* has probably lost parts of its more conservative and corporate readership to the *National Post*, it continues to cater to the Canadian political and intellectual elite, that is, 'readers with university degrees or greater, as well as managers and professionals' (*Globe and Mail Online*, 2003). Despite its leading editorial environment and news of 'national interest' (Kesterton, 1984: 86), the *Globe* is sometimes reproached for being 'Toronto-centric.' By contrast, the *Toronto Star* consciously reports for and from Canada's most multicultural city and caters to a readership that is extremely diverse in social, economic, and ethnic terms. With a total average circulation of half a million copies per day, the *Toronto Star* is Canada's most widely read local newspaper (*Toronto Star Online*, 2004). Adopting a more social-liberal editorial stance than the *Globe*, and insisting on its critical social consciousness – on 'speaking for the powerless' (*Toronto Star*, 1999) – the *Star* seems to be 'perpetually indignant' (Kesterton, 1984: 88).[4]

Obviously, this spectrum, although highly relevant and politically influential, cannot be taken for all media discourses in a regionally extremely diverse country such as Canada. In particular the Prairie provinces are known for their particular view of Canada – a view which is often diametrically opposed to Central Canadian standpoints. As such, the analysis in this book can only exemplify one of many possible representations of Canadian multiculturalism in the vast entity called English Canada.

Steps of Data Selection and Analysis

Concentrating not on 'whether' but on 'how' Canadian national identity is represented as multicultural requires the compilation of a closed corpus of textual data, rather than an open-ended review of supporting and contradictory material. In this study, newspaper articles were selected by keyword search in the *Globe and Mail* on CD-ROM and through the electronic newspaper index *Canadian Virtual Newslibrary* (NewSCan) in the *Toronto Star*.[5] Selecting articles by 'in text search' provided more significant results than concentrating on headlines. I selected my corpus through the four-word combination 'Canada and Quebec and nation and (multiculturalism or pluralism or diversity).'[6] In order to let my data 'speak,' and to provide for the possibility of shifting conceptions of otherness, I have consciously avoided focussing my data collection on pre-identified events or situations of conflict.

In a first step of data collection, I collected 188 *Globe and Mail* articles and 162 *Toronto Star* articles of all genres within the period from 1 January 1992, the year of the pan-Canadian referendum on the Charlottetown Accord, to 31 December 2001. The events on 11 September 2001 led to a change in discourse and brought a definite end to the 'differentialist turn.' All 350 articles were downloaded and printed. Their standard properties (name of newspaper, reporter, type of article, date, etc.) were catalogued. Reading these articles repeatedly in chronological order allowed me to become familiar with the media discourses during the 1990s, and to situate the op-ed pieces within a larger framework of relevant societal debates and events. News articles, book reviews, in-depth reportages, etc. drew my attention to specific events, speeches, and publications. The articles selected by keyword search are distributed relatively evenly over the years. Peaks occur in 1992, the year of the Charlottetown referendum, and in 1995, the year of the Quebec referendum on sovereignty. Towards the end of my investigation period (in the years 2000 and 2001) the number of articles dealing with Quebec in combination with immigration-related ethnic diversity declines.

In a second step of data selection, out of my larger corpus of newspaper articles, 123 op-ed articles have been selected for in-depth examination through Critical Discourse Analysis. I found an investigation of op-ed articles to provide more significant insights than examining news stories.[7] I concentrate on editorials, columns, and letters to the editor. For my analysis, I do not differentiate between opinion genres, because all of them are explicitly and deliberately subjective. They are treated as interconnected elements of a single media text about Canadian multiculturalism and nationhood in the 1990s (Kress, 2000).[8] CDA was applied to 49 *Globe* articles and 74 *Star* articles (23 editorials, 79 columns, and 21 letters to the editor).[9]

It should be underlined that this qualitative study aims to develop and exemplify a *theoretical understanding* of the multicultural reconstruction of Canadian national identity in the 1990s. It does not pretend to produce representative results for which a larger sample and quantitative analysis would have been necessary. A more comprehensive examination of Canadian English-language majority discourses should include not only a variety of newspapers from other Canadian regions but also take account of parliamentary speeches and government documents and publications.

In the following two sections, I will first sketch out the contours of the newspaper sample in terms of the presence and absence of ethnocultural actors in the mainstream press. This section also serves to define the terminology that will be used to describe these actors. I will then introduce three different ideological perspectives that are prevailing in the newspaper sample under investigation.

Presences and Absences

To come into existence and to be able to appropriate material and non-material opportunities, social groups must be *represented*, that is, they must be 'envisioned' or 'imagined' as much as they must be named and spoken of/for. For Pierre Bourdieu, this is the 'political work of *class making*' (1987: 8). It involves the 'construction of [mobilized or "mobilizable"] groups' and 'the imposition of the legitimate vision of the social world and of its divisions' (ibid.: 13). In this section I will briefly outline which collective actors are represented in the corpus of newspaper texts, and which categories are absent. The following descriptions are based on word counts and notes taken during a phase of extensive reading of my textual material. I will also define the terminology that I use to describe Canada's ethnic and national actors.

In general, in the newspaper sample under investigation, Canada is portrayed as an extremely diverse place; social inequalities, regional differences, and cleavages between groups are downplayed. Only close textual analysis reveals the internal and external boundaries of Canada's multicultural nation. Two collectivities deserve particular attention: the United States and Quebec. While their boundaries remain blurred, they are frequently mentioned within my sample and clearly identifiable as ethnonational group categories.

The United States is mentioned at least one time in every second selected article (183 times in total). It constitutes an omnipresent entity that seems to have an important impact on the constitution of the multicultural Canadian nation. On the one hand, the United States is represented as a society marked by harsh individualism and the absence of 'care.' On the other hand, the United States seems to have a strong assimilative capacity and is admired for its internal unity and strong national identity. As Mexico is excluded from the considerations in this book, I will use the terms 'United States' and 'America' synonymously.

In the newspaper sample, the term 'French Canadians' is used in historical accounts of Canadian nation building. In contemporary times, francophones are relegated to the territory of Quebec. With the exception of one *Globe and Mail* column (G-1998-0414), which underlines Franco-Albertans' opposition to Québécois separatism, there is no mention of French-speaking minorities outside Quebec. Quebeckers are cast as a French-speaking population of French ancestry; ethnic and linguistic diversity in Quebec is only referred to when it enters into conflict with the attitudes of 'Québécois de souche.' As an entity, Quebec is often defined by the attitudes imputed to its nationalist, separatist leaders, who seem to subdue (apolitical) 'ordinary Quebeckers.' I use the term 'French Canada' to designate one of the two linguistically defined Canadian 'founding nations.' While Canadians of French Canadian heritage live in all parts of Canada, Quebec is now Canada's only (unilingual) French-speaking province. 'Québécois' designates all habitants living on Quebec's territory, whether they are anglophones, francophones, or 'allophones' (individuals whose mother tongue is other than English or French). 'Francophone Québécois' are all habitants of Quebec who speak French, be they of French, Haitian, Lebanese, Vietnamese, or any other national background. I will use the term 'Franco-Québécois' to designate Quebeckers who self-identify as being of French ancestry.

I use the term 'Canada' to refer to the pan-Canadian society north of the border with the United States. While, officially, the Canadian nation includes Quebec, these two entities are sometimes contrasted. Within the discourse of my sample, the composition of the rest of Canada remains vague. Three categories can be identified: 'English Canadians,' 'ethnic Canadians,' and 'First Nations.'

In the newspaper sample, the term 'English Canadians' is used in historical accounts of Canada and republican discourses that view Canadian nationhood as being constituted by 'English Canadians' (the terms 'Anglo-Celts' and 'WASPs' are also used) and the 'British traditions' of law, order, civility, and tolerance. Typically for Central Canadian newspaper discourses, regional differences do not receive much attention in my sample. 'The West' is sometimes portrayed as a carrier of alterity; Ontario is not invested with any striking characteristics. I use the term 'English Canada' to designate the second Canadian 'founding nation.' I use both terms 'English Canada' and 'English-speaking

Canada' to refer to the society in 'the rest of Canada' where English constitutes the dominant language. The term 'English Canadians' refers to individuals who identify themselves as British in ancestry or 'Canadian' on the census (generally those of several generations' British descent). This group still forms the majority within English-speaking Canada. The term 'English-speaking Canadians' also includes individuals who do not claim to be of British extraction, but whose mother tongue is English and who primarily self-identify – and are commonly identified – as 'Canadian.'[10]

Taken together, the terms 'ethnic Canadians,' 'ethnic groups,' 'ethnic communities,' 'ethnic minorities' appear only 15 times in the newspaper sample. The term 'visible minorities' is used only 7 times. There are also no 'racialized minorities,' no 'people of colour' in my sample. 'Blacks' are mentioned 23 times, but 12 of these counts refer to the United States and one to France. The picture changes dramatically, if the terms 'immigrants' and 'minorities' are used: 88 counts for 'minorities,' 73 for 'immigrants,' 23 for 'refugees.'[11] These numbers reveal that Canadians other than those of British and French origin exist, but that they are rarely named. This might be due to a bias of my research frame, which was designed to capture the multicultural inclusion of ethnic groups rather than their exclusion. However, the absence of ethnic 'groups' may also reflect (1) the recent changes in the multiculturalism program/ideology, where integrated diversity triumphs over structural pluralism (see Chapters 8 and 10); (2) the missing voice of minority groups within the mainstream media, (3) the shifting content of the category 'ethnic groups.'[12] In my analysis, I use the term 'ethnic minorities.' This term (1) refers to a category of people rather than a constituted group, and (2) avoids a clear-cut division between racialized/non-racialized minorities, as the latter cannot be clearly discerned from the newspaper sample.[13]

Although 'First Nations' are mentioned 67 times within my data sample, they are rarely at the centre of attention. Only two *Globe and Mail* columns deal exclusively with First Nations issues: the Nisga'a treaty (G-1998-0917) and the creation of Nunavut (G-1999-0401). First Nations are mentioned with reference to Canadian history, but they are not given agency and prominence in issues related to multicultural nationhood. This observation describes both a limitation of the newspaper sample and a result. The under-representation of Aboriginal peoples in the media is a widely acknowledged indicator of their minority status (Hacket and Gruneau, 2000; Mahtani, 2001; Perigoe and Lazar, 1992).

International comparisons with individual countries or, in general, 'the world' are an important feature of my sample.[14] 'The world' increasingly replaces the United States as a contrasting example; it constitutes the stage on which Canada plays, and the audience that admires Canada's multicultural mosaic and judges its moral worth as a nation.

In sum within the newspaper sample, the boundaries that are constructed are mainly those of the Canadian nation. Although ethnocultural diversity is highlighted, internal divisions are downplayed. Discourses of race, resistance, trinationalism, and colonialism are absent. There are exceptions within the *Toronto Star*, as I will outline in the next section, but even these discourses do not challenge the representation of Canada as a relatively successful, harmonious, and ethnically diverse multicultural nation. Although the mis- and under-representations of ethnic groups and First Nations are unintended effects of my data selection, scholars have identified this as a common feature of Canadian mainstream media discourses (Hacket and Gruneau, 2000; Mahtani, 2001; Perigoe and Lazar, 1992). The missing discussion of regional differences highlights the fact that the sample is made of discourses from Central Canada. In many respects, my sample exhibits thus the characteristic traits of Canadian majority discourses, and this even in regional terms.

Diverging Perspectives

The representation of group relations is impacted by both situational interests (varying with context) and long-term ideas (world views). Both motivate the enunciation. According to Kenneth Gergen (2001), every speech act must establish an endpoint or goal that provides the enunciation with meaning. On the one hand, this endpoint or persuasive goal impacts the strategies that are employed to represent group relations. On the other, the persuasive goal is itself a function of a particular representation of the world, its normative bases and social divisions. Within a sample of opinion discourses from two Toronto-based mainstream newspapers one can expect a relatively small variety of diverging world views. Nevertheless, the media are not monolithic institutions. Thus, even within this segment of majority discourses there is considerable variation.

In order to come to terms with this variation, as a heuristic means, I classified each article according to its main persuasive goal or endpoint. This method was not preconceived, but emerged out of my involvement with the empirical material. I found that it is possible to differentiate between three persuasive goals regarding ethnic diversity and its recognition in the public space: reducing, maintaining, or extending normative pluralism. In Canada, opinions about normative pluralism require further qualification, since different types of pluralist accommodation are negotiated/have already been put in place. We must thus ask: Whose publicly recognized ethnic diversity is to be reduced, maintained, or extended? Distinguishing between the three persuasive goals, I first coded all articles as to whether these goals related primarily to Quebec's and/ or First Nations' claims for multinationalism, or to the multicultural accommodation of 'ethnic Canadians.' This coding produced considerable overlap, which led me to merge some of my categories and to identify three types of majority perspectives within my sample: republican, liberal-pluralist, and liberal-multiculturalist. At a later stage, these classifications were verified and corrected through a rigorous analysis of the prevailing triangular relations (see Chapter 9). I will briefly circumscribe these perspectives.

The discourses in the newspaper sample that pursue the persuasive goal of reducing ethnic pluralism in Canada have been labelled as 'republican.' While they do not necessarily oppose ethnic plurality as such, they claim that its public recognition undermines social cohesion and ultimately leads to the disintegration of the Canadian nation. Although it is possible to identify discourses that target primarily Québécois nationalism and separatism, most of the 'reducing pluralism discourses' (which were later bundled and named 'republican') are as equally opposed to special status for Quebec and First Nations as to multiculturalism as an official policy and blueprint for society.

The discourses in the newspaper sample that pursue the persuasive goal of maintaining the status quo of ethnic pluralism in Canada have been identified as 'liberal-pluralist.' These discourses do not disrupt the dominant narrative of a relatively harmonious Canadian multicultural nation. For them, the 'just balance' between Canadian nationhood, special status for Quebec, self-government rights for First Nations, and multiculturalism has been established. They perpetuate and legitimize the status quo. The status quo refers to a situation where Quebec de facto enjoys more group-based rights of (deeper) structural pluralism than immigrants and ethnic Canadians, even though its status as a 'distinct society' is not constitutionally recognized. Although the failure to include Quebec within the Canadian Constitution is sometimes regretted, no serious arguments are brought forth in favour of granting Quebec the political and economic autonomy it desires.[15] I have decided to use the generic term 'pluralism' for this ideological perspective as it includes both the recognition of national and ethnic minorities.

The discourses in the newspaper sample that pursue the persuasive goal of extending multiculturalism in Canada have been labelled 'liberal-multiculturalist.' They contend that the status quo is insufficient, without, however, resorting to a radical multiculturalism as a strategy of subversion. These discourses claim that immigrants, ethnic Canadians, and 'visible minorities' are still marginalized in the mainstream societies of English-speaking Canada and Quebec, and that more public recognition of immigration-induced ethnic diversity is needed. Within the newspaper sample, there are no strong demands for multinationalism. As a consequence, the category of 'liberal-multiculturalist discourses' only concentrates on articles with the persuasive goal of extending multiculturalism in Canada without reinforcing the recognition of Quebec and Aboriginal peoples as 'nations.'[16] Furthermore, within the newspaper sample, I was unable to identify forceful requests for extending institutional pluralism to ethnic groups of immigrant origin. This absence is most likely related to the fact that I am investigating newspaper texts, thus majority discourses. It is interesting in so far as it evades radical forms of multiculturalism (Bannerji, 2000; Gilroy, 2004) and claims for the extension of democratic institutional pluralism to immigrant groups (Bader, 1995b; Modood, 2005). I therefore use the term 'liberal' to describe the type of multiculturalism at stake.

Sketching the contours of the three perspectives, these descriptions show that there are important variations within my sample. The distribution of the three perspectives is shown in Table 6.1. The table reveals that the republican and the liberal-pluralist discourses are dominant within the sample and equally represented within the two newspapers. Interestingly, articles aiming to extend liberal multiculturalism have only been identified in the *Toronto Star*.

Table 6.1
Number of coded articles according to discursive perspective

	Globe and Mail	*Toronto Star*	*Globe & Star*	
Type of perspective	*N*	*n*	*n*	%
Republican	24	29	53	43.1
Liberal-pluralist	25	26	51	41.5
Liberal-multiculturalist	0	19	19	15.4
Total	49	74	123	100

In Chapter 9, these diverging discourses will be further discussed. For reasons of clarity, they will not be taken into account in Chapters 7 and 8. In the remainder of this chapter, I will develop the theoretical model of pluralism as a set of triangular group relations and explain how it has been used to analyse the textual material.

Main Analytical Model: Pluralism as a Triangular Relation

Us/We Relations in the Multicultural Context

Discourse analysts teach us that national identities are constructed through simultaneously projecting distinction and/or difference to the outside and emphasizing sameness/shared belonging within. Both techniques together produce the uniqueness of the nation, constitute its individuality, and thus, found its right of independent existence within a world of nations (Hall, 1996a; Wodak et al., 1998). Constructing a multicultural nation is therefore a challenging undertaking, which is often viewed either as being incompatible with unified nationhood (Schlesinger, 1998) or as camouflaging homogeneous nationhood under a layer of shallow, inoffensive cultural diversity that mitigates conflict and substantial forms of 'difference' and inequality (Bhabha, 1990b). Indeed, multiculturalism complicates the process of national identity construction because, on the one hand, it must avoid the impression of homogeneity. Advocating internal sameness is an ideological, discursive, and political 'no.' On the other hand, negative or inferiorizing strategies of differentiation are also unacceptable within a multicultural context.

Trying to find a solution to this problem, the political theorist Ian Angus (1997) suggests that a multicultural identity is not made of exclusive 'us/them' relations, but of inclusive 'us/we' relations, which reflect the feeling that we all belong despite our differences. According to Angus, within the multicultural context, the relation between two members of different ethnic groups – which is usually identified as an us/them relation – does not culminate in a synthesis. Synthesis would be characteristic of group relations characterized by interculturalism, hybridity, and/or the idea of the 'melting pot.' This, by definition, should not occur within *multi*culturalism. By the same definition, the multicultural context should also not be characterized by antagonist us/them relations which preclude the emergence of feelings of commonality and shared belonging.

Rather, within the multicultural context the typical antagonist us/ them relation, which characterizes the establishment of group boundaries, is transformed into an us/we relation where 'the 'us' [refers] to one's ethnocultural group and the 'we' [refers] to the multicultural context' of the larger society (Angus, 1998: 84). The multicultural context transforms the role of ethnic tradition, since it presents cultural membership from the outset as one possibility among others, thereby generating (1) an understanding of the particularity/uniqueness of one's culture, and (2) an appreciation of the multicultural context that validates this particular way of life/culture (as it validates all others). As a consequence, 'in the passage from the perception of uniqueness to its justification, the "us" is constituted. In the passage from the "us" to a multicultural context that includes many ethno-cultures, the "we" is formed' (ibid.: 86).[17] In the Canadian context, the us/we relation expresses 'how one can participate in English Canada *through* participation in an ethnocultural group' (ibid.: 85).

Angus' political philosophy of multiculturalism is intriguing as it claims that the inclusion of a culturally different other within a collectively imagined pluralist we-group is possible without the under- or misrepresentation of minorities that is often reported by discourse analysts. To be more precise, Angus reminds us that the standpoint from which individuals or collectivities speak – be they majorities or minorities – is particular. For him, it is the appreciation of the cultural and individual uniqueness of 'us' that sustains the more encompassing inclusive formulation of 'we.' If 'we' want to be pluralist or *multicultural* (and not primarily assimilative, hybrid, *inter*cultural, or melted), 'us' cannot be extended into a 'we,' but must recognize the existence of another particular 'us' within the realm of 'we.' This is an important insight, which can help to improve the empirical analysis of discourse.

Nevertheless, if we look at Angus' concept of us/we relations from the sociological theory that has been elaborated in Chapters 4 and 5, his concept falls short with regard to two considerations. First, his model fails to reflect power relations. If difference is (re)produced within unequal power relations then even us/we relations within the multicultural context can never involve entirely equal participants. Second, Angus' multicultural *philosophy* is a normative model of pluralism, which wants to be universal and therefore fails to recognize its boundaries. The sociological constitution of 'normative' pluralism (in the sense of a prescriptive idea of society building), by contrast, requires the construction of group boundaries through the confrontation with (real or imagined) 'Others.' I will continue to explore these two consid-erations in the following section.

The next section will also bridge the gap between the theory of a 'multicultural we' and the method for its empirical analysis. In fact, while Angus' concept of us/we relations is purely theoretical, the meth-odology of Critical Discourse Analysis, which will be applied to exam-ine the newspaper sample, allows us to trace power inequalities and processes of othering in discourse.

Us/Them Relations in Dominant Discourses

The crucial role of (real or imagined) outsiders in fostering group forma-tion has been discussed in Chapter 4. It is also at the heart of approaches in Critical Discourse Analysis that have recently gained currency in ex-amining inequality and injustice in multicultural societies (Dunn and Mahtani, 2001; Teo, 2000; Potvin, 2008; Henry and Tator, 2002).

Critical Discourse Analysis emerges out of an 'anti-foundationalist' perspective that examines power inequalities in society, such as the theory of majority/minority relations.[18] It is based upon the assumption that language and meaning are both reflections and reproducers of con-crete power relations between social actors.[19] Linda Pietrantonio (1999), for example, shows that unequal social positions are reflected in discur-sive representations where they translate into a dissymmetry in terms of the social norm, agency, and individuation. Thus, a majority status within society is revealed through (1) agency (including historicity and a *faire social*) and (2) individuality/individualization. The absence of these attributes is characteristic of the representation of minorities.[20]

Processes of othering in discourse are thus a crucial part of unequal group relations. In fact, as shown in Chapter 4, collective identities are constructed by differentiating between 'us' and 'them.' The confronta-tion with third persons helps to downplay the internal heterogeneity of collectivities and thereby supports the emergence of a collective identity. Scholars have therefore highlighted the importance of supporting casts for the construction of unified, positively connoted we-groups. Erich Voegelin (1933) underlined the role of Jews as a *Gegenidee* (counter-idea) in Nazi Germany. Lewis Copeland uses the term 'contrast conception' to argue that in the United States 'the Negro [. . .] produces cohesion within white society. The common object of hatred provides a common element of belief and sentiment' (1939: 139). More recently, Edward Said (1994b) proposed that the image of today's valorized Western society can only be upheld through projection of communitarian 'tribalism' upon oriental bodies.

In multicultural societies, however, the explicit articulation of hierarchy, subordination, and dominance is officially discredited. As a consequence, the expression of discriminatory opinions has become more subtle and complex: 'the lexical terms that are likely to be preferred in public today are those that *mitigate and disguise* a speaker's or writer's tendency to discriminate' (Riggins, 1997: 7, original emphasis). Tainted in-group/out-group representations are often achieved through the use of subtle linguistic techniques such as the absence/presence of particular actors or attributes in the text, positively/negatively connoted lexemes, active vs. passive constructions, quantity and details of positive/negative propositions, disclaimers (apparent denials/concessions/empathy), dualisms, etc. These representations are examined by Critical Discourse Analysis, which aims to reveal mitigated forms of othering and discrimination. Teun van Dijk's 'ideological square' demonstrates the underlying systematic: (1) emphasize our good properties/actions; (2) emphasize their bad properties/actions; (3) mitigate our bad properties/actions; and (4) mitigate their good properties/actions (1998: 33).

While Critical Discourse Analysis allows us to identify majority and minority positions within discursive representations of collective identity, in my experience with the newspaper sample under investigation, it proved difficult to apply this approach to understand the construction of a 'multicultural we.' Rather, it seemed to me that that approaches like Teun van Dijk's 'ideological square' was encaging my analysis in a false logic of binaries without allowing to capture the (sometimes) empowering effects for those minorities that are constructed as 'conditional insiders.' From the perspective of Critical Discourse Analysis, they remained purely subordinate categories. Admittedly, they were subordinate in relation to the dominant group. However, in the newspaper sample, there were also minorities that were constructed as being even 'further down the road' in respect of otherness. How was I to account for this difference between diverse minority categories? Classifying all of them as being constructed as 'them' did not seem to do justice to the empirical material.

Put differently, when analysing the collected Central Canadian newspaper discourses, I found that there were often more than two group categories present in the discourse. Thus, there was a dominant category. Often, as I will argue in the following chapters, this dominant category was identified as English Canadian. Then there were at least two or more minority categories. Quite often, the dominant category was the one that represented the social norm. However, the other categories were not simply constructed as minorities. Rather, they were situated in a relationship with each other. In addition to the dominant group, there was a second point of reference. Expressed positively, one minority group was always better than the others, more adapted then the others, culturally closer than the others, etc. Expressed negatively, I found that one group category was usually constructed as more demanding than the others, less grateful than the others, etc. In sum, by means of constructing a contrast with yet another group category ('them'), some group categories became part of 'us,' or – put correctly, they did not quite become 'us': they became unequally included as 'others' within a more or less 'multicultural' we.

Drawing from this experience, we may say that by concentrating only on majority/minority power asymmetries (Pietrantonio, 2000) the theory of majority/minority relations and its predominant operationalization in Critical Discourse Analysis tend to neglect the emancipative potential of unequal inclusion and to blind us to the construction of multicultural alliances.

To overcome this problem, Engin Isin recently argued that the logics of alterity are more nuanced than binaries of inclusion/exclusion, because they embody differentiation and distinction 'as strategies of elective affiliation, recognition, incorporation, and congregation' (Isin, 2002: 25). Based on my experience with the newspaper discourses collected for this study, I concur with Isin that there are different types of outsiders. However, we should be careful not to throw out the baby with the bathwater: analysing social relations in terms of inclusion/ exclusion neither presumes nor produces a binary. Rather, concentrating in our research on merely two groups (re)produces a dualism. If we conceive of the social as a net of multilayered situations of inclusion/ exclusion, we should be able to conceive of a model of discourse analysis that captures instances of conditional inclusion/exclusion. Drawing upon Angus' theory of us/we relations, the theory of majority/minority relations developed in Chapter 4, and its operationalization in Critical Discourse Analysis' focus on us/them relations, I will propose such a model in the section below.

From Binaries to Triangular Relations

To analytically comprehend multicultural identity formation, we have to develop an understanding of inclusion/exclusion that goes beyond binary relations. Rather, what we need is (at least) a triangular relation-ship. These considerations can be summarized by the following (mini-malist) equation:

$$us + others_{1-n} = multicultural \ we \neq them_{1-n}$$

First, in line with the theory developed in Chapter 4, I argue that the relation between the participating members of a 'multicultural we' (us + others$_{1-n}$) must not necessarily be one of equality. In fact, if we assume that ethnic groups are constituted in unequal power relations, the 'multicultural we' can never be entirely free of inequalities, which, in turn, are reflected and reproduced in discourses on nationhood. 'Us' designates the speaking collectivity. I use the term 'others' to designate the included – but never on entirely equal terms – minority group(s). Despite these considerations, I assume that construction of a 'multicul-tural we' is possible in much the same way that other group formations occur, that is, by downplaying (but not erasing) salient differences be-tween individual/collective group members for the purpose of group closure.

Second, this downplaying of internal heterogeneity is only possible through confrontation with third persons. Thus, a 'multicultural we' that allows for internal group-differentiated boundaries and identities (as Angus claims) cannot exist without being bounded by an opposition to real or imagined Others. While others (in lower case) may become seen as part of 'we,' Others (in upper case) are constructed as outsiders (them$_{1-n}$). Both, the included 'others' as well as the excluded 'them,' can refer to one or an indefinite number of groups (implied by the subscript 1–n). 'Them' refers to a real or imagined collectivity that is perceived as 'different.' It can be located inside the national society or outside of a particular set of associative relations. 'Them' are usually represented as the opposite of the 'multicultural we.' As opposite of normative plural-ism, a real or imagined 'them' collectivity is reproached for practising either assimilation or exclusion.

Third, in principle, the 'multicultural we,' is represented as a negoti-ated compromise among equals. It is cherished for its 'uniqueness' and distinguished from competing types of *Gesellschaft* and *Gemeinschaft*, which are both judged as inadequate, deviant, 'too different,' or 'too extreme.' This contrast does not exist prior to the 'multicultural we' but is constructed by its members. It provides the 'multicultural we' with meaning and identity. The 'multicultural we' and its 'Others' (in upper case) always emerge simultaneously in a dialogical manner and consti-tute each other.

In sum, following the theoretical framework developed in Chapter 4, my discourse analysis draws on Guillaumin's (1972) and Pietrantonio's (1999) examinations of unequal majority/minority relations within text. My focus of analysis, however, is slightly different. While these authors concentrate on the exclusion of minority categories from a unified majoritarian 'we,' I am first and foremost interested in the possibilities of *pluralist inclusion* as such. My analysis, therefore, examines the inclusion of some groups through the discursive strategies of contrast and opposition vis-à-vis other groups. I call this 'conditional inclusion.' For reasons that have been explained earlier (see also Chapter 6), I am particularly interested in the impact that representations of 'the French fact' (related to official bilingualism, Québécois nationalism, etc.) have upon the relations between the remaining groups.

Newspaper articles from my sample are identified by first letter of newspaper title – publication year – month and day, for example: G-1997-0701.

In the following section, I will briefly describe how the above-elaborated formula will be applied to the textual material, and how the analysis is pursued throughout the following chapters.

Three Focal Points of Analysis

During a phase of intensive discourse analysis, the model of triangular relations has been applied to 123 articles. For each article, an original analysis was written using the above-described model of triangular relations. Afterwards, this material has been reinterpreted and rewritten to answer my research questions by taking into account the theoretical framework elaborated in Chapters 4 and 5. This led to the development of three focal points of analysis, as shown in Figure 6.1.

1 In Chapter 7, I examine the impact of shifting constructions of 'them' upon representation of the 'multicultural we.' I will not describe the constructed 'contrast conceptions' (Copeland, 1939) in detail. This would be an interesting task, but an exhaustive analysis would lead astray from the main objective of my study. Rather, I examine the functions of these representations for the external boundary construction of multicultural nations.
2 In Chapter 8, I investigate how the discursive logics related to multinationalism (the varying representations of conflict and agreement between pre-established groups) influence the possibilities

Figure 6.1: Model of triangular relations with three focal points of analysis

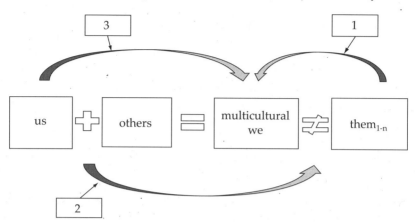

of multicultural inclusion for newcomers. This will allow us to better assess the relationship between multinationalism and multiculturalism.

3 In Chapter 9, I concentrate on the constitution of the 'multicultural we' from within: who and/or what is represented as the 'essence' of Canadianness, and to what extent is this Canadianness characterized as 'multicultural'?

Needless to say, my analysis has also been inspired by an extensive literature review of academic and newspaper texts from Canada and other parts of the world. In all three chapters, references to my review of the academic literature will be used as supplements to provide relevant information and to contrast or confirm the results stemming from the newspaper analysis.

Conclusion

In this chapter, I have elaborated the rationale for an empirical analysis of opinion discourses in two Central Canadian English-language mainstream newspapers, namely, the *Globe and Mail* and the *Toronto Star* between 1992 and 2001. I have also described the sampling methodology, sketched out presences and absences of group categories in the corpus, and identified three diverging perspectives on multiculturalism. Taken together, the presences and absences of actors in the sample, as well as the prevailing ideological perspectives describe both the specific content and the limitations of the newspaper sample. They constitute the background against which the findings of the upcoming analysis must be evaluated.

Second, I have elaborated the theoretical approach and analytical model that has been applied to analyse the textual material. The model of pluralism as a set of triangular relations emerged from the empirical material through extensive reading and analytical testing. At the same time, it is inspired by the sociology of ethnic relations and the pluralization of national identity that has been developed in Chapters 4 and 5. Used as a particular approach of discourse analysis, this model allows us to study the construction of a 'multicultural we' by replacing exclusive us/them binaries with a triangular matrix of group relations.

Three focal points of analysis, described in the section above, will guide the investigation in the following three chapters. Taken together, these chapters will allow us to respond to the research questions that are at the core of this book. They will reveal how a 'multicultural we' is constructed within the selected newspaper discourses, and identify the extent to which representations of Québécois nationalism sustain this construction.

7 Neither 'America' nor 'Quebec'

This is the first of three chapters in which I present the results of a an empirical analysis of opinion discourses in two Central Canadian English-language mainstream newspapers, the *Globe and Mail* and the *Toronto Star*, between 1992 and 2001. The previous chapter provided the rationale for this study, described the sampling method, and discussed the content and limitations of the newspaper sample. Furthermore, it was argued that a particular analytical model, namely, that of pluralism as a set of triangular relations emerged from the empirical material through extensive reading and analytical testing. Employed as a particular approach to discourse analysis, this model allows us to study the construction of a 'multicultural we' by replacing exclusive us/them binaries with a triangular matrix of group relations.

This and the following two chapters reveal how a 'multicultural we' is constructed within the selected newspaper discourses. Particular attention is paid to the extent that representations of Québécois nationalism sustain this construction. Taken together, these chapters will allow us to respond to the research question that is at the core of this book: How do 'we' – the national majority – become multicultural? Put differently, how do (previously constructed) ethnic categories become included into a dominant representation of who 'we' are and/or want to be? In each of these chapters, I will proceed by first reminding the reader of the prevailing literature and/or theoretical context that the empirical analysis is responding to. An overview of these approaches and the 'theoretical puzzles' that emerge from them is provided in Chapter 3. Second, I will present the findings of the empirical study in a way that that is informed by and engages with the identified theoretical challenges at hand. Third, I will address these challenges explicitly and discuss how the empirical study informs our theoretical understanding of multicultural transformations of national identity.

More specifically, in this particular chapter, I will concentrate on the first of three focal points of analysis, which have been described in Chapter 6, and will be further elaborated in the section below.[1]

Context

In their recently published book, André Lecours and Geneviève Nootens (2007) showed that there is a gap in the current literature on nationalism. According to them, most research in the field concentrates on the nationalism of minorities, while the fact that dominant groups are also engaged in practising nationalism is usually forgotten. This oversight is caused by the fact that so-called dominant nationalism is no longer recognized as such once it is accepted by a sufficiently large number of groups within a single state. To achieve this acceptance, dominant nationalisms integrate some cultural elements from minorities. According to Lecours and Nootens, this strategy can also be traced in anglophone- or pan-Canadian nationalism: 'Contemporary Canadian nationalism, for example, should not be viewed as the simple extension of an English-speaking, Protestant "ethnic core." Its articulation includes, in part, bilingualism and multiculturalism' (2007: 26, my translation).

Lecours and Nootens view Anglo-Canadian nationalism as a dominant nationalism which, on the one hand, evolved out of a 'dominant ethnicity' (Kaufmann, 2004: 30) but which, on the other, partially integrated both official bilingualism and multiculturalism. This integrative capacity results, according to Lecours and Nootens, from a double occultation of inherent cultural elements: dominant nationalism presents itself as both patriotism and the location of egalitarian relations between the state and its citizens of diverse origin (2007: 26). National majorities have, in other words, a tendency to portray themselves as universalist, individualist, open, and tolerant. Because they are the most powerful group in the polity, they can reinforce their power through laws and institutions. As a consequence, they reproduce their nationalism without reference to their cultural particularity. And, even if they refer to cultural practices, they do so only to legitimize the established order of society and not, as minority nationalisms do, for the sake of contestation (ibid.: 30). Nonetheless, even dominant nationalisms are culturally specific – and do not, as they like to present themselves, embody some sort of universal civilization. To mitigate this cultural specificity, difference is projected upon minorities: they are viewed as different from the universal norm. The reproach of cultural partisanship is most likely to be used against minorities that are powerful enough to threaten the position of the dominant group.

Lecours and and Nooten's conceptualization of dominant nationalism is closely connected to a line of other approaches that have been discussed throughout this book. In particular, it builds upon the themes that were used to guide the reader through Chapters 4 and 5: the construction of the dichotomies between society/community and civic/ethnic nationalism, as well as their unequal attribution to the cultural and political entities of English-speaking Canada and Quebec. To recall an earlier quotation from the Canadian political scientist John Meisel: 'francophone Quebec still exhibits many of the characteristics of *Gemeinschaft* [. . .] The rest of the country is held together less by emotional ties [. . .] and more by rational pursuit of self-interest' (Meisel, 1999: 113).

Expressions like these reinforce the idea that dominant nationalisms are indeed disconnected from the emotional and cultural ties that typically characterize small groups and face-to-face relations – although, as Meisel admits 'these cannot be dismissed altogether' (Meisel, 1999: 113). Put more strongly, cultural and emotional ties are not absent from English Canadian nationalism, but – as Lecours and Nootens argue – they become camouflaged and reinterpreted as civic ties and patriotism. In this sense, these authors' approach is not very different from the theoretical framework presented in Chapter 5 of this book. The aim there is precisely to go beyond the deconstructions of those often-evoked conceptual dichotomies, locate them within their constitutive power relations, and apply the theory of majority/minority relations to the realm of nation building and pluralism.

Adopting a similar theoretical approach but emphasizing the construction of majority and minority categories in discourse, scholars have recently pointed to the role of Quebec as a constitutive Other of Anglo-Canadian multiculturalism (Lacombe, 1998, 2007; Potvin, 2000a, 2000b; Winter, 2001, see also in Chapter 2 the section 'Dualism versus Multiculturalism?'). In these studies, multiculturalism is presented as an expression of Anglo-Canadian dominant nationalism that comes close to what Richard Day describes as the 'simulation of assimilation of Self to the Other' (2000: 184–99). Put differently, it is assumed that the ethnicization of Québécois nationalism produces an imaginary 'them' or Other with a capital O (*Gegenbild*), whose presence relativizes the difference of immigrants and thereby facilitates their integration into the Anglo-Canadian 'civic' nation. Thereby the latter obtains a multicultural facade, but does not truly subscribe to egalitarian multiculturalism. On the contrary, it continues to strive for the republican dissolution of particular internal group identities.

Taken together, these approaches raise at least two questions: First, did Québécois nationalism during the 1990s serve as a counter-image to the construction of a Canadian 'multicultural we'? Second, is this 'multicultural we' the expression of English Canadian dominant nationalism? How can we theorize its emergence?

In this chapter, I aim to answer these questions by using the analytical model developed in Chapter 6. In particular, I will concentrate upon the impact that constructions of alterity ($them_{1-n}$) have upon representations of the 'multicultural we':

$$us + others_{1-n} = \mathbf{multicultural\ we} \neq \mathbf{them_{1-n}}$$

This focal point of analysis (indicated in bold) was inspired by the finding that, within the examined sample of Central Canadian newspaper discourses, representations of Quebec and the United States emerged as the two most important projections of Otherness of Canadian multiculturalism. This is not a fundamentally new insight. On the contrary, the importance of Canada/U.S. comparisons for the construction of Canadian identity is an established fact in Canadian Studies (Grant, 1965; Lipset, 1990). However, my investigation shows that both conceptualizations discussed earlier – that of Canadian multiculturalism as dominant nationalism and that of Quebec as an ethnicized supporting cast to Canadian multiculturalism – fail to account for Canada/U.S. relations. As a consequence, while these studies can help us to better understand Canadian nationalism, due to their restricted focus, they are unable to theorize its inherent multicultural character.

Finally, a caveat is necessary: the following analysis deals with representations and images that are constructed in Central Canadian opinion discourses about the collective entities at stake, primarily the United States, English-speaking Canada, and Quebec. It is not my aim here to deconstruct these images, but rather to analyse their function for the multicultural transformation of Canadian national identity.

Contrasting these images with statistical data drawn from opinion polls in Canada and the United States, the sociologists Edward Grabb and James Curtis have recently turned several Canadian myths upside down. They maintain that 'English Canadians and northern Americans, despite residing on opposite sides of the official national boundary, share more in common with each other than they do with their fellow citizens from Québec and the American South' (Grabb and Curtis, 2005: 257). In their book *Regions Apart: The Four Societies of Canada and the United States*, Grabb and Curtis argue that the American South, primarily because of the distinctive social and economic conditions associated with slavery, has developed into 'the most conservative, traditional, and insular sub-society' (ibid.: 252). The original quasi-feudal values and institutions in Quebec, by contrast, have shifted dramatically since the 1960s, so that Québécois 'now generally rank as the most liberal, permissive, or tolerant population in North America' (ibid.). Grabb and Curtis conclude that without the these two regions '"pulling" English Canada and the American North away from each other' (ibid.: 256) chances are great that the latter two entities would not be any different at all.

This interpretation, of course, is strongly refuted by pollster Michael Adams (2003), whose recent book rejects the 'myth of converging values.' According to Adams, 'Canadians have sometimes reluctantly, but most often readily, welcomed American capital, technology, consumer products, and popular culture – and yet they have not adopted American values' (2003: 142). This is 'because Canada's founding values, historical experiences, and political institutions are very different from those in the United States and have a greater influence on Canadians' contemporary values than the much vaunted forces of globalization' (ibid.: 143). Drawing on statistical data from the recent decade, Adams observes that 'Canadians and Americans are actually becoming increasingly different from each other' (ibid.: 4).

Despite his objections to Grabb and Curtis' general thesis, Adams does not dispute their argument about liberal attitudes to cultural difference in Quebec. On the contrary, his findings indicate that 'xenophobia is lower in Quebec than in any other Canadian region' (2003: 83).[2] In the wake of Quebec's 'reasonable accommodation crisis' (Potvin, 2008), these findings should be interpreted with caution. Nevertheless, they can still serve to balance some of the representations about Quebec's society and nationalism that we will encounter in the next section.

Let us now turn to the collected *Globe and Mail* and *Toronto Star* opinion discourses from the 1990s. In the next section, three elements will be analysed in particular: First, the particularization of Canada through the confrontation with American nationhood. Second, the ambiguities of recognizing the distinctiveness of Quebec inside Canada. Third, the consequences of projecting Quebec's supposedly 'ethnic' nationalism outside the boundaries of Canadianness.

Analysis

An Alternative Nation-Building Project

'*Americans do not know but Canadians cannot forget* that two nations, not one, came out of the American Revolution. [. . .] Americans are descended from winners, Canadians, *as their writers frequently reiterate*, from losers' (Lipset, 1990: 1, my emphasis). This statement captures both the founding myth of the Canadian nation, and the fundamental power imbalance that inhibits U.S./Canadian relations. While Americans are said to be profoundly ignorant about their northern neighbour, comparisons with the United States are a fact of life for Canada – or, to be precise, for English Canada. Being a minority nation, French Canadians' point of reference is not the United States but *le Canada Anglais* and, to a certain extent, *la France*. By contrast, English Canadians do not seem to have the luxury of 'overlooking' their American neighbour. 'Almost since the beginning of the two societies, Canada has largely been defined in comparison with, and often in contrast to its neighbour to the south' (Grabb and Curtis, 2005: 2).

Within the sample of newspaper articles, there is an abundance of references to the United States. Almost every second article mentions the United States at least once. These references rarely involve elaborate comparisons. That they can be elusive reveals that commentators assume a shared knowledge about Americans. Only when representations of the United States contradict what is collectively accepted, are more elaborate explications given. The omnipresence of references to the United States within constructions of English Canadian identity is a tribute to both the power and geographical and cultural closeness of the United States. In fact, in the two newspapers under investigation, Canadianness is constructed *in relation to* attributes that are imputed to Americans. While there is a tendency to portray Canada as morally superior to the United States, these comparisons are not purely hostile in nature, as the construction of alterity also involves a mixture of envy and admiration. To adapt Liah Greenfeld's (1992) analysis to the Canadian case: Canadians strive to imitate the American model, but they do so with 'ressentiment' because of their factual or perceived impossibility of competing with what is perceived as the more advanced or admirable project model of liberal nationhood in the United States.[3] Thus, one can frequently read in the examined newspaper discourses that the 'Americans, the British, the French, the Russians and the Chinese know who they are' (G-1997-0701). Canadian identity, by contrast is often defined in the negative: 'Unlike 19th-century Americans, we never saw ourselves as the new Athenians' (G-1997-0701). 'Indeed, if the Americans say of themselves, "out of many, one" (e pluribus unum), Canadians say of themselves, "out of many, many." Canada has so encouraged the pursuit of individual identity that it lacks an obvious collective one. Maybe that's why we can't boldly say who we are today' (G-1994-0701).

Within the Central Canadian newspaper discourses examined here, Canada is often constructed as an *alternative* project of nationhood. By being the dominant player on the North American continent, within the print media discourses, the United States acquires the characteristics of a 'majority.' It represents itself – and is represented by others – in universal terms. Being American becomes the social norm while difference is imposed upon others. French Canadians accept this difference more readily as they can easily redefine it from within by mobilizing elements of their language and culture.[4] Within the discourses analysed here, by contrast, many English Canadians seem to be haunted by their commonalities with Americans. As both societies appear to be kindred, if somewhat different, branches from the same Old English tree, English Canadians face the possibility of fusion as well as the threat of assimilation: 'The problem is whether English Canada has enough diversity, or even will, to survive as a distinct society in North America' (G-1992-0404). As an 'imitator' or 'latecomer nation' within the realm of nation building, English and English-speaking Canadians are represented in a way as if they have to legitimize why they want to be an independent nation; they must claim to be 'different but equal.' Being constituted as a 'minoritarian nation' reduces the horizon of possible self-representations. With the claim of 'incarnating humanity' being appropriated by the more powerful American nation, English Canadians and those assimilated to this group are obliged to emphasize their *unique collective identity*, which – in a world of nation-states – usually involves some sort of shared culture or ethnicity. In this sense, the Canadian project of nation building bears more resemblance with the ideal-type of the particularized 'ethnic nation' than the universalist 'civic nation.' Indeed, until much of the 1960s, Canada's project of nationhood had been defined in terms of English civility, norms, and institutions (Breton, 2005: 104–19).

While explicit claims to return to this mono-culturally English definition of Canadian nationhood have become rare in times of political correctness, traces can still be found within the newspaper sample.

Thus, it is argued that Canada 'would be exactly like, if not a part of, the United States; because the institution of the crown and the thinking that goes with it are the only things that separate us from the Americans' (T-1993-0924). Furthermore, 'Anglo-Celtic (or British) Canadians' are represented as having 'given shape to Canada, defined its citizenship, constructed the foundations of the country that the United Nations has labelled the most agreeable in the world' (T-1993-0924). Despite these efforts they are now 'the only people in the country who have only one country. "All immigrants are linked to their ancestral homeland. All Quebeckers have *deux pays*, Canada and that part where they feel *maître chez nous*. All native people retain, at least in their memory, an image of another country. Only English Canadians are here alone, emotionally and psychically"' (G-1995-1205, quoting from Gwyn, 1995).

More frequently than this mono-cultural nostalgia, in the Central Canadian newspaper sample from the 1990s, one finds the claim that English or 'British' culture and institutions have laid the foundations for a 'kinder, gentler nation' in which the harsh side effects of unhampered capitalism and individualism, which are said to shape life in the United States, are softened by social programs, tolerance, and mutual respect. This corresponds to the truism that Canadian nation builders have drawn much of their legitimacy from proposing a compassionate nation where overly modern and individualist forms of society are rejected. Thus, within the two newspapers under investigation, one reads: 'Canada is not a race course for individuals but a community to be built' (T-1992-0214). It 'is a country of democracy and tolerance. Beyond the weather, we reject extremes. Ideology, accent and class aren't very important. We welcome immigrants and protect minorities. We condemn capital punishment and condone abortion' (G-1994-0701). In sum, Canadians 'have struggled to build a nation that is tolerant, humane and deliberately different from the colossus south of the 49th parallel' (T-1993-0525).

Within this type of self-representation, Canada's 'mosaic' of distinguishable ethnic groups plays an important role. The non-assimilation of minority groups is used to underline Canada's distinctiveness vis à vis the American 'melting pot' and staged as a demonstration of Canada's compassionate character.

At least historically, the Canadian approach to ethnic diversity has had less to do with 'compassion' than with compromise. Academic commentators suggest that English Canadians were demographically

incapable and ideologically unwilling to assimilate incoming populations regarded as culturally and racially inferior (Day, 2000). For many
English Canadians, the essential moral feature of the 'Canadian nation'
was being part of the Anglo-Saxon empire and 'race,' which required the
political and economic integration of other peoples within the British
Empire. French Canadians, however, for whom Canada's particular
moral value was associated with the Roman Catholic faith, strongly
rejected assimilation to English Protestantism. Thus, what came to distinguish Canada from other countries in the nineteenth and twentieth
centuries was a 'dualist' compromise: Canada's moral mission was to
give an example to the world of a pacifist union between two 'races'
that were traditionally considered enemies (Lacombe, 2002).

Cultural and structural diversity also became a political strategy to
populate the Canadian West. Immigrants were attracted to Canada on
the promise of being able to practise their culture and religion. Block
settlements, enhancing social and economic stability, were encouraged as they enticed newcomers to settle and remain in Canada even
when economic opportunities tended to make the United States more
attractive (Palmer, 1975). In the newspaper sample, this political dimension of Canada's approach to ethnic diversity is reflected in statements
such as: 'The conscious multiculturalism of the West [. . .] became one
of Canada's competitive advantages in immigration' (G-1999-0701).
Usually, however, the racist or xenophobic dimensions of Canada's
immigration and integration policies are downplayed or portrayed
as having been overcome in more recent times: 'Prior to the 1960s, we
expected immigrants to assimilate; indeed, we tried to keep out any
groups seen as incapable of assimilation [. . .] We now view it as natural
for immigrants to cherish and express their ethnic heritage and identity' (G-2000-1227). The failure of Canadian mono-cultural nation building, if alluded to, is generally redefined in positive terms as a 'happy
coincidence of history' (G-1999-0701). The following quotation uses a
combination of these strategies: 'We can be proud that our ancestors
eschewed conquest and rejected genocide in their relationships with
First Nations, which unhappily was not the case everywhere in the 18th
and 19th centuries. We no longer have the appetite to force assimilation
either. And we know that paternalism is no alternative' (G-1998-0917).

This representation of the relations between colonizers and Aboriginal
peoples in Canada also contains an implicit comparison with the United
States; this comparison is demonstrated by the sentence: 'our ancestors
eschewed conquest and rejected genocide . . . which unhappily was not

the case everywhere.' The strategy to construct American 'bad guys' in order to imagine Canadian 'good guys' with respect to minority integration is an important feature of my newspaper sample. It is, for example, common to read that the United States are 'haunted as ever by the fear of crime and the reality of racism suffered by a massive underclass of Blacks stuck in urban ghettos' (T-1994-0701). The inherent need for this strategy demonstrates that it has become impossible to construct Canadian ethnic relations in entirely positive and harmonious ways: 'While Canada is in no way a model for the way it has treated its native peoples, our country has a much better historical record than the United States' (T-1993-0924).

The same newspaper article from which the above quotation is taken constructs a difference between Americans and Canadians on the three accounts of minority integration that have come to be the 'brand mark' of Canadian ethnic diversity: minority nationalism, Aboriginal peoples, and immigration. It therefore stands for a general tendency to construct 'the Canadian way of dealing with ethnic diversity.' First, the 'protection' of French culture and language through the 1774 Quebec Act is contrasted with 'our republican neighbours, who quickly assimilated their Spanish and Mexican possessions into their American culture' (T-1993-0924). Second, the signing of (subsequently rewritten and ignored) treaties with Aboriginal peoples in Canada is contrasted with the 'Americans claim[ing] "manifest destiny," and slaughter[ing] thousands of natives in their push to gain more land' (T-1993-0924). Third, the 'the tolerance and acceptability of other cultures [rooted] in the Commonwealth' is compared with immigrant assimilation into the American melting pot (T-1993-0924). The series of comparisons leads the author to the following conclusion: 'Canada's monarchy, along with her British parliamentary and judicial systems, have caused *us* to take a different political course than *our* republican cousins to the south, a course for which most Canadians, especially *those* very groups which push for its abolition, *should be grateful*' (T-1993-0924, my emphasis).

Canadian particularity is here constituted through British culture and institutions, which are opposed to (what is claimed to be) the 'American' national idea. The hierarchy of groups is revealed by the distance between 'our' and 'those very groups.' French Canadians, Aboriginals, and immigrants are not included within the 'national we.' Rather, they are outsiders, whose legitimate membership within the nation is dependent on their appreciation of what 'Canada' is doing for them: they 'should be grateful.'

This quotation reveals an intriguing ambiguity. Despite their symbolic exclusion, ethnic and national groups remain important for the construction of the English Canadian national project and its 'difference' from the 'political course' taken by Americans. Without their collaboration and gratefulness, the image of Canada as 'a kinder, gentler nation' is difficult to uphold. Minority complaints discredit the stylized vision of 'Canadian compassion' and thereby undermine the legitimacy of Canadian independent nationhood itself. Since health care and other social programs are eroding due to the neo-liberalization of the welfare state, 'grateful minorities' have come to be an important symbol for Canada's compassionate, tolerant character. Without minority groups thankfully acknowledging the 'privilege' of living in Canada (rather than in the United States), in the examined discourses, little seems to be left to differentiate Canada from the United States: 'We now have a society in English-speaking Canada that often resembles that of the United States, but without the extremes of excellence and despair that exist in that country' (T-1997-0131).

In sum, from the representations in the Central Canadian print media we can conclude that the confrontation with America's dominant project of nationhood has rendered Canada's national majority painstakingly aware of its particularity. To safeguard their project of independent nationhood, English Canadians were forced into collaborations with internal minorities: immigrant populations from other European countries, Aboriginal peoples, French Canadians/Franco-Québécois, immigrant minorities from non-European sources. Over the years, this has led to the development of a national imaginary that pictures Canada as a country favouring group rights approaches. This process has been neither without hesitations nor confrontations.[5] Furthermore, as Etienne Balibar warns us with respect to the extension of citizenship rights to minorities: 'there is nothing automatic, linear, or [. . .] irreversible about this process' (1988: 724).

The Ambiguities of 'Difference Within'

As noted in Chapter 2, scholars arguing from an anti-foundationalist perspective have criticized multiculturalism for being a 'top-down' approach, a government-implemented ideology that culturalizes socioeconomic differences and fails to include grassroots' concerns (Bannerji, 2000). Canadian multiculturalism, so it seems, simulates the assimilation of self to other, while in reality an invisible we-group grants minority rights on a discretionary basis (Day, 2000). Indeed, within the newspaper discourses under investigation, there are some attempts to appropriate multiculturalism and to describe it as a genuinely 'English Canadian invention' (T-1993-0307). However, in the *Globe and Mail* and the *Toronto Star*, French Canadians and/or Quebec are also frequently mentioned. They are said to have played a – positive or negative – role for the constitution of multiculturalism. Within these representations, Franco-Québécois – although white and European – are neither an unambiguous part of the dominant majority, as Bannerji claims, nor were they the first (or second, after Aboriginal peoples) to have been assimilated and rendered into 'canonical selves,' as Day argues (2000: 161, 185). Rather, their position within the constructions of the Canadian multicultural nation remains highly complex and controversial. It seems as if Quebec cannot easily be abstracted from. In the opinion discourses from the *Globe and Mail* and the *Toronto Star* during the 1990s, it continues to be represented as one of the cornerstones of Canadian uniqueness. Its presence not only passively symbolizes Canada's difference from the United States in terms of language and culture, but also actively prevents the Canadian nation-state's collapse and assimilation: Without Quebec 'the rest of the family will splinter because the essential internal balance of the regional pieces of the federation will be gone' (T-1994-0508).

The discourses surrounding the 1992 Charlottetown referendum can serve as an example for the importance of maintaining Quebec's difference within Canada. In 1982, Canada had patriated its Constitution without the consent of Quebec, which rejected the agreement because the newly established Charter of Rights and Freedoms empowers the Supreme Court of Canada to invalidate provincial laws and regulations in the name of individual rights. As mentioned earlier (see Chapter 6), the pan-Canadian referendum on the Charlottetown Accord was the second attempt, after the failed 1987 Meech Lake Accord, to belatedly include Quebec as a 'distinct society' within the Constitution. In several articles, the two newspapers included in my analysis encouraged a Yes vote, thereby demanding loyalty and 'compromise' from ethnic group leaders and 'ordinary Canadians,' who feared that giving special status to Franco-Québécois might create a two-class society and curtail individual rights: 'Is a "distinct society" different from India's caste system or South Africa's apartheid' (T-1992-0828)?

Within this context, both newspapers emphasize the 'Canadian tradition' of 'honourable compromise' between the 'two founding linguistic communities of Canada,' as well as with Aboriginal peoples and 'immigrants from all corners of the world' (G-1992-0702). They portray granting special status to Quebec as the 'right thing to do.' First, it is acknowledged that the British North America Act, which 'established the Canadian tradition of "peace, order, and good government" in the northern part of this continent' (G-1992-0702), would not have been possible without French Canadian support. Second, it is argued that although 'Canada has changed a great deal since 1867, with a belated recognition of the Aboriginal peoples as a third order of government, and constitutional entrenchment of the multiculturalism of new Canadians,' it must not be forgotten that 'French-Canadians were one of the two nations at the table 125 years ago' (T-1992-1015). Finally, Quebec is depicted as having become an 'embattled minority – with a falling birthrate and low immigration' – that is 'trying to stay afloat in a continental sea of Anglophones' and therefore deserves to be 'protect[ed] from further erosion' (T-1992-1015). 'Helping Quebec' by voting in favour of the Charlottetown Accord is described as an act of compassion and, as such, it becomes 'typically Canadian': 'Part of the pride in compromise comes in the honest acknowledgment that *we* care about other people's needs [. . .] *This is the nature of Canada. This has always been the nature of Canada. This is the condition of Canada's survival over time*' (G-1992-1022, my emphasis).

The quotation above reveals common strategies involved in building communities of shared fate: Canada's 'nature' is not only projected into the past and the future, it is also portrayed as the 'condition of [its] survival.' Voting in favour of the Charlottetown Accord becomes a question of life and death, and this not only for English Canadians but also for immigrants and members of ethnic groups within Canada: 'English-speaking Canadians of all origins want to resist the forces of continental integration and keep their country under the control of Canadians' (T-1992-0204). References to the United States within the discourses surrounding the reconstruction of the Canadian nation show that Canada's 'old agenda of balancing group interests' and 'our historical preoccupation with regions and cultures' (G-1992-1022) gain meaning through the presence of a third, dominant group. For one, compared with 'the American emphasis on individual rights' (G-1992-1022), group rights become 'distinctively Canadian.' They are constructed as a national tradition of which dualism – the recognition of Quebec's distinctiveness within Canada – is the archetype because it describes the 'best traditions of our founding leaders, who [. . .] created a country in 1867 by dividing a single province in two' (G-1992-1022).

Second, efforts to include Quebec and Aboriginal peoples into the Constitution and to 'accept less than the fruit that pure principle [of individual equality] would deliver' (G-1992-1022) are presented as being justified in the face of the threat posed by neighbouring America: 'If Canada were to break up into small regional states in the aftermath of Quebec's departure, these would inevitably be absorbed into the United States – a loss not only for us but for the world' (T-1992-0204). Interestingly, a fourth group is drawn into the picture. Portraying 'the world' as a beneficiary of the Canadian experiment downplays the likely impression that minority inclusion is motivated by English Canadian self-interest. Rather, it becomes a question of Canadian moral superiority – vis-à-vis those included and, more importantly, the United States. In this sense, 'the world' becomes an observer and judge of the 'moral worth' of the Canadian nation.

The context of the Charlottetown referendum demonstrates that Canada's *alternative* nation-building project does not only require minority gratefulness but also their active collaboration and compromise. After all, 'Anglo Canadians represent only half of the equation. All the "others" in Canada are no longer others. They are us' (T-1993-0228). Historically, French Canada has been the most powerful internal player who categorically refused to accept to be grateful for and/or collaborate within a Canadian nation defined in mono-culturally 'British' terms. From the very beginning, French Canadians forced a dualist definition of the country – even though it is still a topic of heated debates whether Canada was founded as a partnership between two 'founding nations' (plus Aboriginal 'First Nations') or a series of equal provinces.

The rejection of the Charlottetown Accord through the referendum on 26 October 1992 demonstrated that the question of minority inclusion had become much more complex. The victory of the opponents of the Accord left the federal government without a satisfactory answer to the demand of group-differentiated citizenship rights within a pan-Canadian state (Cook, 1994; Bourque and Duchastel, 1996). The defeat was followed by a shift towards a more integrative, citizenship-based approach towards national identity and multiculturalism (Abu-Laban and Gabriel, 2002). In government documents, cultural group identities and rights are no longer central. Rather, emphasis is placed on the need for overcoming our differences and a shared project of living together in a multicultural society (see also Chapters 2 and 10).

In return, for many Franco-Québécois, the Charlottetown failure was an incentive to continue with the project of building an independent

Québécois nation. On 12 September 1994, the Parti Québécois was elected on the promise of leading the province into independence. Coinciding with the revival of ethnic nationalisms in Eastern Europe and the attempted genocide in Rwanda, this led to a situation where many commentators in the English-speaking rest of Canada felt that Canada had overemphasized diversity and that 'the ability of English Canadians to "imagine" their community by reference to clearly recognizable symbols and practices ha[d] waned' (Ayres, 1995: 185).

Indeed, within the media discourses of my sample, Quebec is attributed a double function: while it is sometimes situated at the heart of positively connoted ethnic diversity, it is as often portrayed as the source for the proliferation of ethnic difference and the failure to have constructed a unified Canadian nation. In the following quotation, the Canadian founding myth is turned on its head. Dualism is here not the quintessence of successful compromise and the moral superiority of Canadian pluralism over the American melting pot, but rather the cause of increasing societal fragmentation: 'The very nature of Canada – founded as an explicit partnership between two distinct peoples in the 1860s – sustains a culture of regional measurement and comparison. The creation of the Official Languages Act in 1969 played this duality out across modern Canada, generating in turn the official multiculturalism policy of 1971, which contributed to the aboriginal self-government movement of the 1980s. Re-asserting the original duality led to the recognition of many more particularities [. . .] Political correctness is but the latest manifestation of the tribalism that is invading everything' (G-1994-0513).

The quotation above constructs a chain reaction from the 'original dualism' on which the country was founded through the British North America Act to the policies of bilingualism, multiculturalism, increasing claims for multinationalism, and 'many more particularities,' such as the women's movement and rights for gays and lesbians. Within this representation, Canada is predestined to break up because of its inability to overcome 'tribalism' and the proliferation of 'difference': 'No country can survive forever such a broad coalition against the very concept of a common interest' (G-1994-0513). The danger of fragmentation is portrayed as being rooted in the intrinsic 'nature' of Canada, of which Quebec is an intrinsic but 'rotten' part. French Canada or Quebec – with its claim for the recognition of distinctiveness – becomes the source for increasing disloyalty to the Canadian nation. 'Feelings of alienation,' which are portrayed as a cancerous disease, are said to originate in

'Quebec, where it is risky to play the national anthem [. . .] The alienation is now spreading like a contagion and our loyalties are shifting to
region and race' (G-1997-0701). As a consequence, 'Canada is suffering
from a fading sense of community, an erosion of self-awareness and a
retreat into sectionalism and ethnicity' (G-1997-0701).

These discourses describe what Wimmer calls the ethnicization or
failed nationalization of politics (2002; see also Chapter 5). Hereby it is
of particular importance that Quebec, for reasons of relative power and
legitimacy, is represented as a minority that can neither be assimilated
nor expelled. As such, it is attributed a double function. It is seen as both
a constitutive part of the nation and its most dangerous inherent enemy.
Situated at the very heart of Canadianness, the presence of Quebec contributes to the possibility of constructing a pan-Canadian community – in
distinction to the image of American individualist society – while, at the
same time, it harbours the dangers of fragmentation as its 'tribalism'
does not allow for the constitution of an overarching pan-Canadian 'national' identity. Quebec's influence upon the proliferation of 'difference'
(in the negative) or 'diversity' (in the positive) is intensified – or even
made possible – by the fact that English Canada itself is striving to be 'different but equal' vis-à-vis the United States. As with all groups who find
themselves in the minority position of a particular relation, the desire
to create a 'radically different kind of North America' (T-1993-0307), the
need to constantly engage in external boundary construction in order to
avoid assimilation, and – consequently – the impossibility of constructing the nation in strictly 'universal' terms, have unintended side effects:
'We have become obsessed with the group; disdaining the universal
ideals of liberalism, we have embraced the relativistic conceits of particularism [. . .] Indeed, we have made an exception of the country itself,
celebrating our inability to bind *ourselves to the ideals that others live by as
a virtue.* [We have made this] part of our unique identity – rather than a
failing [. . .] Having invested our entire nationhood in little more
than being different from Americans, we have nothing to say when
Quebeckers respond: we're different from you' (G-1995-1023, my
emphasis).

This quotation reveals that minority claims for being recognized as
'different but equal have their starting point within the logic of nation-
state formation itself. It thereby brings the predicament of 'alternative
nations' to the point: having to address their particularity in the face
of a powerful Other (who lives by the 'universal ideals of liberalism')
renders them vulnerable to the demands by internal minorities that

operate on the same logic of cultural/national recognition and/or self-determination. Leading to a weakening of the legitimacy of the nation-building project, this 'relativism' can either be viewed as a predicament or as an opportunity. On the one hand, defining the nation in particular terms rather than universal ones may offend internal minorities and exacerbate conflict. On the other hand, it may allow for a more transparent negotiation process about group rights than the pseudo-universalism that can often be observed in strong, majoritarian nations.

In the case of Canada, the new rise of the separatist movement in Quebec in the mid-1990s contributed to the widespread feeling that the country had overemphasized 'diversity' (Ayres, 1995). It is important to remember that separatism is a powerful demonstration of minority alienation. It indicates that minorities are neither grateful nor willing to (further) compromise. As such, far beyond the concrete threat it poses to the unity of the nation, separatism symbolizes the failure of a project that aims to construct 'Canada as the very paragon of modern civilized living: a nation that does not depend upon strength or the threat of strength, that flourishes by diversity, that stands always for the right' (T-1992-0615).

Reclaiming Universalism

The previous section has shown that Quebec's ethnolinguistic 'difference' (and not its 'containment,' as suggested by the proponents of the constitutive-Other or *Gegenbild* theory) plays an important role in the Canadian self-understanding as a multicultural nation that differs notably from the United States. It has also been suggested that this role is neither static nor unambiguous. Starting from the mid-1990s, the image of a supposedly separatist Quebec was created and used more and more strongly to illustrate what a 'multicultural Canada' does not want to be. In fact, the discourses surrounding Canadian nationhood became increasingly more characterized by the construction of an opposition between a tribal ethnocentric Quebec and a culturally diverse, open-minded Canada.

In reaction to Quebec's nationalism, which was (rightfully or wrongfully) interpreted as an affront to Canada's understanding of its mission as a nation, representations of English Canadian nationhood become more and more defensive: 'Strong ideals are often forged in adversity [. . .] With the very existence of the country at stake, we must give new voice to the idea of Canada' (G-1995-1104). Within the examined media discourses, the portrayals of Quebec's separatism during the mid-1990s confirm the strategy outlined in the citation above. From now on, the discourses on Canadian national identity are indeed characterized by a constructed opposition between a supposedly ethnocentric Quebec and a culturally diverse and open Canada (Frisco and Gagné, 1998; Lacombe, 1998, 2007; Potvin, 2000a, 2000b; Winter, 2001).

Lacombe (1998) argues that Québécois 'separatists' are portrayed as pressing for favours that are denied to other Canadians. Their political project is considered to be in disaccord with the socioeconomic realities of a global, modern world; it is further rejected on the ground that French Canadians are no longer culturally and economically oppressed. Québécois politicians are frequently portrayed as charismatic nationalists who are misleading 'ordinary Quebeckers.' It is assumed that only the Canadian framework of federal institutions is able to protect Quebec's 'distinct society' and, by extension, French language and culture in North America. In the newspaper sample under investigation, this type of representations is also frequent. To give an example of the semantics employed: The 'romantic and manipulative demagoguery' of Quebec's politicians is said to leave 'Québecers [. . .] dancing euphorically inside a bubble' (T-1995-1025). Canada, by contrast, is represented as a 'sophisticated, post-industrial state [that] values citizenship more than blood [and] is unified not by race or language, but by memories, rights, ideals and interests' (G-1995-1101). It is a 'multi-ethnic World Nation' (T-1993-0131) whose 'self-defence' is viewed as being legitimized by its superior institutions and the complacent representation of being 'the best country in the world' (T-1995-1025).

The representation of Quebec as 'a tribe of Quebecois with some others living amongst them' (T-1993-0131) seemed to be justified when Quebec's Premier Jacques Parizeau blamed 'money and the ethnic vote' (meaning anglophone Quebeckers and immigrants) for losing the latest referendum on Québécois sovereignty in October 1995 (for details, see Winter, 2007a, and Chapter 2). Although the vote did indeed follow 'ethnic' and residential patterns, Parizeau's statement was entirely inadequate. Protests by Québécois of all origins forced him to resign. Nevertheless, for the Canadian English-language media, his remarks confirmed a long-standing image: 'The Premier did not misspeak himself. In fact, Mr Parizeau was artlessly honest and exquisitely consistent. In singling out immigrants, the English and business – all of whom largely voted no – he shouted his atavistic tribalism' (G-1995-1101). In apparent concessions, it is admitted that the 'the sovereigntists speak of pluralism and diversity.' But 'whatever [their] protests' (G-1995-1101), the independence movement is said to be 'irredeemably narrow, parochial and defensive. It invites Quebeckers to circle the wagons and turn inward, shielded from modernity. It is an old-world vision of the ethnic nation-state, not the new-world civic state' (G-1995-1101).

In a situation of conflict, Quebec is constructed as an 'ethnic nation.' Its independence movement is allegedly motivated by ethnocentrism: 'separatism is a species of ethnic nationalism, by nature exclusionary, intolerant and, in its worst forms, racist' (G-1995-1104). Recalling an earlier quotation which states that Canadians 'have nothing to say when Quebeckers respond: we're different from you' (G-1995-1023) allows us to understand why the ethnicization of separatism is important. Both alternative nation-building projects, Quebec and Canada, operate within the same logic of claiming to be recognized as 'different but equal' in a world of nations. It becomes thus difficult to reject one project without undermining the legitimacy of the other. Constructing a fundamental difference between the 'moral worth' of Canadian and Québécois nationhood helps to solve the problem of legitimacy. First, ethnicizing Quebec's independence movement discredits its right to form a sovereign nation – which could only be achieved at the expense of other minorities and must therefore be prevented. Second, constructing Quebec as a tribal and oppressive 'ethnic nation' provides a supporting cast for redefining Canadian nationhood and 'unity within diversity':

> What do we stand for as a nation? [. . .] *We are against* the idea that people should be treated differently because of their skin colour, language, religion or background. *We are for* the idea that all Canadians should be treated as full citizens [. . .] *We are against* ethnic nationalism, in which people of common ethnicity rule themselves – *masters in their own house. We are for* civic nationalism, in which people of different backgrounds come together under the umbrella of common citizenship to form a community of equals. Ours is a modern nationalism: liberal, decent, tolerant and colourblind. That is what Canada represents to the millions of people who come here from other countries. That is the idea of Canada. (G-1995-1104, my emphasis)

This quotation displays several characteristics that are typical of discourses where the image of a Québécois 'ethnic nation' serves as a contrasting other. First of all, we operate here within the logic of us/them divisions where negative images of 'them' are put forth to facilitate the construction of a positively connoted 'us.' In its quality as an (assumed) 'ethnic nation,' Quebec is considered 'wholly unCanadian' (G-1999-0701) and projected outside the boundaries of Canadianness. It is interesting to note that the slogan 'maîtres chez nous' (masters in our own house) was introduced by the provincial government under Liberal Premier Jean Lesage 1960–66 (Meisel et al., 1999: 169). Branding it as 'ethnic nationalism' does thus not exclusively aim at separatism but also rejects other forms of Quebec's struggle for distinctiveness. In discourses that accept the logic of an ethnic/civic binary between Quebec and Canada, 'Canadians inside Quebec' are part of the Canadian 'we' on the condition that they agree to leave their status as 'Québécois' behind and give priority to 'the idea of Canada.'

Second, the projection of conflict to the outside of Canada's boundaries facilitates the acceptance of a more or less 'multicultural we' within: The real or imagined threat to collective survival creates a commonality that relativizes conflictual relations within an imagined English-speaking Canada. For the national majority, cultural difference and demands for recognition by non-separatist minority groups appear acceptable. For minority groups, the belief that 'ethnic homogeneity' and 'racial discrimination' are worse outside the rest of Canada downplays the severity of inequality (that they experience or hear about) in Canadian society. Thus, through the opposition to a 'tribal' Quebec, Canada's multiculturally imagined nation shines in a new light. Furthermore, placing emphasis on the external boundaries of the nation allows the collective identity within to remain deliberately vague. It thereby provides the nationalized subjects with a maximum of freedom from narrow, reductionist, and uni-dimensional definitions of belonging. Thus, a 'multicultural Canada,' defined primarily through its opposition to 'ethnic nationalism,' is likely to become acceptable to a wide variety of individuals and groups with otherwise conflicting views on Canadian society.

If avoiding fixing or prescribing one's national identity, in principle, produces favourable conditions for pluralist forms of identification, we must also scrutinize the type of multiculturalism at stake: does it still involve a group-rights' approach or are we observing the constitution of a 'new melting pot'? Through the opposition to Québécois 'ethnic nationalism,' the rest of Canada is constructed as both (1) a unified entity beyond regional cleavages, and (2) an ethnically diverse and tolerant 'civic nation.' It is represented as being based upon the principles of merit, colour-blindness, and individual equality. Compared with the representations of Canadianness that were quoted earlier in this book, these latter attributes are not, in themselves, particularly 'Canadian.' Indeed, Canada's 'old agenda of balancing group interests' (G-1992-1022), to recall an earlier quotation, is missing from representations of Canada as a 'civic nation.' Furthermore, Canada's traditional opposition to an 'assimilating' hegemonic American other loses importance here. Difference is no longer claimed by Canada. 'Difference' is now imputed to Quebec and projected outside the boundaries of the Canadian 'national we.' The focus on Quebec frees the Canadian self-understanding from having to emphasize its particularity vis-à-vis the United States. This shift in otherness, and the redefinition of the opposing attributes it implies, allows Canada to reclaim universalism: 'We must show Quebeckers – many of whom have been as appalled as other Canadians at what separatist leaders have been saying – that Canada and Canada alone waves the banner of pluralism and common humanity' (G-1995-1104).

Compared to 'Quebec,' rather than to 'America,' Canada is no longer constructed as an alternative nation. On the contrary, by monopolizing the incarnation of 'common humanity,' Canadian pluralism becomes the point of reference, the social norm. Within this representation, not individuals but collectivities are denied the right to be 'different but equal' as their social organization could never be as good as the 'common humanity' proposed by Canada. There is no space for alternatives – at least none of equal civilizational worth. The newfound Canadian self-confidence reflected in the discourses of the newspaper sample coincides with (and seems to be supported by) an international search for alternative ways of integrating ethnocultural diversity. Afforded the qualities of a typical majority, in several newspaper articles, Canada is presented as a model to the world. Within this logic, Canadianness no longer provides for the possibility of negotiation and compromise; rather, it imposes imitation or assimilation. In the case of Quebec, however, 'taming one's old demons by copying the Canadian model of society' (G-1999-0705) seems precluded. At the end of the 1990s, within the newspaper sample under investigation, recent attempts by the Quebec government to promote an ethnically inclusive definition of Québécois citizenship were (rightly or wrongly) greeted with scepticism.

The Multiculturalization of Canadian National Identity

The preceding analysis provides important insights regarding the multiculturalization of Canadian national identity. In particular, it shows that we require a more nuanced understanding of the underlying processes than that offered by the studies on the relations between Canadian and Québécois nationalism, which were presented at the beginning of this chapter. Two points are particularly noteworthy. First, based on the preceding newspaper analysis, it is not possible to conceptualize Anglo- or pan-Canadian multiculturalism as strictly 'dominant.' Second, we have seen that francophone Quebec and even modest forms of Québécois nationalism do not solely serve as contrasting images of a multiculturally imagined Canada. These two points will be discussed in more detail below.

I will begin with the first of the two points, the representation of Canadian multiculturalism as dominant nationalism (Lecours and Nootens, 2007). The dualism of the sociological categories, 'majority' versus 'minority,' should not make us jump to the conclusion that the social world is also organized in binary categories. On the contrary, the theory of majority/minority relations presupposes a net of overlapping, reinforcing, and balancing majority/minority relations, which does not operate along national borders and boundaries but crosses them. In the social sciences it is therefore important to transcend a 'methodological nationalism,' that is the assumption that the nation/the state/the society is the natural social and political organization of the modern world (Wimmer and Glick Schiller, 2002: 301).

Without taking into account that Canadian nationhood is constructed in relation to an external dominant player, the United States, an important element of the constitutive process of multiculturalism would be missing from our investigation. Imagined Americanness permeates Canada's boundaries and interferes with the representation of internal social group relations. The confrontation with dominant alterity leads to the particularization of the national majority; that is, the need arises to define the 'national we' in relation to an existing social norm. Anglo-Canadian nationalism can therefore not simply be viewed as majoritarian or 'dominant.' With respect to the United States, Canada needs to legitimize its existence and cultural particularity; in relation to the United States, Canadian nationalism becomes minoritarian.

The confrontation with the United States causes a twofold process. By 'naming' the nation's dominant identity, namely, that of English Canada, the cultural traditions of the social entity in question become transparent. On the one hand, attempted group closure always bears the risk of homogenizing internal diversity. In the examined newspaper discourses, this is revealed by traces of nostalgia for an idealized Anglo-Canadian mono-culturalism. On the other hand, the confrontation with the real or imagined dominant player reveals the presence – and/or renders possible the construction – of collective identities within the nation, which would otherwise remain implicit. The particularization of the national majority is a crucial element in making the constitutive processes of group formation *transparent*. It thereby leads to negotiations and pluralist compromise rather than to the assumed cultural neutrality, which is characteristic of purely dominant nationalisms. To put it another way, favourable conditions for holistically defined national identity are created through the confrontation of the national majority with a dominant external player. While this may lead to cultural homogenization, it is also a necessary condition for the multiculturalization of national identity, that is, a national imaginary that involves all groups living on the national territory, and is not only defined in terms of minority rights while taking majority rights for granted.

Furthermore, the preceding print media analysis shows that one group can be constructed as both a majority and a minority at the same time, depending on the constitutive referent. In that sense, Canadian nationalism takes on different expressions which can be qualified as sometimes more minoritarian and sometimes more majoritarian. The analysis suggests that in Canada, in addition to the will to differ from the United States, there is a second factor that contributes to the particularization of the dominant group: the national minorities' ongoing refusal to assimilate. The presence of one or more relatively powerful internal minorities can prevent holistically or culturally defined minoritarian nationalisms from turning ethnocentric or exclusive. As pointed out earlier (see also Chapter 5), to a certain extent, multiculturalism relies upon the failed nationalization of politics (Wimmer, 2002), that is, it takes place in countries where national identity is not framed in a way that gives expression to minority interests and identities. We must not forget that, historically, Canadian national identity was not framed in a way that was meant to reflect minority cultures. On the contrary, timid attempts to pluralize national identity only set in during the 1950s and 1960s (Breton, 2005: 104–19). In this sense, it is of particular importance that Quebec, for reasons of relative power and legitimacy, has become a minority that can neither be assimilated nor expelled.

This brings me to the second point mentioned above, the representation of Quebec as a constitutive Other (Lacombe, 1998, 2007; Potvin, 2000a, 2000b; Winter, 2001). The examination of media discourses has shown that Québécois nationalism is indeed ethnicized. However, it

is not always constructed as total opposition to the multiculturalization of Canadian national identity. In large segments of the examined
discourses, Quebec – even a nationalist Quebec – remains part of a
pan-Canadian identity. Nevertheless, there is an important condition:
Québécois nationalism must remain a secondary, culturally connoted
minoritarian nationalism that accepts the political primacy of Canada
and does not embrace separatism (Winter, 2007b). The recognition of
Quebec as a 'distinct society' within Canada fulfils a twofold function.
On the one hand, francophone Quebec becomes the symbol of Canada's
tradition of 'honourable compromise' and a 'Canadian ethics of care'
that distinguishes Canada from the (supposedly) American 'might
makes right' (T-1993-0924). On the other hand, Quebec's distinctiveness
is portrayed as the starting point of an endless proliferation of group difference that will unavoidably lead to the disintegration of the Canadian
nation. In both cases, the constructed image of Quebec cannot be considered an opposition or *Gegenbild*, but rather constitutes a (positively
or negatively connoted) precedent of multiculturalism (Winter, 2009).

The inherent ambiguity within representations of Quebec in the
English-speaking mainstream media reveals the predicament of nationalisms that deviate from being strictly majoritarian or 'dominant': having to address the nation's particularity in the face of a powerful Other
(in the case of Canada: the United States) prevents them from defining their nation in strict universal, political, or 'civic' terms. Admitting
their own cultural particularity, in turn, renders them vulnerable to the
demands of internal minorities (like, e.g., Quebec) that operate on the
same logic of cultural/national recognition and/or self-determination.
Accommodating group-related difference within the nation thus creates a permanent tension and the constant need to reconstruct the
compromise that constitutes society. In other words, the multicultural
transformation of national identity is inherently dialectic. This can be
interpreted (negatively) as failed nationalization of politics or (positively) as the necessary condition for the constitution of multicultural
group rights.

Finally, the examination of English-language media discourses demonstrates that the nature of Canadian nationalism changes when otherness and conflict are projected outside of the nation. In this case, the
representation of Quebec as an 'ethnic nation' indeed serves as a supporting cast, compared with which British traditions and multicultural
conflicts within the rest of Canada become relative. By taking Quebec as
a point of reference rather than the United States, Canadian nationalism

sheds the burden of particularization. It represents the nation in 'universal,' 'civic' terms as the best possible incarnation of pluralist humanity. Canadian nationalism takes on unequivocally majoritarian traits. However, this change in national self-representation appears to come at the price of a truly multicultural identity: multiculturalism is increasingly represented merely as the diversity of individuals. This 'first level diversity,' as Charles Taylor (1993) has put it, does not differ in a meaningful way from the idea of the American melting pot. Multiculturalism as a 'synthesis,' freed of group identities and inherent tensions, seems therefore to have failed its purpose.

Conclusion

What are then the conclusions that can be drawn from the preceding analysis for the multicultural transformation of national identity? This chapter has demonstrated that the multiculturalization of national identity is located at the intersection of universalistic and particularistic tendencies of national identity formation. As suggested in Chapter 5, multicultural nationalism is universalistic and civic in so far as it presupposes an institutional framework that guarantees individual rights. The latter constitute a key component for the interaction between equal citizens of different ethnic origins. Multicultural nationalism is ethnic or culturally particularistic, in as much as these institutions are not defined as (ethnically, culturally, religiously, and linguistically) neutral, but are regarded as the result of historically grown and permanently changing group relations.

Multicultural nationalism requires a transformation of the national imaginary in pluralist terms. This chapter suggests that this pluralization is neither likely to occur through the ideal-type of dominant nationalism, which strives to define membership in civic and universal terms, nor through the ideal-type of minority nationalism, where boundaries are defined in mono-cultural terms.[6] Rather, the multiculturalization of national identity seems to emerge most easily when the national majority (1) is aware of its own particularity as a group which shares society with others, and (2) does not have the will or power to impose this identity upon all other groups. But, even in this specific case, multicultural identity cannot be produced once and forever, but continues to depend upon dialectic negotiations of multicultural self-representations *in relation* to shifting Others that are constructed as either 'too individualist' or 'too communitarian.' The 'multicultural we' oscillates between these two tendencies, which are necessary for its catalysis. Once this oscillation stops, and the constitutive ethnopolitical conflict is settled, the emerging collective identity can no longer be characterized as truly multicultural.

In Canada the conditions for the development of this multicultural dialectics were favourable during the mid-1990s. On the level of discourse, this is shown in the changing projection of the limits of multiculturalism – namely, cultural assimilation and ethnocentric exclusion of immigrants – on two types of Others: the United States of America and francophone Quebec. Until the early 1990s, Central Canadian English-language print media tended to represent Quebec as a national minority that deserved to be integrated by (if compared with America) 'typically Canadian' pluralist compromise and concessions. In the following years, however, Québécois separatist nationalism was regarded more and more as the enfant terrible of pan-Canadian multicultural identity.

8   To Be or Not to Be Like Quebec

The present chapter is the second of three empirical chapters, in which I present the analysis of keyword-selected opinion discourses on Canadian identity and multiculturalism in the *Globe and Mail* and the *Toronto Star* from 1992 to 2001. The rationale for this study, sampling method, content, and limitations of the newspaper sample, as well as the interpretive scheme that was used for analysis are all described in Chapter 6. In the previous chapter, I discussed how a Canadian 'multicultural we' is constructed *in relation* to images of otherness projected upon the United States of America and francophone Quebec. The analysis presented in this chapter uses a difference lens to examine the multicultural transformation of Canadian identity. It concentrates upon the relationship that is constructed between francophone Quebec and immigrants/ethnic groups. Put differently, I will concentrate on the second of three focal points of analysis elaborated in Chapter 6 and further explained below.[1]

As in the previous chapter, I will first remind the reader of the prevailing literature and/or theoretical context that the empirical analysis is engaging with. Second, I will present the findings of the empirical study in a way that responds to a number of identified theoretical challenges (Chapter 3). Third, I will discuss how the empirical study informs our theoretical understanding of multicultural transformations of national identity. Specifically, in an effort to systematize how the presence of historically established groups – such as francophones/Québécois – impacts upon (de)legitimizations of Canada as a multicultural nation, I will refer to the four hypotheses elaborated in Chapter 5.

Context

During the 1990s, Canadian scholarship produced internationally accepted differentiations between minority nations and immigration-induced ethnic minorities. Charles Taylor's (1993) concept of Québécois and First Nations' 'deep diversity' (versus other Canadians' 'first level' membership in the polity) and Will Kymlicka's (1995) liberal theory of 'multicultural citizenship' are just two of the most common examples.

Taylor underlines francophone Québécois' and Aboriginal peoples' 'deep diversity.' According to Taylor, the members of these two groups are Canadians through their particular group identities, which he qualifies as 'national.' By contrast, for Taylor, other Canadians, even those who have a background of migration and ethnic group membership, are characterized by 'first level diversity.' They are first and foremost Canadians and only secondarily characterized by their country of origin (e.g., Canadian of Italian, Ukrainian, British origin). According to Taylor, these groups' collective ethnic identities do not qualify for the attribute 'national.' This argument is further elaborated in Kymlicka's liberal theory of minority rights. According to Kymlicka, individuals depend upon a 'societal culture,' which makes it possible for them to make meaningful choices about their life in relation to a particular cultural horizon. Kymlicka suggests that national minorities like the francophones in Quebec and Aboriginal peoples have developed such a 'societal culture' over time. Immigrants and their descendants, by contrast, do not possess a 'societal culture' of their own. Even though they often reject full cultural assimilation, according to Kymlicka, immigrants' primary objective is the integration into the host society. For a more detailed discussion of these authors' theories, see Chapter 3.

The contributions of Taylor and Kymlicka are important because – in addition to their intrinsic theoretical value, which is not under examination here – they help to solve a conceptual confusion regarding the distinction between 'national minorities' and 'ethnic minorities' resulting from immigration. This confusion characterized much of the academic and political debates during the 1990s. In fact, abstracting from their theoretical differences, the two authors draw the same conclusion: national minorities are to be distinguished from immigrant groups, even if the latter exist for generations. In comparison with ethnic groups resulting from immigration, national minorities – which emerge through conquest and/or colonization – deserve other rights of collective recognition – including the right for some institutional autonomy. As argued in Chapter 3, from a sociological point of view, this normative conclusion should remain open to negotiation. However, it is accepted, even in sociology, that these two types of minorities feature different empirical characteristics. They differ in their degree of 'institutional completeness' (usually less pronounced in the case of immigrant groups; Breton, 1964) and with respect to the nature of their political claims (usually more strongly oriented towards political autonomy in the case of national minorities).

Although Taylor's and Kymlicka's normative propositions have caused much debate, and although the distinction between national and ethnic groups is now widely accepted in Canada and abroad, one aspect usually gets forgotten: the relationship between different types of national and ethnic movements and their accommodation. Today, there are many countries that feature two or more types of diversity, such as national minorities, Aboriginal peoples, and immigrants. Do these different collectivities, their claims, and accommodations exist completely separately from each other? If not, then what characterizes the relation between these different types of minorities and their (claimed/granted) rights?

On the one hand, the gap in the literature is not surprising, because governments in Canada and abroad tend to elaborate distinct policies for different groups and even deal with them in separate departments and legislative pieces (Kymlicka, 2007). On the other hand, failing to recognize that there is a relation between the construction and expression of different types of diversity is a fundamental departure from the way Canadian multiculturalism was debated after its original implementation in the 1970s. Then, the close connection between Québécois nationalism and the framing, claims making, and recognition of 'the other ethnic groups' – to quote from the title of the fourth volume of the Bi & Bi Commission's report (Royal Commission on Bilingualism and Biculturalism, 1969) – was an issue of much contention (Rocher, 1971; McRoberts, 1997). Today, the presence of a threefold diversity – with respect to Québécois minority nationalism, multicultural immigrant integration, and Aboriginal self-government – is said to have become a characteristic feature of Canadian identity (Kymlicka, 2003). It would therefore be interesting to know if and how these facets of Canadian diversity impact each other – if not in legislative or administrative terms, then at least at the level of discourse.

In this chapter, I focus on one side of this relationship, namely, on the way that representations of Québécois nationalism and, in more general terms, 'the French fact' impact upon the construction of a

Canadian 'multicultural we.' I thereby strive to respond to the research questions that are at the core of this book: How do 'we' – the national majority – become multicultural? And how do representations of Quebec influence this process? The rationale for the upcoming analysis has been developed in Chapter 6. Like in the previous chapter, I will use the model of pluralism as a triangular relation when analysing the sample of newspaper discourses. However, I will focus on a different dimension. Following the methodology developed in Chapter 6, I analyse how the relationship between 'us' and 'others' – here interpreted as multinational compromise (indicated in bold) – impacts the representation and newcomers ('them$_{1-n}$') and their inclusion/exclusion.

$$\text{us} + \text{others}_{1-n} = \textbf{multinational we} \neq \text{them}_{1-n}$$

The analysis in the following section is divided into four parts. I first trace dominant representations of multiculturalism as an extension of Canadian dualism. I then argue that – within this context – both claims for liberal multiculturalism and republican rejections of multiculturalism have commonly pursued the logic of constructing a similarity between Quebec and ethnic groups of immigrant origin. Fourth, I observe a discursive shift that took place in the mid-1990s. Claims for multiculturalism now frequently underline its difference from traditional forms of diversity.

Analysis

The Extension of Dualism and Its Limits

When members of the Royal Commission on Bilingualism and Biculturalism conducted hearings in the Prairies, Canadians of neither British nor French origin confronted them with a question that had a lasting impact on the development of multiculturalism: 'if it is valuable for French Canadians to maintain their distinctive culture and identity, why is it not so for other groups' (Palmer, 1975: 516)? This quotation describes the logic of multiculturalism as an *extension* of dualist citizenship rights. By inserting themselves within the pre-established compromise between the two Canadian 'founding nations,' and by adopting the dominant discourse about language and culture, immigrant groups of predominantly European (but other than French) origin were able to construct themselves as a similar type of 'ethnic minority' as French Canadians. Thereby, they managed to challenge the privileged position of the two 'founding nations' and to convincingly argue that 'ethnic minorities deserve rights too.' Slowly gaining political influence, these 'other ethnic groups' had become a 'third force' in Canadian politics. Their voice provoked the members of the Royal Commission on Bilingualism and Biculturalism, while reiterating their perception of Canada as a bicultural country, to 'take into account the contribution made by the other ethnic groups to the cultural enrichment of Canada' (Royal Commission on Bilingualism and Biculturalism, 1969, vol. IV; cf. Chapter 2).

As argued in Chapter 2, in the political process that followed the commission's recommendations, the various types of ethnonational groups were 'accommodated' differently – and rarely to their full satisfaction. Discrimination against Aboriginal peoples was to be replaced with assimilation in the 1969 White Paper. National dualism was transformed into official bilingualism in the 1969 Official Languages Act. Biculturalism and the Western ethnocultural 'mosaic' were translated into multiculturalism, established as a state policy in 1971. In his speech to the House of Commons in October 1971, Prime Minister Pierre Trudeau declared that 'multiculturalism within a bilingual framework' not only constituted an official state policy but was also 'the very essence of Canadian identity' (House of Commons, 1971: 8580). Though there are two official languages, there is no official culture and no ethnic group should take precedence over any other. This policy marked the passage from assimilationism to normative pluralism in Canada. It was based upon a political choice to move 'from binationalism to bilingualism, and from biculturalism to multiculturalism' (Juteau, 2000a: 18, my translation).

Since then, in dominant discourses, the recasting of Canada's national identity tends to reflect the multicultural input from minority populations. This 'progress' is often represented as a transition from dualism to pluralism: 'The two founding linguistic communities of Canada and its aboriginal people have since become a multicultural society enriched by the arrival of immigrants from all corners of the globe,' proclaimed Canada's head of state, Queen Elizabeth II on her eighteenth visit to Canada in 1992 (quoted in both newspapers; G/T-1992-0702). 'Our history has prepared us to be innovative in the modern world, where diversity counts for so much,' argued Canada's former Governor General Adrienne Clarkson in a Speech from the Throne (Government of Canada, 2004). Indeed, in the 1990s, the representation of a linear evolution from a dualist past to a pluralist present and future became an integral part of the Canadian founding myth:

From the moment of its birth, Canada had a complex, divided personality shared between French settlers and United Empire Loyalists fleeing the

American Revolution [...] By the 1890s, the Governor-General was assuring *immigrants from Europe* to the 'Last Best West' that their languages and religions would be respected *under the umbrella of an English-speaking democracy* on Canada's prairies. The conscious multiculturalism of the West was *a natural extension of the Confederation of the centre* [...] Overlaying all this was *the British connection* [...] By the 1940s, it was clear that many Canadians felt no such connection, and the decades since have allowed it to *gently fade to pastels*. (G-1999-0701, my emphasis)

The proliferation of positively connoted 'diversity' (in contrast to negatively connoted 'difference') is here portrayed as a smooth and effortless 'extension' of Canada's 'complex, divided personality between French settlers and United Empire Loyalists fleeing the American Revolution' (G-1999-0701). In a similar way as described in Chapter 7, we find Canadian multiculturalism emerging quasi 'naturally' from the strange encounter between 'the French fact' and 'Americanness.' The proliferation of ethnic diversity first blossoms under a vaguely defined 'British connection' and then goes hand in hand with an apparently peaceful dissolution of the British 'ethnic nation,' which 'gently fade[d] to pastels.' Conflict and struggle – such as the two conscription crises, the nativist movement, and the internment of 'ethnic Canadians' with roots in 'enemy countries' – are downplayed or relegated to the past. Thus, the 'bitterly partisan [...] deep divisions between the Catholic French and Protestant British' (G-1999-0701) and past injustices towards Aboriginal peoples (Neu and Therrien, 2003) are increasingly superposed by a harmonious multicultural present and future. Canada's trajectory as a nation seems a model evolution from a de facto 'fractious' (G-1999-0701) plural colony (like the one observed by Furnivall, 1939; cf. Chapter 3) to a 'happy' and normatively pluralist society: 'Since 1950, the diversity of people coming to Canada has grown, and the capacity of Canada to accommodate that diversity has been remarkable only to those who do not understand the essence of our history. Living "at some distance together" has been a condition of Canada's existence. It is one of the happiest coincidences of events in the 18th and 19th centuries that this should be so' (G-1999-0701).

Historically, this view provoked much contention among the francophones of Quebec and Aboriginal peoples. Seeing themselves as separate nations and not as immigrant-type ethnic groups, they rejected multiculturalism as a political strategy aiming at the co-optation of 'third force'

Canadians into a white English Canadian majority.[2] Commentators from Quebec have been particularly vocal in expressing their objections: Alluding to the fact that over long periods of time, French Canadians constituted Canada's demographic majority, they claim that 'English Canada has learned to count on immigration' to establish its supremacy over Canadian francophones. 'Without immigration [. . .] there would not be a Canada that is English within terms of its population, language and culture' (Bouthillier, 1997: 18, my translation). As such, 'the federal policy of multiculturalism [. . .] can only relativize and banalize the position and importance of Quebec's particular cultural identity: within Canada, and with the contempt of history, the latter would merely be one particularism among others – one small piece of a huge mosaic' (Corbo, 1996: 100, my translation). In endorsing multiculturalism and the Canadian Charter of Rights and Freedoms, English Canadians are viewed as ratifying 'an alliance among themselves and a very large number of immigrants [. . .] The role of the combatants comprises, above all, speaking English, forcing other people to speak it as well, to accurately reproduce the traditional attitudes of the "English" towards French Canadians, and to lead immigrants to adopt the same strategy' (Schwimmer, 1995: 173, my translation).

While some scholars claim that multiculturalism has (practically or even deliberately) undermined Quebec's distinctiveness in Canada (Rocher, 1971; McRoberts, 1997; Bissoondath, 1994; Angus, 1997) we must not overlook that the dominant Canadian subject is not only anglophone, but also white, European, Christian, and male (Thobani, 2007). Women, racialized minorities, Aboriginal peoples, and religious minorities (these days predominantly Muslims) are still fighting various forms of discrimination within Quebec and the rest of Canada (Helly, 2004; Sharma, 2006; Henry and Tator, 2006; Wood, 2003). In fact, under Canadian law, English and French Canadians enjoy more group rights than other ethnic and national groups. In particular, Charles Taylor's (1993) vision of Québécois and Aboriginal 'deep diversity' has been accused of 'relegate[ing] "the others" to the status of second-class citizens just as it relegates questions of the representation of ethnic/racial minorities to a much lower rank of importance than the representation of [the French and English] "charter groups"' (Stasiulis, 1995: 212). Indeed, within most societies, there is a tendency to take majority rights for granted. As they have come to form the 'normal' pillars of society, they often remain unspecified.

Only when minorities make claims does it become obvious that the 'extension' of majority rights to minorities has clearly defined limits: 'No one *rationally* is going to suggest that Canada establish Islam's sharia law alongside the English common law, the Quebec Civil Code and whatever the nation's aboriginal justice systems evolve. Apart from anything else, it would not be *practical*. This illustrates *private versus public culture* and non-institutionalized versus institutionalized culture. Multiculturalism – for now, at any rate – does not mean that everyone's culture is on the same institutionalized footing as English, French and aboriginal cultures' (G-1994-0617, my emphasis).

This quotation demonstrates that bi- or trinationalism does not automatically and unconditionally translate into pluralism. It also supports the claim that 'multiculturalism has never seriously challenged the pre-eminent position of national politics centred on the French-English cleavage' (Stasiulis, 1995: 203). In the quotation above, trinationalism is 'majoritized' and rendered 'universal' through an argument that evokes 'practicality,' 'rationality,' and the distinction between 'private versus public culture' in order to reject challenges to the status quo. By constructing a fundamental difference between historically grown 'Canadian' institutions and 'everyone [else's private] cultures' the extension of multicultural group rights is reduced from a 'public issue' to a 'private trouble' (Mills, 2000). The 'irrational' extension of rights from dualism and/or trinationalism to multiculturalism is thus blocked. Interestingly, ten years later, the very concrete possibility of using sharia tribunals for the purpose of family arbitration in Ontario became a subject of heated debate (Razack, 2007; Macklin, 2005).

To enforce the distinction between legitimate and illegitimate rights, within the examined newspaper discourses, trinationalism is represented as a 'Canadian' historical compromise and subsumed under the 'personality' of the nation. For this purpose, the harmonious dimensions of compromise are stressed, while the disagreements between the three Canadian nations – precisely with respect to the law, government, commerce, and education – are downplayed: 'Everyone's history is not *Canada's history*. The history of settlement, of how the instruments of social existence were constructed – the law, government, commerce, education and so forth, is the history of Canada and should be the history of *every one* of *us* who lives here' (G-1994-0617, my emphasis). While it is highly unlikely that First Nations and Franco-Québécois would agree with '*the* history of Canada' that is implied in the quotation above, their inclusion within the national compromise is here used to stabilize the status quo. 'National' traditions, historically produced through power relations, circumscribe the extension of pluralism.

As we have seen in Chapter 5, in supposedly 'civic' nations, 'national traditions' tend to be camouflaged as practical, rational solutions (Bader, 1995a). In so-called ethnic nations, they are often legitimized by reference to a shared 'core culture' (Manz, 2004). In Canada, minority rights have been attributed differently to national minorities, on the one hand, and immigrant groups, on the other. This distinction has become legitimized by academic scholarship (Kymlicka, 1995). Whether or not these legitimizations are 'right' or 'wrong' is not of concern here. Rather, I want to emphasize two points. First, as we realize in the case of the 'sharia tribunals,' historically established traditions of rights and recognitions cannot be deduced 'objectively' and fixed forever. Second, the idea of citizenship – which is at stake in these representations – always implies both: to grant rights to those recognized as members (the citizens) and to 'tame and civilize' the citizens' political actions through institutional rules and procedures (Eder, 1998b: 66).

In sum, the discourses analysed in this section suggest that bi- or trinationalism does not automatically lead to a proliferation of rights. Rather, it provides a matrix for the articulation of minority rights. One the one hand, it imposes a logic and terminology into which claims making *must be inserted*. On the other hand, within multinationalism, multiculturalism *can be inserted* as an extension of – rather than a break with – 'tradition.' In the following three sections, these processes will be further explored.

Claims for Multiculturalism

Claims for recognition must not necessarily follow the logic of pluralism. Whether the cause of ethnic groups is best served by group-differentiated rights or 'unhyphenated' equality is still hotly debated, and this even in Canada. Examples from the newspaper sample show that 'unhyphenated Canadianness' within an 'imagined community' that kept its promise of being a strictly 'horizontal comradeship' (Anderson, 1991) without vertical divisions along ethnocultural lines is often represented as the ideal option: 'There are many Canadians including minorities who [. . .] just want to be Canadians, unhyphenated, with all the rights, responsibilities and privileges. They want a Canada where no one is assigned his or her place according to ethnicity. That is what it should be in an ideal world. Unfortunately, the world is far from ideal' (T-1995-0123).

Because Canada's historical evolution is beset with ethnicity, and 'assimilat[ion] into the French or British culture' is rejected, multiculturalism becomes Canada's 'second best' choice. Multiculturalism seems to represent a more inclusive framework than alternative models for Canadian national integration, such as a societal project based on orthodox liberalism and individualism or a societal project based on the recognition of two (or even three) nations (Stasiulis, 1995). As argued earlier, the implementation of multiculturalism in Canada has very much been following the logic of 'minorities deserve recognition, *too*.' This is also reflected in claims for the extension of multiculturalism in the newspaper sample under investigation:

> The founding ethnic groups in Canada, the Inuits [sic] and the Indians, were hyphenated since they belonged to different groups or nations. When the Europeans came, they brought their specific hyphens, too – French and then English, followed by everyone else. Until 1971 biculturalism was acceptable to most. It was felt those who were neither French nor English did not bring anything worthwhile with them. Their culture was looked down on. They were forced to 'assimilate' into the French or British culture. If Bissoondath has his way, would he be able to persuade Quebecers that they should just be Canadians and not French Canadians? Is it realistic to ask them to do so? (T-1995-0123)

Canadian novelist Neil Bissoondath (1994), who is attacked in the quotation above, embraces the binational character of the country but criticizes the multicultural particularization of Canadian identity, including affirmative action programs for members of 'visible minorities.' Interestingly, there are many examples, such as the passage above, where the point of reference are not the taken-for-granted majority rights of English Canadians, but rather the (claimed and partially granted) minority rights of Franco-Québécois. The quotation above stands for a persistent ambiguity that characterizes the discourses of the newspaper sample: are Franco-Québécois preventing the growth of an unhyphenated (non-French, non-British) 'Canadian' identity, or are they the most powerful example of the disenchantment with a seemingly 'universal' Canadian identity? On the one hand, minority nationalism, in particular, 'the province's restrictive French language Bill 101' is being viewed as 'trampling on the democratic rights of those who immigrate to Quebec' (T-1998-0223). From this perspective, the emphasis on bina-tionalism is perceived as an obstacle to the extension of multicultural rights: By 'requiring the children of newcomers (especially minorities) to attend French-only schools, the Bloc government [*sic*]' is accused of 'put[ting] up tremendous hurdles against our nation's multiculturalism and diversity' (T-1998-0223).

On the other hand, it is argued that 'the Quebec issue is just one of the ongoing unsettled questions about how we live together in this land called Canada' (T-1995-0829). From this perspective, the 'Charter of Rights, bilingualism, multiculturalism, aboriginal affairs, and our evolving immigration policy' are merely 'moderate responses' to a growing ethnic diversity (T-1995-0829). In both cases, the representation of minority rights builds upon a similarity between minority nations and ethnic groups. Minorities are perceived as having more power; ethnic minorities are portrayed as having less power. Both, however, are understood as belonging to the same order of group formation. This similarity is then used to argue in favour of increased minority rights: 'People who are not part of the ruling elite in this country do not feel that they fundamentally belong. The "Two Founding Nations" speeches cannot capture the hearts and spirits of French Quebecers who do not have the sense of sharing power. Just as the myth of multicultur-alism is no solace to immigrants confronted with Markham councillors threatening to leave town because so many Chinese are congregating there [...] The separatist movement must be taken as a wake-up call for all Canadians. Its sentiments of alienation are not limited to French Quebecers' (T-1995-1016).

The struggle for rights and recognition of the most powerful minor-ity on Canadian soil, Quebec, is here portrayed as the so-called tip of the iceberg of minority 'alienation.' In stark contrast to the argument against binationalism that was presented earlier, minority nationalism seems here to be spearheading multiculturalism. It is used to draw at-tention to the struggle of those who are less powerful. To foster their rights, a history is constructed to provide the term 'identity politics' with ancestry and legitimacy. The similarity between ethnic groups and Quebec is used to appropriate some of the factual and symbolic power that inhibits francophone Quebec: Critics of multiculturalism say '"iden-tity politics" are new. This is rewriting history. The 1867 Constitution was all about recognizing identities – French and English, Catholic and Protestant, and the four original provinces – each maintaining its iden-tity in a united Canada. One of our great strengths has been that we have been able to recognize identities and accommodate them. It is the failure to recognize one of these identities – Quebec's – that recently brought Canada to the edge' (T-1996-0104).

In addition to claiming legitimacy, the quotation above enunciates an implicit threat: The non-recognition of identities brings Canada 'to the edge'; Québécois separatism constitutes a powerful example. Thus, 'we/you' had better take the claims for multiculturalism seriously! While this type of argument has helped ethnic minorities to challenge the privileged position that is commonly attributed to minority nations, constructing a similarity between ethnic groups and minority nations can also be detrimental. In the following section, I will analyse references to Quebec within conservative rejections of multiculturalism.

Rejections of Multiculturalism

As long as multicultural demands of minorities aim for integration and not for separation, these demands are either accepted and inserted within the logic of extending dualism (as pointed out in the previous section), or they are downplayed and integrated into the logic of dissolving dualism: 'perhaps it is time for us to allow our founding people, the French and the British, to rest in peace. They carved out a country, earned our respect and their place in our history, but they are dead' (T-1993-0321). Indeed, one potential strategy to counter demands for multiculturalism is to dissolve the tradition of multinationalism altogether. This type of reasoning is based on the liberal idea that 'the state has no business in the family trees of the nation' (T-1993-0321), and that Canadians should take 'personal responsibility for our own cultural heritages' (T-1993-0321). In the quotation below, ethnic minorities are integrated as part of 'the people' in a liberal state. However, their membership remains conditional upon the shedding of their particular cultural group-identities:

> Strong forces of nationalism are loose in the land outside Quebec. [...] They express themselves in the desire [...] to be one people in a liberal state, rather than a collection of hyphenated peoples in a vague confederation. (*Many so-called ethnic Canadians feel this way.*) [...] Many Canadian nationalists believe that official bilingualism and its fraternal twin, official multiculturalism, inhibit the growth of a coherent English-speaking nation. They want more emphasis in the public sphere on things we have in common, leaving the nourishment of differences to private lives.

Can this be appreciated in francophone Quebec, which apparently feels the same way about its own society? (G-1992-0111, my emphasis)

Here, a similarity is constructed between official bilingualism, perceived as a concession towards French Canadians, and 'its fraternal twin' multiculturalism, portrayed as concession towards (other) ethnic groups: both policies are perceived as invasions: they 'inhibit the growth of a coherent English-speaking nation.' At the same time, the quotation suggests that ethnic groups living in the rest of Canada and French Canadians living in Quebec belong to different orders: while 'ethnic Canadians' are to be integrated into an English-speaking nation as individuals, 'francophone Québec' is constructed as a separate entity in Canada with 'its own society.'

In the 1990s, scholars increasingly disputed the idea that the liberal state could be both politically bounded and culturally neutral (Taylor, 1995, 2001). As a consequence, both the demands for pluralism, on the one hand, and the opposition to all types of 'groupism,' on the other, became stronger. In Chapter 7, it was argued that Quebec, during this time, is often portrayed as the main source for the proliferation of (negatively connoted) ethnic 'difference' rather than positively connoted 'diversity' (e.g., G-1994-0513, G-1996-0701, G-1997-0701). In addition, in English-speaking Canada – due to the destructive power of Québécois separatism and French Canadians' pioneering role in destabilizing English Canadian identity – the idea of 'Quebec' has become a symbol of social fragmentation. In this situation, minority claims suggesting that 'Quebec's struggle for recognition represents us all' turn out to be detrimental: references to francophone Quebec are now increasingly used with the aim to also reject minority claims for the extension of multiculturalism: 'It may seem outlandish to suggest that Anglo Canadian culture could become marginalized. It is still financially and commercially dominant, and remains on top politically. *A precedent, though, has been set in Quebec.* Until the late 1950s, the famed Anglo Scottish Ascendancy dominated the province's public life. Today, those "White Rhodesians," although still comparatively well-off, are scarcely more influential than are the various expatriate communities in cities like Paris, Rome, London' (T-1993-0228, my emphasis).

This quotation insinuates that increasing multiculturalism may ultimately produce a similar situation to Quebec's Quiet Revolution, where English Canadians have become 'marginalized' by a rising francophone middle class. The notion of a 'precedent' suggests that there is 'proof' that English Canadian culture is under threat, and that what has happened in Quebec may also happen in the rest of Canada – even though 'Anglo Canadian culture [...] is still financially and commercially dominant, and remains on top politically.' In this type of allegation, a parallel is drawn between ethnic groups and minority nations. Thus, explicitly or implicitly, it is suggested that 'our multiculturalism may be turning into multinationalism' (T-1993-0228). On the one hand, ethnic groups are increasingly portrayed as 'diasporic groups' that 'care more passionately about events in their "home" country than in their "adopted" one' (T-1993-0228). On the other hand, the increasing number of non-white Canadians is represented as a cultural-linguistic take-over of/on Canadian soil: 'If an "ethnic" community becomes larger than the European-descended community, it will grow more assertive. It will see no reason to defer to a culture that has fewer adherents than its own. It might change the local bylaw so that it can cut down as many trees as it wants. It might want offices and schools to close on its holidays and to remain open on holidays it doesn't celebrate. It might decide to make its language official and have it spoken in the legislature, placed on public signs, and compulsory in schools' (Stoffman, 2002: 134–5).

Although the threatening Other is here identified as non-European, the situation described alludes to English Canada's experience with Quebec and thereby evokes memories of struggle, negotiation, 'second-class citizenship,' and the threat of separation. As a powerful symbol of the weakening of English Canadian dominance, interpreted as 'societal disintegration,' francophone Quebec is constructed as an awful example of what 'true multiculturalism' (Stoffman) in response to immigration-related ethnic diversity may lead to. In some cases, the similarity between ethnic groups and Quebec is direct ('ethnic groups may become like Quebec'). In other cases, more cautiously, an indirect similarity is constructed through parallel outcomes of the two types of minority claims: 'Multiculturalism, along with other factors such as our passive acceptance until very recently that Quebecers had a unilateral right to decide whether to cease being Canadians, has made our common citizenship insubstantial or weightless' (T-1997-0219). Whether the similarity is direct or indirect, in both cases, the overall logic remains unchanged: ethnic groups and minority nations are constructed as belonging to the same order of group formations; multiculturalism is merely an extension of dualism. What is altered in these representations – in contrast to those evoked to claim multiculturalism – are merely the normative connotation of pluralism (reducing rather than enhancing equality) and the projected outcome (societal fragmentation instead of integration).

'Ethnic Minorities Don't Ask for Self-Government'

In reaction to these reproaches, ethnic minorities have underlined their devotion and loyalty to Canada as a nation. However, for a long time, their assurances did not seem to be convincing. This situation changed in the second half of the 1990s. In the empirical material, a discursive shift can be observed from 'multicultural minorities want/ deserve the same cultural rights as francophones' to 'multicultural minorities do not make the same political claims as Quebec.' Within this new representation of ethnic relations in Canada, a fundamental difference is constructed between Quebec's 'separatist minority nationalism' and a multicultural pan-Canadianism concerned with immigration-related ethnic diversity: 'Those who blame multiculturalism and the lack of Canadian loyalty from ethnic communities need only look at the Parti Quebecois' assessment of its recent attempt to break up Canada. One blamed the ethnic vote and another blamed the "ravages of multiculturalism" for keeping Canada united. When the chips were down, the ethnic vote was 100 per cent pro-Canada' (T-1996-0104, my emphasis).

The comparison with Franco-Québécois who, in the 1995 Quebec referendum on sovereignty, voted 60 per cent in favour of separation, allows ethnic minorities to shed the stigma of being catalysts for social fragmentation. The facts are on their side. During the referendum, 95 per cent of Quebec's non-francophone population voted indeed against separation (Drouilly, 1997). This new type of representation provides them with a tremendous increase in legitimacy. Here, ethnic minorities are no longer conditional insiders at the margins of the dualist nation. Rather, they are portrayed – and portray themselves – as multicultural allies of the pan-Canadian nation: 'The biggest challenge to Canadian citizenship comes not from the new minorities but our oldest ones- the aboriginals and the English and the French [. . .] "National minorities," in the words of Will Kymlicka of Queen's University [. . .] insist on nation-to-nation negotiations in the "multi-nation state" that is Canada. But immigrants, *Canadians by choice rather than the accident of birth,* make no such demands. They *don't ask for self-government.* They are *not potentially secessionist;* in fact, *those in Quebec are in the forefront of fighting separatism'* (T-2000-1105, my emphasis).

This quotation reveals that two events, not one, came to the support of the reframing of multicultural claims making within Canadian majority discourses: the 1995 Quebec referendum, and the publication of Will Kymlicka's influential philosophy of *Multicultural Citizenship* in the same year. Kymlicka's distinction between rights granted to minority nations, Aboriginal peoples, and ethnic groups of immigrant origin has been interpreted (negatively) as fixing a hierarchy of rights in favour of minority nations and Aboriginal peoples. Nevertheless, the quotation above shows that it can also be used (positively) to distance minority groups of immigrant origin from the potentially secessionist intentions of minority nations. Ethnic groups 'don't ask for self-government' and political autonomy. Rather their claims for multicultural rights should be interpreted, according to Kymlicka (1995), as quests for more inclusion. Thus, the 'attachment of recent immigrants to their old homelands' is said to 'rarely detract from their Canadian-ness' (T-2000-1105). Rather, it is claimed that these sentiments 'reinforce' recent immigrants' commitment to Canada. Although 'newer minorities' may be on different sides of global conflicts,' within the Canadian context, they are said to 'keep a peaceful distance from each other' (T-2000-1105). The distinction between 'new and old minorities' is then further elaborated: 'Newer minorities are not transplanting "old country" troubles here, as the old ones did. Nor are they narrow regionalists. They strongly identified with Pierre Trudeau precisely because of his pan-Canadian vision (not, as some shoddy commentaries had it, because he "let them" into Canada). Immigrants are less complaining and less demanding than the native-born. Yet they are routinely maligned for a multitude of sins, including cheapening our citizenship [...] We may need to revisit the subservient role we have assigned to the non-Aboriginal, non-Quebecois and non-English minorities, particularly the newer immigrants' (T-2000-1105).

This quotation demonstrates a new stream of minority claims. Within the context of a Canadian 'dual majority' (Anctil, 1984), claims are no longer made on the basis of similarity with the established groups, but rather on the basis of difference. 'The newer immigrants' are portrayed here as 'the better Canadians,' as they are 'less complaining and less demanding' than the members of the so-called founding nations. As pan-Canadianists, they have 'helped [to] make Canada what it is – the best nation in the world' (T-1998-0614), and have 'chosen' it as their 'new country because Canada is a beautiful, marvellous and very special place to live' (T-2001-0424). In these discourses, the rejection of being 'trapped in an old model' of diversity is flanked by an increasing valorization of 'choice.'

On the one hand, this highly liberal understanding of multiculturalism is seriously challenging the notion that 'blood is stronger than water.' The immigrants of today are said to be more committed than the established groups precisely because they are, to recall an earlier quotation, 'Canadians by choice rather the accident of birth' (T-2000-1105).[3]

On the other hand, it would be false to assume that the new 'multiculturalist discourses' in the mainstream media radically displace the idea of Canada as we have come to know it. On the contrary, representations of 'multicultural Canada' tend to avoid the impression that Canada has become a 'virtual address' (G-1997-0701). Rather, we are said to experience 'the emergence of a new diversified nation. This diversity includes people of other races, religions, and ideas' (T-2001-0424). The 'growing diversity, especially Toronto's (48 per cent immigrant, 41 per cent visible minorities) [is held up] as a model for the world' (T-1998-0614) and bounded through contrast:

> Toronto [...] has [...] grown into the most cosmopolitan place on Earth, miraculously with none of the tensions experienced by other major metropolises. Similarly, the characteristics of peace, order and good government helped us through the *crises created by the tribalism of Quebec separatists* [...] What is new is the *creeping Americanization of Canada* – the growing gap between the haves and the have-nots; the de-legitimization of government; and the division of society into Us vs. Them, by demonizing the weak [...] Neo-conservatives complain that Canadians are far too generous with the unemployed, the welfare moms, the poor, the refugees. But such *critics, who draw their inspiration from America, expose not a Canadian malaise but their own colonized minds.* (T-1998-0701, my emphasis)

The quotation above, even though it stresses the importance of urban multi-ethnic cosmopolitanism, also expresses a profound commitment to the 'traditional' meaning of Canadian nationhood. Situated between 'the tribalism of Quebec separatists' and the 'neo-conservative' 'American' individualization of 'McWorld' (Barber, 2001), Canada remains a compromise between diverse types of diversity: an increasingly multicultural national identity smoothly superposes (rather than radically displaces) the idea of a 'community of communities.'[4]

Not all discourses in favour of Canada's 'new' multiculturalism share this view. Some consider binationalism as clearly outdated: 'The media portray our French-English conflict as the number one political issue [...] When will [they] accept the fact that Canada's political and social map is not the same as it was years ago?' (T-2001-0424). Nevertheless, the idea of Canada as an ethnically diverse 'united nation' (T-2001-0424) is never challenged. On the contrary, multiculturalism 'if properly developed, directed and used' is considered 'an asset' of nation building and not a 'liability' (T-1995-0123).

The 'Dual Majority' as a Discursive Matrix in the 1990s

In a widely cited article, Pierre Anctil (1984) describes the relations between ethnic groups in Montreal in terms of a 'dual majority' of anglophones and francophones, which positively impacts the creation of a separate sociocultural space for ethnic groups of neither French nor British (nor Aboriginal) origin. Anctil writes: 'The hypothesis that the situation of a dual ethnic majority produces a positive outcome for third communities arises very clearly from the recent literature on this subject. [It is as if] by attracting all attention, the political and legal confrontation between old stock Francophones and Anglophones freed in Quebec a well-defined sociocultural space that Allophones [of immigrant origin] had been able to occupy alone' (1984: 450).

Anctil's observation stems from a time when the relationship between French/English dualism and multiculturalism was still hotly debated, and this particularly in the province of Quebec. Interestingly, the preceding analysis of Central Canadian newspaper discourses showed that – even in the 1990s – references to Québécois minority nationalism and, to a much lesser degree, Aboriginal peoples, are still employed to foster both legitimizations and delegitimizations of Canada as a multicultural nation. These findings demonstrate how important it is to overcome the radical analytical split between multinationalism and multiculturalism when examining questions of immigrant integration. 'Host societies' are not homogeneous entities and, at least in the Canadian case, different types of diversity and their accommodations do not seem to exist parallel to each other without ideological, discursive, and presumably, political interaction.

Although immigrants may demand different types of rights and pursue different political goals than minority nations, they often become ethnicized after their immigration in a way that resonates with a society's previously established 'cultural compromise' (Wimmer, 2002). Framed as 'ethnic groups,' their claims must then be voiced – and are interpreted – in ways that take into account previously established discourses, as anything else would not be understood. Adapting to these discourses, it is only logical that spokespersons of ethnic groups and associations try to borrow from the authority and legitimacy attributed to movements that are (rightly or wrongly) viewed as predecessors. In this sense, previously established minority accommodations – such as multinationalism – impact on multiculturalism in response to immigrant integration. They constitute a set of rules and mental paths, which at a given time, and for a particular set of social relations, frame the possibilities and limits of both immigrants' multicultural identities and the types of accommodation that will eventually be built into images of the nation.

In Chapter 5, four hypotheses on the potential impact of multinationalism upon multiculturalism were developed. It was suggested that *agreement* over the recognition of historically established ethnic or 'national' groups – such as Quebec – can (1) be meaningless or even detrimental to the recognition of newcomers, or (2) lead to an extension of pluralist rights. Furthermore, it was suggested that *conflict* over the recognition of historically established ethnic or 'national' groups – such as Quebec – can (3) render the recognition of newcomers extremely difficult or (4) favour their integration as 'contingent insiders.' How do these hypotheses relate to the multicultural transformation of Canadian identity in the newspaper discourses under investigation?

First, the preceding analysis challenges the commonplace representation of multiculturalism as an extension of French/English dualism. Previously recognized multinationalism leads neither automatically nor fully to an extension of multicultural rights and recognition. As long as the members of the dominant group – whether or not the latter consists of a singular or a 'dual' majority – agree upon their respective roles and privileges as 'founders' of the nation, the extension from binationalism to trinationalism and/or multiculturalism remains cumbersome and incomplete. In this case, as described in hypothesis (1), 'ethnic groups' of immigrant origin are merely 'conditional insiders' with less important collective rights than Canada's so-called founding nations.[5]

In the discourses examined here, binationalism as a compromise imposes a logic and terminology into which demands for the accommodation of newcomers *must be inserted* (since anything else would be politically marginalized). In Canada, the dominance of the 'Quebec question' has produced a situation where ethnic diversity is predominantly framed in terms of culture, language, and, to a lesser extent, regional/territorial autonomy.[6] In the newspaper sample under investigation, issues of 'race' and racialization – forms of exclusion that concern primarily Canada's newer immigrants (but also long-term residents of, e.g., Chinese or African background) – are largely absent. With culture, ethnicity, language and nationhood as dominant paradigms of pluralism, it remains difficult to bring the fight against racial and religious discrimination to the fore in dominant (media) discourses (Bannerji, 2000; Henry et al., 2000).

Second, the fact that recognized bi- or trinationalism circumscribes the expression of legitimate diversity does, however, not imply that it cannot serve as a template for the extension of minority rights. Hypothesis (2) states that traditional multinationalism provides an extendable ideological and discursive matrix that is favourable for the implementation of multiculturalism. Within a context of a 'dual majority,' claims for/from ethnicized groups follow the logic of *extending* recognition to other minority groups: a similarity is established between immigrant organizations and the so-called founding nations. As argued above, in Canada, this similarity is reflected in the use of the term 'ethnic groups' to describe immigrant organizations.

Interestingly, multicultural claims making seldom attacks the 'unnamed' majority rights enjoyed by English Canadians. Rather, in the examined newspaper discourses, what causes contention is the fact that 'both Francophones and Aboriginals assert their primacy over immigrants' (T-1995-1016). The presence of 'named' (claimed/granted) minority rights serves as a better target for criticism than camouflaged mono-nationalism.[7] Because the cultural particularity of at least one of the majorities must be rendered explicit (rather than camouflaged as universalism), multinationalism allows multiculturalism to be inserted as an extension of – rather than a break with – 'tradition.' Indeed, in the examples provided above, legitimizations of multiculturalism are often phrased in the logic of 'minorities deserve recognition too.' The proliferation of ethnic plurality becomes thus a broadening of the dualist compromise: it fosters Canadianness rather than circumventing it. Within this logic, the adaptation of multiculturalism does not displace or explode the notion of Canadianness. Rather, it embellishes and *complements* multinationalism.

Third, the constructed similarity between immigrant groups and Canada's minority nation(s) also has a down side. In times of conflict, the link between multinationalism and multiculturalism can easily be reversed. When the members of established groups fail to agree on their respective privileges, the 'problems' associated with minority nationalism are sometimes projected upon ethnic minorities. In the newspaper sample at hand, particularly during the first half of the 1990s, the (real or imagined) similarity between ethnic groups and French Canadians is often abused. Images of Québécois nationalism are inflicted upon immigrant and ethnic minorities with the purpose of discrediting the idea of Canada as a multicultural nation. This corresponds to hypothesis (3), which states that national majorities tend to secure their superiority by inflicting stigmata developed in reference to 'deviant minorities' upon newcomers. Indeed, in the newspaper sample investigated here, Québécois nationalism and separatism are often used as a symbol for conflict and political mobilization along 'ethnocultural' lines. The idea of a logical similarity between multinationalism and multiculturalism persists, but it is now used to make an argument against all types of group rights.

That negative attributes associated with old minorities can easily become imposed upon new minorities shows that multinationalism as an historically established compromise does not predetermine attitudes towards newcomer adaptation and integration. Once established, the similarity between ethnic groups and (alienated) minority nations may not only be used to extend rights to minorities but also to deny minority rights altogether. Immigrant minorities may therefore have an interest in dissociating themselves from the allegation that they follow in the footsteps of the countries' 'older' ethnonational groups. The examined newspaper discourses suggest that this dissociation took place in the 1990s.

Fourth, for the proponents of multiculturalism, the pronounced conflict between the two Canadian 'founding nations,' highlighted by the 1995 referendum on Quebec's sovereignty, increased the urgency of rejecting the thesis that the recognition of immigration-related ethnic diversity necessarily produces societal fragmentation. As a consequence, within the examined discourses from the *Globe and Mail* and the *Toronto Star*, the logic that 'ethnic minorities are like Quebec' became disrupted. From the second half of the 1990s onwards, pan-Canadian multiculturalism became more and more legitimized not by its similarity with multinationalism but by its difference.

Indeed, compared with minority nations' quests for political autonomy and separation, ethnic groups' demands for 'polyethnic' and 'representation' rights, as Kymlicka (1995) puts it, appear relatively harmless. In the newspaper discourses, while multinationalism becomes marginalized because of its inherent potential for conflict, ethnic minorities are increasingly represented as the 'true' carriers of diversity. *Their* 'multiculturalism' is positioned socially between (as 'glue') and morally above (as the 'visible face' of the nation) the quarrelsome 'founding nations.' As such, it is portrayed as a favourable element of *unity* and as an element that invests Canadian identity with meaning. This situation reminds of hypothesis (4), which states that the confrontation between established groups may create a context where newcomers have a stronger bargaining power to negotiate for multicultural rights and recognition.

The empirical material analysed here suggests that two events in the 1990s contributed to dissociating multiculturalism from the stigma of causing social fragmentation. First, the 'ethnic vote' in opposition to Quebec's independence in the 1995 referendum allowed ethnic groups to be represented, and to represent themselves, as loyal citizens who support the project of pan-Canadian nationhood and are, therefore, to be preferred over (supposedly) 'quarrelsome separatist Québécois.' Second, Will Kymlicka's influential theory of multicultural citizenship, published in 1995, provided the distinction between ethnic groups and minority nations with academic authority. Constituted in opposition to – rather than an extension of – 'dualism' multiculturalism became invested with legitimacy and moved from a discourse at the margins to a social imaginary at the centre.

Conclusion

In Chapter 5, I developed four ideal-typical scenarios or 'hypotheses' regarding the relationship between multinationalism and multiculturalism. In the preceding discussion, it became obvious that all four of them resonate with the discourses on Canadian national identity in the 1990s. How is this possible, and what does it teach us for future investigations? The preceding analysis reminds us of four points.

First and foremost, no compromise is unanimous. There are always two dimensions embedded within the notion of compromise: relative agreement and relative compromise. Thus, the notion of a French/English 'dual majority' as relative agreement reserves privileges for the two Canadian 'founding nations' that are inalienable to 'ethnic groups' and have only been granted to a much lesser extent to Canada's Aboriginal peoples. It also imposes a logic and terminology into which newcomers' claims making *must be inserted* if it wants to be successful in the political arena. By contrast, the 'dual majority' as relative conflict produces a situation where at least one of the two majorities' cultural particularity cannot be camouflaged – as it is typically the case with 'dominant nationalism' (Lecours and Nootens, 2007) – but is rendered explicit for the sake of its own identity formation and/or claims making. In this sense, the 'dual majority' provides a discursive matrix for the extension of minority rights. For that purpose, the distinction between ethnic groups and the privileged (minority) nation becomes deconstructed.

Nevertheless, once established, the similarity between ethnic groups and minority nations can also be used, by the opponents of pluralism – for delegitimizing minority rights altogether. This leads me to my second point. As I will show more explicitly in the next chapter, there are always multiple voices and diverging appreciations of the historically established compromise. Thus, even in a relatively small and homogeneous sample of Central Canadian newspaper articles, we can distinguish between proponents and opponents of multiculturalism who adopt different logics for the sake of constructing their argument.

Third, as shown by the preceding analysis, the relations between the established groups do not remain static. As their relation changes – a change that may even be catalyzed by the influx of newcomers – the prospects of multiculturalism may also be affected. For example, in Canada, at a particular point in time, it became increasingly common sense that minority nations and ethnic groups do not belong to the same order of groups: they do not ask for the same rights, and according to some, they do not 'deserve' the same rights. While this could be read as a 'concession' towards Quebec and First Nations, who have been insisting on their 'special status' for a long time, in the mid-1990s, the distinction became acceptable to ethnic groups to the extent that it helped them to rid claims for multicultural recognition of the stigma of 'social fragmentation.'

Finally, while the words may stay the same, their meaning and connotations may change over time. Thus, when Pierre Anctil, in 1984, suggested that the presence of a French/English 'dual majority' in Montreal had a pluralism-enhancing impact, he clearly had in mind the emergence of 'third communities' (1984: 450). The pan-Canadian multiculturalism expressed in this newspaper sample, however, is made of individuals – immigrants and members of minorities – rather than communities. Within the examined discourses, the notion of Canada as a 'community of communities' becomes increasingly superimposed by 'unity in (individualist) diversity.' Indeed, while we are observing the development of two – fairly independent – English-speaking and French-speaking societies within Canada, something else seems to have happened to multiculturalism: if it was ever perceived in terms of groups or group rights, this clearly is no longer the case within the newspaper sample examined here. In the following chapter, I will trace the different meanings of multiculturalism in more detail.

9 Who Constitutes Multiculturalism? Divergent Perspectives

This is the last of three chapters in which I present an empirical analysis of opinion discourses in two Central Canadian English-language mainstream newspapers, the *Globe and Mail* and the *Toronto Star* in the 1990s. For information on the study's rationale, the sampling method, an overview of the general content, and the limitations of the newspaper sample, see Chapter 6. The same chapter develops the analytical model of pluralism as a set of triangular relations, which is used in all three chapters to interpret the empirical material.

By situating the construction of a 'multicultural we' within triangular relations of 'us,' 'others,' and 'them,' the analysis in this book emphasizes the shifting and multiple dimensions that underscore representations of 'who we are and/or want to be.' It focuses on the construction of pluralist alliances, rather than on identifying strategies of othering, which are inherent to binary us/them relations. Chapter 7, examines how shifting contrasts with 'them' impact on the representation of diversity within the multicultural nation. Chapter 8 investigates how the discursive logics related to multinationalism (and its varying degrees of conflict and agreement) influence the (de)legitimization of multiculturalism as a normative framework for immigrant integration and national identity.

The present chapter explores a third angle. The analysis concentrates on the construction of a 'multicultural we' not by comparison, but through constitution 'from within.' What is at stake here is the internal dimension of the ethnic boundary and its (supposedly) multi-ethnic composition. The questions I ask are: Who/what is represented as the 'essence' of Canadianness? To what extent is this Canadianness characterized as 'multicultural'? Methodologically, the chapter highlights the last of three focal points of analysis, which have been described in Chapter 6. Further details will be provided in the section below.[1]

As in the previous empirical chapters, I will remind the reader of the literature and context that this particular chapter is responding to. Details are provided in Chapters 2, 3 and 6. I will then present the find-ings of the empirical study in a way that speaks to the identified gaps in the literature and the questions raised by them. Third, I will sum-marize my findings and discuss how this particular analysis adds yet another piece to our understanding of the multicultural transformation of national identity.

Context

Canada's media are required by law to represent the country's eth-nic and cultural diversity. Section 3 of the Canadian Broadcasting Act states that programming and employment opportunities should 'serve [...] and reflect [...] the linguistic duality and multicultural and multiracial nature of Canadian society and the special place of aboriginal peoples within that society' (Canada, 1991). Despite these provisions, a review of the scholarly literature reveals widespread discontent. To put it with Dunn and Mahtani: 'One would anticipate that media portrayal of ethnic minorities would be less disparaging within a society defined as multicultural. However, media research-ers indicate the opposite is occurring' (Dunn and Mahtani, 2001: 6). In fact, 'media representations of minorities border on the questionable at best, reprehensible at worst' (Fleras and Kunz, 2001: vii).

The systematic under- and misrepresentation of ethnic minorities in the mass media (Mahtani, 2001) is attributed to the fact that Canada's traditional sociocultural elites have maintained substantive control over key institutions. According to the critics, Canadians of French and British descent continue to decide over content and form of media dis-courses. They are therefore in a position to reinterpret public symbols in their own favour (Royal Commission on Newspapers, 1981; Karim, 1993: 202). For Henry and Tator, 'the tremendous concentration of media ownership among the White male corporate elite, most of whom hold conservative or neoconservative values, represents a serious threat to a pluralistic democratic state' (2002: 39). These authors maintain that the mainstream media's trivialization, culturalization, and depoliticization of minority concerns and contributions to Canadian society influence the attitudes of both those who see themselves as 'mainstream society' and those who are depicted as 'different.'

A closer look at those who are depicted as 'different' reveals that scholarship on minority representations in the Canadian mainstream media is broadly divided into two bodies of literature. Most research is concerned with the under- and misrepresentation of Aboriginal peoples and 'visible minorities.' Here is not the place to review this literature in detail. However, four groups deserve to be mentioned, as they seem to be particularly vulnerable to racial stereotyping in the mainstream media. Researchers underline the centrality of conflict in the few existing media representations of Aboriginal peoples (Grenier, 1992; Perigoe and Lazar, 1992; Skea, 1993). They argue that portrayals of Chinese and Asian Canadians shift between the images of illegal refugees and 'boat people,' on the one hand, and wealthy entrepreneurs building 'monster houses,' on the other (Ma and Hildebrandt, 1993; Li, 1994; Hier and Greenberg, 2002; Greenberg and Hier, 2001; Greenberg, 2000). Scholarship also shows an over-representation of Blacks in news coverage on sports, crime, and, poverty (Henry et al., 2000; Henry and Tator, 2002, 2006). Since 11 September 2001, Muslims have been subjected to intense scrutiny almost everywhere in the Western world. Researchers find that associations between Islam, terrorism, and the oppression of women are particularly frequent (Bullock and Jafri, 2001; Jefferess, 2002; Jiwani and Dakroury, 2009; Karim, 1997, 2003).[2]

Considerably less scholarship deals with the under- and misrepresentation of francophones and/or Québécois in English-speaking mainstream media (Bright et al., 1999; Lacombe, 1998; Morris, 1984, 1989, 1995; Potvin, 2000a, 2000b; Robinson, 1998; Siegel, 1996). Arthur Siegel (1996) maintains that Canadians live in two hermetically sealed media worlds – one English-speaking, the other French-speaking – which cover the same issues from divergent and often ethnocentric perspectives. The few studies on representations of francophone Quebec within the English-speaking print media – particularly those concentrating on the 1990s – have been reviewed earlier in this book (Chapters, 2, 3, and 7). In addition to those accounts, it has been observed that the English-language news media tend to frame minority language rights as a 'Quebec issue.' Concerns of the anglophone (and allophone) community in Quebec have accordingly taken centre stage in the Canadian English-language media while similar complaints made by francophone communities in the rest of Canada are regularly downplayed (Hacket and Gruneau, 2000: 173–5). Furthermore, in the *Globe and Mail*'s op-ed pages Canadian federalism is said to gain increasingly pan-Canadian nationalist overtones. Sylvie Lacombe argues that in the rest of Canada sympathy for Quebec's struggle for sovereignty is declining and that the notion of 'letting Quebec go' is no longer limited, like it was before, to Canada's Western provinces (Lacombe, 2007: 1).

By and large, there are two difficulties or flaws with these bodies of literature. First, as Mahtani (2001) observes, many of the recent studies on media/minority relations in Canada follow Teun van Dijk's structuralist take on media reporting (1991), which is concerned with both surface representations and underlying meanings. While this approach allows us to analyse negative and positive descriptions of a group within a document or text, it inadvertently reinforces the binaries of us/them that it helps to discover. As argued in Chapter 6, many approaches in Critical Discourse Analysis (CDA) examine how images of 'us' and 'them' are (re)produced in dominant discourse. They concentrate on in-group/out-group relations, but rarely account for multiple groups and their (constantly changing and highly contextual) relations. Furthermore, many authors locate the (main) dividing line between the white majority, on the one hand, and racialized Canadians, on the other. As a consequence, there are few comparisons between (racialized) minority group representations (e.g., are some groups more included/ excluded than others?), and scholarship on media/minority relations almost never includes linguistic minorities, such as francophones.

Second, a similar reproach can be made to the studies that fall within the realm of, broadly speaking, 'French/English relations' and their representations in the media. Here, scholars point to the othering of francophones – particularly Québécois nationalists – in relation to an amalgamated 'rest of Canada.' Concentrating purely on the dualism between Canada's so-called founding nations and its linguistic and/ or political expressions, these studies rarely pay attention to the larger dynamics of Canadian pluralism, which includes Aboriginal peoples, ethnic groups, and racialized minorities.

In sum, there is a persistent gap between the two bodies of literature. While scholars in both camps draw our attention to very important cleavages in Canadian society, it would be desirable to combine these perspectives and show how these dividing lines may reinforce or, in some instances, potentially ease each other. To put it bluntly, while, according to some authors, the English-speaking mainstream media appear to be profoundly racist, according to others, they seem to be fundamentally opposed to the French fact, specifically to anything that has to do with Quebec's political quest for independence.

If these accounts are correct, then the question emerges whether there is any chance at all that a 'multicultural we' is constructed in the Central Canadian newspaper discourses examined in this study. Should the answer be an unexpected Yes, we can further wonder whether this 'multicultural we' only serves as a means of co-opting immigrants into an English Canadian project of society – either for the sake of ethnic categorization and the perpetuation of white supremacy (as the first perspective implies) or (as the second view suggests) with the aim to marginalize Quebec linguistically and/or politically?

In Chapter 6, I have already hinted at the fact that the mainstream media should not be interpreted as monolithic institutions. Even within a relatively small sample of opinion pieces from two Central Canadian newspapers collected over a period of ten years, I discerned a variety of voices, which I then categorized as three dominant perspectives on multiculturalism and national identity. To establish this categorization, I first heuristically identified each article's discursive 'endpoint' or 'goal' (Gergen, 2001). I then refined this classification by means of a rigorous discursive analysis of the prevailing triangular relations within the newspaper texts.

A quick reminder may be helpful. Roughly 40 per cent of the articles view pluralism as harmful to Canadian nationhood. In principle, discourses classified as 'republican' aim to reduce both national dualism and multiculturalism. Another 40 per cent of the articles view a 'pluralist compromise' as characteristic of Canadian nationhood. This 'liberalist-pluralist' perspective promotes the maintenance of the status quo of current multicultural *and* multinational arrangements. Less than 20 per cent of the collected articles argue that Canada is constituted through ethnic diversity that is related to (recent) immigration. This 'liberal-multiculturalist' perspective was only identified in *Toronto Star* articles. It claims that the current arrangements are insufficient, and that multiculturalism's role within Canadian identity must be extended.

These diverging discourses and their unequal distribution in the two newspapers suggest that there is no uniform representation of the relationship between multiculturalism and Canadian national identity. Even within this study's relatively narrow focus on two newspapers from Central Canada, we have to differentiate between the different ways in which a 'multicultural we' may or may not be constituted from within the 'ethnic boundary.' In other words, there are at least three perspectives on who/what constitutes the essence of Canadianness. And in each case, we have to critically examine if and to what extent this Canadianness is characterized as 'multicultural.' The focal point of analysis (indicated in bold) is thus the cultural/ideological 'content' of the 'multicultural we' and the group(s) identified as 'us.'

$$\text{us} + \text{others}_{1-n} = \textbf{multicultural we} \neq \text{them}_{1-n}$$

In the following section, I will examine the three majority perspectives in more detail. For each perspective, I will trace the underlying 'ideal-type' by asking the following two questions: What is the ideological essence of the discourse? And: Who is 'we'? Since ideological orientations are always adapted to specific circumstances and changing contexts, I will also discuss each perspective's 'strategic variations.' Finally, in keeping with this book's core questions, I will trace the symbolic role attributed to 'the French fact'/Quebec. The ways in which these four dimensions interrelate vary for each perspective.

Analysis

Discourses Adopting a Republican Perspective

The type of discourse that I identify as 'republican' oscillates between seemingly neutral Canadian patriotism and explicitly English Canadian nationalism. On the one hand, it seems to be 'a better, finer, nobler thing to love Canada – not the land or the people, but the idea – than to seek only dumb contentment of huddling together with our own kind' (G-1995-1023). In many republican discourses, a deliberate attempt is made to abstract from the cultural characteristics of (English) Canada. Here, the nation becomes merely the 'largest act of empathy of which we are yet capable' (G-1995-1023). On the other hand, these discourses are never too far away from the conviction that 'the glue that is holding Canada together [...] is the culture and the values of English Canadians' (T-1993-0307). This inherent ambiguity reminds us of the proximity in practice, if not in theory, between a republican 'civic' understanding of nationhood and a culturally motivated 'ethnic' interpretation of the nation (see Chapter 5). In both sub-currents of the republican perspective, national unity is viewed as the quintessential guarantor of a superior – 'most tolerant, most liberal and least racist' (T-1993-0307) – form of society, which is 'rooted neither in homogeneity nor in diversity, but in humanity' (G-1995-1023). The Canadian nation, supposedly the best possible approximation of universalism, also allows for individual emancipation: 'We have created a country in which, more nearly so than anywhere else I know of, everyone can be whatever they want to be' (T-1993-0307).

The representation of Canadian nationhood as being primarily constituted through British or English Canadian culture and institutions produces fears about fragmentation and disintegration. The public recognition of ethnocultural diversity is seen as undermining social cohesion and as ultimately leading to the disintegration of the Canadian nation, which would be detrimental to all members of society, the majority and minorities alike. Indeed, in the republican discourses of the newspaper sample, any type of 'groupism' – whether it comes in the form of Québécois nationalism or the recognition of ethnic group identities through multiculturalism – is rejected. For the republican perspective, in its purest form, the 'secessionists in Quebec [...] do not represent the only danger' of national disintegration (G-1996-0701). Rather, this perspective postulates 'a broad coalition' among minority groups where Québécois 'separatists' 'make tacit common cause with the cries of interest groups, the demands of victims and the carping of the regions' (G-1996-0701). In other words, the discourses of the republican perspective in the newspaper sample are as equally opposed to special status for Quebec as to multiculturalism as an official policy and national ideology.

Within this representation of Canada, English Canadians are never viewed as 'different' or located at the margins of the Canadian nation. On the contrary, in its ideal-typical form, the republican perspective constructs an opposition between *ideal citizens,* explicitly or implicitly identified as white anglophone British Canadians, and an undifferentiated marginalized *rest.* In fact, the centre of the Canadian majority, which does not participate in the 'broad coalition against the very notion of common interest' (G-1994-0513) is comprised of uncomplaining male WASPs: 'everyone else is a victim' (T-1993-0307). Canada is here characterized by unmarked whiteness: 'For about three decades, beginning with the accusations of having been unfair to *francophones,* and on down to today's charge of practicing "systemic racism," WASPs have [unjustifiably] been identified as the sole source of all of Canada's social and political ills' (T-1993-0307).

Furthermore, the centre of the English Canadian nation is located in Ontario, which is said to be the only province that does not complain and claim regional particularity (G-1997-0605). The geographical, emotional, and irrational boundaries of 'regions' are here opposed to the rational, political delimitations of 'provinces' – attributes which are said to reflect the character of the inhabitants. These undertones remind us of the fact that the discourses of the sample are produced for and from Central Canada, the country's centre of political power.

In its ideal-typical form, the 'Canadian we' identified in the republican perspective is thus highly ethnocentric and opposed to any sort of group-based pluralist arrangements. Nevertheless, in times of distress, this perspective also accommodates strategic alliances between *ideal citizens* ('us') and varying segments of *the rest* ('others' and 'them'). Two variations can be observed:

In some cases, ethnic minorities' multicultural demands are rejected with reference to the 'Canadian tradition,' which includes francophones and First Nations together with English Canadians (and white Europeans who assimilate into this culture). Ethnic minorities, by contrast, are identified as 'them.' In other cases, Québécois aspirations of independent nationhood are said to be realizable only at the expense of English Canada's open, tolerant or even 'multicultural' society, which then includes ethnic minorities and First Nations along with English Canadians (and those accepting the primacy of Canadian nationhood). I will briefly give examples of the two variations. Let me start with the following quotation:

> Our multiculturalism may be turning into multinationalism. It hasn't happened yet [...] But more and more Canadians care more passionately about events in their 'home' country than in their 'adopted' one [...] A growing number of Canadians simply haven't been here long enough to have learned about Canada. As our ethnic communities expand in size and coherence, it becomes easier for individuals to live in the country while remaining outsiders, emotionally and psychically. *Most will become North Americans all right, or their children will, since the continental culture is so magnetic. But this isn't the same as their becoming Canadian in the sense of identifying with our history, our unique struggles and challenges.* (T-1993-0228, my emphasis)

Here, ethnic minorities are cast as outsiders through the construction of an opposition between those who 'haven't been here long enough to have learned about Canada' and those who are 'naturally' or have become 'Canadian in the sense of identifying with *our* history, *our* unique struggles and challenges.' Elsewhere, the columnist explains that 'what has for so long defined Canada' includes 'French-English relations' and the 'problems of native peoples' (T-1993-0131). Implicitly or explicitly,

Quebec and First Nations are here 'contingent insiders' whose presence is included within 'the Canadian tradition,' even if the acknowledgment of *their* 'unique struggles and challenges' remains at its margins. Within this logic, 'the 1867 architects, out of necessity, preserved what was already in place. Without the minority-education [and other dualist] guarantees – couched in religious terms but in reality referring to the French and English – there would have been no Confederation, no Canada' (G-1996-1122; my emphasis). Dualism is perceived as a historical liability which cannot be avoided but which must certainly not be 'extended' to other groups who may 'expand in size and coherence' and then make similar demands as francophones in Quebec.[3]

In the sample of newspaper discourses under investigation, the second variation of the republican perspective was more frequent. Particularly since the mid-1990s, ethnic minorities are attributed the position of conditional insiders, since they appear less 'deviant' if compared with an ethnically closed, French-speaking, 'separatist' Quebec. Under these circumstances, and within a climate of international praise for Canadian multiculturalism (Fontaine, 1995; Rotte, 2002), the republican perspective no longer opposes the notion of a multicultural society as such, but portrays it as being constituted through British culture and institutions: 'Multiculturalism [. . .] is a unique, English Canadian invention. It exists nowhere else in the world, including in *Quebec* [. . .] But this kind of Canada can only exist – outside of *Quebec* – within the template provided by the values and culture of English Canada. Also, by its sense of being heir to an historical continuum that stretches back to the Loyalists and their decision to come north to try to create a radically different kind of North America [. . .] If those qualities, and sense of historical purpose, go, everything goes' (T-1993-0307, my emphasis).

While this vision of society seems more inclusive than the previously described English Canadian ethnocentrism, it remains a strongly patronizing perspective of the 'multicultural we.' English Canadian *Gemeinschaft* constitutes here the multicultural *Gesellschaft*, which is then able to integrate limited expressions of other group-based identities. Lip services such as the following reveal the embedded inequality within this construction of 'multiculturalism': 'The injunction of our multiculturalism law – that "there is no such thing as an official culture" – gives our own "old stock," the Anglo-Celts, no greater claim to "own" the country than a Somali refugee just off the boat' (T-1993-0131). Constructing refugees as 'boat people' shows little respect for their individual and/or collective histories (Somali refugees in the mid-1990s did not come to Canada by boat). It confirms Eva Mackey's (1999) observation that English Canadians are still viewed as the representatives of Canadian culture in relation to which all other cultures are constructed as constituting the 'multicultural.' Furthermore, this vision of decorative 'multiculturalism' derives much of its constitutive force from contrast: 'Canada today is [. . .] composed of two quite dif- ferent kinds of societies – an ethnic, European-style, nation in Quebec, and a "rest of Canada" that is well on the way to becoming a multiethnic World Nation' (T-1993-0131).

Within the discourses of the republican perspective, Quebec not only serves as a contrast but also as a negative example. While globalization and non-Western immigrants who 'live in the country while remaining outsiders, emotionally and psychically' are often portrayed as Canada's most important challenge in the future, 'dualism' has acquired a strong symbolism. In some cases, portraying francophone Quebec as the incarnation of anti-Canadianism, republican discourses construct a causal link between the 'very nature of Canada – founded as an explicit partnership between two distinct peoples' (G-1994-0513) – and increasing national disintegration (see Chapter 8). The presence of Quebec is portrayed as the *starting point* for unavoidable fragmentation, which spreads 'like a contagion' by shifting loyalties 'to region and race' (G-1997-0701). In other cases, the reference to Quebec's growing influence and power (and English Canadians' 'decline') is used to reject minorities' claims for multiculturalism. In these cases, Québécois nationalism is constructed as a 'precedent' (T-1993-0228) of how 'multiculturalism may be turning into multinationalism' (see Chapter 7).

Concluding from the representations of Quebec as an incarnation of alienation and disintegration, one should assume that the discourses of the republican perspective would wholeheartedly embrace a Canada without Quebec. Dualism would then neither hinder English Canadian community closure vis-à-vis the United States nor 'contaminate' immigrants, 'ethnic Canadians,' regions, and 'interest groups' by initiating demands for rights and recognition. Paradoxically, in the sample of newspaper discourses, only few columnists insist that 'there is life after and apart from Quebec and we could survive their independence a good deal more effortlessly than Quebec itself could' (T-1997-0131). In general, the discourses are characterized by the fear that Canada could 'be torn apart and, very possibly, should Quebec actually leave, be scattered to the global winds' (T-1995-0913).

For a perspective that views English Canadian culture and values as Canada's 'national glue,' the fear about Quebec's separation comes as a surprise. Why is Quebec's presence important for a Canadian nation defined in English Canadian terms? Three arguments can be found in the newspaper sample: 'Quebec's separation' would reduce Canada's reputation in the world. It 'would destroy our own civil society and, therefore, our ability to continue to help other societies become more civil' (T-1995-0913). It would also divide Canada geographically: 'Thus, should the Cree of Nouveau Quebec vote to separate, as they may well do, Canadians would welcome them back into Confederation because, to our great psychic self-interest, this curious country would once again stretch from sea to sea' (T-1994-0511). Furthermore, Quebec's separation would reveal the cleavages within the rest of Canada: 'The notion of a "rest of Canada" is quite unlikely. There will more likely be independent options for British Columbia, Alberta and Ontario, along with a new Republic of Quebec' (T-1994-0508).

In sum, the construction of Canadianness in the discourses of the republican perspective comes closest to traditional representations of homogeneous nationhood. Three main strategies are employed to construct Britishness as irreplaceable and to position it at the centre of Canadian society.[4] First, English Canadian cultural particularity is downplayed, so that Britishness becomes the condition of shared humanity; second, it is suggested that Britishness constitutes an open and possibly 'multicultural' society; third, minorities are denied the society-constituting capacities that are attributed to English Canadians.

Relying on the construction of a Canadian essence to constitute both society and its unity renders the relationship between Canadianness and diversity inherently problematic. Representations of Canadianness as being rooted in Britishness therefore require the limitation and reduction of ethnic plurality and pluralism, which are both seen as posing a threat to social cohesion and unified nationhood. In the republican discourses from the *Globe and Mail* and the *Toronto Star*, 'diversity' is often portrayed in broad and general terms, referring not only to Quebec, First Nations, and immigrant-origin ethnic groups, but also to provinces, regions, and 'interest groups,' such as women, and 'Westerners' from the Prairie provinces who, although predominantly English-speaking, are often denied the status of intrinsic Canadianness (G-1997-0605). Although none of the articles in the corpus argues openly for ethnic homogeneity and Anglo-conformity, Canada's centre (i.e., British culture, institutions, and ideology) is represented as being in constant danger of erosion. This fear of fragmentation leads to jealousy over the United States' strong national identity.

Discourses Adopting a Liberal-Pluralist Perspective

In the newspaper sample under investigation, the republican perspective competes with other types of discourses that can be defined as liberal-pluralist. These discourses celebrate (limited amounts of) ethnic diversity and aim to maintain the status quo of pluralism in Canada. For these discourses, the 'just balance' between Canadian nationhood, special status for Quebec, self-government rights for First Nations, and multiculturalism has been established. The status quo refers to a situation where Quebec de facto enjoys more rights and recognition than ethnic groups, even though its status as a 'distinct society' is not constitutionally recognized. Although the failure to include Quebec within the Canadian Constitution is regretted within this perspective, in the discourses of the sample, no strong arguments are brought forth in favour of granting Quebec the political and economic autonomy it desires.

Rather than identifying a particular group or cultural quality (such as Britishness) as the guarantor of 'unity in diversity,' in the liberal-pluralist perspective *compromise* is portrayed as Canada's constitutive essence. In principal, this compromise involves the *active* collaboration of different types of ethnic/national groups. In other words, the multicultural *Gesellschaft* is supposed to be constructed through multiple and normatively equal forms of *Gemeinschaft*. Built upon the stylization of compromise, within this discourse, integrated ethnic diversity is viewed as intrinsically Canadian, while the failure to achieve compromise is portrayed as undermining the very idea of Canadianness. As a consequence, attempts to unsettle current arrangements are viewed with suspicion.

Practically, however, ethnic/national minorities are not included on equal terms within the social norm. Normative positions are rooted in socially constituted ethnic/national groups, which are factually unequal. The liberal-pluralist perspective reflects the power inequalities that still persist in Canadian society, even though it strives to mitigate and downplay them. Quebec, First Nations, and ethnic groups are represented as having less agency and being closer to irrational, ethnic forms of *Gemeinschaft* than the English Canadian majority. Compared to the dominant representations in the republican perspective, within liberal-pluralist discourses the division between 'us' and 'others' is a fine line. Because the promoted vision of Canada as a pluralist nation requires at least two parties (in compromise) to be situated within the (multi)ethnic boundary, modestly 'different' insiders ('others') enjoy a privileged position. Nevertheless, even within the liberal-pluralist perspective, English Canadians are never positioned as *outsiders* to the Canadian nation. They remain at the core of Canadianness, even though they are not *imagined* as being there alone.

This imagination of egalitarian pluralist compromise within Canada is created through diverse discursive strategies. The most important one is contrast. In Chapter 7, I discussed how the imaginary of the multicultural nation is created through shifting oppositions with assumed assimilationism (attributed to the United States) and assumed ethnocentrism (attributed to Quebec). A second strategy of staging successful pluralism involves the relegation of ethnic conflict and inequality to the past. In Chapter 8, I argued that Canada's trajectory as a nation is often represented as an ongoing evolution of increasing diversity and tolerance. Usually, this evolution involves a transition from (sometimes 'fractious, quarrelsome') dualism to relatively integrated, peaceful multiculturalism (see, e.g., G-1994-0914, G-1999-0701). In these discourses, constituting, contrasting otherness is no longer situated outside the boundaries of the nation, but rather projected upon 'our' racist past:[5] *'Prior to the 1960s, we* expected immigrants to assimilate; indeed, *we* tried to keep out any groups seen as incapable of assimilation. *Now* that means learning one or both official languages and adopting liberal democratic values; *once it also meant* becoming indistinguishable from native-born citizens in their style of speech, clothes, diet, political views, work habits, family size and leisure activities. [...] *We* repudiated this approach in 1971, when Canada became the first country to adopt a federal multiculturalism policy' (G-2000-1227, my emphasis).

The representation of Canadian diversity in the quotation above views pluralism as a linear evolution: past injustices have been rectified, and Canada is now travelling progressively towards more and more inclusiveness. Minorities' struggles and efforts in achieving equal rights without assimilation are here downplayed. Indeed, within the discourses of the liberal-pluralist perspective, multicultural rights tend to be 'given to *them* by an Invisible Self group,' as Richard Day (2000: 215–16) claims. Minorities are still at the receiving end of social action, whereas unmarked Canadians 'had to continually adapt and innovate to meet the challenge of accommodating diversity while respecting individual rights and maintaining stable political institutions' (G-2000-1227). That these institutions are thoroughly British, Protestant, and male-dominated seems to be entirely 'forgotten.'

Representations of Canada's proliferation of diversity (and diversity accommodation) also tend to neglect that dualism was 'enriched' rather than supplemented by multiculturalism. While both original 'founding nations' still enjoy substantial collective rights – far more than ethnic minorities – only Quebec's are cast as 'minority rights' and carefully distinguished from those 'granted to' Aboriginal peoples and immigrant minorities. Minority rights are here portrayed as static, 'normal' categories outside the realm of negotiation and power relations. This strategy describes the simultaneous construction of diversity and its containment through classification (as claimed by many anti-foundationalist approaches; cf. Day, 2000; Bannerji, 2000; discussed in Chapter 3).

Yet another frequent strategy of portraying Canadian diversity in harmonious terms is the depolitization and culturalization of 'difference.' Pluralism – the term is rarely used in these representations – becomes here a multicultural, multiracial 'heaven on earth':

> My neighbourhood [in Toronto] has a little bit of everyone from everywhere. The same block on my street has million-dollar mansions and subsidized apartments. You can walk to Thai food, sushi, Italian, and superior baguettes [. . .] the boardwalk at the bottom of my street [. . .] is the crossroads of the world. On Canada Day, it looks like a poster for multinational harmony. There are nearly naked people playing volleyball on the sand, and three-generation clans who come to spend the day strolling and picnicking and napping. Along the boardwalk, the teenage boys and girls hold hands and kiss, defying all the lines of culture and colour [. . .] Muslim women in their head coverings and ankle-length skirts walk their thoroughly Canadian children to school. Sometimes, there is a woman shrouded in a *burka,* walking three steps behind her husband. A few years from now, their kids will be sneaking down to the boardwalk on a summer weekend to show their bellybuttons. (G-2001-0701)

In the quotation above, Toronto in the year 2001 is described as a place without class barriers and ethnic segregation; different forms of 'diversity' contribute to the charm and the richness of life in the city: there is plenty of exotic food; half-naked people move playfully in the sun; a multiplicity of cultures, sexes, and generations render life interesting; the rich and the poor live peacefully next to each other. While the columnist seems to be committed to multicultural food and intercultural/interracial hybridity, we can also trace a hidden assumption of assimilation: 'Muslim women in their head coverings and ankle-length skirts' are opposed to 'their thoroughly Canadian children.' Why are *burka*-wearing Muslim women not considered 'Canadian'? What will happen if these women's children do not adhere to 'Canadian' 'mainstream' values ('show their bellybuttons')?[6] This type of implicit assumption is typical for discourses that cast ethnic diversity in terms of folklore: they depoliticize ethnic group membership and avoid addressing questions of inequality and discrimination. This way it becomes possible to represent national and ethnic group relations in Canada as relatively integrated 'diversity' that does not disrupt the inherent 'unity' of the nation.

In sum, conflict and unequal relations between English Canadians and other ethnonational groups still persist within the liberal-pluralist perspective, even though they are mitigated. The 'multicultural we' only seemingly includes all participants of the pluralist compromise on supposedly equal terms. Furthermore, the compromise between 'us' and 'others' (in lower case) is reinforced through the construction of 'them.' Two strategic variations can be identified for this perspective. The first situates the 'French fact' and the recognition of Quebec closer to the centre than other forms of diversity and diversity accommodation. The second variation, on the contrary, cements the multicultural alliance between English Canadians and ethnic groups by opposing it to Québécois 'ethnic nationalism' and 'separatism.' Both strategies have been discussed in Chapter 7. Here, I will only briefly discuss how, within liberal-pluralist discourses, representations of Quebec provide a frame for the integration of ethnocultural diversity.

On the one hand, the British and the French still play the major roles within the Canadian founding myth, even though narratives also stress the presence of Aboriginal peoples and other ethnic groups. As discussed in Chapter 8, ideologically and discursively, dualism provides a matrix into which multiculturalism is integrated as a 'natural extension' (G-1999-0701) rather than a forced break with tradition. Within these discourses, Quebec is located at the centre of Canadianness. Ethnic minorities (as well as English Canadians) are urged to respect this position – even only out of self-interest – since, within this logic, only a united Canada can assure their cultural protection:

What would *the world* have lost [if Quebec had separated]? The hope that different peoples with different religions, cultures and languages can find in each other not just tolerance, not even just respect, but *part of who they are*. For 350 years, aboriginal peoples, French Canadians, English Canadians and people from every quarter of the globe *have together made a country* that *at its finest moments* defines itself through its diversity. *Were it not for English or* [sic] *French together*, such moments would not have been imaginable *on the continent*. If Canada aspires to be a place where religions, cultures, languages intersect, inform each other and live together, Quebec's presence is at the very heart of it all. (T-1995-1218, my emphasis)

In this quotation, pluralist compromise formally involves equally (in historical chronology) 'aboriginal peoples, French Canadians, English Canadians and people from every quarter of the globe.' At the same time, the contributions of 'English [and] French together' are especially underlined. Their collaboration constitutes Canada and its uniqueness not only 'on the continent' (i.e., vis-à-vis the United States) but also in 'the world.' This ambiguity is characteristic of the liberal-pluralist perspective which is always concerned about striking a balance between unity and diversity, and therefore also reluctant to grant ethnic minorities full equality in terms of structural group rights. While English Canadians' group rights often remain unspecified in liberal-pluralist discourses, the minority rights of Aboriginal peoples and, particularly, Quebec receive more attention. In the passage above, 'Quebec's presence is at the very heart of it all.' In comparison with the republican perspective, this is a fundamental difference, because in the liberal-pluralist perspective it is not English or French Canadians' cultural properties that constitute Canadianness but the compromise struck between them. Canada is here 'constituted by the diversity of people in its midst,' and among those, 'the people of Quebec [. . .] make possible who we all are' (T-1995-1218). In these quotations, the ambiguities between unity and diversity, as well as between individuals and groups are evident. Ultimately, these ambiguities are the reason why certain expressions of 'difference' cannot be tolerated, and why, in the liberal-pluralist perspective, references to Quebec not only constitute Canadian pluralism but also define its limits: While separatism fails to cherish the pluralist compromise that constitutes Canadianness, ethnic nationalism is rejected for advocating an 'anti-liberal' culture of ethnic homogeneity, intolerance, and disrespect for individual rights (Cook, 1995; Hartney, 1995; Ignatieff, 1994).[7]

In sum, within the liberal-pluralist perspective, dualism serves as a symbol of both Canada's historical constitution as a nation and its potential death as a nation. The 'dualist frame' that is constructed around tolerable expressions of ethnocultural difference corresponds to what Homi Bhabha has called 'an attempt both to respond to and to control the dynamic process of the articulation of cultural difference, administering a *consensus* based on a norm that propagates cultural diversity' (Bhabha, 1990c: 208, original emphasis). The 'dualist frame' operates in two directions. It prescribes ethnic groups what they may and may not do (e.g., demand the status of minority nations), and it informs Quebec about the limits of national self-government rights.

Discourses Adopting a Liberal-Multiculturalist Perspective

In the sample of newspaper discourses, the republican and liberal-pluralist perspectives are dominant with just over 40 per cent of articles each. These discourses are spread evenly over the ten-year period from 1992 to 2001 and have been identified within both newspapers. While the two dominant perspectives are thus able to impose their logic upon the discussion of nationhood and pluralism in the media and, presumably, considerable segments of the public space, they also keep each other at bay. This is why the emergence of a third perspective, towards the late 1990s, is important – even though, in the newspaper sample, this perspective is not very significant in quantitative terms.

Roughly 15 per cent of the newspaper articles in the sample pursue the goal of extending multiculturalism in Canada. These discourses oppose and reject both English Canadian mono-culturalism and national dualism. They contend that the status quo of diversity accommodation in Canada is insufficient. While the vision of Canada as an egalitarian 'unity in diversity' finds support in discourses that argue from a liberal-multiculturalist perspective, this ideal is portrayed as not yet been achieved. Rather, since immigrants, non-French, non-English 'ethnic Canadians' of immigrant background, and 'visible minorities' are viewed as still being marginalized in the mainstream societies of English Canada and Quebec, more public recognition of immigration-induced ethnic diversity is demanded.[8] In fact, if the liberal-pluralist perspective fetishizes 'pluralist compromise' as the essence of Canadianness, the liberal-multiculturalist perspective highlights ethnic diversity and its recognition in the public space. Here, liberal (and thus highly individualist) 'multiculturality' as such, rather than carefully manufactured agreements between groups, is represented as the essence of Canadian nationhood.

While voices for and from multicultural minorities within the mainstream press should not come as a surprise in an officially multicultural country, their presence seems to be a fairly recent phenomenon, at least if one judges from discussions in the academic literature. It seems thus telling that, within the sample of newspaper discourses, the liberal-multiculturalist perspective has only been identified in articles from the *Toronto Star*. In the sample, the portrayed 'us' in these discourses claims to represent 'immigrants and visible minorities in every sphere of Canadian society in every part of the country' (T-2001-0424). This 'majority of Canadians' is said to not even want to hear about 'nonsense political problems' such as 'Quebec sovereignty and separation' because 'our whole society is advancing toward a better and united Canada' (T-2001-0424). These discourses seem to reflect the confidence and social standing of a highly educated multicultural urban elite: 'We want more educated and wealthy immigrants to come to Canada. We do not take anymore the "wretched refuse" (to quote from the Statue of Liberty). Are they going to embrace wholeheartedly the British and French culture in Canada or would they want to maintain some of their culture and traditions? The "wretched refuse" would have happily embraced biculturalism, lock, stock and barrel' (T-1995-0123).

Furthermore, it is argued that 'if minorities become more accepted in Canadian society [...] employment equity policies in the long run will become superfluous' (T-1995-0123). The 'newer immigrants' do not seem to need the support of their 'ethnic communities' any longer. Rather, they underline the importance of 'let[ting] *each Canadian* speak the language of *his or her choice* and live and work in peace and tranquility with each other in *one new nation* made up of people with different cultures and backgrounds' (T-2001-0424, my emphasis). As mentioned in Chapter 8, only very few discourses in the sample actually claim group rights (e.g., T-1992-1104, T-1995-0811). Much more common are individualist rejections of being treated as 'second-class citizens': 'Newcomers are [said to be] guests in the Canadian house and had better behave. This is obviously still true of refugees. But they constitute barely one-eighth of our annual intake of 200,000 immigrants. For most others, especially the well-educated and skilled in high-tech and information technology, *coming to Canada is a contract; they trade their talents for membership in a great nation*' (T-2000-1105, my emphasis).

The quotation above underlines the trend towards an increasingly liberal conception of 'multicultural nation building.' It also reminds us of the fact that that the media sample is constituted out of majority discourses: While well-educated immigrants may 'trade their talents for membership in a great nation,' unskilled refugees remain 'guests' and 'had better behave.' In the context of globalization, where states compete for attracting highly skilled 'designer immigrants' (Simmons, 2010), the dividing line presented in the mainstream media is no longer one between established groups and newcomers, but rather between those who can and those who cannot 'pay' for their membership in the nation.

Despite the fact that these urban discourses in favour of multiculturalism seem to be wholeheartedly 'buying into' the ideology of 'selling diversity' (Abu-Laban and Gabriel, 2002), they remain *Toronto Star* discourses in so far as they reject strong neo-liberal tendencies, which are stereotyped as 'creeping Americanization' (T-1998-0701). Thereby, the 'traditional' Canadian 'we' is reaffirmed:

America remains transfixed by white-black relations – a legacy of slavery. Lately, it has also been preoccupied with its growing Hispanic population. It has little time for its rich diversity, pretending that its melting-pot model is doing its alchemy, when it's clearly not. Americans are as proud of their hyphens as multicultural Canadians, and want their cultural, ethnic, religious and other identities acknowledged. Britain's integration of immigrants is hampered by its colonial attitudes and still strong class divisions. Germany and France continue to keep millions of Turks and others as second-class citizens in ghettoes that are ticking time bombs. Canada's successful transition to a confident, cosmopolitan society is a tribute to our temperament – peaceful, egalitarian – and sound policies. (T-1998-0614)

This quotation demonstrates how, within discourses of the liberal-multiculturalist perspective, multicultural Canada's uniqueness is contrasted to United States – portrayed as assimilationist – and several European countries – represented as ethnically exclusionary. Like in the two dominant perspectives, Canada is also described as having left its old (ethnocentric) self behind. It is portrayed as successfully constituting itself as a 'confident, cosmopolitan society.' Furthermore, within the liberal-multiculturalist perspective, 'multicultural Canadians' can easily be proud of both 'their hyphens' and their Canadian heritage of 'peace, order, and good government,' which has here been disguised as 'peaceful, egalitarian temperament' and 'sound policies.' Although 'evidence is mounting that unemployment levels among newer immigrants and Canadian-born visible minorities are very high' (T-1998-0614), within the liberal-multiculturalist discourses of the sample, the notion of racism within Canada is largely avoided (Henry et al., 2000; Henry and Tator, 2006). As such, these discourses do not radically contradict the republican and liberal-pluralist perspectives. Rather, they respond and reproduce these dominant discourses while still adding a new dimension, which is best described as a constant push towards defining Canadianness in the 'multicultural' terms of a highly diverse urban 'immigrant' population.

In principle, the liberal-multiculturalist perspective insists that Canada was never constituted by a single group. It argues for the equality of ethnic minorities within the Canadian nation by emphasizing the contributions of ethnic minorities and immigrants. In some instances, within these discourses, one finds attempts of constructing minority coalitions between ethnic minorities and francophone Québécois. As argued in Chapter 8, in these cases, 'the Quebec issue' is portrayed as 'a wake-up call for all Canadians' (T-1995-1016) and as 'just one of the ongoing unsettled questions about how we live together in this land called Canada' (T-1995-0829). After all, liberal-multiculturalist claims making takes place in the context of a 'dual majority' (Anctil, 1984), and Quebec, in terms of political power and clout, has been spearheading minority quests for recognition. In Chapter 8, I therefore argued that multicultural claims in Canada have traditionally followed the logic of 'ethnic minorities deserve rights too.'

Despite the attempts to construct parallels between French Canadians/ Québécois and (other) ethnic groups, francophones' aspirations to power and recognition are viewed with suspicion. Therefore, in practice, liberal-multiculturalist discourses typically oppose – rather than celebrate (as a precedent) – minority rights for Quebec. Underlining the 'ethnic' dimensions of Québécois nationalism, the liberal-multiculturalist perspective insists that Quebec's project of society is oppressive and prevents 'Quebec's minority immigrants from contributing to their society with their rich cultural heritages' (T-1998-0223). Furthermore, 'while sovereignists feel Quebec is not properly respected, their own treatment of minorities is not stellar' (T-1995-0829).

Overall, the liberal-multiculturalist perspective challenges the predominance of dualism in two ways: first, by claiming the same or similar rights for ethnic minorities as those claimed by/granted to

Canada's 'minority nations,' and second by opposing the fragmenting, separatist overtones inherent to minority nationalism and demands for 'self-government rights.' In Chapter 8, I examined how the rejection of separatism is used to support the representation of ethnic groups as being loyal to Canada. By being better Canadians than 'Québécois separatists,' ethnic groups are portrayed as having earned their place at the table. As a consequence, they can no longer be legitimately portrayed as outsiders. While the first strategy claims a similarity between diverse types of minorities, the second strategy constructs a difference between the integrative demands of immigrant minorities and the potentially 'destructive' quarrels of the established groups: 'The new diversified Canada is more generous, friendly, understanding and religiously and ethnically more tolerant than [. . .] the Canada of the past' (T-2000-0424).

'Multiculturalism' as the Smallest Common Denominator

By analysing the representations of included, conditionally included, and excluded groups, in this chapter, I have identified three different perspectives on multiculturalism. The findings of this analysis are schematically summarized in Table 9.1. The table shows the most common representations of group relations within each perspective.[9] It demonstrates the difficulty of constructing the internal dimension of the ethnic boundary from within the dominant group. In fact, even within a relatively small and homogeneous sample of English-language newspaper discourses, there is no unified vision of the relationship between Canadian identity and multiculturalism. While all three identified ideological perspectives construct a 'Canadian we' by *contrasting* the inclusion of second groups within the multicultural context to 'deviant' third parties, they do so by adopting very different – even contradicting – premises.

Table 9.1 reveals both the heterogeneity of discourses within each ideological perspective and the overlap of representations across perspectives that this heterogeneity generates. Specifically, in Row 2, the Table 9.1 reveals a new insight: the equation 'English Canadians + ethnic minorities = multicultural we ≠ Quebec' is the only constellation that can be found in all three perspectives. It is the only representation that 'makes sense' for republican, liberal-pluralist, and liberal-multiculturalist discourses. Put differently, positioning Quebec as an outsider ('them') is the location where the otherwise divergent

Table 9.1
Representations of group relations in Canada within three types of discourse

Representations of group relations		Perspectives identified within two Canadian mainstream newspapers		
we = us + others ≠ them		Republican Discourse	Liberal-Pluralist Discourse	Liberal-multiculturalist Discourse
Canadianness	≠ them	Canada = British culture & institutions	Canada = pluralist compromise	Canada = diversity
1 English Canadians + Quebec + ethnic Canadians	≠ US, 'the world'	— (Canada is constituted through Britishness)	Aboriginals, Francophones, Anglophones, and immigrants play significant part in Canadian society	(Immigrants help to build the country)
2 English Canadians + ethnic minorities	≠ Quebec	Quebec is a hindrance to English Canadian community closure; it thereby puts at risk one of the most tolerant countries in the world	1) Quebec is an essential part of Canada, but separatism is un-Canadian 2) Quebec's rationalism is ethnic; this shows us our virtues; we Canadians are for pluralism	1) Quebec oppresses immigrants in Quebec, whereas Anglo Canadians are more tolerant 2) Quebec wants to separate, immigrants don't; therefore they are better Canadians than the Québécois
3 English Canadians	≠ ethnic minorities + Quebec	1) Quebec is the starting point of disintegration (worst Other) and collaborates with 'special interest groups' 2) Immigration destroys Canada's cultural glue; the new ethnic groups will become like Quebec		

#					
4	English Canadians + Quebec	≠ ethnic minorities	Immigrants cannot ask for the same rights as Quebec because Quebec co-constitutes the country (immigrants must adapt and learn Canadian history, etc.)	Quebec deserves more rights than immigrants because Anglos and Quebec constituted the country	— (this representation of Canada is opposed)
5	Quebec + ethnic minorities	≠ English Canadians	—	—	Quebec's nationalism/ separatism is a sign that all minorities feel alienated; discriminating Anglos ≠ good Canadians
6	ethnic minorities	≠ English Canadians + Quebec	—	—	Immigrants are better Canadians because they do not import old conflicts (like the British & French); are 'carriers' of true ethnic diversity
7	Quebec	≠ English Canadians + ethnic minorities	PARADOX: English Canadians must be tough on separatism; BUT 'if Quebec goes, so goes everything': neither immigrants nor English Canadians can maintain Canadian dream without Quebec	—	—

perspectives 'meet.' The preceding analysis thereby allows us to better understand how and why the 'multicultural we' comes to be constituted as the 'smallest common denominator' of otherwise conflicting perspectives on Canadian identity. In the remainder of this section, I will summarize the findings of the preceding analysis and discuss their consequences for the multicultural transformation of Canadian identity in the 1990s.

It is important to underline that Quebec is attributed an ambiguous role within all three discourses. On the one hand, it represents Canada's *locus classicus* of 'community' (*Gemeinschaft*) and is therefore deeply associated with a collective Canadian 'we.' In republican discourses, it sometimes enjoys the 'protection' and 'tolerance' of English Canadians. In liberal-pluralist discourses, Quebec co-constitutes both Canadian nationhood and pluralism. In liberal-multiculturalist discourses, Quebec is an important predecessor in terms of minority accommodation. On the other hand, Quebec is also attributed the position of 'them' – the Other (with a capital O) to the Canadian nation. For republican discourses Québécois 'difference' always bears the risk of fragmentation. In the liberal-pluralist and the liberal-multiculturalist perspectives, Québécois 'deep diversity' as such does not have negative connotations. However, for defendants of liberal-pluralism, the prospects of separation and 'ethnic nationalism' are intolerable. In liberal-multiculturalist discourses, it is mainly the prospect of a potentially ethnically oppressive Quebec that prevents ethnic minorities from sympathizing with francophones' quest for rights and recognition.

The analysis further suggests that portraying multiculturalism positively as an extension of dualism, as practised by liberal-pluralist discourses, does not necessarily lead to its widespread acceptance. Neither of the so-called founding nations that historically agreed upon French/English dualism as a compromise is homogeneous or united. There exists a multiplicity of different voices in both English Canada and Quebec. Some of this variety, with respect to a particular segment of Central Canadian newspaper discourses, has been revealed through the empirical study presented here. In their ideal-typical forms, the three perspectives identified in the newspaper sample differ considerably. Let me briefly recapitulate the most important findings from the preceding analysis.

First, in republican discourses, Britishness constitutes the Canadian nation and, to a certain extent, also 'multiculturalism.' Republican discourses never represent English Canadians as being located outside the

Canadian nation.[10] Within republican discourses, English Canadians tend to occupy the centre position. Multiculturalism is here associated with fragmentation. In the few cases where it is not outright rejected, multiculturalism is portrayed as being constituted through British 'tolerance' and 'civility.' In their purest form, republican discourses construct an opposition between English Canadians 'and the rest' (Row 3 in Table 9.1). However, in situations of distress, there are variations of this theme and strategic alliances are constructed between English Canadians and either francophones/Québécois or ethnic minorities (Rows 2 and 4).

Second, in liberal-pluralist discourses, Canadianness is constituted through pluralist compromise, which provides a privileged position to the two 'founding nations' and, to a lesser extent, First Nations. Within this perspective, there are no representations where one single ethnic group constitutes Canadianness. In liberal-pluralist discourses, compromise is perceived as the essence of Canadian nationhood, and compromise requires at least two parties to be involved. Interestingly, Row 5 in Table 9.1 also remains empty within this discourse. Thus, within this perspective, too, English Canadians are never positioned as outsiders to Canada. Furthermore, in liberal-pluralist discourses, dualism remains an important element of the pluralist compromise. Quebec – more often than ethnic minorities – is here represented as being close to the centre (Row 4). However, separatism also constitutes a powerful symbol of the limits of pluralism (Row 2). In principle, these discourses strive for a balanced representation of group relations. Trying to mitigate multiculturalism's underlying (and ongoing) power relations, they tend to fetishize multicultural harmony.

Third, in its ideal-typical form, the liberal-multiculturalist perspective identifies Canadianness as the liberal expression of diversity of, mostly, immigrant minorities. It promotes the idea of a new diversified and 'united' 'multicultural people,' which nevertheless is only loosely bounded. In principle, ethnic minorities can thus occupy the centre of Canadianness alone (Row 6). However, ethnic minorities are more often represented as being situated at the margins from whence they make claims to the centre position (Row 4).[11] The liberal-multiculturalist perspective rejects the representation of multiculturalism as a cause of fragmentation, as well as the legitimacy of dualism alone (its prioritization over multiculturalism). Often, preferential treatment of French Canadians and/or francophone Québécois is opposed (Row 2). In few cases, alliances between ethnic minorities and francophones are constructed (Row 5).

These three types of discourse mutually contradict, reinforce, and respond to each other in a circular way. In the newspaper sample, the most important flow of arguments leads from discourses that constitute Canadianness in terms of British culture and institutions to discourses that view Canada as being historically constituted through dualist compromise (and not necessarily through English Canadian culture). From here, as shown in Chapter 8, the flow leads to liberal-multiculturalist claims that Canada is mainly about ethnic diversity (and not merely about French/English dualism). Within the limits of the empirical study, the two dominant perspectives, the republican and the liberal-pluralist perspectives, hold each other at bay. The republican perspective simply reverses the image of a positively connoted extension of dualism. With roughly 42% each, the two perspectives are in balance: anti-pluralists oppose pro-pluralists.

On the one hand, in this scenario, the relatively small portion of liberal-multiculturalist discourses (15.4%), identified in the *Toronto Star*, shifts the balance towards pro-pluralism, more precisely, towards immigration-related multiculturalism. On the other hand, this perspective alone is unable to change the dominant logic. As long as liberal-multiculturalist claims operate along the lines of 'minorities deserve rights too (like Quebec),' ethnic minorities continue to carry the stigma of being 'fragmentationalists.' In fact, in reaction to demands for the extension of multiculturalism, republican discourses reproach ethnic Canadians for causing national disintegration 'like Quebec.' Associating ethnic groups closely with Quebec, they claim that multiculturalism causes the 'potentiation' of fragmentation. The liberal-multiculturalist perspective, in return, rejects this reproach but struggles with shedding the stigma of compartmentalization.

The empirical study suggests that, in the 1990s, it is disagreement and competition – not compromise – between those who hold the power in Canadian society that opens a space for political newcomers to insert and assert themselves. For multiculturalism to move from a discourse at the margins (liberal-multiculturalist perspective) to a discourse invested with legitimacy at the centre (supported by the liberal-pluralist and republican perspectives), the dualist compromise that previously united the dual majority must cease to be sustained by (some) members of one or both 'founding nations.' In English-speaking Canada, this was the case when, starting with the 1994 election of the Parti Québécois in Quebec, 'deep diversity' was no longer associated merely with the idea of a 'distinct society.' Rather, framed as anti-liberal, oppressive, and separatist, Québécois 'ethnic nationalism' became perceived as putting the 'survival of the nation' at stake (see Chapter 7).

The 'intolerable' nationalism of Quebec increased the need for strategic variations within each perspective. Table 9.1 draws our attention to a particular representation of group relations: 'English Canadians + ethnic minorities = multicultural we ≠ Quebec' (Row 2 in Table 9.1) is the only constellation that is present within all three perspectives. Francophone Quebec is here positioned as Other ('them') to the multicultural alliance between English Canadians and ethnic groups. Within the limits of the newspaper sample, this constellation represents the 'smallest common denominator' of republican, liberal-pluralist, and liberal-multiculturalist discourses. It describes, however, not an ideal-type of any of the three perspectives (which are Row 3 for the republican perspective, Row 1 – or, within limits, Row 4 – for the liberal-pluralist perspective, and Row 6 for the liberal-multiculturalist perspective). Rather, it describes a strategic adaptation of an ideological perspective to a particular sociopolitical context.

This insight enhances our understanding of boundary construction from within: at the inside of the ethnic boundary a multitude of diverse and diverging historical and cultural representations are mobilized. What is ultimately brought to the fore, and becomes significant for the group's self-representation, is not necessarily a particular 'dominant representation' (as suggested by the media studies cited at the beginning of this chapter), but an element that – in given historical constellation – becomes acceptable to a critical mass of group members. It is a minimal agreement and not necessarily a dominant principle, which will then undergo further alterations when confronted with external representations of the groups' identities.

Constructing a contrast between a supposedly ethnically oppressive Quebec and a multicultural Canadian nation serves different purposes in different discourses: In the republican perspective, designating Québécois nationalism as separatist and 'ethnic' serves to highlight the danger of fragmentation. It also helps to portray Canadian society as more tolerant and inclusive (than ethnic nations), and to depict multiculturalism as a 'unique English Canadian invention' (T-1993-0307). In the liberal-pluralist perspective, Québécois 'deep diversity' does not have negative connotations as such. However, separation and 'ethnic nationalism' are intolerable. Here, the opposition to Quebec's potentially separatist and ethnic nationalism serves to demonstrate the limits of pluralism and to distinguish between acceptable and unacceptable expressions of ethnocultural difference. Separatism is here deemed as 'wholly unCanadian' (G-1999-0701). Besides, distinguishing between 'potentially separatist minority nations' and 'multiculturally integrating ethnic groups' raises the public acceptance of a moderate unifying multiculturalism.

From the liberal-multiculturalist perspective, opposing Québécois 'ethnic nationalism' and separatism allows ethnic groups to be represented as the non-separatist 'better Canadians' whose multicultural integration fosters 'unity in diversity.' This representation stabilizes the precarious position of immigrants and other minorities as 'conditional insiders.' Within the newspaper sample examined here, liberal-multiculturalist discourses remain quantitatively marginal. As mentioned above, they cannot 'stand on their own' but have to strategically align themselves with (at least) one of the more powerful discourses. There are surprisingly few complaints about racism within the discourses that operate from a liberal-multiculturalist perspective. While this absence may be an unintended effect of the sampling method, it is more likely that radical multiculturalism – like the one that can be found in anti-foundationalist approaches – was not allowed into the two newspapers' opinion pieces, because it would not have resonated with the mainstream newspapers' editorial stances. Similarly, liberal-multiculturalist claims that explicitly challenge both Québécois *and* English Canadians' hegemonic status as Canada's ideal citizens remain marginal within the sample: attacks more often target Québécois minority rights than unacknowledged English Canadian majority rights. Thereby, liberal-multiculturalist claims become acceptable even for the defendants of the other two dominant perspectives, republicanism and liberal-pluralism. As a consequence, otherwise divergent discourses on Canadian identity find themselves agreeing in at least one point: an opposition to a (real or imagined) Québécois 'them.'

These findings help us to understand why, in the late 1990s, multiculturalism is much more popular in Canadian public discourses than it was in previous decades (Karim, 2002; see also Chapter 10). However, it would be false to assume that the collective rejection of 'ethnically motivated separatism' erases the fundamental differences between the republican, liberal-pluralist, and liberal-multiculturalist perspectives. On the contrary, differences continue to persist. The common point of rejection can merely serve as a shared point of departure for new negotiations about the type of society Canadians want to live in. But at least a mono-cultural national self-understanding seems to be increasingly banned from dominant discourses in the Central Canadian print media. As a consequence, members of ethnic and racialized minorities slowly obtain the possibility to negotiate the nature of multicultural rights and recognition 'from within.'

That we find the liberal-multiculturalist perspective predominantly in the *Toronto Star* suggests that recent immigrants and members of previously marginalized communities have started to appropriate a platform – at least in one of Canada's most ethnically diverse cities – from which they are able to voice concerns and make them heard. Future research must analyse how representative these voices in the mainstream media are, whose concerns and opinions they reflect, and how much they have to comply with dominant discourses and/or the editorial stance of the newspaper.

Conclusion

This chapter is the last of three chapters presenting the findings of an empirical analysis of opinion discourses in two Central Canadian English-language mainstream newspapers, the *Globe and Mail* and the *Toronto Star* in the 1990s. After having examined how multiculturalism is constituted in relation to its others (Chapter 7) and how its (de)legitimization is impacted by binationalism (Chapter 8), in this chapter, I examined the construction of a 'multicultural Canada' from within the ethnic boundary. The internal dimension of the group boundary is the outcome of shifting social relations, group formations, and negotiated representations of the world. As we have seen in the preceding analysis, the elements that become staged as 'national' are extracted out of discursive conflicts. Therefore, in this chapter, the divergent voices within the media were situated at the centre of attention. Applying the model of triangular relations to the textual material and concentrating on the relation between representations of 'us' and those of multiculturalism, I identified three ideal-typical perspectives in the examined Toronto-based newspapers, namely, republicanism, liberal-pluralism, and liberal-multiculturalism. While these ideological perspectives are characterized by deep cleavages, in the late 1990s, the idea of Canada as a multicultural nation reunited them not for reasons of profound conviction, but as a 'smallest common denominator.'

While these findings nuance popular claims that the idea of multiculturalism is deeply entrenched in the Canadian psyche, there is reason to believe that even a relatively shallow commitment to a multicultural – rather than to a mono-, bi-, or tri-national – Canada provides members of ethnic and racialized groups with an 'allocation of symbolic resources' (Breton, 1984), and allows them to redefine Canadianness from within. Future research must investigate to what extent (1) issues of 'racial' diversity will be incorporated into representations of the Canadian nation and (2) whether group rights are still claimed and/or granted.

The emergence of multiculturalism as a 'smallest common denominator' will be further explored in the following chapter – the first of two concluding chapters. There, I will discuss how the findings of the empirical case study expand the theoretical framework developed earlier, and allow us to better understand the consolidation of multiculturalism as a social imaginary in Canadian dominant discourses in the 1990s.

PART IV

Conclusions

10   The Social Constitution
of a Pluralist 'We'

The transformation of national identity in pluralist terms is a complex process. What seems to matter most is the emergence of an understanding that multiculturalism is not just about 'them' and their rights, but also what defines 'us.' Although Western European governments have reluctantly admitted that they, too, have become countries of immigration, they have so far failed to construct new multicultural identities for their countries. Canada, by contrast, has done precisely this: it has adopted multiculturalism not only as a policy towards minorities but also as a basic feature of shared identity (House of Commons, 1971: 8580). According to numerous opinion polls, Canadians are doing fairly well in identifying themselves as multicultural, and support was rising throughout the 1990s (Dasko, 2003; Harell, 2009; Jedwab, 2005; see also Chapter 2). How did this happen? Where does the widespread acceptance of a multicultural identity in Canada come from, particularly at a time when many Western countries are poised to abandon multiculturalism?

Answers to these questions involve many different dimensions, such as a country's demographic composition, its history of ethnocultural diversity, the state of the economy, and practices of governance. This book has concentrated on a particular factor impacting the multiculturalization of national identity, namely, multiculturalism's integration within a country's historically established set of ethnocultural relations and their contemporary representations within public space. More specifically, it has examined the following question: how and under what circumstances do (previously constructed) ethnic categories become included into a dominant representation of who 'we' are and/or want to be? Incorporating the results from an analysis of Central Canadian

English-language newspaper discourses into a neo-Weberian theory of ethnocultural pluralism, this book has proposed a threefold approach to the multiculturalization of national identity: as being shaped by extranational and intranational relations of power and alterity; as being heavily influenced by minority nationalism and shifting relations between a country's previously established dominant groups; and as being constructed within diverging and sometimes conflicting discourses on nationhood and belonging. These three dimensions of multicultural identity are not only mediated by binary us/them relations. Rather, the inclusion or exclusion of some groups takes always place in the presence of others, in relation to whom the suitability of those to join or not is judged and decided. Therefore, this book proposes a model of pluralism as a triangular relation.

This concluding part contains two chapters. In Chapter 10, I will revisit the model of pluralism as a set of triangular relations and show its advantages over liberal-culturalist and anti-foundationalist approaches. Drawing upon this model, I will then extrapolate from the preceding analysis to propose an interpretation of the multicultural transformation of pan-Canadian identity in the 1990s. In Chapter 11, I situate the Canadian experience with multicultural identity formation in a larger international context.

Revisiting the Pluralism Model

Too Much Concession?

This book has taken its starting point from a perspective that embraces pluralism optimistically. From a sociological point of view, it locates processes of ethnicization at the heart of unequal social relations and thus considers them inevitable. From a normative point of view, it cherishes both the multiplicity of different views, values, languages, cultures, ways of life, etc. and their non-violent, egalitarian integration within liberal democratic societies. Taken together, these two statements produce a contradiction. If ethnocultural difference is, at least in part, (re)produced in unequal social relations, how can it be integrated in an egalitarian way?

This is where the paradigm of pluralism comes into play. Pluralism encourages the expression of ethnic diversity within the public space. As such, it aims to provide a modest remedy against the effects of nationalist exclusion, which always favours some groups (and their cultures and views of society) over Others ('them'). Although pluralism may be defined in a purely normative way (e.g., as emphasizing our 'unity within diversity'), in this book, it has not been elevated above the level of social relations. On the contrary, it has been conceptualized as being produced by and through social relations and their representations within discourse. Defined in a sociological way that follows the tradition of Max Weber's sociology of ethnic relations, pluralist societies – although encouraging the expression of diversity within the public space – will never be entirely free from power relations and inequality as cultures, values, and other markers of 'ethnicity' do not exist independently from the collectivities that either promote or disqualify them.

The Weberian perspective favoured in this book does not deny the existence of different cultures, languages, religions, etc. However, it does not view them as producing clashes of values or civilizations (Huntington, 1996; Sniderman and Hagendoorn, 2007). Rather, it poses that the elements which become invested with meaning – selected historical events, particular features of religious faith, certain phenotypical characteristics – are chosen and reinforced within unequal social relationships (see Chapter 4). It is in relationships between individuals that categories are developed to distinguish between potential insiders and outsiders, patterned action orientations emerge, and groups are constituted. Those in power (the majority) tend to view themselves in universal terms and to impose difference upon others (minority categories). This being said, minorities also have agency in forming social relationships and in (re)articulating what defines them. Arguably, they often rely upon (previously imposed) communitarian elements for the means of self-identification and empowerment, but other strategies of subversion are also open to them (Wimmer, 2008; Safran, 2008). Furthermore, from the perspective of the dominant group – which has been under scrutiny in this book – different minority categories are weighted against each other, and some of them may become included on a conditional basis.

These considerations are at the heart of the model of pluralism as dynamic sets of triangular group relations developed in this book. In its minimalist form, this model can be summarized in the following schematic way: pluralist we = us + others ≠ them. Earlier in this book, I have verbalized this formula in the following way: Two or more groups – come together – enter in negotiation processes about pluralist collaboration – not because they are equal in terms of power or similar in terms of 'culture,' but because they are confronted with a (real or

imagined) third group that forces the national majority to give concessions to minority groups – or to attempt their co-optation, as the glass
is always either half full or half empty.

The simple formula receives its analytical strength from the Weberian
framework that informs the various 'players' involved. Let me briefly
remind the reader that, obviously, the model does not simply pit clearly
defined (ethnic) groups against each other in a static way. Rather, it
views these entities as being constituted within unequal social relations
as described above (and in more detail in Chapters 4 and 5).[1] The terms
'us,' 'them,' 'others' are proxies that operate interchangeably. Which
category of 'others' is included conditionally within the pluralist we,
and which is excluded – and thus constructed as 'them' or 'Other' (with
a capital O) – is not fixed in time. The choice of 'others'/'them' is neither limited by national boundaries (Chapter 7) nor restricted to certain
types of national/ethnic minority groups (Chapter 8). Furthermore, the
categories associated with each proxy and the representation of their relation to each other vary within different types of discourse (Chapter 9). In
sum, the model of pluralism as a triangular relationship can be used to
describe an array of overlapping – reinforcing and/or contradicting –
social relationships and their representations.

To situate the conceptualization of pluralism as a triangular relation
within the wider picture of contemporary approaches to ethnic diversity, we may say that the model developed here bonds with a new
stream of intersectional analyses, which Leslie McCall has framed as
'intercategorical approaches' (2005).[2] These approaches begin with the
observation that relationships of inequality among already constructed
social groups do exist – as imperfect and ever-changing as these group
constellations may be – and take those relationships as the centre of
analysis: 'The concern is with the nature of the relationships among social groups and, importantly, how they are changing, rather than with
the definition or representation of such groups per se' (ibid.: 1785).

By making relations between groups centre stage and by provisionally
accepting the use of categories (such as – in this book – ethnic groups,
English Canadians, and francophones/Québécois) for the sake of analysis, intercategorical approaches distinguish themselves from earlier
and more widely known analyses of intersectionality – identified by
McCall as anti-categorical and intracategorical approaches – in which
unequal power relations between social groups tend to act merely as
background, contextual, discursive, or ideological factors. Like other
intercategorical approaches of intersectionality, the model of pluralism

as a triangular relation concentrates on the complexity of relationships between multiple social groups and categories, and not (as in anti-categorical and intracategorical approaches) on complexities within single social groups, categories, or both. Therefore, as McCall specifies, the subject is multigroup, and the method is systematically comparative (rather than single case intensive).

Concession versus Containment

Defined along the lines of Weberian sociology, the conceptualization of pluralism as a triangular relation overcomes the impasse between those who theorize multiculturalism as (justified) concession and those who conceive it as an ideology of containment. First, contrary to the liberal-culturalist approaches described in Chapter 3, within the Weberian framework privileged here, individuals are not viewed as necessarily needing a particular 'culture' to thrive. Rather, our attention is directed to the relevant, constitutive *relations* that produce minority and majority categories along the lines of 'race,' culture/ethnicity, gender, and class. Multiculturalism is thus not motivated by the coexistence of particular, sometimes conflicting 'cultures.' On the contrary, it is considered legitimate because its aim is to moderately alleviate the effects of nationalist closure and discrimination that are inflicted on individuals on the basis of ascribed membership without enforcing assimilation. Put differently, if there would not be (or not have been) discrimination of ethnic, racial religious, etc. categories, normative pluralism would not be necessary. But because processes of ethnicization are part and parcel of our social relations (as described in Chapter 4), normative pluralism presents itself as mediator.

For those familiar with Weberian sociology and Weber's notion of value pluralism it should not come as a surprise that the approach developed here also takes offence at the under-theorization of conflict and struggle in liberal-culturalist theories of multiculturalism where recognition appears to be given automatically to minority categories ('others') by a culturally emancipated benevolent majority ('us'). The model of pluralism as a triangular relation challenges the view that multiculturalism (or any other form of minority accommodation) is granted voluntarily as a 'concession.' Rather, for pluralism to come into being, it must be claimed by the minority, which 'seeks toleration for its differences on the part of the dominant group' (Wirth, 1945: 354).[3] To what extend this claim is granted depends upon complex negotiations, which take place in the presence of (real or imagined) third persons ('them'). By theorizing pluralism not as an abstract principle but as a *negotiated compromise* between the majority and a particular minority group (or groups) in relation to outsiders ('them'), the sociological approach developed here overcomes the invisibility and assumed neutrality of the dominant group that is striking in liberal-culturalist theories of minority rights (see critique by Day, 2000: 209–22). Put differently, if we theorize (claimed or granted) minority rights, we cannot let (factual) majority rights go unnoticed. The confrontation with third persons, which is a necessary element in our model of pluralism, prevents us from making this mistake: it provides a context to the negotiated compromise and shows that the groups in question do only exist *in relation* to each other ('pluralist we') in the presence of outsiders.

Second, if the advocates of multicultural concessions under-theorize the role of power in the articulation of pluralism, those who theorize multiculturalism as nothing more than a strategy of containment also remain caught in binaries. Here, the dominant group receives all the visibility, while the agency and heterogeneity of minorities are neglected (Bannerji, 2000; Day, 2000; McFarlane, 1995). Historically, in the Canadian context (as explained in Chapter 2), some immigrant groups asked for multicultural recognition, others favoured anti-racism, and yet others viewed all these measures as undermining the special status of national minorities. Did the dominant group try to co-opt minority members by granting specific rights to the most vocal and powerful immigrant groups? Most likely, it did. Did the dominant group try to contain minority demands by pitting one group against another? Most likely, it did. Did, nonetheless, some minority groups and/or individuals benefit from this process of pluralizing Canadianness? Most likely, they did and still do. Furthermore, some members of the dominant group certainly felt and feel that they were and are losing out by making 'too many concessions.' Nevertheless, they also benefited from multiculturalism in some other ways (e.g., its positive impact on immigration). As Max Weber has put it, a relatively stable social order – as Canadian multiculturalism has now been for more than forty years – relies upon a minimum of 'voluntary obedience' of its members. An overwhelmingly large group of individuals must have an 'interest,' however defined, in accepting the status quo and subjectively believing in its legitimacy (Weber, 1978: 212; 1980: 121). Therefore, conceptualizing multiculturalism merely as containment in binary terms does not get to the core of the issue.[4]

In this book, a theoretical model has been developed that aims to overcome the binary that is inherent in the previous theorizations by asking the question of concession versus containment in a different way: When and why does which group get included in or excluded from a Canadian 'multicultural we' in relation to whom? I do not pretend that the illustrative case study of two newspapers – which is a highly specific segment of majority discourse – and the triangular relationships detected therein provide us with a full picture of the Canadian 'reality.' The empirical findings in this book can only serve as a proxy to illustrate the complexity of the multiculturalization of national identity, which involves many more minority and majority categories and their representations – not only in multiple majority discourses but also in minority contestations.

Despite these limitations, the theorization of pluralism as a set of overlapping, triangular relations provides some answers to the theoretical puzzles identified in Chapter 3. In the next section, I will show that it also offers a fresh view on the multiculturalization of Canadian identity during the 1990s.

The Multiculturalization of Canadian National Identity

The Consolidation of Multiculturalism in Dominant Discourses

In the early 1990s, the same wave of criticism that brought a strong backlash against multiculturalism in countries like the Netherlands and Australia, also affected Canada. Widespread concerns about Canada's 'balkanization' prompted the 1991 Spicer Commission to recommend refocusing multiculturalism policy in a way that would 'welcome all Canadians to an evolving mainstream' (Citizens' Forum on Canada's Future, 1991: 129). The public mood also helps explain why the proposed 1992 Charlottetown Accord did not mention multiculturalism, and why, in 1993, the Progressive Conservative Pre-election Cabinet (overseen by Prime Minister Kim Campbell) disbanded Multiculturalism and Citizenship as a separate department only two years after its creation.[5]

The incoming federal Liberals under Prime Minister Jean Chrétien in 1993 did not reinstate a separate Department of Multiculturalism but placed it within the newly created Department of Canadian Heritage (overseen by a secretary of state, a junior minister not represented in the Cabinet). This shift can be read as highly symbolic as it foreshadowed the emphasis that the Liberal government (in power until 2006) placed on fostering an 'attachment to Canada' (Canadian Heritage, 1998: 2). In 1995, the Liberal government commissioned a review of the multiculturalism program. In reaction to what has become known as the Brighton Report (Canadian Heritage, 1996) the new multiculturalism program, announced in 1997–98, subsumed the expression of ethnocultural diversity under the notion of shared Canadian identity,[6] restricted funding for ethnocultural groups, and reduced the budget for multiculturalism from $27 million in the early 1990s to $18.7 million in 1996–97 (Abu-Laban and Gabriel, 2002: 15).

At the same time, however, public support for immigration, ethnic and racial diversity, and multiculturalism had been growing steadily over the 1990s (Dasko, 2003; Harell, 2009; Jedwab, 2005; see also Chapter 2). There is evidence that Canadians are more supportive of multiculturalism and immigration than people are in other industrialized countries (Adams, 2007; Hiebert et al., 2003; Ward and Masgoreth, 2008). Furthermore, scholars from a wide variety of disciplines agree that multiculturalism has indeed become an important dimension of pan-Canadian identity (see contributions to Stein et al., 2007). As mentioned earlier in this book (Chapter 2), while the 'end of the differentialist turn' (Brubaker, 2001: 531) had devastating effects on the multiculturalism policies in many European countries, in Canada, public support for multiculturalism merely 'dipped' temporarily in the early 1990s and then rose to unprecedented heights. Even in government discourses, multiculturalism regained its prominence in the second half of the 1990s, although dubiously lauded as enhancing Canada's economic competiveness and as a means of casting Canada as a world leader in diversity management (Abu-Laban and Gabriel, 2002: 117).

These contradictory tendencies are poignantly summarized by Karim Karim: Paradoxically, 'as the bureaucratic target for anti-multiculturalism attacks has shrunk, Canada is increasingly described as a multicultural country in current dominant discourses' (2002: 454; see also Karim, 2008).

As argued in Chapter 2, there are numerous factors that facilitate the emergence of multiculturalism in the Canadian context, such as Canada's history of immigration, its geographical location, and the type of immigrants it attracts. Canada's minority 'rights revolution,' its increasing 'reality' of ethnic and racial diversity, and intergenerational change (Harell, 2009) have also been evoked to explain the consolidation of multiculturalism as a societal ethos and discourse about national identity in the 1990s. This book has concentrated on the level of discourse and the deployment of constitutive Others to investigate the multiculturalization of Canadian national identity. It has been particularly interested in the impact of Québécois nationalism upon the construction of a Canadian 'multicultural we.'

Extrapolating from the newspaper discourses examined in earlier chapters, this book suggests that the renewal of Québécois nationalism in the 1990s had an important impact upon the multiculturalization of Canadian identity in public discourse. The analysis thereby challenges the now-widespread assumption that the accommodation of national minorities and ethnic groups happens in hermetically closed 'silos' with little interaction (Kymlicka, 2007: 39). Admittedly, minority groups often differ as to their historical origins (e.g., colonization, conquest, immigration), their institutional completeness, the types of rights they demand (e.g., anti-racism, cultural maintenance, institutional separation), and the government departments that have been charged with dealing with their accommodation (e.g., Indian and Northern Affairs for Aboriginal peoples, Intergovernmental Affairs for Quebec, Citizenship and Immigration, as well as previously Canadian Heritage for immigrants and ethnic groups). Nevertheless, while different types of minorities may be analytically different, they are still closely interrelated in public perceptions and discourse. To name but a few reasons for these relations: As newcomers to the political arena, immigrants are framed in – and adapt to – the ways in which previous ethnic minorities have come to be constituted. Claims making and changes in any type of minority accommodation affect the balance of power between the remaining groups and lead to new negotiations. Proponents and opponents of multiculturalism deliberately blur the differences between minority nations and immigrant groups to make their cases. By tracing the ways in which these diverse minorities and their accommodations are constituted in relation to each other, the book provides another piece of the puzzle as to why multiculturalism in Canada was on the rise at a time when it was in decline almost everywhere else in the world.

On the one hand, scholars have found that the primacy of a centralized (historically English Canadian) state over the provinces already intensified in Central Canadian English-language discourses about national identity during the 1980s (Denis, 1993; Lacombe, 2007). On the other hand, my own reading of the examined newspaper discourses suggests that, until the early 1990s, Quebec tended to be represented as a national minority that is at the heart of Canadian identity and that needs to be accommodated by 'typically Canadian' pluralist compromise and concessions. Both are said to distinguish the 'Canadian' way of dealing with ethnic diversity from the 'American' one. With respect to multiculturalism, Quebec was then overwhelmingly represented as a predecessor of diversity proliferation with contradictory normative connotations. For some commentators, particularly from the political right, the rights claimed by and partially granted to a francophone · Quebec such as 'official bilingualism and its fraternal twin, official multiculturalism' (G-1992-0111) are at the heart of centrifugal powers undermining social cohesion. The image created here is that of a deadly spiral towards fragmentation/identity politics and the destruction of society (G-1997-0701).

For other commentators, located closer to the political centre and left, the successful compromises reached to accommodate Quebec's cultural and linguistic difference have helped to prepare the rest of Canada to deal with the challenges of newer sources of ethnocultural diversity, particularly those that are produced through immigration at a time of globalization (i.e., the 'cultural distance' and variety of sending countries; Cameron, 2007). These latter discourses are also typical of government representations of Canadian national identity.[7]

The continued presence of these types of discourse in the public realm contradicts the claim of a fundamental opposition between a francophone, nationalist Quebec and the rest of Canada. Quebec is neither entirely 'contained' nor solely constructed as mirror image. On the contrary, the 'French fact' – (re)produced predominantly in Quebec – continues to be viewed as a cornerstone of Canadian identity.[8]

This being said, towards the mid-1990s, a change of discourse could be noticed. Québécois separatist nationalism – as opposed to the simple notion of 'the French fact' – came to be regarded more and more as the enfant terrible of Canadian multiculturalism. In discourses from the political right, references to Quebec served no longer solely to point out the root cause for social disintegration, but also, increasingly, as an 'awful example' of what multiculturalism as a normative framework for dealing with ethnocultural diversity may lead to (T-1993-0228). Furthermore, in discourses from the political centre and left, even commentators embracing pluralism as a normative value per se, started to refer to Quebec in order to distance themselves from ethnically motivated nationalism and separatism, on the one hand, and to illustrate the limits of diversity accommodation, on the other (Young, 1997: 156).

The rejection of 'ethnic nationalism' gained particular salience against the backdrop of international events, such as the rise of nationalisms in the former Soviet Union after the fall of the Berlin Wall in 1989, the 1994 Rwandan genocide, and ethnic cleansing during the 1996–99 Kosovo war. At the same time, from the perspective of many European countries, finally accepting the fact that refugees and former guest workers were there to stay, Canada gained a reputation as 'the place where multiculturalism actually worked.'[9] These external factors contributed to rendering the expression of nostalgia for Anglo-conformity within representations of Canadian identity increasingly unpopular.

On the domestic front, the potential scenario of a separating Quebec (shaking up the very foundation on which the Canadian state is built) and the growing number of immigrants 'from all over the world' (see note 7 of this chapter) produced a situation where English Canadians were in desperate need of rethinking their national identity beyond expressions of mono-culturalism (Resnick, 1994). In this context, the notion of a 'multicultural Canada' gained new appeal. On the one hand, a seemingly ethnoculturally oppressive Quebec is no longer viewed as the (positively or negatively connoted) predecessor of multiculturalism, but rather constructed as the mirror image of the nation that English Canada wants to be and/or stands for (Winter, 2009). On the other hand, compared with a hostile, French-speaking, and potentially separating Quebec, the claims for cultural maintenance and non-discrimination by English-speaking (-learning) immigrants did appear harmless and 'integrative.'

English Canadian attitudes vis-à-vis Quebec hardened in the wake of the 1995 Quebec referendum on sovereignty-partnership (Lacombe, 1998; Potvin, 2000a; Bright et al., 1999; Longstaff, 1996). The referendum's narrow defeat sent a shock wave through the rest of Canada.' The 'Parizeau gaffe' (El Yamani, 1996) – Quebec's premier blaming 'money and the ethnic vote' for the loss of the referendum – reinforced the image of a fundamental difference between Quebec and the rest of Canada. At a time of political adversary, the long-standing images of a Québécois *Gemeinschaft* (community) and a Canadian English-speaking *Gesellschaft* (society) – to use John Meisel's comparison (1999: 113, cited in Chapter 4) – became exacerbated. While Quebec was increasingly described as a narrow-minded 'ethnic nation' (G-1995-1101), the rest of Canada was portrayed as an open, tolerant 'multi-ethnic World Nation' (T-1993-0131). In academia too, the civic, pluralist nature of Québécois nationalism was (rightly or wrongly) put into question (Cook, 1995; Elmer and Abramson, 1997; Ignatieff, 1994; 2000; Webber, 1999).

The publication of Will Kymlicka's influential *Multicultural Citizenship* in 1995 gave academic authority to the widely shared impression that the multicultural rights demanded by immigrant groups and ethnic associations were indeed fundamentally different from the 'self-government rights' claimed by the Franco-Québécois and, in a less threatening way, by Canada's First Nations. The paradigm change within the academy was echoed in public discourse and also made its way into media representations of Canadian diversity. In academia, Kymlicka's theory has been criticized for privileging minority nations (Parekh, 2000; Walker, 1997). In Canadian public discourse, however, his distinction was increasingly used to distance ethnic groups of immigrant origin from the potentially secessionist intentions of minority nations – and thus to liberate them from the stigma of causing 'social fragmentation' (see Chapter 8).

In addition, Kymlicka's scholarly distinction was forcefully underlined by Canadians' experience with the so-called ethnic vote in the 1995 Quebec referendum on sovereignty. While Quebec's premier had to resign over his ill-suited comments in the referendum night, 95 per cent of Quebec's non-francophone population voted indeed against separation (as opposed to 60% of Franco-Québécois). The voting pattern in the 1995 referendum was a powerful example of both the 'destructive' potential of a self-government demanding minority nation, on the one hand, and the 'unifying' pan-Canadianism expressed by Canadians of immigrant origin, on the other.[10] The symbolic importance of this widely recognized demonstration of loyalty to Canada should not be underestimated. It fed into a new political assertiveness of 'ethnic Canadians' of immigrant origin, primarily in Canada's major cities. Underlining the many contributions that immigrants – new Canadians as well as those who are not (yet) Canadian citizens – make to Canadian society, in the city of Toronto, for example, initiatives are currently under way to provide non-citizens with local voting rights (Omidvar, 2008; Siemiatycki, 2007).

In the newspaper sample examined in this book, this change in public discourse is highlighted in two ways. First, a new strand of discourse emerges (only) in the *Toronto Star*, which expresses liberal-multiculturalist claims. This perspective quantitatively changes the balance between republican and liberal-pluralist discourses in favour of a national self-understanding that embraces multiculturalism. Second, the idea of a multicultural Canada becomes accepted even in discourses that previously rejected all types of 'groupism' and drew parallels between

Franco-Québécois and ethnic groups. Not surprisingly, these three majority perspectives expose different views as to who is unconditionally included within the 'Canadian we' and which groups should be 'grateful' for being accommodated (see Chapter 9). Nevertheless, these different perspectives 'meet' in their rejection of ethnically motivated nationalism and separatism. As the analysis in Chapter 9 suggests, over the course of the 1990s, a vaguely defined multiculturalism emerges as the 'smallest common denominator' of otherwise diverging perspectives on Canadian nationhood. This confirms Desmond McNeill's (2006) research. McNeill finds that 'the most successful ideas are not those that are most analytically rigorous but those that are most malleable, achieving consensus by conveying different meanings to different audiences' (2006: 334).

Obviously, these results must be treated with caution because of the limitations of the sample. However, they help us to better understand the consolidation of multiculturalism as an element of Canadian identity in the late 1990s. In particular, the analysis warns us to be careful with interpreting the current public support for multiculturalism as a wholehearted and unambiguous expression of deep-seated cultural tolerance and a readiness to grant far-reaching 'concessions' to minorities.[11] Although official representations of Canadian values and national identity would like to have it this way, the consolidation of multiculturalism as a part of Canadian identity is better characterized as a lukewarm compromise, which, while not purely accidental, owes much of its existence to a series of lucky, unintended circumstances.

Stating that the idea of a 'multicultural Canada' became consolidated in dominant discourses during the second half of the 1990s requires two important qualifications, which I will briefly discuss below.

The 'Containment' of Québécois Separatism

The first qualification of the statement that multiculturalism became 'consolidated' in dominant discourses relates to the representation of Quebec. In this book, it has been shown that, in opposition to those for whom multiculturalism is merely part of a 'politics of containment' towards Quebec (Gagnon, 2003: 306), Québécois nationalism is not solely constructed as a mirror image to the imagined Canadian nation. On the contrary, in liberal-pluralist discourses, a French-speaking Quebec and its nationalism remain at the heart of pan-Canadian identity. The same, however, does not hold true for Québécois nationalism when it is expressed as separatism. Even the most sympathetic representations of Canada as a multinational state reject the idea of an independent Quebec. Figuratively speaking, within the sample of newspaper discourses examined here, a 'separatist Quebec' is never included – not even conditionally – within the 'Canadian we.' This representation within discourse reflects the political events in the second half of the 1990s and their ongoing ramifications.

In the months and years following the 1995 Quebec referendum on sovereignty several political measures were adopted.[12] One of them was a call to the Supreme Court of Canada to rule on the legality of a unilateral declaration of independence. On 20 August 1998, the Supreme Court of Canada ruled that Quebec could not unilaterally secede from Canada, neither according to the Canadian Constitution nor according to international law. The decision of the Court was univocal as to the interpretation of the laws. Nevertheless, it also invited Quebec and the rest of Canada to find creative and democratic ways to assure the continuation of Canada and the pluralist society/societies that it has come to stand for. According to James Tully, the Secession Reference describes Canada's constitutional democracy not as an attained end-state but as 'a "global system of rules and principles" for "the reconciliation of diversity with unity" by means of "continuous processes" of democratic discussion, negotiation and change' (2000: 4).[13]

By refusing to define Canadianness in clear-cut terms and by emphasizing the need for ongoing negotiations of who 'we' are, the Secession Reference is very much in line with the interpretation of pluralism that has been advanced in this book. However, prescribing and, at the same time, circumscribing creative and democratic negotiations by law is a difficult process. The Clarity Act (Bill C-20), proposed by the federal Liberals and adopted by Parliament in June 2000, stipulates the rules for a future referendum on Quebec sovereignty. It implements provisions for a 'clear' referendum question and a 'clear' majority of votes. Not surprisingly, interpretations of the Clarity Act differ: For some commentators, mainly from Canada outside of Quebec, the act assures the continuity of a united Canada (Ryan, 2000); for other critics, mainly those within Quebec, the act imposes one fixed definition of clarity: 'debate is ended and democracy, even as the Court defined it, is stifled' (Rocher and Verrelli, 2003: 233).

In addition to 'containing' Québécois separatism by law, the federal government also engaged in a massive campaign to increase the visibility and popularity of the federal government in all spheres of life by spending large amounts of money on the distribution of Canadian flags, sponsorship of Canada Day festivities, and the promotion of federal government services (Turp, 2000). Described as 'Plan B' (Gibson, 1994), the 'sponsorship program' (1996–2004) was established as an effort to promote national unity and to raise the profile of the federal government, particularly in the province of Quebec. In the rest of Canada, the sponsorship program went hand in hand with the federal government's initiative to foster an attachment to Canada. This initiative had been placed under the mandate of the Department of Canadian Heritage.[14] In Quebec, by contrast, it aimed particularly at removing nationalist spokespersons from the public eye, at drawing attention to the Government of Canada's contributions to Québécois industries and cultural activities, and at countering the efforts of the province's Parti Québécois government to promote independence (Gagnon, 2003). Commentators have therefore qualified the sponsorship program as an attempt by the federal government to monopolize the status of being the only legitimate 'national' government, and to undermine the development of a Québécois 'national' identity (Labelle and Rocher, 2004).

In 2004, it was revealed that the efforts to promote Canadian 'national' unity operated at the limits of legality. During the 'sponsorship scandal,' broad corruption was discovered in the program's operations. Illicit and even illegal activities within the administration of the program involved the misuse and misdirection of public funds intended for government advertising in Quebec (Fraser, 2004). Such misdirections included sponsorship money awarded to advertising firms in return for little or no work, the which firms maintained Liberal organizers or fundraisers on their payrolls or donated back part of the money to the Liberal Party. The investigations by federal Auditor General Sheila Fraser and, subsequently, the Gomery Commission affected the Liberal Party of Canada. They became a significant factor in the lead-up to the 2006 federal election where, after more than twelve years in power, the Liberals were defeated by the Conservatives.

In 2006, the struggle for Québécois nationhood was put back on the political agenda when Michael Ignatieff reintroduced the idea of recognizing Quebec as a nation in an attempt to garner Quebec support in his Liberal Party leadership bid. The Bloc Québécois subsequently proposed to pass a motion on the issue in Parliament. In a surprising political move, Conservative Prime Minister Stephen Harper tabled his own 'pan-Canadian' version of the motion, which stated that 'the Québécois form a nation within a united Canada.' On 27 November

2006, the Canadian House of Commons passed this motion with 266 to 16 votes in favour. It should be added that the Conservative minority government under Stephen Harper owed much of its electoral success to the backlash in popularity suffered by the federal Liberals in the wake of the 'sponsorship scandal,' particularly in Quebec. Since then, in the rest of Canada, and most importantly in the Prairie provinces, the Conservatives have been reproached for wooing Quebec.

On the one hand, the motion on national recognition can be seen as a concession to Québécois nationalists.[15] On the other hand, it can also be interpreted as yet another attempt to 'contain' Québécois separatism, and this not only by emphasizing the last four words of the motion ('within a united Canada') but also by referring to the 'Québécois' as 'a people' and not to the province of Quebec with its territory and institutions. Indeed, in English-speaking Canada, the use of the French word 'Québécois' (rather than Quebeckers) in the English version of the motion was widely debated. In particular, it was interpreted as referring to 'pur laine Québécois, those residents of Quebec who can trace their roots back to New France' (*Winnipeg Free Press*, 2006: A11). Was the avoidance of the term Quebeckers deliberate? Was it to suggest that anglophones and allophones (Quebeckers of non-French, non-British, non-Aboriginal origin) in Quebec are not to be part of the 'Québécois nation'?[16] If yes, the Canadian Parliament under the leadership of Stephen Harper would have practised what Weber describes as the 'ethnicization' of political or economic competitors (here: Québécois separatists) with the aim of achieving their marginalization (Chapter 4).

In summing up this section, we may thus conclude that the consolidation of multiculturalism within dominant Canadian discourses during the 1990s does include, to a limited degree, the expression of Québécois nationalism. It nonetheless continues to hold very strong reservations vis-à-vis the expression of separatism and representations of Canada's and Quebec's national identities on equal footing.

The 'Decommunitarization' of Multiculturalism

The second qualification that has to be made when stating that the idea of a 'multicultural Canada' became consolidated in dominant discourses during the second half of the 1990s relates to the definition of multiculturalism itself. As mentioned in Chapter 2, Canadian multiculturalism policy is to be understood as an integral part of the human rights revolution, and as an extension of – and not a break with – the culture of rights. As such, commentators have insisted that multicultur-alism's legal framework does not subdue the individual to the group even though the policy recognizes the importance of cultural com-munities (Kymlicka, 1998).[17] While this clarification is important, it is interesting to note that during the first twenty years of its existence, the policy was cast in the language of ethnocultural communities, even though it never specifically guaranteed group rights.[18] To give some examples: In the fourth volume of their report, the Royal Commission on Bilingualism and Biculturalism recommended to take into account 'the contributions of other ethnic groups' (Royal Commission on Bilingualism and Biculturalism, 1969, vol. IV). Announcing the 1971 multiculturalism policy in Parliament, Prime Minister Pierre Trudeau famously stated that 'there is no official culture, nor does any ethnic group take precedence over any other' (House of Commons, 1971).[19] The 1988 Multiculturalism Act, which replaced the 1971 policy and gave a firm legislative basis to multiculturalism, holds it to be the policy of the Government of Canada 'to recognize the existence of communities whose members share a common origin and their historic contribution to Canadian society, and enhance their development' (Canada, 1988).

The language of ethnocultural communities was abandoned, at the very latest, in the Liberal government's response to sharp critiques of multiculturalism in the early 1990s (Bibby, 1990; Bissoondath, 1994). In the Brighton Report and in Canadian Heritage's subse-quent Multiculturalism Program Review (Canadian Heritage, 1996) the language of communities is missing. As mentioned earlier, the new policy goals emphasize the mandate to ensure that 'people of all background feel a sense of belonging and attachment to Canada' (Canadian Heritage, 1998: 2). Reacting to the proposed policy changes, the Canadian Ethnocultural Council (CEC), an umbrella organization for ethnocultural minority organizations, criticized the new program as a 'movement away from the [Multiculturalism] Act.' The CEC ar-gued that the revised program 'dilutes multiculturalism in Canada and diminishes the role and ability of Canada's ethnocultural communities to contribute to the national enterprise' (Kordan, 1997: 138). Among other things, the CEC regrets the reduced level of funding and the logic of funding allocations (ad hoc project–oriented rather than com-munity organization–oriented). According to the CEC, the new pro-gram shows 'a decided lack of interest [on behalf of the Government of Canada] in engaging Canada's ethnocultural groups in a full and equal partnership' (ibid.: 140).[20]

In a recent study of the nature of the associations and the projects receiving funding through the multiculturalism program between 1983 and 2002, Marie McAndrew and her colleagues (2005) come to a similar conclusion. They find that in 2001–02, more than 80 per cent of the funding was spent on projects that aimed at bringing Canadian society more in tune with increasing ethnocultural and 'racial' diversity by transforming public opinion and institutions. Interestingly, this task is neither assigned to mono-ethnic associations (serving a single ethnic group) nor mainstream organizations (serving the larger Canadian population). Rather, McAndrew et al. find that, in 2001–02, more than 65 per cent of the funding handed out by the multiculturalism program was attributed to multiethnic organizations (representing a coalition of ethnocultural groups), whereas mono-ethnic groups received less than 10 per cent of the funding: 'To put it schematically, it seems that [mono-ethnic] communities – which, in the past, were primarily concerned with guaranteeing the survival of their language and culture and/or the resolution of specific [discrimination/integration] problems – were gradually given the mandate to form broad alliances in order to foster the transformation of society by supporting the government in its management of public opinion' (McAndrew et al., 2005: 68, my translation).

This development can be evaluated in several ways. Some readers may criticize it for ridding ethnic groups and associations of their capacity of building and maintaining their own institutions and priorities in favour of taking on tasks of public governance, which, in principle, are the responsibility of (different levels of) the government. Others may feel that the new funding priorities should be praised for fostering interethnic contact and coalitions as means of integrating minorities and reinforcing social cohesion. Finally, in light of the drastic budget cuts, one may also question the future of the multiculturalism program as such. To put it with McAndrew and her colleagues: 'one wonders whether, during the year 2000, the [federal] government is not slowly putting the policy to sleep, ready to be forgotten, without that any official announcement was made in this respect' (ibid.: 68, my translation).

The recent policy changes left ethnic groups and 'visible minorities' – who have almost completely replaced mono-ethnic organizations of European background – basically without financial support to cover operational costs of their organizations. It is therefore surprising, as McAndrew et al. (2005: 68) note, that during the 1990s the protest by the various ethnic groups and associations has been relatively weak.

These scholars suggest that the lack of protest is, in fact, a direct outcome of the new funding priorities, which 'plunge ethnic associations in a perpetual race in search of funding for specific projects and gives them little opportunity to address more essential but less immediate stakes' (ibid., my translation). Put differently, ethnic associations are increasingly losing their institutional completeness. The more they depend upon ad hoc projects funded by the government, the less likely they are able to take on radical positions and assume their role as interest groups (ibid.: 70).

The findings of the print media analysis conducted for this book (see Chapters 8 and 9) resonate with the developments observed by McAndrew et al. (2005), Kordan (1997), Abu-Laban and Gabriel (2002), and others. The consolidation of multiculturalism as an integral part of Canadian national identity in the 1990s seems to be strongly related to its increasing 'de-communitarianization.' To the extent that Quebec and other groups, whose demands for recognition are oriented along communitarian ideals became staged as outsiders and unacceptable forms of alterity, 'integrative' multiculturalism gained in appeal. At the same time, the type of 'multiculturalism' that is promoted publicly has increasingly lost the right to bear its name – at least in so far as its raison d'être is not only defined as encouraging the cultural integration of immigrants, but also as the promotion of group identities and institutionally supported diversity.

In general, after the 1992 Charlottetown referendum, very few of the examined newspaper articles from the *Globe and Mail* and the *Toronto Star* use the language of ethnocultural communities. While, in republican discourses, Franco-Québécois and ethnic groups continue to be cast as 'special interest groups' operating against 'common goals' at the pan-Canadian level, both liberal-pluralist and liberal-multiculturalist discourses prefer, since the second half of the 1990s, the liberal language of 'unity in diversity' over the more communitarian notion of Canada as 'community of communities.'

Furthermore, up to the mid-1990s, Canadian multiculturalism largely followed the logic that immigrants deserved the same – or at least similar – cultural recognition and rights as members of the French Canadian minority. In the wake of the 1995 Quebec referendum on sovereignty, by contrast, the proponents of multiculturalism insisted (rightly or wrongly) upon a fundamental difference between integrative liberal multiculturalism, on the one hand, and separatist nationalism, on the other (Kymlicka, 1995). In other words, constituted in opposition to – rather than in extension of – French/English 'dualism' and its 'out-dated' communitarian understanding, multiculturalism became con-solidated as a descriptive element of Canadian national identity.

Indeed, from the perspective of many 'visible minorities,' multicul-turalism represents a more inclusive framework than alternative mod-els for Canadian national integration, such as a societal project based on orthodox liberalism and individualism, on the one hand, or a so-cietal project based on the recognition of one, two, or three nations, on the other (Stasiulis, 1995). However, in the long run, this inclusive framework seems to come at the price of group identities. The liberal-multiculturalist perspective identified in the *Toronto Star*, suggest that immigrants, who had formerly claimed equal rights in comparison to French Canadians and Franco-Québécois are, in the second half of the 1990s, mostly concerned with underlining the liberal attitudes of im-migrant organizations and their members, their rejection of ethnocen-trism, and their desire for integration into (rather than separation from) a non-assimilative 'multicultural Canada.' The prioritization of 'choice' over the 'accident of birth' and the logic of 'trading one's talents for membership in a great nation' both point to a this new trend. Whether this trend is to be viewed positively as leading towards stronger equal-ity among individuals and a more integrated society, or whether it is viewed critically as eroding substantive diversity by undermining the possibility for alternative, parallel institutions is in the eye of the be-holder. Ironically, even though the *Toronto Star* vows to 'speak for the powerless' (*Toronto Star*, 1999), the new discourse that emerges from its opinion pages in the late 1990s very much reflects the framing of multiculturalism in liberal, individualist, and entrepreneurial terms that had then been promoted by the Liberal government for over a de-cade (Abu-Laban and Gabriel, 2002). As such, the newspaper represen-tations of ethnic minorities examined here underline the findings by McAndrew et al. (2005) that the late 1990s and early 2000s were charac-terized by relatively little protest against the abandonment of specific group rights – as the language of groups seems no longer adequate for the demands of members of immigrant minorities.

Although more research is necessary to confirm this thesis, we may ask for the potential causes of this shift in discourse. Do the new funding priorities of the multiculturalism program since 1997 – the preference for project-based multiethnic coalitions – indeed undermine ethnic mi-norities' capacity to organize as 'groups,' as suggested by McAndrew et al. (2005)? Or does the new discourse in the *Toronto Star* point to the changing nature of immigration in Canada? Given the large numbers of recent immigrants, is there an emerging 'super-diversity' (Vertovec, 2007), which makes it increasingly difficult to sustain a logic of (fairly homogeneous) 'ethnic groups'? Indeed, the members of minorities classified as 'ethnic groups' are increasingly characterized by class differences (e.g., between workers and entrepreneurs), regional ('ethnic') differences, and legal status differences (e.g., between refugees, temporary workers, and permanent residents). Or does the discourse identified in the *Toronto Star* merely reflect an inherent bias of the newspaper sample? Newspaper discourses are, after all, dominant discourses. Even if the *Toronto Star* prides itself in giving voice to minorities, it does not capture the attitudes of the most vulnerable members of minority populations. Only the most powerful representations make it into the mainstream media. Furthermore, the *Toronto Star* provides a city perspective, where social relations are traditionally characterized by more anonymity and individualism. Would the results of this study differ if the so-called ethnic press and/or local newspapers from rural regions had been examined?

While future research is necessary to inquire about the changing nature of ethnic 'groups' and their representations by spokespersons, it should be noted that the language of groups has recently made its way back into the political arena, albeit with altered connotations. After the attacks on the World Trade Center in New York City and the Pentagon in Washington on 11 September, 2001, the subsequent U.S.-led 'war on terrorism' and other acts of violence committed by Muslim fundamentalists (the London and Madrid bombings, the murder of Theo van Gogh in the Netherlands, etc.), religion – particularly Islam – has become an even stronger marker of 'difference' and discrimination than skin colour and 'race.' At the same time, Muslim immigrants have come to settle permanently in populations in Europe and North America and are therefore more likely to require institutional support to practice their religion and to sustain certain dimensions of their culture (Zolberg and Woon, 1999). As a consequence, they are increasingly asking for 'group rights.' This should not come as a surprise as religion can serve in a meaningful way to reconstruct ethnic boundaries from within. Religion binds communities and provides the means for *collective* empowerment, and this much more so than any collective opposition against racialization – the colour of one's skin does not have any meaning outside a context of domination/subordination (Chapter 4) – that marked the 1980s and 1990s.

To conclude, despite these two qualifications – the containment of Quebec separatism and the decommunitarization of multiculturalism – can we still talk about a 'consolidation' of multi in public discourses? I answer this question in the affirmative. First, we have to take into account the fact that public discourse is composed of multiple perspectives. Within these perspectives, simultaneous yet contradictory tendencies of 'containment' and 'concession' reinforce each other and produce semantic shifts, as well as redefinitions. Second, these developments are not necessarily linear. In fact, extrapolating from the analysis in this book, I argue that the conflict between Canada's so-called founding nations has helped to render immigrant multiculturalism socially acceptable by underlining its liberalism and inclusiveness. While it contributed to the time lag with which questions of 'Muslim communitarianism' have come to the fore in Canada, the general understanding of multiculturalism was – and still is – unable or unwilling to reintegrate the claims for parallel institutions (structural pluralism), as the debates about 'Sharia tribunals' in Ontario (2005) and 'Reasonable Accommodation' in Quebec (2007–08) have shown. With Muslims now being the primary targets cast as the multicultural society's anti-liberal, communitarian Other ('them'), the debate in Canada seems to have arrived – slightly belatedly – at the same issues that have recently tormented the European disputes over multiculturalism.

Is there something that we can learn from the preceding analysis when we situate the Canadian case in a comparative perspective? In the next chapter, the last one of this book, I will briefly address this question. I will argue that there are at least two fields in which the insights gained in this book can make meaningful contributions: the analysis of the recent trend towards citizenship testing in European countries, and the study of immigrant integration in historically diverse and/or 'multinational' societies.

11 Comparative Perspectives

The Renationalization of Citizenship

In the late 1990s, Will Kymlicka predicted that 'liberal culturalism' was becoming an emerging consensus among scholars and policy makers in the field of immigration and citizenship (Kymlicka, 2001, chapter 2; originally published in 1998). Several years into the new century, Kymlicka withdrew from this position and admitted that he might have been too optimistic (2005). Despite Kymlicka's disappointment with the backlash against multiculturalism in many countries, we may say that his earlier prediction still holds true. Liberal-culturalism has become a widely accepted paradigm in public opinion and politics – however, the signs have been turned around. Today, it is no longer (different types of) ethnic minorities whose accommodations attract our intellectual curiosity, our intuitive sympathy, and our political efforts. Rather, the pivotal community to stabilize, unify, and protect seems to be yet again: the nation.

Although the terrorist attacks in Washington and New York on 11 September 2001 were more a symbol and catalyst of change than they were in themselves a root cause of the new developments, they represent in many ways an important caesura. When, on 12 September 2001, the publishers of the two leading dailies in Italy and France headlined their front-page editorials with the same words: 'We Are All Americans' (Colombani, 2001; de Bortoli, 2001)[1] they enacted the climax of the belief in the possibilities and moral superiority of the 'civic nation.' In principle, the civic nation (as explained in Chapter 5) is said to be artificial, universalist, and individualist. It stands for equality without relevance of social determinations such as ethnicity, gender, class, descent, or status, and democracy as the outcome of rational deliberations among free individuals. After the horrors of Nazi fascism and the Holocaust, which discredited all romanticist nostalgia for the idea of nations based on shared language and ethnocultural roots, the ideal-type of the civic nation has become the beacon of the West, where it is usually associated with the idea of a secular state governed by elected representatives.

In the beginning of the new century, however, the triumph of the civic nation is being fundamentally challenged. In the aftermath of the events of 11 September 2001, and in a climate of islamophobia and fear of terrorism, the discussion about 'who we are and want to be' as a community (Habermas, 1990: 151) has taken a new turn. While immigration remains a necessity in many countries because of demographic changes and labour market pressures, as well as continuing humanitarian imperatives, the liberalization of immigration and naturalization policies has brought with it increasing concerns about social cohesion, adherence to basic liberal democratic values, and security. As a consequence, the multiculturalization of ('our') national societies in Western immigrant-receiving societies is increasingly viewed with concern. Do 'we' want to become pluralist, if this means that 'we' have to give up 'all' our cultural, religious, and linguistic particularities? In reaction to immigration perceived as a threat and/or the impacts of globalization pushing towards supra-national and administrative powers, the dominant populations in many countries have recently reacted by underlining – much more strongly than before – their national character.

Both reacting to and shaping public opinion, in recent years, many governments, particularly in Europe, have rendered their immigration and naturalization policies more restrictive. The Netherlands, for example, has gone so far as demanding persons that apply for immigration from abroad – mainly for the sake of family reunion – to take an integration test even before setting foot in the country (Van Oers, 2008). Since 2006, would-be immigrants are required to acquire a basic knowledge of the Dutch language and society in their country of residence (Netherlands, *Wet Inburgering Buitenland*, 2006). In Denmark, requirements for naturalization have also been sharpened (Ersbøll, 2006: 105). Over the past decade, stipulations on language proficiency, the loss of nationality, and financial self-sufficiency have been introduced (Ersbøll, 2006). Denmark now demands that applicants for citizenship must sign a declaration of loyalty indicating that they will 'work actively for the integration of myself and my family into Danish society' (Fekete, 2006: 3). This reminds one of Quebec, where, since

1 January 2009, applicants for immigration are required to sign a 'declaration on the common values of Quebec society' (Gouvernement du Québec, 2009). Even in Canada, the federal government amended the Citizenship Act on 17 April 2009 to restrict the possibility of passing on of Canadian citizenship to endless generations born abroad ('first-generation-limitation').[2] These changes demonstrate a 'philosophical shift from naturalization as a "tool" of integration to naturalization as "end-point" of successful integration' and 'citizenship as the first price' (Joppke, 2008a: 16).

Admittedly, a complete return to the quintessential 'ethnic nation' bound by blood and/or narrowly defined cultural belonging does no longer seem viable, not even in Europe (Joppke, 2008b; Wright, 2008; Faist, 2009). Defining the nation as a community of blood-brothers no longer resonates with the vast majority of the population.[3] It is certainly not a feasible option in terms of policy making and legislation. Even Germany, viewed by many as the notorious prototype of the 'ethnic nation,' introduced a new citizenship law in 2000, which stipulates substantial *ius soli* provisions (Palmowski, 2008) and lays out criteria for naturalization (amended in 2008, Bundesministerium der Justiz, 2008; cf. Michalowski, 2007). Nevertheless, while the late 1990s and early years of the new millennium have been characterized by a growing assumption that immigration and nationality laws of Western democratic states were converging on liberal ('civic') norms of equality and inclusiveness (Joppke, 2007a; 2007b; Heckmann and Schnapper, 2003; Joppke and Morawska, 2003), in many European countries, including Germany, the original opening towards immigration and multiculturalism has recently been retracted (Winter, 2010). Concerns about adequate language and literacy, immigrants' adherence to basic liberal democratic values, and the promotion of both the rights and responsibilities of citizenship have been elevated to 'national preoccupations.'

As a consequence, several countries have recently introduced integration policies and citizenship tests that measure immigrants' adequate skill of a national language, civic knowledge, and value compatibility (Kiwan, 2008; Spencer, 2008; Laversuch, 2008; Löwenheim and Gazit, 2009; Wright, 2008). Some scholars characterize this trend as a general 'retreat of multiculturalism' and a reinforcement of the liberal state (Joppke, 2004; Barry, 2001);[4] others speak of the renationalization of citizenship (Jacobs and Rea, 2007; Fekete, 2006). The insights gained in this book allow us to comment on this trend. Obviously, this is not the place to analyse the transformation of national identity and citizenship in European countries.

Nonetheless, on the basis of the preceding analysis, I will briefly sketch out some new questions and directions for future research.

   In Chapter 7, it was argued that Canadian multiculturalism corresponds neither to the ideal-type of majoritarian or 'dominant' nationalism – which expresses itself through laws and institutions without reference to cultural particularity – nor to that of minoritarian nationalism, where belonging is defined in biological or narrowly defined cultural terms.[5] Rather, representations of the 'multicultural we' oscillate between two conceptions of how and what we do *not* want do be, namely, an individualist, open society without shared values, trust, and compassion, on the one hand, and a closed ethnocentric community where tradition is valued more than individual freedom, on the other. Through this oscillation 'our' perfect balance between national identity and cultural tolerance is produced. Furthermore, it was argued that, in the Canadian case, the confrontation with an external Other – in the form of dominant American nationhood – leads to the realization of the cultural particularity of the dominant group. This and the strong presence of minority groups within Canada – of which francophone Quebec is politically the most effective – produces the view that the national majority shares 'its' society with others. The particularization of the national majority has therefore been viewed as a condition to render negotiation processes around citizenship, identity, and belonging transparent, and as preventing the rights of majorities from remaining unnamed and/or camouflaged and, thus, taken for granted.

   This reminder shows that the Canadian discourses examined in this book exemplify many of the experiences that other countries, particularly in Europe, are currently struggling with. On the one hand, there are strong incentives to 'open' national societies and imaginaries to external forces, which are usually summarized under the heading of 'globalization.' In the context of the European Union (EU), these external factors are also laws and regulations that 'harmonize' national legislations across Europe and bring them in line with the goals set by the European Commission. The initial difficulties in ratifying the Lisbon Treaty in the Netherlands, France, and Ireland have therefore also been interpreted as backlashes against what is perceived as a threat to national identity (McLaren, 2004; Schmidtke, 2005; Westin, 2008). In other words, due to the ongoing integration of Europe, some populations experience a stronger awareness of their particular culture, values, traditions, etc. On the other hand, within the countries that are part of the EU, many of those who had previously been 'others' in legal and symbolic terms have become part of 'us.' Most citizens of EU member states can now travel freely within Europe and also enjoy the right to live and work in the country of their choice within the EU (Maas, 2008). Even though third country nationals – individuals who do not hold citizenship of one of the member states – remain largely excluded from the benefits of EU citizenship, some of the former immigrants and their children have started to naturalize, although in much smaller numbers than immigrants in Canada. Furthermore, as a result of sinking birth-rates and skill shortages, the need for immigration will not go away soon (Commission of the European Communities, 2003: 9–17).

Viewed from this angle, the recent introduction of 'citizenship trajec-tories' in many European countries can be seen as part of the negotiation process between national majorities and their others, those within the borders of the nation-state and those that are (in legal and/or symbolic terms) situated outside it. From the line of argument drawn from the analysis of Canadian newspaper discourses earlier in this book, renation-alizing conceptions of citizenship is not necessarily a step towards the elimination of pluralism as such. On the contrary, if done carefully and within limits, it can actually serve as the precondition of fruitful debate. Rather than pretending to universalism, by rendering cultural claims and rights of the majority explicit, citizenship would become adapted to national contexts. Not surprisingly, in many of the countries that devel-oped integration tests for would-be citizens, much of the surrounding debate centred less on the immigrants than on visions of who/what 'we' are and want to be (Davy, 2008; ngo-online, 2006). This resonates with one of the conclusions drawn in Chapter 7: that the ideal-type of the pluralist nation is civic or associative in so far as it supposes an institu-tional framework, which guarantees the individual rights; but that it is ethnic or communitarian in so far as it does not present this framework as being (ethnically, culturally, religiously, linguistically) neutral, but as coming from processes of historically specific group relations.

This being said, there is a strong risk for the renationalization of citi-zenship to be 'overdone.' To give some examples, in many of the newly implemented citizenship trajectories, citizenship is viewed as having to be 'deserved' and framed as an end goal of – and not as a means for – integration. The emphasis on language competences may be read as fostering social and labour market integration, but mono-lingualism also reminds us of nineteenth-century nation building, which started on the premise of *un peuple, un territoire, une langue*. Some of the citizen-ship tests check for attitudes and an adherence to the core values of the society that would-be citizens are about to join. It is often forgotten that today's societies are marked by a variety of social divisions and highly diverging discourses about 'our' core values. As a consequence, rather than being a balance of give and take – a two-way process – between the host society and the newcomers (Commission of the European Communities, 2003), much of the burden of 'integration' is placed on immigrants who may keep some of their (inter)cultural business competences, but must adapt quickly to the culture and values of their new country. As Thomas Faist puts it: 'good citizens are now not only those who support themselves economically and have no criminal record, but they must also prove that they speak the national language' (2009: 178). A set of questions arises from these observations: Are these new approaches to citizenship indeed 'contextualizing universalism' and 'balancing ethnic heterogeneity and nationalism'? Or are they reintroducing a mix of nineteenth-century type (homogeneous) nationalism? Or, on the contrary, does the pendulum swing more towards a new nationalism based on neo-liberal ideology?

Reacting to these changes in policy and discourse, astute observers have suggested that 'diversity' has become 'a new mode of incorporation' (Faist, 2009). Thomas Faist convincingly argues that the notion of diversity expresses the 'semantic shift from the recognition of collective identity to that of individual competences' (ibid.: 177). Intriguingly, this shift seems only to apply to immigrants and minorities. While institutions of the dominant group are being demanded to adapt to increasing (individual) 'diversity,' the institutions themselves are not multiplied. More importantly, the dominant society and its identity continue to be cast in terms of 'core values' and 'social cohesion.' Here, a critical assessment of the newly introduced citizenship trajectories and their 'oscillation' between civic turn (Mouritsen and Jørgensen, 2008) and renationalization (Jacobs and Rea, 2007) in terms of a triangular relationship could bring some interesting insights.

A second field of study where the insights gained from the research presented in this book can make a meaningful contribution is the study of multiculturalism within divided societies and/or multinational states.

Immigrant Integration in Historically Diverse Societies

The analysis in this book has also shown that that different types of national and ethnic diversity, their representations and accommodations, do not – as their treatment in the current literature suggests – exist separately from each other. On the contrary, in the Canadian context, Québécois minority nationalism and multiculturalism have historically been characterized by a strong logical, discursive, and political interdependence. While this interdependence may no longer be as vivid and immediate as it was during the 1970s, when the multiculturalism policy was first implemented, the print media analysis in this book has shown that it continued to exist during the 1990s. Once more, 11 September, 2001 is likely to represent a caesura in this regard. More research is necessary to show whether and how the discourse has changed after the revival of religion as an important dividing line between insiders and outsiders of the nation. What do these insights teach us for the analysis of immigrant integration and multicultural accommodation in other countries and contexts and cross-national perspectives?

It is now commonplace to hear that, largely as a result of immigration, most contemporary societies in the West are characterized by ethnic diversity. It is equally commonplace to hear that the integration of immigrants and 'their' diversity is to be regarded as a 'two-way process' by which both the immigrants and the members of the so-called host society make mutual adjustments. What is often forgotten is that these same host societies are not homogeneous. Rather, they are often characterized by significant levels of social divisions which are also understood in 'ethnic' terms. As argued in Chapter 3, in political science the terms 'multinational states' or 'divided societies' refer to states or regions (such as Canada, Northern Ireland, South Africa, Bosnia-Herzegovina), which are characterized by deep social cleavages based on ethnic difference. However, historically established divisions that are understood in ethnic, linguistic, and/or religious terms must neither be understood as 'national' nor must they always result in violent conflict. They can also be cast as societal pillars (as in the Netherlands), religious dualism (as in Germany and Switzerland), linguistic pluralism (as in Switzerland, Belgium, and the United Kingdom). Furthermore, they can also exist in relatively peaceful countries. Many countries are divided along regions that used to have connotations of 'ethnic' separateness and were later transformed into administrative units, and many have historically incorporated minorities (such as the Sami in Sweden, Norway, and Finland; the Roma in the Czech Republic, and other countries in Eastern Europe, African Americans and Natives in the United States, etc.). The realization that immigrants often find themselves in societies characterized by some sort of social division along ethnic lines changes our traditional understanding of 'integration.' What does it mean to 'integrate' into a society which is not itself integrated? Into which segment of society are immigrants supposed to 'integrate'?

The recognition that previously established 'ethnic' divisions exist within our societies also alters both our understanding of the multicultural transformation of national identity and the way in which 'diversity' and diversity management are framed. Being incorporated as 'traditions' within the organization of the nation-state, historic group relations and their meanings – such as those imbedded in French/English dualism – impact upon newcomer integration and potential reinventions of who 'we' are and want to be.[6] As newcomers to the social and political arena of established societies, immigrants are perceived and classified *in relation to* existing divisions and social categories. At the same time, immigrants adapt to societal discourses – either in the hope to borrow some of the authority and the legitimacy from movements that are seen as predecessors, or in an attempt to distance themselves from widely despised rebellious ethnicities. As such, taking stock of social divisions along ethnic lines is an important starting point for the analysis of multicultural claims making of immigrants and immigrant organizations (Koopmans et al., 2005; Landolt et al., 2009; Wayland, 1995).

The analysis in this book suggests that the presence of historically recognized multinational regimes is likely to facilitate the multicultural integration of newcomers. In Chapter 8, for example, it has been shown that multicultural claims making in the print media seldom questions 'unnamed' majority rights (e.g., those enjoyed by English Canadians). Rather, presence of the 'named' (claimed/granted) minority rights of francophones and Aboriginal peoples provides a better reference for attack than camouflaged mono-nationalism. Furthermore, in Canada, at the time of the implementation of multiculturalism as a policy (1971), the historically established segments of society were defined in linguistic-cultural terms. As a consequence, it was relatively easy to assert claims cast in ethnocultural terminology, while the demands for anti-racism and remedies against the devastating consequences of colonial oppression tended to be ignored (Bannerji, 2000; Razack, 2002; Thobani, 2007). In other words, in Canada, multicultural immigrant 'integration without assimilation' (Ossenberg, 1964: 204) seems to have benefited from national dualism (better: trinationalism) and a situation characterized by 'a considerable amount of competition' between two dominant majorities with their 'virtually separate social systems [and] their own economic, educational, social, and cultural institutions' (ibid.: 205).

Nevertheless, the research conducted for this book does not warrant the elevation of this particular causal relationship to the status of a general principle. Sure enough, it could be argued that almost all countries that are known for having implemented multicultural policies for the sake of immigrant integration – Canada, the Netherlands, Sweden, Australia, the United Kingdom – are also characterized by a fair share of national minorities and other historically-established diversity.[7] But not in all of these countries has the implementation of multiculturalism been publicly portrayed as a 'natural outgrowth' of historically pluralist arrangements, and we should be careful to reduce it to the latter. In fact, multiculturalism in response to immigration is neither *exclusively* triggered by historical and/or 'multinational' diversity,[8] nor is it a *necessary* outcome of historically recognized diversity. The latter claim can be illustrated by the Swiss case. Although having implemented generous accommodations of its historic German, French, Italian, and Romansh groups, Switzerland is known for being resolutely opposed to immigrant multiculturalism (D'Amato, 2009).[9] As such, the analysis in this book can only suggest that the relationship between the recognition of 'ethnic,' religious, or linguistic divisions within diverse societies (including 'multinational' regimes) and multicultural policies is characterized by certain 'elective affinities,'[10] which do not extend into mandatory causal relationships.

More comparative research is necessary for the elaboration of a comprehensive set of patterns that characterize the relationship between historically recognized ('national') diversity and multiculturalism in response to immigration. Nonetheless, the analysis conducted here reveals a series of factors that should be taken into account when examining the relations between different types of diversity and their accommodations. For example, a first task when analysing the framing of immigrants and their (claims for) multicultural integration should be to determine whether national minorities' ethnocultural difference is 'extended' to immigrant minorities, so that they are situated within a common matrix or tradition of pluralist arrangements.

Second, if a logical, discursive, political relationship between immigrants and pre-existing ethnic/national divisions is established, it matters whether the compromise reached by historically established ('national') groups is characterized primarily by agreement or by a certain amount of non-violent conflict that may impact the multicultural accommodation of immigrants. The analysis of the Canadian case in the 1990s (as well as in the 1970s) suggests that conflict between established groups can be favourable for the establishment of immigrant multiculturalism for two reasons: (1) It helps to uncover and 'name' some cultural accommodations – or injustices – that otherwise would remain camouflaged by presumed universalism; and (2) conflict between established groups increases the need for allies. Reference to countries like Switzerland and the Netherlands, where the established groups are relatively satisfied with the current arrangements, can serve to support this hypothesis. Taking a look at Belgium, by contrast, tells us that the outcomes of multinational struggle are highly contextual. Although Belgium is characterized by a deep cleavage between its historical groups, only the Flemish side has opted for some sort of multiculturalism. Wallonia, by contrast, practises more French-style assimilation (Jacobs, 2008). Thus, it remains uncertain whether the power of immigrant groups as potential allies of the multinational adversaries facilitates the implementation of multicultural rights or leads to assimilation. Because, if in the case of conflict, the established groups are unsatisfied with the principle of pluralism in its implemented state, they may, in fact, be reluctant to grant any substantial form of diversity accommodation to incoming populations.[11] An answer to this question can only be determined on a case-by-case basis.

A third element to be taken into account when analysing attitudes towards immigrants in historically diverse societies is the fact that neither the established groups nor the newcomers are homogeneous and politically united entities. As a consequence, we will rarely find a real-life situation that is characterized by full agreement between all segments of society. In other words, once a logical connection between national and ethnic minorities is established, in public discourse there will always be the latent possibility that stereotypes related to national minorities become extended to ethnic minorities with the intention of disqualifying their claims for recognition (as depicted by Elias and Scotson, 1994; and described in Chapter 5). This phenomenon is most likely to be observed in times of rising conflict between the established groups.

Fourth, the relations between the old and new diversities are not static. On the one hand, the influx of new populations impacts the power relations between the established groups. On the other hand, changing relations of disagreement and compromise between the established groups also influence these groups' attitudes towards the integration of newcomers. The recent demise of multiculturalism in the Netherlands is a powerful example. A society that is increasingly viewed as depillarized and secular also sheds its inclination to grant differential rights to newcomers on the basis of their religious beliefs (Rath et al., 1996). The developments in the Netherlands suggest that the multiculturalization of national identity need not necessarily be linear. Because no compromise is eternally stable, as historic group relations are reinterpreted, the conditions for multiculturalism also change.

Fifth, although immigrant minorities may have been originally situated within a common matrix of traditional pluralist arrangements, this does not mean that immigrant multiculturalism cannot develop dynamics of its own. Confirming findings related to funding and programming issues in practice (McAndrew et al., 2005), the analysis in this book suggests that, over the course of the 1990s, a change in the semantics of multiculturalism in dominant discourses has taken place, from group rights to the accommodation of individual diversity. There is evidence that this change of orientation is part of a growing international trend where 'diversity' – rather than multiculturalism – is promoted as a new 'mode of immigrant integration' (Faist, 2009).

It remains to be seen, in Canada and elsewhere, how minorities – ethnic and national – will react to this change in policy orientation. Will there be new alliances between, for example, national and religious minorities organizing as groups and asking for separate institutions? Or will previously united groups and associations splinter because of increasing 'super diversity' (Vertovec, 2007) and immigrants' preference for individual rather than group accommodation? Both developments would alter not only the premises upon which multiculturalism – in theory and practice – was originally developed, but also change the ways in which multiculturalism relates to the pluralist transformation of national identity.

Notes

1. How Do 'We' Become Pluralist?

1 This study comprises 350 keyword-selected newspaper articles out of which 123 op-ed pieces have been submitted to Critical Discourse Analysis. Newspaper discourses only constitute a small segment of dominant discourses. Besides, they vary regionally and follow a corporate agenda.
2 A rationale for the research strategy – its advantages and limitations – can be found in Chapter 6.

2. A Canadian Paradox

1 Particularly since the events of 9/11, the right-wing populist campaign of Pim Fortuyn, and the recent assassination of film-maker Theo van Gogh, 'a dramatic change occurred first in political rhetoric and increasingly also in policy recommendations and actual implementation of new policies' (Bader, 2005a: 9). In the Netherlands, multiculturalism is claimed to be responsible for high unemployment and crime rates among immigrants and home-grown terrorism, as well as geographical segregation and a 'clash of values' between native Dutch (*autochtonen*) and non-Western immigrants and their descendants (*allochtonen*).
2 The largest group enumerated by the census consisted of just over 10 million people who reported Canadian as their ethnic ancestry. The other most frequently cited origins were English (6.6 million), French (4.9 million), Scottish (4.7 million), Irish (4.4 million), German (3.2 million), Italian (1.4 million), Chinese (1.3 million), North American Indian (1.3 million), Ukrainian (1.2 million), and Dutch (1.0 million).

3 The category of 'visible minorities' is an ambiguous construct. The criteria of 'visibility' refer sometimes to skin colour (e.g., Blacks), sometimes to cultural belonging and/or religion (e.g., Arabs and South Asians), and sometimes to the nationality of origin (e.g., Chinese).

4 This ethnic diversity plays particularly out in Canada's metropolitan areas of Toronto, Vancouver, Montreal, and Calgary. The province of Ontario is home to more than half of Canada's 'visible minority' population. Most of them live in Toronto.

5 Figure 1 uses data from Environics Focus Canada surveys, which are based on samples of 2,000 Canadians. The data were accessed through the Canadian Opinion Research Archive (CORA) based at Queen's University (http://www.queensu.ca/cora). The graphic shows that support for multiculturalism policy was at its lowest in 1994 (35.6%); it then rebound quickly to 45.3% in 2003. Donna Dasko (2003) arrives at similar outcomes when tracking levels of approval of the federal policy of multiculturalism.

6 This being said, even the obvious advantages of Canada's geographical boundaries do not necessarily prevent moral panics related to the seemingly unhindered and massive influx of undocumented immigrants (see Hier and Greenberg, 2002; Greenberg, 2000, for the case of the 'Chinese boat people').

7 Veit Bader, e.g., argues that the land borders of both Canada and the United States can be controlled: 'the American-Mexican border is, in contrast to the predominant rhetoric, in my view, as open or closed as it fits the U.S.' (2005a: 9).

8 This being said, the United States has also implemented 'multicultural' policies, albeit on the local or state level, and more often these are framed as 'affirmative action measures'; for Canada/United States comparisons see Reitz and Breton (1994), Bloemraad (2006), and Grabb and Curtis (2005).

9 The term 'third force' is attributed to Senator Paul Yuzyk. He introduced this term in his first speech before the Senate on 3 May 1964 (Kelner and Kallen, 1974: 33).

10 The point system was legally enshrined by the 1976 Immigration Act. For a critical view, see Simmons (1998).

11 Interpreted as an attempt to bring about the assimilation of Aboriginal peoples, the Statement of the Government of Canada on Indian Policy was later abandoned (Weaver, 1981; Wotherspoon and Satzewich, 1993; Cairns, 2000).

12 The Charter aligns the Canadian political system with the American one in having a schedule of individual rights offering a basis for juridical review of legislation at all levels of government.

13 The preferred metaphor in interculturalism is that of a tree into which vari- ous rootstocks are grafted: A solid Québécois core culture is to be enriched by the contributions from minority cultures (McAndrew, 1996).

14 While the question in the 1980 referendum on Quebec's sovereignty suggested to negotiate 'sovereignty-association' with the Canadian government, the referendum question in 1995 proposed 'sovereignty' along with the pos- sibility of a Quebec-Canada partnership. The result of the 1995 referendum prompted Quebec's Premier Jacques Parizeau to blame 'money and the ethnic vote' (meaning anglophone Quebeckers and immigrants) for losing the referendum. Indeed, although the vote followed 'ethnic' and residen- tial patterns, Quebeckers of all origins criticized Parizeau's statement and forced him to resign (El Yamani, 1996). The outcome of the referendum has been accepted as the result of a democratic voting process. There were no violent attacks or open hostility against potential adversaries.

15 See Bernard (1996) for an analysis of the debates surrounding the referendum.

16 For a critical analysis of National Flag Day, see Rukszto (1997); for an anal- ysis of the sponsorship scandal, see Turp (2000, 2001); for an opposition to the reform of multiculturalism policy, see (Kordan, 1997).

17 In Quebec, by contrast, between 1996 and 2003, the governing Parti Québécois focused on the construction of a Québécois citizenship. Within this approach pluralism is gradually replaced with the ideal of creating a universal 'national *Québécois* subject [which] can neither be ethnic nor Canadian' (Juteau, 2002: 451; original emphasis).

18 For post-referendum relations between Quebec and the rest of Canada, see Trent et al. (1996), McRoberts (1997: 245–76), and Gibbins and Laforest (1998).

3. Theoretical Puzzles

1 Quite often, the debates on multiculturalism are framed in terms of politi- cal theory and philosophy. Sociologists, although not silent on these issues (Juteau, 1998, 1999b, 2000b; Helly, 2003; Eder, 1998a; Eder and Giesen, 2001; Wieviorka, 2001), have had less impact on public debates and politi- cal outcomes.

2 Studying Indonesian society in the 1930s, John S. Furnivall (1939) found different ethnic groups living side by side without substantial interaction other than occasional encounters in the marketplace. Whereas social rela- tions within each ethnic community were guided by distinct moralities according to religion and kinship order, there was no moral control of

conduct for intergroup relations in the marketplace. Furnivall argued that the participating segments in the 'plural society' would, in fact, constitute separate societies were they not bound together by outside pressure, i.e., the colonial power which imposed a Western superstructure of capitalism. Without an overarching social consensus – and the normative framework that informs social (and not only economic) life in society – plural societies are characterized by 'economic symbiosis and mutual avoidance, cultural diversity and social cleavage' (Kuper, 1997: 222).

3 Scholars associated with the 'functionalist school of pluralism' are Raymond Aron, William Kornhauser, S.M. Lipset, Edward Shils, and William McCord. This tradition dates back to the works of Alexis de Toqueville.

4 Bader (1995b) differentiates between four types of societies. The imperial model, based on domination and segregation (apartheid as a state policy, e.g., former South Africa), the 'ethnonationalist' model (*ius sanguinis*, e.g., Germany), the republican model (*ius solis*, e.g., France), and the pluralist, multi-ethnic, multicultural model (*ius solis*, e.g., North America, Australia).

5 On the one hand, Bader distinguishes 'democratic institutional pluralism' (DIP) and illiberal and often profoundly racist undemocratic institutional pluralism (IP), which characterized the plural society. On the other, he argues that DIP is much better equipped to cope with factual cultural diversity than its modern counterpart: institutional monism (2003: 132).

6 Civil citizenship addresses individual rights, i.e., the freedom of speech, thought, and faith, as well as rights to property, contract, and justice. Political citizenship comprises the right to participate in public decision making, i.e., to vote and to become elected. Social citizenship, finally, includes the right to security, welfare, and to 'share to the full in the social heritage and to live the life of a civilized being according to the standards prevailing in the society' (Marshall, 1973: 78).

7 Marshall limits his argument to the employment sector – where equal treatment of individuals with unequal abilities produces a hierarchical status structure (1973: 120–1).

8 In the philosophies of Hegel and Rousseau we find the idea that in order to transcend their particularities and act on the basis of a 'general will' citizens need to be 'equal,' i.e., similar. Those who do not fit this image are excluded from the citizenship and the public realm on the grounds of 'difference,' i.e., the assumption that they cannot adopt the general point of view.

9 Taylor does not use the term 'multinational,' but uses the language of two societies within Canada instead (1994: 60).

10 Strictly individualistic conceptions of the good life may indeed preclude important shared community values that are necessary for individual well-being. Besides, liberal individuals fail to promote social cohesion and a shared collective identity: 'shared values are not sufficient for social unity'; rather, the 'missing ingredient seems to be the idea of shared identity' (Kymlicka, 1995: 188).

11 Taylor's differentiation between second- and first-level diversity thus translates into Will Kymlicka's liberal theory of minority rights.

12 Concepts like Homi Bhabha's hybridity and 'third space' (1990c, 1998; Childs and Williams, 1997; Papastergiadis, 1998) or Stuart Hall's creolization and 'new ethnicities' (1990, 1992, 1996a) imply the idea that cultural hybridity is able to subvert fixed categories of ethnicity and 'difference.'

13 For Nancy Fraser 'the politics of recognition and the politics of redistribution appear to have mutually contradictory aims' (1998: 24). Whereas the politics of recognition promote group differentiation, the claims for redistribution call for the elimination of arrangements that underpin group specificity.

14 Or, in the case of postmodern authors, the material and historical rootedness of ethnic group formation, as well as the social and political continuity of imposed identities are underestimated.

15 See also Day's (2002) response and Angus' (2002a) reply.

16 For a discussion of Barry's *Culture and Equality,* see Barry et al. (2002) and Kelly (2002).

17 Similar concerns for 'unjust' multicultural policies and group rights have been raised with respect to affirmative action programs in the United States (Schlesinger, 1998), and in the Canadian context, with respect to the supposedly illiberal nature of Quebec language laws and their impact on the members of anglophone and allophone minority groups within the province (Hartney, 1995).

18 Republican notions of citizenship, such as Jürgen Habermas' (1994) well-known *Verfassungspatriotismus* (i.e., the loyalty to a constitutional political community) and the French idea of *civisme* (i.e., a civic or public feeling; Schnapper, 1994) describe an overarching civic identity that unites the members of the nation beyond their cultural and social differences and aims to integrate minorities by means of common political values. For a discussion of the differences between liberal and republican conceptions of citizenship, see Weinstock (2000).

19 Some political theorists have therefore developed models that highlight individual agency and interaction within civil society (Walzer, 1995; Mouffe, 1992a). Mouffe theorizes the political realm as a discursive

surface. Mouffe's analysis demonstrates that individuals have multiple identities and allegiances that are not necessarily fixed and exclusive but rather fluid, overlapping, and complementary. It also reveals that political coalition building – a fundamental element of democracy – is based on processes of negotiation and identification.

20 Integration is not synonymous with assimilation, as the former is said to involve a two-way adaptation by both immigrants and the host society.

21 Ethnic associations, e.g., are usually assumed to do both: promote the community's cultural life, language, and values, *and* facilitate the social, economic, and political integration of immigrants and their descendants into mainstream institutions.

4. Social Relations and Processes of Ethnicization

1 Other commentators, by contrast, contend that Québécois 'now generally rank as the most liberal, permissive, or tolerant population in North America' (Grabb and Curtis, 2005: 252; see also Adams, 2003).

2 Tönnies and his followers were the last generation of authors who could innocently glorify the bonds of *Gemeinschaft* and kinship ties. After the horrors of Nazism and the Holocaust, most intellectuals came to favour the virtues of *Gesellschaft*'s individualism over the holism implicit to the notion of *Gemeinschaft* (e.g., Popper, 1950). Only very recently have commentators again evoked positively connoted notions of community (Huntington, 2004; Putnam and Feldstein, 2004).

3 Weber's scepticism and criticism of rationalization is evident in evocations like the famous 'iron cage.' Nevertheless, the communal ethic is not missing from his writings. Weber's nationalism – expressed in his 1895 inaugural lecture, in his political writings during the First World War, and in a few scientific texts such as his 'Intermediate Reflections' – has led some scholars to question even the validity of his analytical sociology (Mommsen, 1965: 132–3; Paré, 1999).

4 If possible, I refer to the English translation of Weber's works. The second page number refers to the German original of the respective texts.

5 The term 'social relation' denotes the existence of a probability that meaningful social action oriented towards the action of others will occur (Weber, 1978: 26–7; 1980: 13).

6 This common interpretation of Tönnies' terms is nevertheless unintended by the author who wants his concepts to be seen as processes (Nisbet, 1966: 79).

7 I will use interchangeably *Vergemeinschaftung*, communalization, and communal relations. I will refer to *Vergesellschaftung* also as association and associative relations.

8 I will use the terms 'monopolistic closure,' 'social closure,' and 'group closure' interchangeably. All terms refer to the *attempted* monopolization of
   power, status, and resources. For Weber, social relations are always open/
   closed in various degrees. On the one hand, the smallest degree of closure
   merely involves the definition of a collectivity's objectives. This implies an
   identification of insiders without the group being opposed to the inclusion
   of potential newcomers. On the other hand, the act of closure is never total
   (Bader, 1995b: 59). Although 'excluded' (from certain resources, opportunities, jobs, symbolic and political representations, etc.) minorities usually
   remain 'included' in the larger social net. (That is why they are 'minorities'
   and not, e.g., independent nations.) Some scholars therefore prefer the
   concept 'marginalization' (De Rudder et al., 2000).
9 Where the underlying differences between status groups are held to be
   'ethnic' (i.e., in terms of common descent), Weber anticipates a social stratification similar to that of Indian 'castes,' i.e., a social order that is guaranteed not merely by conventions and laws, but also by a particular belief
   system (Weber, 1978: 933; 1980: 536; Weber speaks of 'religious sanctions').
   While we may reject this terminology as outdated, ideologies like racism,
   nationalism, and the essentialization of group differences are serving similar purposes of normalizing or 'sanctioning' unequal power relations (for a
   typology of legitimizations for exclusion, see Bader, 1995b: 64).
10 The literary translation of the German term *Gemeinschaftshandeln* is 'community action.' This implies that a communal relationship is necessary to
   initiate collective action.
11 Romila Thapar (1980) cautions that Weber's studies on the Indian caste
   system rely on ideologically biased sources, that Weber overestimates
   the impact of religion, and that he accepts the racially distinct character
   of upper and lower castes. While Thapar is certainly right on the first
   and second points, I hold her to be mistaken on the last. Weber is particularly interested in the creation of a status system through social – not
   biological – causes.
12 I would argue that these relative majority/minority dispositions can be associated with the premises of modern Enlightenment-influenced culture
   ('life as a supreme value') and the external and internal forms of counter-
   Enlightenment that it provokes (Taylor, 2001).
13 Minority groups are incited to identify themselves in more rigid and essentialist and exclusive terms than majority groups for several reasons.
   First, they are classified in essentialist terms by the dominant group, and
   this classification has both ideal and material consequences. The social
   mark attributed to minorities may be internalized by group members, and
   it may lead to increased intergroup relations. Or, as shown in the case of

racialized minorities (and women), individuals stigmatized as minorities may not share many commonalities (other than the stigma) that could be used for the creation of a less essentialist identity. For group action, they may therefore resort to relatively meaningless, imposed characteristics. Second, even if they manage to develop a positively connoted alternative identity, the appeal to 'common descent' is a powerful tool for political mobilization, since it touches individuals' instincts of 'survival' and provides moral legitimacy even to ruthless struggles, such as wars, which are declared as self-defence. Third, and maybe most importantly, minorities lack the power and the means to 'go large'; given the symbolic space being occupied by the majority's appropriation of universalism, 'late coming' minorities are doomed to accept the prevailing model (assimilate) or to insist on the (equal) value of their particularity: they claim to be different but equal.

14 *Gemeinsamkeit* should not be translated as 'community,' 'membership,' or 'identity' as the translators of *Economy and Society* propose.

5. Nationalist Exclusion and Its Remedies

1 Elsewhere, I have attempted a 'Weberian' response to the question of multi-nationalism (Winter, 2004, chapter 3). On the one hand, strictly exegetically speaking, Weber remains ambivalent towards the coexistence of multiple nations within a single state. Although he admits that the state must not necessarily be a nation-state but 'can serve the cultural interests of several nationalities' (1988a: 128, my translation), he does not develop an ethos of multicultural nation building and, even less so, of multinationalism. Weber conceives ethnic pluralism only within the framework of competition and unequal power relations. He therefore goes only so far as to argue that it may well be 'in the interests of its dominant nationality' if the state fosters the loyalty of smaller nationalities by catering to their 'cultural interests' (ibid.: 128, my translation). On the other hand, for Weber, the state obtains its legitimacy from serving the cultural interests of its subjects, and – with increasing 'democratization of culture' (1946: 176; 1969b: 484) – from serving the cultural interests of all its subjects. Denying recognition to large segments of the population would thus significantly reduce the state's legitimacy and, therefore, potentially lead to its own demise.

2 Weber also describes the nation as 'a community of sentiment (*gefühls-mäßige Gemeinschaft*) which would adequately manifest itself in a state of its own' (1946: 176; 1969b: 484). This definition emphasizes the close connection between ethnic/national communalization and its rational

organization through the state. In this chapter, I do not have the space to investigate the relation between the idea of the nation and the state. Elsewhere, I have traced the trajectory from ethnic group formation to the institutionalization of the nation's political and rational organization (Winter, 2004, chapters 2, 3).

3 Brubaker views 'ethnic' here in the sense of ethnically exclusive. For me, ethnicity is not necessarily associated with racializing tendencies and cultural exclusion; rather, it refers to a particular and particularizing dimension of our humanity (Juteau, 1999a: 77–102).

4 Greenfeld replaces the civic/ethnic dichotomy with a threefold distinction. According to her, England and the United States have both developed 'individualistic-civic' forms of nations, whereas nationhood in France describes a 'collectivistic-civic' project, and the Russian and German nations are 'collectivistic-ethnic.'

5 Once collective imaginaries are embodied in national laws and practices, they are difficult to change and, as powerful structures, develop a dynamic of their own. That is why, to give an example, a country like Germany struggled over an extended period of time to liberalize its blood-based citizenship law (*ius sanguinis*), even though few arguments in favour of an 'ethnically homogeneous nation' have been found in recent public discourse (Gerdes and Faist, 2006).

6 Published while the world was still in shock about *Gemeinschaft* pushed to extremes during Nazism and the Holocaust, Kohn's work acquires a strongly normative undertone and lends itself to the portrayals of a civilized, 'modern' inclusive West versus a backward, barbarian 'rest' characterized by traditionalism and ethnic hatred (Chatterjee, 1986: 2–3). At about the same time, Karl Popper (1950) draws a clear-cut dividing line between Western, modern, individualist, and emancipated society and backward, holist communities. More recently, Samuel Huntington (1996), in *Clash of Civilizations*, and Benjamin Barber (2001), in *Jihad vs. McWorld*, follow this trend.

7 Although Switzerland does not fulfil the criteria of a majoritarian nation-state in the traditional sense, its leading elites have managed to bridge existing cleavages by distributing wealth and political representation equally (Stojanovic, 2006; see also Chapter 11).

8 While this theoretical model helps to understand the strong opposition towards multiculturalism in the United States (other than as a strategy of resistance), it does not account for the relatively successful attempt to institutionalize multiculturalism in the United Kingdom (Runnymede Trust: Commission on the Future of Multi-Ethnic Britain, 2000). Since the United

Kingdom is already a composite state internally, it would be interesting to explore the relationship between this traditional type of pluralism and the establishment of multiculturalism (see discussion in Chapter 11).

9 The type of nation that Greenfeld (1992) identifies as 'collectivistic-civic' seems to come closest to this model. The term 'collectivistic-civic' implies that the nation as a whole is viewed as a collective individual (rather then an association of individuals), while the definition of the criteria of membership in the nation remains civic (rather than ethnic). According to Greenfeld, France constitutes such a type of nation. However, France has managed to avoid the 'ethnicization of politics,' and French republicanism remains strongly opposed to any form of ethnic pluralism (Simon and Sala Pala, 2009).

10 See note 1 of this chapter.

11 'Implicit multiculturalism' involves cultural and political pluralism. Its structural and normative dimensions, however, are weak. In 'implicit multiculturalism,' structural pluralism is viewed – normatively – as a transitional means which should eventually be replaced by assimilation. If kept durably, structural pluralism is likely to produce some sort of pluralization of national identity; it would become 'explicit.'

12 While it seems more difficult to change stable institutionalized structures, they are sometimes altered or replaced through extraordinary political efforts. In comparison, mental frames appear to be more malleable and adaptable to institutional change implemented 'from above.' However, mental frames may also be rigid and do not always follow government legislation (as demonstrated by the persistence of racism and xenophobia in many egalitarian polities). In any case, their transformation is a mandatory requirement for the long-term success of any type of institutional change. For different views on national path dependency and religious diversity, see Bader (2007) and Koenig (2007).

13 In his study on immigrant integration in 'bicultural Montreal' and 'monocultural Toronto,' Ossenberg (1964: 203) arrives at contradictory conclusions. Although native language retention and ethnic reading habits were stronger among immigrants in Montreal, they seem to assimilate (measured as interaction between immigrants and Canadian-born friends) more rapidly than immigrants in Toronto, who expose a greater tendency to isolation and perpetuation of ethnic customs and family traditions.

6. How Do 'We' Become Multicultural?

1 As mentioned in Chapter 2, Quebec's national identity is also pluralist. Compared with Canadian multiculturalism, Québécois interculturalism

places a stronger emphasis on shared language and immigrant integration (Gagnon and Iacovino, 2005; Juteau, 2002).

2 Conducting a study on the relationship between academic research and public policy development (Winter, 2002), the answer that I heard most often from government stakeholders was: 'Get it in the newspapers, then it's on our desk the next morning and we'll have take it into account.'

3 Canada's mainstream media are required by law to represent the country's ethnic and cultural diversity (Canada, 1991). Nevertheless, my focus on the mainstream press reduces the extent to which minority voices are captured by the data sample. Due to the slow multiculturalization of Canadian institutions, few editorialists and columnists, and even fewer media owners are members of 'visible minorities' (Henry, 2002). Scholars have also argued that under- and misrepresentations of ethnic minorities in the press are a frequent phenomenon (Fleras and Kunz, 2001). There are nevertheless exceptions, particularly with the *Toronto Star*. I will discuss this further below. See also Chapter 9.

4 I have chosen the *Toronto Star* over the *Toronto Sun* (a local tabloid-style newspaper) because of its greater circulation and its stronger intellectual competitiveness with national newspapers like the *Globe and Mail*. With regards to ethnic pluralism, content, and editorial strategies the *Globe and Mail* and the *Toronto Star* vary greatly. This being said, my study has not been designed as a comparison of the two newspapers.

5 Sometimes, search engines vary in their output. News indexes tag and incorporate articles differently. NewSCan seems to produce the most reliable, comprehensive, and accessible full text results in comparison with LexisNexis, NewsDisk, and equivalent indexes.

6 The terms 'multiculturalism or pluralism or diversity' cover a broad range of Canada's ethnic group relations. Strictly speaking, 'multiculturalism' does not refer to Quebec and First Nations. 'Diversity' and 'pluralism,' however, are not restricted to ethnic group relations but include political, regional, cultural, and gender differences. The terms 'Canada' and 'Quebec' orient the search towards articles pertaining to the pan-Canadian context. The term 'nation' reduces the number of articles that deal uniquely with ethnic folklore, cuisine, and festivals. I tested the adequacy of my keywords by executing various searches with diverse keyword combinations. Comparing the results of these searches served as a control mechanism and allowed me to develop an understanding of the relevant debates over time.

7 Opinion discourses in the mainstream press aim for widely accessible in-depth analyses, sustained reflection, and authoritative interpretation on

important political issues like nationhood, Quebec, and multiculturalism. In a city where 42% of the population are first-generation immigrants and are thus less likely to be schooled in Canada, opinion discourses in the mainstream media are an important medium not only of information about Canada but also of normative evaluation of group relations within society.

8 This method corresponds best to the goal of this study. The names of the journalists and commentators are not revealed. It is at stake here neither to determine a specific newspaper discourse nor to evaluate the political attitudes of individual journalists. Rather, the analysis concentrates on extracting the argumentative strands present in the media text. These serve as proxy for a Central Canadian dominant, politically liberal discourse on multiculturalism. The examination of a newspaper-specific opinion discourse or that of particular commentators would have required a different method of analysis and text selection.

9 Twelve articles (five *Globe* articles and seven *Star* articles) were eliminated because they did not relate to the theme of my study. Four *Toronto Star* 'news' articles were included because they were particularly relevant to my study. There are irregularities with respect to article genres in the *Toronto Star*. Sometimes, articles are classified differently in different newspaper editions, genres shift over time as new rubrics and new series are introduced, and irregular contributions by columnists are classified not within 'Opinion' or 'Comment' but as 'News' or 'Context' articles.

10 The term 'English Canadians' remains ambiguous as the markers of English Canadian identity have shifted from religion (Catholic/Protestant division) through language (French/English division), and culture (English Canadians/multicultural groups) to race (white Canadians/visible minorities). The term 'English Canada' suggests a stronger imprint from Canadians of British ancestry than the term 'English-speaking Canada,' which alludes to the ethnocultural diversity within. Within the data sample, a clear-cut separation between English Canadians, ethnic groups of European origin, and racialized minorities is sometimes difficult. In my analysis, I will point out ambiguities where they occur.

11 Attempts to discern the national and ethnic backgrounds of minorities and immigrants in Canada through word searches in the sample did not provide significant insights. There are Ukrainians (29 counts), Italians (12), Germans (11), Greeks (7). Furthermore, Asians ('Chinese,' 'Korean,' 'Asian') scored 13 counts; 'Islam/Muslims,' 7; Latinos, 7; Africans ('African,' 'Somali'), 5; and Caribbeans, 2. By contrast, the term 'multiculturalism' is accounted for 170 times and 'Canada' scores 837 times.

12 White Caucasian immigrants have become increasingly assimilated into the two majorities, i.e., into English Canadians in the rest of Canada and into French Canadians in Quebec. The new 'third force' is constituted by 'newer immigrants and Canadian-born visible minorities' (T-1998-0614), i.e., it comprises racialized Canadians of fairly heterogeneous backgrounds. This heterogeneity renders group closure extremely difficult.

13 I do not differentiate between different types of immigrant categories (e.g., between immigrants of European and non-European origin, or between the so-called non-white 'visible minorities'). This differentiation would require a different thematic orientation of discourse analysis, which is not the goal of this book. In fact, the separation between different categories ('immigrants,' 'visible minorities,' 'Caucasians,' etc.) is often blurred. This is partly due to a laissez-faire attitude in newspaper discourses; in other instances the blurring of categories serves particular political functions.

14 'The world' is too vague a category to be described here. Most comparisons target European countries, but there is no clear pattern. In the analysis, I will point out the discursive functions of 'the world' and the countries that are used for comparison.

15 A number of articles, particularly those relating to the 1992 Charlottetown referendum, emphasize the importance of Quebec for Canadian nationhood and pluralism. However, they propose to formalize the status quo rather than to go beyond it.

16 The absence of voices for and from Quebec in my empirical material (with very few exceptions, mainly in the very early 1990s) confirms the existence of separate public spaces within the rest of Canada and Quebec (Hacket and Gruneau, 2000). It is also telling that there were no voices from Aboriginal peoples in the media sample.

17 Here, the 'multicultural we' is articulated from the standpoint of particular group membership and affectivity within a majority or minority group. The appreciation of uniqueness – and of the surrounding context – constitutes the condition for a universal approach to equality. Particularity and universality, membership in *Gemeinschaft* and in *Gesellschaft,* in the 'us' and in the 'we' are thus not mutually exclusive. Rather, for Angus, one is the condition for the emergence of the other.

18 For a definition and discussion of anti-foundationalist approaches, see Chapter 3.

19 In Chapter 3, I discuss the theory of majority/minority relations in detail. The naturalization of minority categories is revealed through three elements: (1) the representation of minorities as objects or their 'status of thing' (*statut de la chose*); (2) the 'design of order' (*pensée d'ordre*), i.e., the

argument that the status quo has always been and should not be changed; and (3) the assumption of 'endogenous determinism' (*programmé de l'intérieur*), which portrays minority groups as being 'acted upon' rather than acting (Guillaumin, 1995: 217).

20 First, the occultation of a historical past indicates 'a tendency towards naturalization' (Pietrantonio, 1999: 125, my translation). Having a (national) past, a history, always implies the existence of a social process and thus of agency rather than a fixed, naturalized state of being. While national majorities are characterized by agency, the latter is absent or limited when it comes to minority groups: 'le group dominant se définit par des mécanismes créateurs d'histoire. [Si les] dominés sont *dans* la nature et la subissant, ... les dominants surgissent de la Nature et l'organisent' (Guillaumin, 1992: 71, 78, original emphasis). Second, the naturalization of minority categories and their lack of agency also prevent their individualization. Minority group members are seldom viewed as individuals, but rather identified through the particular attributes imputed to the collectivity that they are perceived to be a part of.

7. Neither 'America' nor 'Quebec'

1 Let me remind the reader that newspaper articles from the sample are identified by 'first letter of newspaper title – publication year – month and day.' Articles are not included in the Bibliography. They can be traced by their date of publication.

2 For empirically based comparisons of immigrant integration in Canada and the United States see, e.g., Reitz and Breton (1994) and Bloemraad (2006). For an analysis of representations of Canadian multiculturalism in Quebec, see Nugent (2006).

3 Greenfeld shows that different types of national identity emerge through imitation and transformation. Historically, Greenfeld argues, national elites have drawn important national models from other countries with 'ressentiment' because they were torn between admiration for the superior model and a subjective feeling of inferiority caused by factual inequality between the model and its local implementation (1992: 15–16; see also Chapter 5).

4 For French Canadians, constructing a difference from Americans is less pressing as their cultural particularity is manifest in their distinct language. That is why, as *Globe and Mail* columnist Jeffrey Simpson observes, the mythical 'Joe' in the famous Molson beer advertisement only speaks for three-quarters of Canada's population: 'Quebeckers, after all, don't define themselves against the United States. If anything, they define themselves against the rest of Canada' (2000).

5 It also remains a question of debate, whether or not this national self-understanding actually translated into policies such as multiculturalism and the Canadian Constitution (Bourque and Duchastel, 1995; Gagnon and Iacovino, 2005).

6 I would like to reiterate that we are dealing here with ideal-typical descriptions of different forms of nationalism. Ideal-types are abstract constructs that (1) do not exist in this form in reality, and (2) do not claim to be exhaustive descriptions of reality. On the contrary, ideal-types are merely of heuristic value. They are meant to improve our understanding of the social world through comparison (Weber, 1988b).

8. To Be or Not to Be Like Quebec

1 Let me remind the reader again that newspaper articles from the sample are identified by 'first letter of newspaper title – publication year – month and day.' Articles are not included in the Bibliography. They can be traced by their date of publication.

2 Aboriginal peoples were mentioned neither in the 1969 Official Languages Act nor in the 1971 declaration of multiculturalism. Being of relative little importance to Canadian political life in the 1960s (Laczko, 1997: 4), their leaders fought a largely unnoticed fight against the assimilationism of the federal government's 1969 White Paper. The latter proposed the elimination of all government arrangements that specifically addressed Native affairs, including the Indian Act and the very existence of a Department of Indian Affairs (Government of Canada, 1969; Cairns, 2000: 51–3).

3 In Chapter 10, I will further discuss the inherent liberalism of the 'new' claims for multiculturalism.

4 In the column at stake, 'the concept of Canada' is indeed described as 'centrist and egalitarian: a compact between various regions and people, the Canadian-born and the foreign-born; a balance between individual and collective rights; and a collectivist commitment to look after the needy without violating their dignity' (T-1998-0701).

5 An ambiguity exists with respect to Aboriginal peoples. They are commonly viewed as Canada's First Nations and – as opposed to 'ethnic groups' of immigrant origin – enjoy a limited number of self-government rights. Nevertheless, de facto, their members are often more deprived in many respects than many Canadians of immigrant origin (Wood, 2003). This speaks to the well-known fact that legal status is a necessary but not sufficient dimension of citizenship (Kymlicka and Norman, 1994).

6 To oppose biculturalism, immigrants of predominantly European origin historically adopted the language of multi*culturalism*. To oppose

binationalism, Aboriginal peoples demanded to be viewed as Canada's First *Nations*.

7 This has prompted Seymour Martin Lipset to claim that French Canadians in Canada, like Blacks in the United States 'are 'unmeltable ethnics' who have legitimated cultural autonomy for other non-Anglo-Saxon Canadians' (Lipset, 1990: 182).

9. Who Constitutes Multiculturalism? Divergent Perspectives

1 It should be recalled that newspaper articles from the sample are identi-fied by 'first letter of newspaper title – publication year – month and day.' Articles are not included in the Bibliography. They can be traced by their date of publication.

2 Under- and mis-representations of minorities have also been revealed in the French-language media in Quebec (Potvin, 2008).

3 The quotation above also recalls the precarious situation of Canadian na-tionhood on the North American continent. It is considered insufficient if immigrants will simply adapt to the 'magnetic continental culture' and become 'North Americans.' Rather, they should also identify with 'our his-tory, our unique struggles and challenges' as Canadians vis-à-vis the more powerful United States. We are used to hearing precisely the same claim from Québécois nationalists who want immigrants in Quebec to not merely become 'Canadians' but also to identify with 'our history, our unique strug-gles and challenges' as 'Québécois.'

4 Interestingly, republican discourses locate 'Britishness' not 'Englishness' at the core of Canada's national identity. 'Canada's monarchy, along with her British parliamentary and judicial systems' (T-1993-0924) are seen as constitut-ing Canada's difference from the United States. It is 'the British connection' (G-1999-0701) that binds Canada together. Even in liberal-multiculturalist discourses, immigrants are portrayed having been 'forced to "assimilate" into the French or British culture' (T-1995-0123). These representations are not without slippages. Sometimes, 'Anglo-Celtic (or British) Canadians' are viewed as having 'given shape to Canada, defined its citizenship' (T-1993-0924), but it is 'English Canadians' who are – in contrast to immigrants and Franco-Québécois – in Canada 'alone, emotionally and psychically' (G-1995-1205). Furthermore, the representation of 'bitterly partisan [. . .] deep divisions between the Catholic French and Protestant British' (G-1999-0701) neglects the fact that not all British subjects are Protestant, such as the Irish. A more detailed analysis would be necessary to explain these representations. Lacombe's (1998, 2002) research confirms these findings. She also finds that the quality of these Canadian institutions used to be attributed to their genuinely 'British' character.

5 Often both strategies – the construction of past and neighbouring other-ness – are employed simultaneously.

6 It is doubtful that they will become 'patriotic' cabdrivers like the ones described further along in the same column: Taxi drivers (whose origins are described as Bangladeshi, Afghani and Indian) 'all think Canada is the greatest nation in the world, even if it lets them down sometimes' (G-2001-0701). Given that many of these drivers are highly educated engineers or physicians who came to Canada only to find out that their credentials are not recognized in their new country of residence, they have indeed been 'let down' by Canada.

7 These discourses were particularly common in the 1990s. Today, anti-liberalism is often uniquely associated with Islam (Helly, 2004; Karim, 2003).

8 Within the newspaper sample, demands for binationalism or multination-alism are rare. The absence of voices for and from Quebec in the collected empirical material (with few exceptions in the very early 1990s) confirms the existence of separate public spaces within Quebec and the rest of Canada (Hacket and Gruneau, 2000).

9 In this study, I have concentrated on group relations rather than cul-tural content. Table 9.1 also summarizes some of the attributes that are associated with 'francophone Quebec' (e.g., French language and cul-ture, separatism, ethnic nationalism, etc.). They vary within and across perspectives.

10 Row 7 in Table 9.1 describes an exception in this regard. Above, I have dis-cussed this representation as a paradox of English Canadian nationhood.

11 The equation 'English Canadians + Quebec ≠ ethnic Canadians' therefore only exists in the negative.

10. The Social Constitution of a Pluralist 'We'

1 None of the proxies 'us,' 'others,' and 'them' refers to an externally clearly identifiable and internally homogeneous entity or group. The model of triangular relations conceptualizes them as being constituted in unequal power relations, which always involve both symbolic and material dimen-sions (as implied in Weber's concept of the 'status group'). Because dif-ferent forms of power (e.g., economic, political, or cultural-symbolic) are closely interrelated, we can theorize recognition as both a prerequisite for and a consequence of redistribution (and vice versa).

2 For an overview of the history of intersectional analyses with a par-ticular reference to their development in Canada and Quebec, see Ann Denis (2008).

3 Today, the idea of 'tolerance' is often rejected as it presumes the acceptance of a power inequality between those who tolerate and those at the
receiving end of 'toleration' (Brown, 2006; Lewis, 2005; Mirchandani and
Tastsoglou, 2000).

4 It should be acknowledged that these conceptualizations of multiculturalism as a strategy of minority containment often start by arguing that social
divisions in the Canadian settler society have been fundamentally marked
by the ideology of 'race.' These studies have the merit of demonstrat-
ing the impact of racism, in theory and practice, for modern societies – of
which Canada is no exception (Bannerji, 2000; Goldberg, 2002; Guillaumin,
1972; McFarlane, 1995; Thobani, 2007). This perspective, which has been
neglected here, lends itself to an interpretation, where the social is ideologically structured in binary terms of white ('us') and Black ('them').
Unfortunately, these approaches often neglect that (1) there are also 'others'
in diverse shades of brown (to stick to the simplistic colour scheme), and
(2) that discrimination based on skin colour – although deeply ingrained in
modern social thought – is sometimes 'trumped' by other forms of discrimination; e.g., those based on gender and religion.

5 After having passed the 1988 Multiculturalism Act in 1989 the Progressive
Conservative government of Brian Mulroney introduced legislation that
created a separate Department of Multiculturalism and Citizenship. This
legislation came into effect in 1991.

6 The redesigned multiculturalism program, announced in 1997–98, was pre-
mised on three goals: identity, civic participation, and social justice. 'Identity'
is described as: 'fostering a society that recognizes, respects, and reflects a diversity of cultures such that people of all backgrounds feel a sense of belonging and attachment to Canada' (Canadian Heritage, 1998: 2).

7 E.g., in a recent Speech from the Throne, former Governor General I.E.
Adrienne Clarkson declared: 'We have a society [. . .] in which Aboriginals,
Francophones, Anglophones – and immigrants from all over the
world – play a significant part. Our history has prepared us to be innovative
in the modern world, where diversity counts for so much' (Government of
Canada, 2004).

8 In other words, the image of Quebec as a 'predecessor' of diversity accommodation that is being used here does not suggest that regional linguistic diversity and – depending on the type of discourse, even 'national'
multiplicity – is to be fully replaced by multiculturalism. However, see
qualification below.

9 E.g., in Britain, Bhikhu Parekh, the principal author of the report on *The
Future of Multi-Ethnic Britain* (Runnymede Trust: Commission on the Future

of Multi-Ethnic Britain, 2000), suggests 'that a formal declaration of multiculturalism in Britain – in the model of the Canadian Multiculturalism Act – would constitute a "statement of who we are"' (*Daily Telegraph*, 10 October 2000, cited in Fortier, 2001: 5).

10 It is often forgotten – and unfortunately not captured by this media analysis – that new Canadians in Quebec were not the only group that expressed a strong pan-Canadianism. Canada's First Nations were also united in their opposition to a separate Quebec. On 24 October 1995, the Cree held a separate referendum on the issue. Cree voters were asked: 'Do you consent, as a people, that the Government of Quebec separate the James Bay Crees and Cree traditional territory from Canada in the event of a YES vote in the Quebec referendum?' The Cree voted 93.6% to stay within Canada. Of 6,380 eligible voters, 77% participated in the Cree referendum (Wherrett, 1996: 5–6).

11 The interpretation of multiculturalism as a fairly shallow consensus in Canadian public opinion is supported by the fact that at the moment of editing this manuscript we are experiencing yet another wave of multicultiphobia (Ryan, 2010: 199–206).

12 As mentioned in Chapter 2, two other measures were a resolution in Parliament recognizing Quebec as a 'distinct society' within Canada, and the 1997 Calgary Declaration (not ratified by Quebec) in which the provinces recognized the 'unique' character of Quebec while affirming the equality of all provinces (Trent et al., 1996; Gibbins and Laforest, 1998).

13 In concrete words, the Court states: 'The clear repudiation by the people of Quebec of the existing constitutional order would [...] place an obligation on the other provinces and the federal government to acknowledge and respect that expression of democratic will by entering into *negotiations* [...] The [...] Canadian constitutional order cannot remain indifferent to the *clear* expression of a *clear* majority of Quebecers that they do no longer wish to remain in Canada' (Supreme Court of Canada, 1998: 28–9, my emphasis).

14 One of the adopted measures was, e.g., the declaration of 15 February as National Flag of Canada Day only three months after the Quebec Referendum (Rukszto, 1997).

15 Many reactions to the motion support this view. To give some examples: Phil Fontaine, Chief of the Assembly of Canada's First Nations demanded that Aboriginal peoples' uniqueness should also be recognized. Intergovernmental Affairs Minister Michael Chong resigned on the grounds that he could not support a resolution that he described as a vindication of ethnic nationalism.

16 In French, the word Québécois is commonly understood to be inclusive of the increasingly diverse population of the province. Cutting Quebeckers

off from the non-ethnic 'civic' dimensions of their social existence reduces them to a group characterized by cultural and linguistic particularities. In other words, they are first ethnicized and then charged with practising 'ethnic nationalism.'

17 In its forty years of existence, Canadian multiculturalism policy has also undergone important changes with respect to its definition and scope (Helly, 2001; Juteau, 1997b; Kobayashi, 1993; Winter, 2007a).

18 Critics have pointed to a deliberate political shift from the equality of groups to the equality of individuals (1969 White Paper), languages (1969 Official Languages Act), and cultures (1971 Multiculturalism) (McAndrew, 1996; Juteau, 1997b; McRoberts, 1997; Gagnon and Iacovino, 2005).

19 Although it must be added that Trudeau also insisted that 'no citizen or group of citizens is other than Canadian' (House of Commons, 1971).

20 The Canadian Ethnocultural Council also challenged the idea of social cohesion underlying the new program. It insisted: 'Social cohesion can neither be imposed nor manufactured. It emerges naturally from the experience of daily affirmation which comes from full participation as diverse, culturally constituted beings' (Kordan, 1997: 138).

11. Comparative Perspectives

1 The two dailies are *Le Monde* and *Corriere della Sera*. The publishing date of the piece in *Le Monde* is 13 September. However, this journal distributes its editions after noon on the day before the published date. The 13 September issue was thus distributed on 12 September.

2 However, the amendments to C-37 also restored the citizenship of Canadians who unintentionally lost their membership in the Canadian nation (Canada, 2009; Winter, forthcoming).

3 E.g., in Germany, 25% of all families (with children who are younger than 18 years of age) are characterized as having 'a background in migration' (Statistisches Bundesamt Deutschland, 2007).

4 Although recognizing a 'remarkable counter-trend toward more restrictiveness,' these scholars reject the notion of a 'restrictive turn' as the current immigration, integration, and naturalization policies remain embedded within a liberal framework (Joppke, 2008a: 1).

5 It may be necessary to reiterate, once more, that ideal-types are abstract constructs that serve to demonstrate logical tendencies only. They must not be used in a deterministic way to describe outcomes of social processes in the empirical world (Weber, 1988b).

6 While racial ideologies imported from Europe have originally shaped the relations between Aboriginal peoples and French/British colonizers, these historic group relations have left their mark on how 'we' imagine our country today. Thus, in Canada, the fairly recent immigrant-targeting multiculturalism is intrinsically linked to the context of colonization and the ideological mindset of a white settler society (Razack, 2002; Stasiulis and Yuval-Davis, 1995; Thobani, 2007).

7 The Netherlands institutionalized religious-ideological 'pillarization'; in Sweden we find the Sami and the Finnish minority; in Australia Aboriginal peoples are less powerful than in New Zealand, but they are also recognized; the United Kingdom is – as implied in its name – divided into several kingdoms and has granted its 'nested nations' diverse linguistic rights and devolved parliaments.

8 As argued in Chapter 2, there are many factors that impact the development and success of multiculturalism.

9 Switzerland manages the potentially divisive force of its 'own' multinational, multireligious diversity through institutional solutions, legal provisions, and administrative compromises that do not lie in cultural factors (Stojanovic, 2006). Downplaying the existence of (and the need for) any kind of culturalist identity formation, the Swiss uphold a 'strict separation of how indigenous and immigrant groups are [perceived and, consequently,] treated' (Helbling, 2008: 123).

10 Max Weber uses the term 'elective affinities' to describe the relationship between the underlying belief system of certain forms of Protestantism and the capitalist enterprise. While he reveals the 'affinities' between the ideal-typical modes of social action resulting from Protestantism and capitalism, he denies that there is a *necessity* in this relationship. Unfortunately, Weber never defines this term (Howe, 1978; McKinnon, 2010).

11 Furthermore, if we think of a place like Northern Ireland before 1998, the idea of 'conflict' must be qualified. There cannot be immigrant multiculturalism when (parts of) the established groups are fighting each other with firearms and bombs. 'Conflict' between established groups can only be conducive for immigrants' minority rights if it refers to legitimate political adversaries in a peaceful democratic state.

Bibliography

Abu-Laban, Yasmeen, & Gabriel, Christina. (2002). *Selling Diversity: Immigration, Multiculturalism, Employment Equity, and Globalization.* Peterborough: Broadview.

Abu-Laban, Yasmeen, & Stasiulis, Daiva. (1992). 'Ethnic Pluralism under Siege: Popular and Partisan Opposition to Multiculturalism.' *Canadian Public Policy /Analyse de Politiques* 18/4: 365–86.

Adams, Michael. (2003). *Fire and Ice: The United States, Canada and the Myth of Converging Values.* Toronto: Penguin.

– (2007). *Unlikely Utopia: The Surprising Triumph of Canadian Pluralism.* Toronto: Viking.

Anctil, Pierre. (1984). 'Double majorité et multiplicité ethnoculturelle à Montréal.' *Recherches sociographiques* 25: 441–56.

Anderson, Benedict. (1991). *Imagined Communities: Reflections on the Origin and Spread of Nationalism.* 2nd ed. London: Verso.

Angus, Ian. (1997). *A Border Within: National Identity, Cultural Plurality, and Wilderness.* Montreal and Kingston: McGill-Queen's University Press.

– (1998). 'The Originality of the Multicultural Context.' In D. Haselbach (ed.), *Multiculturalism in a World of Leaking Boundaries.* Münster: Literatur Verlag, 65–99.

– (2002a). 'Abyss, or a Located Ethnics? Reply to Day.' *International Journal of Canadian Studies / Revue internationale d'études canadiennes* 26: 133–6.

– (2002b). 'Cultural Plurality and Democracy.' *International Journal of Canadian Studies / Revue internationale d'études canadiennes* 25: 69–85.

Anisef, Paul, & Lanphier, Michael C. (eds.). (2003). *The World in a City.* Toronto: University of Toronto Press.

Arat-Koc, Sedef. (1999). 'Coming to Terms with Hijab in Canada and Turkey: Agonies of a Secular and Anti-orientalist Émigré Feminist.' In

A. Heitlinger (ed.), *Émigré Feminism: Transnational Perspectives*. Toronto: University of Toronto Press, 173–88.

Ayres, Jeffrey M. (1995). 'National No More: Defining English Canada.' *American Review of Canadian Studies* 25/2&3: 181–201.

Back, Les. (1999). 'Rights and Wrongs: Youth, Community and Narratives of Racial Violence.' *Finding the Way Home*. Working Paper 4. London: Centre for New Ethnicities Research.

Bader, Veit M. (1991). *Kollektives Handeln: Protheorie sozialer Ungleichheit und kollektiven Handelns II*. Opladen: Leske & Budrich.

– (1995a). '"Benign State-Neutrality" versus "Relational Ethnic Neutrality," Part I: Dilemmas of Affirmative Action.' Paper presented at Organizing Diversity – Migration Policy and Practice: Canada and Europe, Berg en Dal, Netherlands, 8–12 Nov.

– (1995b). *Rassismus, Ethnizität, Bürgerschaft: Soziologische und Philosophische Überlegungen*. Munster: Westfälisches Dampfboot.

– (2003). 'Democratic Institutional Pluralism and Cultural Diversity.' In C. Harzig & D. Juteau (eds.), *The Social Construction of Diversity: Recasting the Master Narrative of Industrial Nations*. New York: Berghan, 131–67.

– (2005a). 'Dutch Nightmare? The End of Multiculturalism?' *Canadian Diversity / Diversité canadienne* 4/1: 9–11.

– (2005b). 'Reasonable Impartiality and Priority for Compatriots: A Criticism of Liberal Nationalism's Main Flaws.' *Ethical Theory and Moral Practice* 8: 83–103.

– (2007). 'Introduction: Governance of Islam in Europe. The Perils of Modeling.' *Journal of Ethnic and Migration Studies* 33/6: 871–86.

Balibar, Etienne. (1988). 'Propositions on Citizenship.' *Ethics* 98: 723–30.

Bannerji, Himani. (2000). *The Dark Side of the Nation: Essays on Multiculturalism, Nationalism and Gender*. Toronto: Canadian Scholars' Press.

Banton, Michael. (2007). 'Max Weber on "Ethnic Communities": A Critique.' *Nations and Nationalism* 13/1: 19–35.

– (2008). 'The Sociology of Ethnic Relations.' *Ethnic and Racial Studies* 31/7: 1267–85.

Barber, Benjamin R. (2001). *Jihad vs. McWorld: Terrorism's Challenge to Democracy*. New York: Ballantine.

Barry, Brian. (2001). *Culture and Equality*. Cambridge: Harvard University Press.

Barry, Brian, David Miller, Judith Squires, Oliver Schmidtke & James Tully. (2002). 'Review Symposium on Brian Barry: Culture and Equality.' *Ethnicities* 2/2: 261–87.

Bauböck, Rainer. (1998). 'Sharing History and Future? Time Horizons of Democratic Membership in an Age of Migration.' *Constellations* 4/3: 320–45.

- (2002). 'Farewell to Multiculturalism? Sharing Values and Identities in Societies of Immigration.' *Journal of International Migration and Integration* 3/1: 1–16.
- (2005). 'If You Say Multiculturalism Is the Wrong Answer, Then What Was the Question?' *Canadian Diversity / Diversité canadienne* 4/1: 90–3.

Bauder, Harald, & Semmelroggen, Jan. (2009). 'Immigration and Imagination of Nationhood in the German Parliament.' *Nationalism and Ethnic Politics* 15/1, 1–26.

Bauer, Otto. (2000). *The Question of Nationalities and Social Democracy.* Translated by H. Fischer. Minneapolis: University of Minnesota Press.

Baumeister, Andrea T. (1999). 'Multicultural Citizenship, Identity and Conflict.' In J. Horton & S. Mendus (eds.), *Toleration, Identity and Difference.* New York: St Martin's Press, 87–102.

Beiner, Ronald (1995). 'Why Citizenship Constitutes a Theoretical Problem in the Last Decade of the Twentieth Century.' In *Theorizing Citizenship.* Albany: State University of New York Press, 1–28.

Bernard, Paul. (1996). 'Canada as a Social Experiment.' *Canadian Journal of Sociology* 21/2: 254–58.
- (1999). 'La cohésion sociale: Critique dialectique d'un quasi-concept.' *Lien social et politiques* 41: 47–59.

Bhabha, Homi K. (1990a). 'DissemiNation: Time, Narrative and the Margins of the Modern Nation.' In H.K. Bhabha (ed.), *Nation and Narration.* London: Routledge, 290–322.
- (ed.). (1990b). *Nation and Narration.* London: Routledge.
- (1990c). 'The Third Space: Interview with Homi Bhabha.' In J. Rutherford (ed.), *Identity: Community, Culture, Difference.* London: Lawrence & Wishart, 207–21.
- (1998). 'Culture's in Between.' In D. Bennett (ed.), *Multicultural States: Rethinking Difference and Identity.* London and New York: Routledge, 29–36.

Bibby, Reginald W. (1990). *Mosaic Madness: The Poverty and Potential of Life in Canada.* Toronto: Stoddart.

Bickerton, James. (2007). 'La gestion du nationalisme majoritaire au Canada.' In A. Lecours & G. Nootens (eds.). *Les Nationalismes majoritaires contemporains: identité, mémoire, pouvoir.* Montreal: Québec Amérique, 217–70.

Billig, Michael. (1995). *Banal Nationalism.* London: Sage.

Birch, Anthony H. (1989). 'Reflections on Ethnic Politics.' In A.C. Cairns, J.C. Courtney, P. MacKinnon, H.J. Michelmann & D.E. Smith (eds.), *Citizenship, Diversity, and Pluralism: Canadian and Comparative Perspectives.* Montreal and Kingston: McGill-Queen's University Press, 58–71.

Bird, Karen. (2005). 'Multiculturalism in Denmark.' *Canadian Diversity / Diversité canadienne* 4/1: 39–42.

Birnbaum, Pierre. (1996). 'Sur la citoyenneté.' *L'Année Sociologique* 46/1: 57–85.

Bissoondath, Neil. (1994). *Selling Illusions: The Cult of Multiculturalism in Canada*. Toronto: Penguin.

Bloemraad, Irene. (2006). *Becoming a Citizen: Incorporating Immigrants and Refugees in the United States and Canada*. Berkeley: University of California Press.

Bommes, Michael, & Halfmann, Jost. (1994). 'Migration und Inklusion: Spannungen zwischen Nationalstaat und Wohlfahrtsstaat.' *Kölner Zeitschrift für Soziologie und Sozialpsychologie* 46/3: 406–24.

Bourdieu, Pierre. (1987). 'What Makes a Social Class? On the Theoretical and Practical Existence of Groups.' *Berkeley Journal of Sociology* 32: 1–18.

Bourne, Randolph. (1977). 'Transnational America.' In E.O. Hansen (ed.), *Randolph Bourne: The Radical Will. Selected Writings 1911–1918*. New York: Urizen, 248–64.

Bourque, Gilles, & Duchastel, Jules. (1995). 'Pour une identité canadienne post-nationale, la souveraineté partagée et la pluralisé des cultures politiques.' *Cahiers de recherche sociologique* no. 25: 17–58.

– (eds.) (1996). *L'identité fragmenté: Nation et citoyenneté dans les débats constitutionnels canadiens 1941–1992*. Montreal: Fides.

Bouthillier, Guy. (1997). *L'obsession ethnique*. Outremont: Lanctôt.

Breton, Raymond. (1964). 'Institutional Completeness of Ethnic Communities and Personal Relations of Immigrants.' *American Journal of Sociology* 70/2: 193–205.

– (1984). 'The Production and Allocation of Symbolic Resources: An Analysis of the Linguistic and Ethnocultural Fields in Canada.' *Canadian Review of Sociology and Anthropology* 21/2: 123–44.

– (2005). *Ethnic Relations in Canada: Institutional Dynamics*. Montreal and Kingston: McGill-Queen's University Press.

Breuer, Stefan. (1996). 'Von Tönnies zu Weber: Zur Frage einer "deutschen Linie" der Soziologie.' *Berliner Journal für Soziologie* 6/2: 227–45.

Bright, Robert, Elaine Coburn, Julie Faye, Derek Gafijczuk, Karen Hollander, Janny Jung & Helen Syrmbos. (1999). 'Mainstream and Marginal Newspaper Coverage of the 1995 Quebec Referendum: An Inquiry into the Functioning of the Canadian Public Sphere.' *Canadian Review of Sociology and Anthropology* 36/3: 313–30.

Brown, Wendy. (2006). *Regulating Aversion: Tolerance in the Age of Identity and Empire*. Princeton: Princeton University Press.

Brubaker, Rogers. (1992). *Citizenship and Nationhood in France and Germany*. Cambridge: Harvard University Press.

– (1999). 'The Manichean Myth: Rethinking the Distinction Between "Civic" and "Ethnic" Nationalism.' In H. Kriesi, K. Armingeon, H. Siegrist &

A. Wimmer (eds.), *Nation and National Identity: The European Experience in Perspective.* Zurich: Rüegger, 55–71.

– (2001). 'The Return of Assimilation? Changing Perspectives on Immigration and Its Sequels in France, Germany and the United States.' *Ethnic and Racial Studies* 24/4: 531–48.

Bullock, Katherine, & Jafri, Gul. (2001). 'Media (Mis)Representations: Muslim Women in the Canadian Nation.' *Canadian Women Studies* 20/2: 35–40.

Bundesministerium der Justiz. (2008). Einbürgerungstestverordnung vom 5. August 2008 (BGBl. I S. 1649). EinbTestV: 05.08.2008. Retrieved 6 Oct. 2008 from http://bundesrecht.juris.de/bundesrecht/einbtestv/gesamt.pdf.

Cairns, Alan C. (2000). *Citizens Plus: Aboriginal Peoples and the Canadian State.* Vancouver: UBC Press.

Cameron, David Robertson. (1990). 'Lord Durham Then and Now.' *Journal of Canadian Studies* 25/1: 5–23.

– (2007). 'An Evolutionary Story.' In J. G. Stein, D. R. Cameron, W. Kymlicka, J. Meisel, H. Siddiqui & M. Valpy (eds.), *Uneasy Partners: Multiculturalism and Rights in Canada.* Waterloo: Wilfrid Laurier University Press, 71–94.

Canada. (1982). Constitution Act. Retrieved 3 June 2005 from http://laws.justice.gc.ca/en/charter/.

– (1988). *Canadian Multiculturalism Act, Chapter 24, an Act for the Preservation and Enhancement of Multiculturalism in Canada.* Ottawa: Queen's Printer.

– (1991). *Broadcasting Act 1991.* Retrieved 7 March 2004 from http://laws.justice.gc.ca/en/b–9.01/text.html

– (2009). *Bill C–37, Amendment to the Citizenship Act, S.C. 2008, c. 14.* Retrieved 9 March 2010 from http://www2.parl.gc.ca/HousePublications/Publication.aspx?DocId=3437373&Language=e&Mode=1.

Canadian Heritage. (1996). *Strategic Evaluation of Multiculturalism Programs. Prepared for Corporate Review Branch, Department of Canadian Heritage: Final Report.* Ottawa: Brighton Research.

– (1997–98). *Measures Adopted by the Government of Canada, # 381.* Ottawa. Retrieved 9 June 2004 from http://culturecanada.gc.ca/keyrefsearch.cfm?query=veterans&pr=CHRWALK&prox=page&rorder=500&rprox=500&rdfreq=500&rwfreq=500&rlead=500&sufs=0&order=r&mode=simple&cq=&lang=eng&cmd=context&id=47ba72a053.

– (1998). *1996–1997: 9th Annual Report on the Operation of the Canadian Multiculturalism Act.* Ottawa: Minister of Public Works and Government Services Canada.

Chatterjee, Partha. (1986). *Nationalist Thought and the Colonial World: A Derivative Discourse?* Minneapolis: University of Minnesota Press.

Childs, Peter, & Williams, Patrick. (1997). 'Bhabha's Hybridity.' In *An Introduction to Post-Colonial Theory*. London: Prentice Hall, Harvester Wheatsheaf, 122–56.

Choudhry, Sujit. (2002). 'National Minorities and Ethnic Immigrants: Liberalism's Political Sociology.' *Journal of Political Philosophy* 10/1: 54–78.

Citizens' Forum on Canada's Future. (1991). *Report to the People and the Government of Canada*. Ottawa: Supply and Services. Retrieved 23 March 2004 from http://www.solon.org/Constitutions/Canada/English/Committees/Spicer/.

City of Toronto. (2006). *Toronto's Racial Diversity*. Retrieved 9 Aug. 2007 from http://www.toronto.ca/toronto_facts/diversity.htm.

Cohen, Phil. (1999). 'Strange Encounters: Adolescent Geographies of Risk and the Urban Uncanny.' *Finding the Way Home*. Working Paper 3. London: Centre for New Ethnicities Research.

Collacott, Martin. (2002). *Canada's Immigration Policy: The Need for Major Reform*. Vancouver: Fraser Institute.

Colombani, Jean-Marie (2001). 'Nous sommes tous des Américains.' *Le Monde*, 13 Sept.

Commission of the European Communities. (2003). *On Immigration, Integration and Employment*. Retrieved 6 Aug. 2004 from http://ec.europa.eu/justice_home/funding/. . ./com_2003_336_final.pdf.

Cook, Curtis. (ed.). (1994). *Constitutional Predicament: Canada after the Referendum of 1992*. Montreal and Kingston: McGill-Queen's University Press.

Cook, Ramsay. (1995). *Canada, Quebec and the Uses of Nationalism*. 2nd ed. Toronto: McClelland & Stewart.

Copeland, Lewis C. (1939). 'The Negro as a Contrast Conception.' In E.T. Thompson (ed.), *Race Relations and the Race Problem: A Definition and an Analysis*. Durham: Duke University Press, 152–79.

Corbo, Claude. (1996). *Lettre fraternelle, raisonnée et urgente à mes concitoyens immigrants*. Outremont: Lanctôt.

Courchene, Thomas J. (1986). 'Market Nationalism.' *Policy Options* 7: 7–12.

Coutu, Michel, Dominique Leydet, Guy Rocher & Elke Winter. (2001). 'Introduction.' In M. Coutu, D. Leydet, G. Rocher & E. Winter (eds.), *Max Weber: Rudolf Stammler et le matérialisme historique*. Paris: Éditions du Cerf et de l'Université Laval, 1–89.

D'Amato, Gianni. (2009). 'Switzerland: A Multicultural Country without Multicultural Policies?' In S. Vertovec & S. Wessendorf (eds.), *The Multiculturalism Backlash: European Discourses, Policies and Practices*. London: Routledge, 130–51.

Dasko, Donna. (2003). 'Public Attitudes towards Multiculturalism and
    Bilingualism in Canada.' Paper presented at Canadian and French
    Perspectives on Diversity, Ottawa, 16 Oct. Retrieved 16 Sept. 2007 from
    http://www.queensu.ca/cora/_files/diversity_dasko.pdf.
Davis, Howard D. (1985). 'Discourse and Media Influence.' In T.A. van Dijk
    (ed.), *Discourse and Communication: New Approaches to the Analysis of Mass
    Media Discourse and Communication.* Berlin: de Gruyter, 45–59.
Davy, Ulrike. (2008). 'Einbürgerung in Deutschland – blinde Flecken in einem
    Rechtsstaat.' *Die Verwaltung* 41/1: 31–62. Retrieved 10 Nov. 2008 from http://
    www.atypon – link.com/DH/doi/abs/10.3790/verw.41.1.31.
Day, Richard J.F. (2000). *Multiculturalism and the History of Canadian Diversity.*
    Toronto: University of Toronto Press.
– (2002). 'Can There be a Postcolonial Multiculturalism? A Response to Ian
    Angus.' *International Journal of Canadian Studies / Revue internationale d'études
    canadiennes* 26: 127–32.
de Bortoli, Ferruccio. (2001). 'Siamo tutti americani.' *Corriere della Sera,*
    12 Sept., 1. Retrieved 18 Nov. 2009 from http://archiviostorico.corriere.it/
    2001/settembre/12/SIAMO_TUTTI_AMERICANI_co_0_01091210126.shtml.
De Rudder, Véronique, Christian Poiret & François Vourc'h. (2000). *L'inégalité
    raciste: L'universalité républicaine à l'épreuve.* Paris: Presses Universitaires de
    France.
Delanty, Gerard. (2003). 'The Persistence of Nationalism: Modernity and
    Discourses of the Nation.' In E.F. Isin & G. Delanty (eds.), *Handbook of
    Historical Sociology.* London: Sage, 287–300.
Denis, Ann. (2008). 'Review Essay: Intersectional Analysis – A Contribution
    of Feminism to Sociology.' *International Sociology* 23/5: 677–94.
Denis, Serge. (1993). 'L'analyse politique critique au Canada anglais et la ques-
    tion du Québec 1970–1993.' *Revue québécoise de science politique* 23: 171–209.
Dietz, Mary. (1992). 'Context Is All: Feminism and Theories of Citizenship.'
    In C. Mouffe (ed.), *Dimensions of Radical Democracy: Pluralism, Citizenship,
    Community.* London: Verso, 63–85.
Doucet, Michael J. (2001). 'The Anatomy of an Urban Legend: Toronto's
    Multicultural Reputation.' *CERIS Working Paper Series* no. 91. Retrieved
    2 Jan. 2002 from http://ceris.metropolis.net/Virtual%20Library/other/
    doucet3.html.
Drouilly, Pierre. (1997). *Indépendance et démocratie: Sondages, élections et référen-
    dums au Québec.* Montreal: L'Harmattan.
Dumont, Louis. (1979). 'L'Allemagne répond à la France: Le peuple et la nation
    chez Herder et Fichte.' *Libre* no. 6: 233–50.

- (1986). 'A National Variant, I: German Identity – Herder's Volk and Fichte's Nation.' In *Essays on Individualism*. Chicago: University of Chicago Press, 113–32.

Dunn, Kevin, & Mahtani, Minelle. (2001). 'Media Representations of Ethnic Minorities.' *Progress and Planning* 55/3: 163–71.

Eder, Klaus. (1998a). '(Staats)Bürgerschaft – ein analytisch brauchbares Konzept für die Soziologie?' *Berliner Journal für Soziologie* 8/4: 445–52.

- (1998b). 'Warum ist Migration ein soziales Problem? Von einer politischen Ökonomie zu einer politischen Soziologie der Migration.' In M. Bommes & J. Halfmann (eds.), *Migration in nationalen Wohlfahrtsstaaten: Theoretische und vergleichende Untersuchungen*. Osnabruck: Universitätsverlag Rasch, 63–79.

Eder, Klaus, & Giesen, Bernhard. (eds.). (2001). *European Citizenship between National Legacies and Postnational Projects*. Oxford: Oxford University Press.

Eder, Klaus, Bernhard Giesen, Oliver Schmidtke & Damian Tambini. (2002). *Collective Identities in Action: A Sociological Approach to Ethnicity*. Aldershot: Ashgate.

El Yamani, Myriame. (1996). 'De la gaffe politique à l'exclusion: Le marquage du "nous" et du "eux" à travers les discours et stratégies médiatiques de "L'affaire Parizeau" au Québec.' In K. Fall, R. Hadj-Moussa & D. Simeoni (eds.), *Les convergences culturelles dans les sociétés pluriethniques*. Quebec: Presses de l'Université Laval, 191–217.

Elias, Norbert, & Scotson, John L. (1994). 'Introduction: A Theoretical Essay on Established and Outsider Relations.' In *The Established and the Outsiders: A Sociological Inquiry into Community Problems*. London: Sage, xv–lii.

Elmer, Greg, & Abramson, Bram. (1997). 'Excavating Ethnicity in Québécois.' *Quebec Studies* 23: 13–28.

Entzinger, Han. (2003). 'The Rise and Fall of Multiculturalism: The Case of the Netherlands.' In C. Joppke & E. Morawska (eds.), *Toward Assimilation and Citizenship: Immigrants in Liberal Nation-States*. Basingstoke: Palgrave, 59–86.

Ersbøll, Eva. (2006). 'Denmark.' In R. Bauböck, E. Ersbøll, K. Groenendijk & H. Waldrauch (eds.), *Acquisition and Loss of Nationality*, vol. 2, *Country Analyses: Policies and Trends in 15 European Countries*. Amsterdam: Amsterdam University Press, 105–48.

Esser, Hartmut. (1988). 'Ethnische Differenzierung und moderne Gesellschaft.' *Zeitschrift für Soziologie* 17: 235–48.

Faist, Thomas. (2009). 'Diversity – a New Mode of Incorporation?' *Ethnic and Racial Studies* 32/1: 171–90.

Fekete, Liz. (2006). 'Enlightened Fundamentalism? Immigration, Feminism and the Right.' *Race and Class* 48/2: 1–22.

Fennema, Meindert, & Tillie, Jean. (2001). 'Civic Community, Political Participation and Political Trust of Ethnic Groups.' *Connections* 24/1: 26–41.

Fichte, Johann Gottlieb. ([1808] 1978). *Reden an die deutsche Nation.* 5th ed. Hamburg: Felix Meiner.

Fleras, Augie, & Kunz, Jean Lock. (2001). *Media and Minorities: Representing Diversity in a Multicultural Canada.* Toronto: Thompson.

Fontaine, Louise. (1995). 'Immigration and Citizenship in Canada and Belgium: Is the Canadian Model of Citizenship Useful for the European Union?' In M. Martiniello (ed.), *Migration, Citizenship and Ethno-National Identities in the European Union.* Aldershot: Avebury, 93–102.

Fontaine, Louise, & Shiose, Yuki. (1991). 'Ni Citoyens, ni Autres: La catégorie politique "communautés culturelles."' In D. Colas, C. Emeri & J. Zylberberg (eds.), *Citoyenneté et nationalité: Perspectives en France et au Québec.* Paris: Presses Universitaires de France, 435–43.

Fortier, Anne-Marie. (2001). *Multiculturalism and the New Face of Britian.* Lancaster University Press. Retrieved 5 March 2002 from http://www.comp. lancs.ac.uk/sociology/afortier.html.

Fraser, Nancy. (1998). 'From Redistribution to Recognition? Dilemmas of Justice in a "Post-Socialist" Age.' In C. Willet (ed.), *Theorizing Multiculturalism: A Guide to the Current Debate.* Oxford: Blackwell, 19–49.

Fraser, Sheila. (2004). 'Auditor General's Report 2004.' *CBC News Online,* 11 Feb. Retrieved 8 April 2005 from http://www.cbc.ca/news/background/ auditorgeneral/report2004.html.

Frisco, Pierre, & Gagné, Jean-Simon. (1998). 'Le Québec vu par le Canada anglais: La haine.' *Voir (L'hebdomaire culturel),* 18 June, 12.

Fulford, Robert. (2006). 'How We Became a Land of Ghettos.' *National Post,* 12 June, A19.

Furnivall, John S. (1939). *Netherlands India: A Study of Plural Economy.* Cambridge: Cambridge University Press.

– (1945). 'Some Problems of Tropical Economy.' In R. Hinden (ed.), *Fabian Colonial Essays.* London: Allan & Unwin, 161–84.

– (1948). *Colonial Policy and Practice: A Comparative Study of Burma and Netherlands India.* Cambridge: Cambridge University Press.

Gagnon, Alain-G. (2003). 'Undermining Federalism and Feeding Minority Nationalism: The Impact of Majority Nationalism in Canada.' in A.-G. Gagnon, M. Guibernau & F. Rocher (eds.), *The Conditions of Diversity in Multinational Democracies.* Montreal: Institute for Research on Public Policy (IRPP), 295–312.

Gagnon, Alain-G., Montserrat Guibernau & François Rocher (2003). *The Conditions of Diversity in Multinational Democracies.* Montreal: IRPP.

Gagnon, Alain-G., & Iacovino, Raffaele. (2005). 'Interculturalism: Expanding the Boundaries of Citizenship.' In R. Máiz & F. Requejo (eds.), *Democracy, Nationalism and Multiculturalism*. London: Frank Cass, 25–42.

Gagnon, Alain-G., André Lecours & Geneviève Nootens. (eds.). (2007). *Les Nationalismes majoritaires contemporains: Identité, mémoire, pouvoir*. Montreal: Québec/Amérique.

Gagnon, Alain-G., & Tully, James. (eds.). (2001). *Multinational Democracies*. Cambridge: Cambridge University Press.

Gerdes, Jürgen, & Faist, Thomas. (2006). 'Von ethnischer zu republikanischer Integration: Der Diskurs um die Reform des deutschen Staatsangehörigkeitsrechts.' *Berliner Journal für Soziologie* 16/3: 313–35.

Gergen, Kenneth. (2001). 'Self-Narration in Social Life.' In M. Wetherell, S. Taylor & S. J. Yates (eds.), *Discourse Theory and Practice: A Reader*. London: Sage, 247–260.

Gibbins, Roger, & Laforest, Guy. (eds.). (1998). *Beyond the Impasse: Toward Reconciliation*. Montreal: IRPP.

Gibson, Gordon. (1994). *Plan B: The Future of the Rest of Canada*, Vancouver: Fraser Institute.

Giesen, Bernhard, & Junge, Kay. (1998). 'Nationale Identität und Staatsbürgerschaft in Deutschland und Frankreich.' *Berliner Journal für Soziologie* 8/4: 523–37.

Gilroy, Paul. (2004). *After Empire: Multiculture or Postcolonial Melancholia*. London: Routledge.

Glazer, Nathan. (1997). *We Are All Multiculturalists Now*. Cambridge: Harvard University Press.

Glazer, Nathan, & Moyinhan, Daniel Patrick. (1963). *Beyond the Melting Pot: The Negroes, Puerto Ricans, Jews, Italians, and Irish of New York City*. Cambridge: MIT Press.

Globe and Mail. (2003). 'New Canada Series,' 7–30 June.

Globe and Mail Online. (2003). 'Why Advertise in the Globe and Mail Newspaper?' 15 Aug. Retrieved 5 April 2003 from http://www.theglobeand mail.com/advertise/whyGlobeNewspaper.html.

Goldberg, David Theo. (2002). 'Racial States.' In J. Solomos (ed.), *A Companion to Racial and Ethnic Studies*. Oxford: Blackwell, 233–58.

Gordon, Milton. (1981). 'Models of Pluralism: The New American Dilemma.' *Annals of the American Academy of Political and Social Science* 454: 178–88.

Gouvernement du Québec. (2009). Immigration et Communautés culturelles. *Demande de certificat de sélection*. A-0520-CF (2009-02). Retrieved 5 Feb. 2009 from www.micc.gouv.qc.ca/ . . . /Mesures-ValeursCommunes-Brochure 2008.pdf.

Government of Canada. (1969). *Statement of the Government of Canada on Indian Policy*. Ottawa: Queen's Printer.

– (2004). *The Speech from the Throne*. Ottawa: Office of the Prime Minister, 2 Feb.

Grabb, Edward, & Curtis, James. (2005). *Regions Apart: The Four Societies of Canada and the United States*. Don Mills: Oxford University Press.

Granatstein, Jack L. (2007). *Whose War Is It? How Canada Can Survive in the Post-9/11 World*. Toronto: HarperCollins.

Grant, George. (1965). *Lament for a Nation: The Defeat of Canadian Nationalism*. Princeton: Van Nostrand.

Green, Joyce. (2005). 'Self-Determination, Citizenship, and Federalism: Indigenous and Canadian Palimpsest.' In M. Murphy (ed.), *Reconfiguring Aboriginal-State Relations*. Kingston: Institute for Intergovernmental Relations, 329–52.

Greenberg, Joshua L. (2000). 'Opinion Discourse and Canadian Newspapers: The Case of the Chinese "Boat-People."' *Canadian Journal of Communication* 25/4: 517–37.

Greenberg, Joshua L., & Hier, Sean P. (2001). 'Crisis Mobilization and Collective Problematization: "Illegal" Chinese Migrants and the Canadian News Media.' *Journalism Studies* 2/4: 563–83.

Greenfeld, Liah. (1992). *Nationalism: Five Roads to Modernity*. Cambridge: Harvard University Press.

Grenier, Marc. (1992). 'The Centrality of Conflict in Native-Peoples Coverage by the *Montreal Gazette:* War-zoning the Oka Incident.' In M. Grenier (ed.), *Critical Studies of Canadian Mass Media*. Toronto: Butterworths, 273–99.

Guérard de Latour, Sophie. (2009). *Vers la république des différences*. Toulouse: Presses Universitaires du Mirail.

Guibernau, Montserrat. (2006). 'National Identity, Devolution and Secession in Canada, Britain and Spain.' *Nations and Nationalism* 12/1: 51–76.

Guillaumin, Colette. (1972). *L'idéologie raciste: Genèse et langage actuel*. The Hague: Mouton.

– (1992). *Sexe, race et pratique du pouvoir: L'idée de nature*. Paris: Côté-femmes.

– (1995). *Racism, Sexism, Power and Ideology*. London: Routledge.

Guiraudon, Virginie, Karen Phalet & Jessika ter Wal. (2005). 'Monitoring Ethnic Minorities in the Netherlands.' *International Social Science Journal* 57/183: 75–87.

Gwyn, Richard. (1995). *Nationalism without Walls: The Unbearable Lightness of Being Canadian*. Toronto: McClelland & Stewart.

Habermas, Jürgen. (1990). *Die nachholende Revolution: Kleine politische Schriften VII*. Frankfurt: Suhrkamp.

– (1994). *Faktizität und Geltung: Beiträge zur Diskurstheorie des Rechts und des demokratischen Rechtsstaats.* Frankfurt: Suhrkamp.

Hacket, Robert A., & Gruneau, Richard. (2000). *The Missing News: Filters and Blind Spots in Canada's Press.* Ottawa: Canadian Centre for Policy Alternatives.

Hage, Ghassan. (1998). *White Nation: Fantasies of White Supremacy in a Multicultural Society.* Annandale: Pluto Australia, Comerford and Miller.

Hall, Stuart. (1990). 'Cultural Identity and Diaspora.' In J. Rutherford (ed.), *Identity: Community, Culture, Difference.* London: Lawrence & Wishart, 222–37.

– (1992). 'New Ethnicities.' In J. Donald & A. Rattansi (eds.), *Race, Culture and Difference.* London: Sage, 252–9.

– (1996a). 'Introduction: Who Needs "Identity"?' In P. Du Gay (ed.), *Questions of Cultural Identity.* London: Sage, 1–17.

– (1996b). 'The Question of Cultural Identity.' In S. Hall, D. Held, D. Hubert & K. Thompson (eds.), *Modernity: An Introduction to Modern Societies.* Cambridge: Oxford University Press, 595–634.

– (1997). *Representation: Cultural Representations and Signifying Practices.* London: Sage.

Haque, Eve. (2005). *Multiculturalism within a Bilingual Framework: Language and the Racial Ordering of Difference and Belonging in Canada.* Doctoral dissertation, Department of Sociology and Equity Studies in Education, OISE, University of Toronto.

Harell, Allison. (2009). 'Minority-Majority Relations in Canada: The Rights Regime and the Adoption of Multicultural Values.' Paper presented at the Canadian Political Science Association Annual Meeting, Carleton University, Ottawa, 27–9 May.

Hartney, Michael. (1995). 'Some Confusions Concerning Collective Rights.' In W. Kymlicka (ed.), *The Rights of Minoritiy Cultures.* New York: Oxford University Press, 202–27.

Harzig, Christiane. (2004). *Einwanderung und Politik: Historische Erinnerung und Politische Kultur als Gestaltungsressource in den Niederlanden, Schweden und Kanada.* Göttingen: V&R unipress.

Hechter, Michael. (1975). *Internal Colonialism: The Celtic Fringe in British National Development, 1536–1966.* Berkeley: University of California Press.

– (1987). *Principles of Group Solidarity.* Berkeley: University of California Press.

Heckmann, Friedrich, & Schnapper, Dominique. (eds.). (2003). *The Integration of Immigrants in European Societies: National Differences and Trends of Convergence.* Bamberg: European Forum for Migration Studies.

Helbling, Marc. (2008). 'Variations across Space, Persistance over Time.' *Canadian Diversity / Diversité canadienne* 6/4: 121–4.

Helly, Denise. (1999). 'Une injonction: Appartenir, participer. Le retour de la cohésion sociale et du bon citoyen.' *Lien social et politiques* 41: 35–46.

– (2001). 'Primauté des droits ou cohésion sociale? Les limites du multiculturalisme canadien 1971–1999.' In M. Wieviorka & J. Ohana (eds.), *La différence culturelle: Une reformulation des débats. Colloque de Cerisy*, Paris: Balland, 414–27.

– (2003). 'Social Cohesion and Cultural Plurality.' *Canadian Journal of Sociology* 28/1: 19–42.

– (2004). 'Are Muslims Discriminated against in Canada since September 2001?' *Canadian Ethnic Studies* 36/1: 24–47.

Helly, Denise, & Van Schendel, Nicolas. (2001). *Appartenir au Québec: Citoyenneté, nation et société civile. Enquête à Montréal, 1995.* Quebec: Presses de l'Université Laval.

Henry, Frances. (2002). 'Canada's Contribution to the "Managment" of Ethno-Cultural Diversity.' *Canadian Journal of Communication* 27: 231–42.

Henry, Frances, & Tator, Carol. (2002). *Discourses of Domination: Racial Bias in the Canadian English-Language Press.* Toronto: University of Toronto Press.

– (2006). *Racial Profiling in Canada: Challenging the Myth of 'a Few Bad Apples.'* Toronto: University of Toronto Press.

Henry, Frances, Carol Tator, Winston Mattis & Tim Rees. (2000). *The Colour of Democracy: Racism in Canadian Society.* 2nd ed. Toronto: Harcourt Brace.

Herder, Johann Gottfried von. ([1773] 1968). *Von deutscher Art und Kunst.* Darmstadt: Wissenschaftliche Buchgesellschaft.

Hiebert, Daniel, Jock Collins & Paul Spoonley. (2003). 'Uneven Globalization: Neoliberal Regimes, Immigration, and Multiculturalism in Australia, Canada, and New Zealand.' *RIIM Working Papers Series* 03–05: 1–31.

Hier, Sean, & Greenberg, Joshua. (2002). 'News Discourse and the Problematization of Chinese Migration to Canada.' In F. Henry & C. Tator (eds.), *Discourses of Domination: Racial Bias in the Canadian English-Language Press.* Toronto: University of Toronto Press, 138–62.

Hirschman, Albert O. (1991). *Deux siècles de rhétorique réactionnaire.* Paris: Fayard.

Holton, Robert. (2003). 'Max Weber and the Interpretative Tradition.' In G. Delanty & E.F. Isin (eds.), *Handbook of Historical Sociology.* London: Sage, 27–38.

House of Commons. (1971). *Debates.* Ottawa: Queen's Printer, 8 Oct.

Howe, Richard Herbert. (1978). 'Max Weber's Elective Affinities: Sociology within the Bounds of Pure Reason.' *American Journal of Sociology* 84/2: 366–85.

Huntington, Samuel P. (1996). *The Clash of Civilizations and the Remaking of World Order.* New York: Simon & Schuster.

– (2004). *Who Are We? The Challenges to America's National Identity.* New York: Simon & Schuster.

Hussain, Asifa, & Miller, William. (2006). *Multicultural Nationalism: Islamophobia, Anglophobia, and Devolution.* Oxford: Oxford University Press.

Ignatieff, Michael. (1994). *Blood and Belonging: Journeys into the New Nationalism.* Toronto: Penguin.

– (2000). *The Rights Revolution.* Toronto: Anansi.

Isin, Engin F. (2002). *Being Political: Genealogies of Citizenship.* Minneapolis: University of Minnesota Press.

Isin, Engin F., & Wood, Patricia K. (1999). *Citizenship and Identity.* London: Sage.

Jacobs, Dirk. (2008). 'Belgium and Its Struggle with Citizenship.' *Canadian Diversity / Diversité canadienne* 6/4: 28–31.

Jacobs, Dirk, & Rea, Andrea. (2007). 'The End of National Models? Integration Courses and Citizenship Trajectories in Europe.' *International Journal on Multicultural Societies* 9/2: 264–83.

Jakubowicz, Andrew. (2005). 'Multiculturalism in Australia: Apogee or Nadir?' *Canadian Diversity / Diversité canadienne* 4/1: 15–18.

Jedwab, Jack. (2005). 'Neither Finding nor Losing Our Way: The Debate over Canadian Multiculturalism.' *Canadian Diversity / Diversité canadienne* 4/1: 95–102.

Jefferess, David. (2002). 'The Borders of Compassion: The Canadian Imaginary and Its External Others.' *International Journal of Canadian Studies/ Revue internationale d'études canadiennes* 25: 43–67.

Jenkins, Richard. (1997). *Rethinking Ethnicity: Arguments and Explorations.* London: Sage.

Jenson, Jane. (2002). 'Identifying the Links: Social Cohesion and Culture.' *Canadian Journal of Communications* 27: 141–51.

Jhappan, Radha. (1993). 'Inherency, Three Nations and the Collective Rights: The Evolution of Aboriginal Constitutional Discourse from 1982 to the Charlottetown Accord.' *International Journal of Canadian Studies/Revue internationale d'études canadiennes* 7–8: 225–60.

Jiwani, Yasmin, & Dakroury, Aliaa. (eds.). (2009). 'Veiling Differences: Mediating Race, Gender and Nation in Canada.' Special Issue of *Global Media Journal. Canadian Edition* 2/2.

Joppke, Christian. (1998). 'Multiculturalism and Immigration: A Comparison of the United States, Germany and Great Britain.' In D. Jacobson (ed.), *The Immigration Reader: America in a Multidisciplinary Perspective.* Oxford: Blackwell, 285–319.

– (2002). 'Multicultural Citizenship.' In B.S. Turner (ed.), *Handbook of Citizenship Studies*. London: Sage, 245–58.
– (2004). 'The Retreat of Multiculturalism in the Liberal State: Theory and Policy.' *British Journal of Sociology* 55/2: 237–57.
– (2007a). 'Beyond National Models: Civic Integration Policies for Immigrants in Western Europe.' *Western European Politics* 30/1: 1–22.
– (2007b). 'Transformation of Citizenship: Status, Rights, Identity.' *Citizenship Studies* 11/1: 37–48.
– (2008a). 'Comparative Citizenship: A Restrictive Turn in Europe.' *Law and Ethics of Human Rights* 2/1: 1–41.
– (2008b). 'Immigration and the Identity of Citizenship: The Paradox of Universalism.' *Citizenship Studies* 12/6: 533–46.
Joppke, Christian, & Morawska, Ewa. (eds.). (2003). *Toward Assimilation and Citizenship: Immigrants in Liberal Nation-States*. Basingstoke: Palgrave.
Juteau, Danielle. (1993). *L'intégration dans une société pluraliste: Les relations inter-communautaires au Québec – un diagnostic qualitatif*. Montreal: Gouvernement du Québec, Ministère des Communautés Culturelles et de l'Immigration.
– (1996). 'Theorizing Ethnicity and Ethnic Communalisations at the Margins: From Quebec to the World System.' *Nations and Nationalism* 2/1: 45–66.
– (1997a). *Citizenship Rights, Integration and Multiculturalism*. In A. J. Peck & R. Maiworm (eds.). *Multiculturalism in an Age of Xenophobia: Canadian, American, and German Perspectives*. CD-ROM 31, Cincinnati: American Jewish Archives.
– (1997b). 'Multicultural Citizenship: The Challenge of Pluralism in Canada.' In V.M. Bader (ed.), *Citizenship and Exclusion*. London: Macmillan, 96–112.
– (1998). 'Les enjeux de la citoyenneté: Un bilan sociologique.' In J.H. Black et al. (eds.), *Les enjeux de la citoyenneté: Un bilan interdisciplinaire – A Multidisciplinary Approach*. Montreal: Immigration et métropoles, 47–72.
– (1999a). *L'ethnicité et ses frontières*. Montreal: Presses de l'Université de Montréal.
– (1999b). 'Le multiculturalisme est-il compatible avec l'idée moderne de la citoyenneté?' In I. Simon-Barouh & V. De Rudder (eds.), *Migrations inter-nationales et relations interethniques: Recherche politique et société – actes du colloque Migrations internationales et relations interethniques, Rennes 18–19–20 septembre 1997*. Paris: L'Harmattan, 227–35.
– (2000a). 'Du dualisme canadien au pluralisme québécois.' In M. McAndrew & F. Gagnon (eds.), *Relations ethniques et éducation dans les sociétés divisées (Québec, Irlande du Nord, Catalogne et Belgique)*. Paris: L'Harmattan, 13–26.
– (2000b). 'Les défis de l'option pluraliste.' In M. Venne (ed.), *Penser la nation québécoise*. Montreal: Québec/Amérique, 199–214.

- (2002). 'The Citizen Makes an Entrée: Redefining the National Community in Quebec.' *Citizenship Studies* 6/4: 441–58.
- (2003). 'Differentiation, Social Policy, and Citizenship Rights.' In D. Juteau (ed.), *Social Differentiation: Patterns and Processes*. Toronto: University of Toronto Press, 253–60.

Juteau, Danielle, Marie McAndrew & Linda Pietrantonio. (1998). 'Multiculturalism à la Canadian and Intégration à la Québécoise: Transcending Their Limits.' In R. Bauböck & J. Rundell (eds.), *Blurred Boundaries: Migration, Ethnicity and Citizenship*. Aldershot: Ashgate, 95–110.

Juteau-Lee, Danielle. (1979). 'La sociologie des frontières ethniques en devenir.' In D. Juteau-Lee (ed., with L. Laforge), *Frontières ethniques en devenir/Emerging Ethnic Boundaries*. Ottawa: Éditions de l'Université d'Ottawa, 1–19.

Kalberg, Stephen. (1989). 'Max Webers historisch-vergleichende Untersuchungen und das "Webersche Bild der Neuzeit": Eine Gegenüberstellung.' In J. Weiss (ed.), *Max Weber heute*. Frankfurt: Suhrkamp, 425–44.
- (1994). *Max Weber's Comparative-Historical Sociology*. Cambridge: Polity.
- (2000). 'Max Weber.' In G. Ritzer (ed.), *The Blackwell Companion to Major Social Theorists*. Oxford: Blackwell, 144–204.

Kallen, Horace. (1915). 'Democracy versus the Melting Pot: A Study of American Nationality.' *Nation*, 18 and 25 Feb. Retrieved 5 Jan. 2008 from http://www.expo98.msu.edu/people/Kallen.htm.

Kanstroom, Daniel. (1993). 'Wer sind wir wieder? Laws of Asylum, Immigration, and Citizenship in the Struggle for the Soul of the New Germany.' *Yale Journal of International Law* 18: 155–211.

Kaplan, William. (2006). 'Is It Time to Close Hotel Canada?' *Maclean's*. 25 Dec. Retrieved 10 Jan. 2009 from http://www.macleans.ca/canada/national/article.jsp?content=20061225_138563_138563.

Karim, Karim H. (1993). 'Constructions, Deconstructions and Reconstructions: Competing Canadian Discourses on Ethnocultural Terminology.' *Canadian Journal of Communication* 18/2: 197–218.
- (1997). 'The Historical Resilience of Primary Stereotypes: Core Images of the Muslim Other.' In S.H. Riggins (ed.), *The Language of Politics of Exclusion: Others in Discourse*. London: Sage, 153–82.
- (2002). 'The Multiculturalism Debate in Canadian Newspapers: The Harbinger of a Political Storm?' *Journal for International Migration and Integration* 3/3&4: 439–55.
- (2003). *Islamic Peril: Media and Global Violence*. Updated ed. Montreal: Black Rose Books.

- (2008). 'Press, Public Sphere, and Pluralism: Multiculturalism Debates in Canadian English-Language Newspapers.' *Canadian Ethnic Studies / Études ethniques au Canada* 40/1–2: 57–78.

Kaufmann, Eric P. (ed.). (2004). *Rethinking Ethnicity: Majority Groups and Dominant Minorities.* London: Routledge.

Kelly, Paul Joseph. (ed.). (2002). *Multiculturalism Reconsidered: Culture and Equality and Its Critics.* Malden: Polity, Blackwell.

Kelner, Merrijoy, & Kallen, Evelyn. (1974). 'The Multicultural Policy: Canada's Response to Ethnic Diversity.' *Journal of Comparative Sociology* 2: 21–34.

Kent, Tom. (2008). 'Canada Is Much More Than a Hotel; If They Are Not Ready to Commit to a Citizenship That Has Real Consequences, Immigrants Should Move On.' *Globe and Mail*, 26 April, A25.

Kernerman, Gerald. (2005). *Multicultural Nationalism: Civilizing Difference, Constituting Community.* Vancouver: UBC Press.

Kesterton, Wilfred H. (1984). *A History of Journalism in Canada.* Ottawa: Carleton University Press.

Kivisto, Peter, & Faist, Thomas. (2010). *Beyond a Border: The Causes and Consequences of Contemporary Immigration.* Thousand Oaks: Sage.

Kiwan, Dina. (2008). 'A Journey to Citizenship in the United Kingdom.' *International Journal on Multicultural Societies* 10/1: 60–75.

Knöbl, Wolfgang. (2003). 'Theories That Won't Pass Away: The Never-Ending Story of Modernization Theory.' In G. Delanty & E.F. Isin (eds.), *Handbook of Historical Sociology.* London: Sage, 97–107.

Kobayashi, Audrey. (1993). 'Multiculturalism: Representing a Canadian Institution.' In J. Duncan & D. Ley (eds.), *Place/Culture/Representation.* London: Routledge, 205–31.

Koenig, Matthias. (2007). 'Europeanising the Governance of Religious Diversity: An Institutionalist Account of Muslim Struggles for Public Recognition.' *Journal of Ethnic and Migration Studies* 33/6: 911–32.

Kohn, Hans. (1955). *Nationalism: Its Meaning and History.* Princeton: Van Nostrand.

Koopmans, Ruud, & Statham, Paul. (2003). 'How National Citizenship Shapes Transnationalism: Migrant and Minority Claims-Making in Germany, Great Britain and the Netherlands.' In C. Joppke & E. Morawska (eds.), *Toward Assimilation and Citizenship: Immigrants in Liberal Nation-States.* Basingstoke: Palgrave, 195–238.

Koopmans, Ruud, Paul Statham, Marco Giugni & Florence Passy. (2005). *Contested Citizenship: Immigration and Cultural Diversity in Europe.* Minneapolis: University of Minnesota Press.

Kordan, Bohdan S. (1997). 'Multiculturalism, Citizenship and the Canadian Nation: A Critique of the Proposed Design for Program Renewal.' *Canadian Ethnic Studies* 29/2: 136–43.

Kress, Günther. (2000). 'Text as the Punctuation of Semiosis: Pulling at Some of the Threads.' In U. Meinhof & J. Smith (eds.), *Intertextuality and the Media: From Genre to Everyday Life*. New York: Manchester University Press, 132–54.

Kuper, Leo. (1997). 'Plural Societies.' In M. Guibernau & J. Rex (eds.), *The Ethnicity Reader: Nationalism, Multiculturalism and Migration*. Cambridge: Polity, 220–8.

Kymlicka, Will. (1995). *Multicultural Citizenship: A Liberal Theory of Minority Rights*. Oxford: Clarendon.

– (1998). *Finding Our Way: Rethinking Ethnocultural Relations in Canada*. Toronto: Oxford University Press.

– (2001). *Politics in the Vernacular: Nationalism, Multiculturalism, and Citizenship*. New York: Oxford University Press.

– (2003). 'Being Canadian.' *Government and Opposition* 38/3: 357–85.

– (2004). 'Marketing Canadian Pluralism in the International Arena.' *International Journal* 59/4: 829–52.

– (2005). 'The Uncertain Futures of Multiculturalism.' *Canadian Diversity / Diversité canadienne* 4/1: 82–5.

– (2007). 'Ethnocultural Diversity in a Liberal State: Making Sense of the Canadian Model(s).' In K.G. Banting, T. J. Courchene & F. L. Seidle (eds.), *Belonging? Diversity, Recognition and Shared Citizenship in Canada*. Montreal: IRPP, 39–86.

– (2009). 'The Rise and Fall of Multiculturalism? New Debates on Inclusion and Accommodation in Diverse Societies.' In S. Vertovec & S. Wessendorf (eds.), *The Multiculturalism Backlash: European Discourses, Policies and Practices*. London: Routledge, 32–49.

Kymlicka, Will, & Norman, Wayne. (1994). 'Return of the Citizen: A Survey of Recent Work on Citizenship Theory.' *Ethics* 104: 352–81.

Labelle, Micheline, & Rocher, François. (2004). 'Debating Citizenship in Canada: The Collide of Two Nation-Building Projects.' In P. Boyer, L. Cardinal & D. Headon (eds.), *From Subjects to Citizens: A Hundred Years of Citizenship in Australia and Canada*. Ottawa: University of Ottawa Press, 263–86.

Labelle, Micheline, François Rocher, Ann-Marie Field & Jean-Claude Icart. (2007). *Le concept d'interculturalisme en contexte québécois: Généalogie d'un néologisme*. Rapport présenté à la Commission de consultation sur les pratiques d'accommodement reliées aux différences culturelles (CCPARDC), 21 Dec. Montreal: Centre de recherche sur l'immigration, l'ethnicité et la citoyenneté, UQAM. Retrieved 15 March 2008 from http://www.accommodements. qc.ca/documentation/rapports/rapport-3-rocher-francois.pdf.

Labelle, Micheline, François Rocher & Rachad Antonius. (2009). *Immigration, diversité et sécurité: Les associations arabo-musulmanes face à l'État au Canada et au Québec.* Quebec: Presses de l'Université du Québec.

Lacombe, Sylvie. (1997). 'Imperial Loyalism: The English Canadian Ideal of Christian Universality.' In C. Coates (ed.), *Imperial Canada 1867–1917.* Edinburgh: Centre of Canadian Studies, University of Edinburgh, 187–95.

– (1998). '"Le couteau sous la gorge" – Ou la perception du souverainisme québécois dans la presse canadienne-anglaise.' *Recherches sociographiques* 39/2–3: 271–90.

– (2002). *La rencontre de deux peuples élus: Comparaison des ambitions nationale et impériale au Canada entre 1896 et 1920.* Quebec: Presses de l'Université Laval.

– (2007). 'La perception du souverainisme québécois dans le *Globe and Mail* dix ans après le référendum de 1995: Du syndrome post-traumatique au repli légaliste.' *Canadian Journal of Media Studies* 2/1: 1–39.

Laczko, Leslie S. (1994). 'Canada's Pluralism in Comparative Perspective.' *Ethnic and Racial Studies* 17/1: 20–41.

– (1997). 'Attitudes towards Aboriginal Issues in Canada: The Changing Role of the Language Cleavage.' *Quebec Studies* 23: 3–12.

Landolt, Patricia, Luin Goldring & Judith Bernhard. (2009). 'Between Grassroots Politics and the Ethnicizing Imperative of the Multicultural State: Latin American Immigrant Organizations in Toronto.' *CERIS Working Paper Series* no. 73: 1–25.

Laversuch, Iman Makeba. (2008). 'Putting Germany's Language Tests to the Test: An Examination of the Development, Implementation and Efficacy of Using Language Proficiency Tests to Mediate Germany Citizenship.' *Current Issues in Language Planning* 9/3: 282–98.

Lecours, André, & Nootens, Geneviève. (2007). 'Comprendre le nationalisme majoritaire.' In A.-G. Gagnon, A. Lecours & G. Nootens (eds.), *Les Nationalismes majoritaires contemporains: Identité, mémoire, pouvoir.* Montreal: Québec/Amérique, 19–45.

Lewis, Gail. (2005). 'Welcome to the Margins: Diversity, Tolerance and Policies of Exclusion.' *Ethnic and Racial Studies* 28/3: 536–58.

Li, Peter (1994). 'Unneighbourly Houses or Unwelcome Chinese: The Social Construction of Race in the Battle over "Monster Homes" in Vancouver, Canada.' *International Journal of Comparative Race and Ethnic Studies* 1/1: 14–33.

Liddle, Rod (2004). 'How Islam Killed Multiculturalism.' *Spectator*, 1 May. Retrieved 5 April 2005 from http://www.lewrockwell.com/spectator/ spec289.html.

Lijphart, Arend. (1968). *The Politics of Accommodation: Pluralism and Democracy in the Netherlands*. Berkeley: University of California Press.

Lipset, Seymour Martin. (1990). *Continental Divide: The Values and Institutions of the United States and Canada*. New York: Routledge.

Lithman, Yngve. (2005). 'Multiculturalism in Norway.' *Canadian Diversity / Diversité canadienne* 4/1: 53–6.

Longstaff, Stephen A. (1992). 'The Quebec-Canada Crisis.' *New Politics* 4/1: 27–40.

– (1996). 'Canada: The Referendum Aftermath.' *New Politics* 5/4: 44–58.

Löwenheim, Oded, & Gazit, Orit. (2009). 'Power and Examination: A Critique of Citizenship Tests.' *Security Dialogue* 20/2: 145–67.

Lütsch, Julia. (2004). 'Die Wurzeln des Multikulturalismus – der ukrainisch-kanadische Beitrag zur Multikulturalismusdiskussion in den 1960er Jahren als ein Beispiel für die "Dritte Kraft."' *Zeitschrift für Kanada-Studien* 24/2: 99–117.

Ma, Jianming, & Hildebrandt, Kai. (1993). 'Canadian Coverage of the Ethnic Chinese Community: A Content Analysis of the *Toronto Star* and the *Vancouver Sun*, 1970–1990.' *Canadian Journal of Communication* 18: 479–96.

Maas, Willem. (2008). 'Migrants, States, and EU Citizenship's Unfulfilled Promise.' *Citizenship Studies* 12/6: 583–96.

Mackey, Eva. (1999). *The House of Difference: Cultural Politics and National Identity in Canada*. London: Routledge.

Macklin, Audrey. (2005). 'Multiculturalism in a Time of Privatization: Faith-Based Arbitration and Gender Equality.' *Canadian Diversity/Diversité canadienne* 4/3: 75–9.

Maddibo, Amal. (2006). *Minority within a Minority: Black Francophone Immigrants and the Dynamics of Power and Resistance*. New York: Routledge.

Mahtani, Minelle. (2001). 'Representing Minorities: Canadian Media and Minority Identities.' Paper presented at the Canadian National Metropolis Conference, Halifax, 1–2 Nov.

Máiz, Ramón, & Requejo, Ferran. (2005). 'Introduction.' In R. Máiz & F. Requejo (eds.), *Democracy, Nationalism and Multiculturalism*. London: Frank Cass, 1–12.

Malesevic, Sinisa. (2004). *The Sociology of Ethnicity*. London: Sage.

Mann, Michael. (1996). 'Ruling Class Strategies and Citizenship.' In M. Bulmer & A.M. Rees (eds.), *Citizenship Today: The Contemporary Relevance of T.H. Marshall*. London: UCL Press, 125–44.

Manz, Stefan. (2004). 'Constructing a Normative National Identity: The Leitkultur-Debate in Germany, 2000/2001.' *Journal of Multilingual and Multicultural Development* 25/5&6: 481–96.

Marshall, Thomas Humphrey. (1973). 'Citizenship and Social Class.' In *Class, Citizenship and Social Development*. New York: Doubleday, 71–134.

Martiniello, Marco. (1996). 'La question nationale belge à l'épreuve de l'immigration.' In A. Dieckhoff (ed.), *Belgique: La force de la désunion*. Brussels: Complexe, 85–104.

– (1998). 'Culturalisation des différences, différenciation des cultures dans la politique belge.' *Les Cahiers du CERI* 20: 1–41.

McAll, Christopher. (1990). *Class, Ethnicity, and Social Inequality*. Montreal and Kingston: McGill-Queen's University Press.

McAndrew, Marie. (1996). 'Canadian Multiculturalism and Québec Interculturalism: Myths and Realities.' *Zeitschrift für internationale erziehungs- und sozialwissenschaftliche Forschung* 13/2: 265–83.

– (2003). 'Immigration, Pluralism and Education.' In A.-G. Gagnon (ed.), *Quebec: State and Society*. Montreal: Québec/Amérique, 345–68.

McAndrew, Marie, Denise Helly & Caroline Tessier. (2005). 'Pour un débat éclairé sur la politique canadienne du multiculturalisme: Une analyse de la nature des organismes et des projets subventionnés (1983–2002).' *Politique et sociétés* 24/1: 49–71.

McCall, Leslie. (2005). 'The Complexity of Intersectionality.' *Signs: Journal of Women and Culture in Society* 30/3: 1771–1800.

McFarlane, Scott Toguri. (1995). 'The Haunt of Race: Canada's Multiculturalism Act, the Politics of Incorporation and Writing thru Race.' *Fuse* 18/3: 18–31.

McKinnon, Andrew M. (2010). 'Elective Affinities of the Protestant Ethic: Weber and the Chemistry of Capitalism.' *Sociological Theory* 28/1: 108–26.

McLaren, Lauren M. (2004). 'Opposition to European Integration and Fear of Loss of National Identity: Debunking a Basis Assumption Regarding Hostility to the Integration Project.' *European Journal of Political Research* 43: 895–911.

McNeill, Desmond. (2006). 'The Diffusion of Ideas in Development Theory and Policy.' *Global Social Policy* 6/3: 334–54.

McRoberts, Kenneth. (1997). *Misconceiving Canada: The Struggle for National Unity*. Toronto: Oxford University Press.

Meinecke, Friedrich. (1922). *Weltbürgertum und Nationalstaat: Studien zur Genesis des deutschen Nationalstaates*. Munich: R. Oldenburg.

Meisel, John (1999). 'The Making of the Welfare State.' In J. Meisel, G. Rocher & A. Silver (eds.), *As I Recall: Si je me souviens bien. Historical Perspectives*. Montreal: IRPP, 109–113.

Meisel, John, Guy Rocher & Arthur Silver. (1999). *As I Recall. Si je me souviens bien. Historical Perspectives.* Montreal: IRPP.

Michalowski, Ines. (2007). *Integration als Staatsprogramm.* Berlin: LIT Verlag.

Mills, C. Wright. ([1959] 2000). *The Sociological Imagination.* Oxford: Oxford University Press.

Milner, Henry. (2001). 'Civic Literacy in Comparative Context: Why Canadians Should Be Concerned.' *Policy Matters / Enjeux publics* 2/2: 1–42.

Mirchandani, Kiran, & Tastsoglou, Evagelia. (2000). 'Toward a Diversity beyond Tolerance.' *Studies in Political Economy* 61: 49–78.

Modood, Tariq. (2005). *Multicultural Politics: Racism, Ethnicity, and Muslims in Britain.* Minneapolis: University of Minnesota Press.

– (2007). *Multiculturalism: A Civic Idea.* Cambridge: Polity.

Mommsen, Wolfgang J. (1965). 'Diskussion zum Thema "Max Weber und die Machtpolitik."' In O. Stammer (ed.), *Max Weber und die Soziologie heute. Verhandlungen des 15. deutschen Soziologentags.* Tubingen: J.C.B. Mohr, 130–8.

Moodley, Kogila. (1982). 'Canadian Multiculturalism as Ideology.' *Ethnic and Racial Studies* 6/3: 320–31.

Morris, Raymond N. (1984). 'Canada as a Family: Ontario Responses to the Québec Independence Movement.' *Canadian Review of Sociology and Anthropology* 21/2: 181–201.

– (1989). *Behind the Jester's Mask: Canadian Editorial Cartoons about Dominant and Minority Groups 1960–1979.* Toronto: University of Toronto Press.

– (1995). *The Carnivalization of Politics: Quebec Cartoons on Relations with Canada, England and France (1960–1979).* Montreal and Kingston: McGill-Queen's University Press.

Mouffe, Chantal (1992a). 'Democratic Citizenship and the Political Community.' In C. Mouffe (ed.), *Dimensions of Radical Democracy: Pluralism, Citizenship, Community.* London: Verso, 225–39.

– (ed.). (1992b). *Dimensions of Radical Democracy: Pluralism, Citizenship, Community.* London: Verso.

Mouritsen, Per, & Jørgensen, Knud Erik. (eds.). (2008). *Constituting Communities: Political Solutions to Cultural Conflict.* Basingstoke: Palgrave Macmillan.

Nagel, Joane. (1994). 'Constructing Ethnicity: Creating and Recreating Ethnic Identity and Culture.' *Social Problems* 41/1: 152–276.

Netherlands, The (2006). *Wet inburgering in het buitenland.* Den Haag: Staatsblad van het Koninkrijk der Nederlanden, 28, 31 January. Retrieved 22 June 2008 from http://www.eerstekamer.nl/9370000/1/j9vvhwtbnzpbzzc/vgxun70y4d51.

Neu, Dean, & Therrien, Richard. (2003). *Accounting for Genocide: Canada's Bureaucratic Assault on Aboriginal People.* Black Point: Fernwood.

ngo-online. (2006). *Schwer auch für Deutsche: Lehrerverband nennt Einbürgerungs-Fragebogen 'recht anspruchsvoll.'* Retrieved 23 March 2008 from http://www.ngo-online.de/ganze_nachricht.php?Nr=13183.

Nielsen, Kai. (1998). 'Un nationalisme culturel, ni ethnique ne civique.' In M. Sarra-Bournet (ed.), *Le pays de tous les Québécois*. Montreal: Bibliothèque nationale de Québec, 143–59.

Nimni, Ephraim. (1999). 'Nationalist Multiculturalism in Late Imperial Austria as a Critique of Contemporary Liberalism: The Case of Bauer and Renner.' *Journal of Political Ideologies* 4/3: 289–314.

– (2006). 'Constitutional or Agonistic Patriotism? The Dilemmas of Liberal Nation States.' In P. Mouritsen & K.E. Jørgensen (eds.), *Constituting Communities: Political Solutions to Cultural Conflict*. Basingstoke: Palgrave Macmillan, 94–116.

Nisbet, Robert A. (1966). *The Sociological Tradition*. New York: Basic Books.

Nugent, Amy. (2006). 'Demography, National Myths, and Political Origins: Perceiving Official Multiculturalism in Quebec.' *Canadian Ethnic Studies* 38/3: 21–36.

Okin, Susan Moller. (2002). '"Mistresses of Their Own Destiny": Group Rights, Gender and Realistic Rights of Exit.' *Ethics* 112/2: 205–32.

Omidvar, Ratna. (2008). 'Think Global, Vote Local.' *Canadian Diversity / Diversité canadienne* 6/4: 161–3.

Ong, Aihwa. (1996). 'Cultural Citizenship as Subject Making: Immigrants Negotiate Racial and Cultural Boundaries in the United States.' *Current Anthropology* 37/5: 737–62.

Oommen, T.K. (2001). 'Situating Ethnicity Conceptually.' *Ethnicities* 1/1: 13–15.

Ornstein, Michael. (2006). *Ethno-Racial Groups in Toronto, 1971–2001: A Demographic and Socio-Economic Profile*. Toronto: York University, Institute for Social Research.

Ossenberg, Richard. (1964). 'The Social Integration and Adjustment of Post-War Immigrants in Montreal and Toronto.' *Canadian Review of Sociology and Anthropology* 1/4: 202–14.

Palmer, Howard. (1975). 'Mosaic versus Melting Pot? Immigration and Ethnicity in Canada and the United States.' *International Journal* 31/6: 488–528.

Palmowski, Jan. (2008). 'In Search of the German Nation: Citizenship and the Challenge of Integration.' *Citizenship Studies* 12/6: 547–63.

Papastergiadis, Nikos. (1998). 'Ambivalence in Identity: Homi Bhabha and Cultural Theory.' In *Dialogues in the Diasporas: Essays and Conversations on Cultural Identity*. London: River Oram, 10–52.

Paré, Jean-Rodrigue. (1999). *Les visages de l'engagement dans l'oeuvre de Max Weber: La nation, la culture et la science*. Montreal: L'Harmattan.

Parekh, Bhikhu. (1995). 'Cultural Diversity and Liberal Democracy.' In D. Beetham (ed.), *Defining and Measuring Democracy*. London: Sage, 199–212.

– (1997). 'Dilemmas of a Multicultural Theory of Citizenship.' *Constellations* 4/1: 54–62.

– (2000). *Rethinking Multiculturalism: Cultural Diversity and Political Theory*. Cambridge: Harvard University Press.

Park, Robert E. (1950). 'The Nature of Race Relations.' In *Race and Culture*. New York: Free Press of Glencoe, 81–137.

Parsons, Talcott. (1967). *Sociological Theory and Modern Society*. New York: Free Press.

– (1969). 'Full Citizenship for the Negro American?' In *Politics and Social Structure*. New York: Free Press, 252–91.

Pateman, Carole (1988). *The Sexual Contract*. Cambridge: Polity.

Patez, Fabrice. (1998). 'Quelques remarques sur l'imaginaire national.' *Les Cahiers du Ceriem* no. 3: 3–13.

Penninx, Rinus. (1996). 'Immigration, Minorities Policy and Mutliculturalism in Dutch Society since 1960.' In A. Heller, R. Bauböck & A. R. Zolberg (eds.), *The Challenge of Diversity: Integration and Pluralism in Societies of Immigration*. Aldershot: Avebury, 187–206.

Perigoe, Ross, & Lazar, Barry. (1992). 'Visible Minorities and Native Canadians in National Television News Programs.' In M. Grenier (ed.), *Critical Studies of Canadian Mass Media*. Toronto: Butterworths, 260–72.

Pfaff-Czarnecka, Joanna. (2004). 'Diversity, Immigration, and National Identity in Switzerland.' *Canadian Diversity / Diversité canadienne* 3/2: 77–80.

Phillips, Anne. (1993). 'Citizenship and Feminist Theory.' In *Democracy and Difference*. Cambridge: Polity, Blackwell, 75–89.

– (2007). *Multiculturalism without Culture*. Princeton: Princeton University Press.

Piché, Victor. (2003). 'Un siècle d'immigration au Québec: De la peur à l'ouverture.' In V. Piché & C. Le Bourdais (eds.), *La démographie québécoise: Enjeux du XXIe siècle*. Montreal: Presses de l'Université de Montréal, 225–63.

Pietrantonio, Linda. (1999). *La construction sociale de la (dé)légitimation de l'action positive ou l'envers de l'égalité*. Doctoral dissertation, Département de sociologie, Université de Montréal.

– (2000). 'Une dissymétrie sociale: Rapports sociaux majoritaire/minoritaires.' *Bastidiana: Racisme et relations raciales* nos. 29–30: 151–76.

Pogge, Thomas. (2003). 'Accommodation Rights for Hispanics in the United States.' In W. Kymlicka & A. Patten (eds.), *Language Rights and Political Theory*. New York: Oxford University Press, 105–22.

Popper, Karl Raimund. (1950). *The Open Society and Its Enemies*. London: Routledge.

Porter, John. (1965). *The Vertical Mosaic: An Analysis of Social Class and Power in Canada*. Toronto: University of Toronto Press.

Potvin, Maryse. (2000a). 'Les dérapages racistes à l'égard du Québec au Canada anglais depuis 1995.' *Politique et Sociétés* 18/2: 101–32.

– (2000b). 'Some Racist Slips about Québec in English Canada between 1995 and 1998.' *Canadian Ethnic Studies* 32/2: 1–26.

– (2008). *Crise des accommodements raisonnables: Une fiction médiatique*. Montreal: Athenas.

Putnam, Robert D., & Feldstein, Lewis M. (2004). *Better Together: Restoring the American Community*. New York: Simon & Schuster.

Rath, Jan. (2005). 'Against the Current: The Establishment of Islam in the Netherlands.' *Canadian Diversity / Diversité canadienne* 4/3: 31–4.

Rath, Jan, Rinux Penninx, Kees Groenendijk & Astrid Meijer. (1996). *Nederland en zijn Islam: Een ontzuilende Samenleving reaggert op het onstaan van een Geloofsgemeenschap*. Amsterdam: Het Spinhuis Amsterdam.

Räthzel, Nora. (1997). *Gegenbilder: Nationale Identitäten durch Konstruktion des Anderen*. Opladen: Leske & Budrich.

Rawls, John. (1971). *A Theory of Justice*. Boston: Belknap.

Razack, Sherene. (ed.). (2002). *Race, Space and the Law: Unmapping a White Settler Society*. Toronto: Between the Lines.

Reitz, Jeffrey G., & Banerjee, Rupa. (2007). 'Racial Inequality, Social Cohesion and Policy Issues in Canada.' In K.G. Banting, T. J. Courchene & F. L. Seidle (eds.), *Belonging? Diversity, Recognition and Shared Citizenship in Canada*. Montreal: IRPP, 547–59.

Reitz, Jeffrey G., & Breton, Raymond. (1994). *The Illusion of Difference: Realities of Ethnicity in Canada and the United States*. Toronto: C.D. Howe Institute.

Renan, Ernest. (1991). 'Qu'est-ce qu'une nation?' In P. Forest (ed.), *Qu'est-ce qu'une nation? Littérature et identité nationale de 1871–1914. Textes de Barrès, Daudet, R. de Gourmont, Céline*. Paris: P. Bordas, 31–43.

Renaud, Jean. (2001). *Ils sont maintenant d'ici: Les dix premiers années au Québec des immigrants admis en 1989*. Quebec: Les publications du Québec.

Resnick, Philip. (1994). *Thinking English Canada*. Toronto: Stoddart.

Rex, John. (1986). *Race and Ethnicity*. Milton Keynes: Open University Press.

– (1997). 'The Concept of a Multicultural Society.' In M. Guibernau (ed.), *The Ethnicity Reader: Nationalism, Multiculturalism and Migration*. Cambridge: Polity, 205–19.

Riggins, Stephen Harold. (1997). 'The Rhetoric of Othering.' In S.H. Riggins (ed.), *The Language of Politics of Exclusion: Others in Discourse*. London: Sage, 1–30.

Roach, Kent. (2003). *September 11: Consequences for Canada*. Montreal and Kingston: McGill-Queen's University Press.

Robinson, Gertrude Joch. (1998). *Constructing the Quebec Referendum: French and English Media Voices*. Toronto: University of Toronto Press.

Rocher, François. (ed.). (1992). *Bilan québécois du fédéralisme canadien*. Montreal: VLB Éditeur.

Rocher, François, & Verrelli, Nadia. (2003). 'Questioning Constitutional Democracy in Canada: From the Canadian Supreme Court Reference on Quebec Secession to the Clarity Act.' In A.-G. Gagnon, M. Guibernau & F. Rocher (eds.), *The Conditions of Diversity in Multinational Democracies*. Montreal: IRPP, 209–37.

Rocher, Guy. (1971). 'Les ambiguïtés d'un Canada bilingue et multiculturel.' *Revue de l'Association canadienne d'éducation de langue française* 1/3: 21–3.

– (2000). 'Droits fondamentaux, citoyens minoritaires, citoyens majoritaires.' In M. Coutu, P. Bosset, C. Gendreau & D. Villeneuve (eds.), *Droits fondamentaux et citoyenneté: Une citoyenneté fragmentée, limitée, illusoire?* Montreal: Éditions Thémis, 23–42.

Rodal, Berel. (1991). 'Das kanadische Rätsel: Zwei Konzepte nationaler Existenz.' In E. Fröschl, M. Mesner & U. Ra'anan. (eds.), *Staat und Nation in multi-ethnischen Gesellschaften*. Vienna: Passagen-Verlag, 225–48.

Rotte, Ralph. (2002). 'Introduction: What Can German Migration Policy Learn from Other Countries?' In R. Rotte & P. Stein (eds.), *Migration Policy and the Economy: International Experiences*. Neuried: ars et unitas, 9–16.

Royal Commission on Bilingualism and Biculturalism. (1969). *Report of the Royal of Royal Commission on Bilingualism and Biculturalism*. Ottawa: Supply and Services Canada.

Royal Commission on Newspapers. (1981). *Report*. Ottawa: Supply and Services Canada.

Rukszto, Katarzyna. (1997). 'National Encounters: Narrating Canada and the Plurality of Difference.' *International Journal of Canadian Studies / Revue internationale d'études canadiennes* 16: 149–62.

Runnymede Trust: Commission on the Future of Multi-Ethnic Britain (2000). *The Future of Multi-Ethnic Britain. The Parekh Report*. London: Profile Books.

Ryan, Claude. (2000). *Consequences of the Quebec Secession Reference: The Clarity Bill and Beyond*. Toronto: C.D. Howe Institute.

Ryan, Phil. (2010). *Multicultiphobia*. Toronto: University of Toronto Press.

Safran, William. (2008). 'Names, Labels, and Identities: Sociopolitical Contexts and the Question of Ethnic Categorization.' *Nationalism and Ethnic Politics* 15/4: 437–61.

Said, Edward W. (1994a). *Culture and Imperialism*. New York: Vintage.

– (1994b). *Orientalism*. New York: Vintage.

Salomon, Albert. (1935). 'Max Weber's Sociology.' *Social Research* 2: 60–73.

Sandel, Michael. (1982). *Liberalism and the Limits of Justice*. Cambridge: Cambridge University Press.

Schermerhorn, Richard A. (1970). *Comparative Ethnic Relations: A Framework for Theory and Research*. New York: Random House.

Schlesinger, Arthur M. Jr. ([1991] 1998). *The Disuniting of America: Reflections on a Multicultural Society*. New York: W.W. Norton.

Schmidtke, Oliver. (2005). 'Re-mapping Europe: Collective Memory and Identity in an Enlarged European Union.' *Eurostudia* 1/1: 1–10.

Schmitt, Irina, & Winter, Elke. (2009). 'Current Debates on Citizenship and Belonging: Multiculturalism, Gender and Sexuality.' In K.-D. Ertler & H. Lutz (eds.), *Canada in Grainau. Le Canada à Grainau. A Multidisciplinary Survey of Canadian Studies after 30 Years. Tour d'horizon multidisciplinaire d'Études canadiennes, 30 ans après*. Vienna: Peter Lang, 129–53.

Schnapper, Dominique. (1994). *La communauté des citoyens: Sur l'idée moderne de nation*. Paris: Gallimard.

– (1998). 'Beyond the Opposition: Civic Nation versus Ethnic Nation.' In J. Couture, K. Nielsen & M. Seymour (eds.), *Rethinking Nationalism*. Calgary: University of Calgary Press, 219–34.

Schwimmer, Éric. (1995). *Le syndrome des Plaines d'Abraham*. Montreal: Boréal.

Seymour, Michel, Jocelyne Couture & Kai Nielsen (1998). 'Introduction: Questioning the Ethnic/Civic Dichotomy.' In J. Couture, K. Nielsen & M. Seymour (eds.), *Rethinking Nationalism*. Calgary: University of Calgary Press, 1–61.

Shachar, Ayelet. (2001). *Multicultural Jurisdictions: Cultural Differences and Women's Rights*. Cambridge: Cambridge University Press.

Sharma, Nandita. (2006). *Home Economics: Nationalism and the Making of 'Migrant Workers' in Canada*. Toronto: University of Toronto Press.

Siegel, Arthur. (1996). *Politics and the Media in Canada*. 2nd ed. Toronto: McGraw-Hill Ryerson.

Siemiatycki, Myer. (2007). 'Invisible City: Immigrants without Voting Rights in Urban Ontario.' *Our Diverse Cities* 4: 166–8.

Silverman, Max. (1996). 'The Revenge of Civil Society.' In D. Cesarani & M. Fulbrook (eds.), *Citizenship, Nationality and Migration in Europe*. London: Routledge, 146–58.

Simmons, Alan B. (1998). 'Racism and Immigration Policy.' In V. Satzewich (ed.), *The Sociology of Racism in Canada*. Toronto: Thompson, 87–114.

– (2010). *Immigration and Canada: Global and Transnational Perspectives*. Toronto: Canadian Scholars' Press.

Simon, Patrick, & Sala Pala, Valerie. (2009). '"We're Not All Multiculturalists Yet": France Swings between Hard Integration and Soft Anti-discrimination.'

In S. Vertovec & S. Wessendorf (eds.), *The Multiculturalism Backlash: European Discourses, Policies and Practices*. London: Routledge, 92–110.

Simon, Pierre-Jean. (1983). 'Le sociologue et les minorités: Connaissance et idéologie.' *Sociologie et Sociétés* 15/2: 9–21.

– (1997). *Histoire de la sociologie,* vol. 2. Paris: Presses Universitaires de France.

Simpson, Jeffrey (2000). 'My Name Is Joe, and I Am Canadian.' *Globe and Mail,* 20 April, A15.

Singer, Brian. (1996). 'Cultural versus Contractual Nations: Rethinking Their Opposition.' *History and Theory* 35/3: 309–37.

Skea, Warren H. (1993). 'The Canadian Newspaper Industry's Portrayal of the Oka Crisis.' *Native Studies Review* 9/1: 15–27.

Smith, Anthony D. (1986). *The Ethnic Origins of Nations*. Oxford: Blackwell.

Sniderman, Paul M., & Hagendoorn, Louk. (2007). *When Ways of Life Collide: Multiculturalism and Its Discontents in the Netherlands*. Princeton: Princeton University Press.

Soroka, Stuart, Richard Johnston & Keith G. Banting (2007). 'Ties That Bind? Social Cohesion and Diversity in Canada.' In K.G. Banting, T. J. Courchene & F.L. Seidle (eds.), *Belonging? Diversity, Recognition and Shared Citizenship in Canada*. Montreal: IRPP, 561–600.

Spencer, Sarah. (2008). 'Citizenship: The U.K. Experience.' *Canadian Diversity/ Diversité canadienne* 6/4: 125–8.

Stasiulis, Daiva. (1995). '"Deep Diversity": Race and Ethnicity in Canadian Politics.' In M. Whittington & G. Williams (eds.), *Canadian Politics in the 1990s*. Toronto: Nelson, 191–217.

Stasiulis, Daiva, & Jhappan, Radha. (1995). 'The Fractious Politics of a Settler Society: Canada.' In D. Stasiulis & N. Yuval-Davis (eds.), *Unsettling Settler Societies: Articulations of Gender, Race, Ethnicity and Class*. London: Sage, 95–131.

Stasiulis, Daiva, & Yuval-Davis, Nira. (eds.). (1995). *Unsettling Settler Societies: Articulations of Gender, Race, Ethnicity and Class*. London: Sage.

Statistics Canada. (2006). *Canada's Ethnocultural Mosaic: 2006 Census. Findings.* Retrieved 4 July 2007 from http://www12.statcan.ca/english/census06/analysis/ethnicorigin/index.cfm.

Statistisches Bundesamt Deutschland. (2007). *Pressemitteilung Nr.183 vom 04.05.2007*. Retrieved 4 Dec. 2008 from http://www.destatis.de/jetspeed/portal/cms/Sites/destatis/Internet/DE/Presse/pm/2007/05/PD07__183__12521, templateId=renderPrint.psml.

Stein, Janice Gross. (2007). 'Searching for Equality.' In J.G. Stein, D. R. Cameron, W. Kymlicka, J. Meisel, H. Siddiqui & M. Valpy (eds.), *Uneasy Partners:*

Multiculturalism and Rights in Canada. Waterloo: Wilfrid Laurier University Press, 1–22.

Stein, Janice Gross, David Robertson Cameron, Will Kymlicka, John Meisel, Haroon Siddiqui & Michael Valpy. (eds.). (2007). *Uneasy Partners: Multiculturalism and Rights in Canada.* Waterloo: Wilfrid Laurier University Press.

Stevenson, Nick. (1997). 'Globalization, National Cultures and Cultural Citizenship.' *Sociological Quarterly* 38/1: 41–66.

Stoffman, Daniel. (2002). *Who Gets In? What's Wrong with Canada's Immigration Program and How to Fix It.* Toronto: Macfarlane Walter & Ross.

Stojanovic, Nenad. (2006). 'Direct Democracy: A Risk or an Opportunity for Multicultural Societies? The Experience of the Four Swiss Multilingual Cantons.' *International Journal on Multicultural Societies* 8/2: 183–202.

Stolcke, Verena. (1997). 'The "Nature" of Nationality.' In V. Bader (ed.), *Citizenship and Exclusion.* London: Macmillan, 61–80.

Stratton, Jon, & Ang, Ien. (1998). 'Multicultural Imagined Communities: Cultural Difference and National Identity in the USA and Australia.' In D. Beetham (ed.), *Multicultural States: Rethinking Difference and Identity.* London: Routledge, 135–62.

Supreme Court of Canada (1998). *Reference re Secession of Québec,* 1998rcs2-217. 20 August. Retrieved 5 May 2001 from http://csc.lexum.umontreal.ca/en/1998/1998scr2-217/1998scr2-217.pdf.

Tamir, Yael. (1999). 'Siding with the Underdogs.' In J. Cohen, M. Howard & M. C. Nussbaum (eds.), *Is Multiculturalism Bad for Women? Susan Moller Okin with Respondents.* Princeton: Princeton University Press, 47–52.

Taylor, Charles. (1993). *Reconciling the Solitudes: Essays on Canadian Federalism and Nationalism.* Montreal and Kingston: McGill-Queen's University Press.

– (1994). 'The Politics of Recognition.' In A. Gutmann (ed.), *Multiculturalism and the "Politics of Recognition."* Princeton: Princeton University Press, 25–73.

– (1995). 'Democratic Exclusion (and Its Remedies?)' In R. Bhargava, A. K. Bagchi & R. Sudarshan (eds.), *Multiculturalism, Liberalism and Democracy.* Oxford: Oxford University Press, 138–63.

– (2001). 'The Immanent Counter-Enlightenment.' In R. Beiner & W. Norman (eds.), *Canadian Political Philosophy: Contemporary Reflections.* Oxford: Oxford University Press, 386–400.

Teo, Peter. (2000). 'Racism in the News: A Critical Discourse Analysis of News Reporting in Two Australian Newspapers.' *Discourse & Society* 11/1: 7–49.

Thapar, Romila. (1980). 'Durkheim and Weber on Theories of Society and Race Relating to Pre-colonial India.' *UNESCO Sociological Theories: Race and Colonialism.* Poole: Sydenhams Printers, 93–116.

Thobani, Sunera. (2007). *Exalted Subjects: Studies in the Making of Race and Nation in Canada.* Toronto: University of Toronto Press.

Tönnies, Ferdinand. ([1887] 1991). *Gemeinschaft und Gesellschaft: Grundbegriffe der reinen Soziologie.* (1935) 8th ed. Darmstadt: Wissenschaftliche Buchgesellschaft.

Toronto Star. (1999). 'We'll Continue to Speak for the Powerless.' Insight/News, 2 Jan.

– (2001). 'Newspapers Called Key to "Civic Literacy."' News, 27 July, A08.

Toronto Star Online. (2004). 'Media Kit 2004.' Retrieved 15 Aug. 2004 from http://www.thestar.com/NASApp/cs/ContentServer?pagename=tsmediakit/Render&c=Page&cid=1078234009627; 5 Jan. 2005 from http://www.thestar.com/NASApp/cs/ContentServer?pagename=tsmediakit/Render&c=Page&cid=1078234009627.

Trent, John E., Robert Young & Guy Lachapelle (eds.). (1996). *Québec-Canada: What Is the Path Ahead? / Québec-Canada: Nouveaux sentiers vers l'avenir?* Ottawa: University of Ottawa Press.

Troper, Harold. (2003). 'Becoming an Immigrant City: A History of Immigration into Toronto since the Second World War.' In P. Anisef & M.C. Lanphier (eds.), *The World in a City.* Toronto: University of Toronto Press, 19–62.

Tully, James. (2000). 'The Unattained Yet Attainable Democracy: Canada and Quebec Face the New Century.' Paper presented at Les Grandes Conférence Desjardins, Montreal, 23 March. Retrieved 4 Feb. 2009 http://francais.mcgill.ca/qcst/publications/desjardins/.

Turner, Bryan S. (1990). 'Outline of a Theory of Citizenship.' *Sociology* 24/2: 189–217.

Turp, Daniel. (2000). *La nation bâillonnée: Le plan B ou l'offensive d'Ottawa contre le Québec.* Montreal: VLB Éditeur.

– (2001). *Le droit de choisir: Essais sur le droit du Québec à disposer de lui-même – The Right to Choose. Essays on Quebec's Right of Self-Determination.* Montreal: Les Éditions Thémis.

Tyrell, Hartmann. (1994). 'Max Webers Soziologie – eine Soziologie ohne "Gesellschaft."' In G. Wagner & H. Zipprian (eds.), *Max Webers Wissenschaftslehre: Interpretation und Kritik.* Frankfurt: Suhrkamp, 390–414.

Van den Berghe, Pierre L. (1967). 'Pluralisme social et culturel.' *Cahiers internationaux de sociologie* 43: 67–78.

van Dijk, Teun A. (1991). *Racism and the Press.* London: Routledge.

– (1998). 'Opinions and Ideologies in the Press.' In A. Bell & P. Garret (eds.), *Approaches to Media Discourse.* Oxford: Blackwell, 21–63.

Van Oers, Ricky. (2008). 'From Liberal to Restrictive Citizenship Policies: The Case of the Netherlands.' *International Journal on Multicultural Societies* 10/1: 40–59.

Vertovec, Steven. (2007). 'Super-Diversity and Its Implications.' *Ethnic and Racial Studies* 30/6: 1024–54.

Vertovec, Steven & Wessendorf, Susanne (eds.) (2009). *The Multiculturalism Backlash: European Discourses, Policies and Practices.* London, New York: Routledge.

Voegelin, Erich. (1933). *Rasse und Staat.* Tubingen: J.C.B. Mohr.

Walker, Brian. (1997). 'Plural Cultures, Contested Territories: A Critique of Kymlicka.' *Canadian Journal of Political Science* 30/2: 211–34.

Walzer, Michael. (1995). 'The Civil Society Argument.' In R. Beiner (ed.), *Theorizing Citizenship.* Albany: State University of New York Press: 153–74.

Ward, Colleen, & Masgoreth, Anne-Marie. (2008). 'Attitudes toward Immigrants, Immigration and Multiculturalism in New Zealand: A Social-Psychological Analysis.' *International Migration Review* 42/1: 227–48.

Ward, John. (2004). 'War on Terrorism: Washington Feels Canada Gets Free Ride on Defence: Former Top U.S. Adviser.' *CNEWS – World*, 26 April. Retrieved 4 March 2005 through Factiva newspaper index.

Waters, Mary C. (1990). *Ethnic Options: Choosing Identities in America.* Berkeley: University of California Press.

Wayland, Sarah Virginia. (1995). *Immigrants into Citizens: Political Mobilization in France and Canada.* Doctoral dissertation, Department of Government and Politics, University of Maryland. Rertrieved 5 March 2006 http://ceris. metropolis.net/Virtual%20Library/other/wayland1/wayland1j.html.

Weaver, S. (1981). *Making Canadian Indian Policy: The Hidden Agenda 1968–1970.* Toronto: University of Toronto Press.

Webber, Jeremy. (1999). 'Just How Civic Is Civic Nationalism in Québec?' In A.C. Cairns, J. C. Courtney, P. MacKinnon, H. J. Michelmann & D. E. Smith (eds.), *Citizenship, Diversity, and Pluralism: Canadian and Comparative Perspectives.* Montreal and Kingston: McGill-Queen's University Press, 87–107.

Weber, Max. ([1912] 1946). 'Max Weber's Comment on a Paper by Karl Barth.' In H.H. Gerth & C.W. Mills (eds.), *From Max Weber: Essays in Sociology.* New York: Oxford University Press, 176–9.

– ([1910] 1969a). 'Redebeitrag.' In S. Deutsche Gesellschaft für (ed.), *Verhandlungen des Ersten Deutschen Soziologentages vom 19.–22. Oktober 1910 in Frankfurt a.M. Reden und Vorträge von Georg Simmel, Ferdinand Tönnies, Max Weber, Werner Sombart, Alfred Ploetz, Ernst Troeltsch, Eberhard Gothein,*

Andreas Voigt, Hermann Kantorowicz und Debatten. Frankfurt: Verlag Sauer & Auvermann, 151–65.

– ([1912] 1969b). 'Webers Kommentar zu Paul Barths "Die Nationalität in ihrer soziologischen Bedeutung."' *Schriften der Deutschen Gesellschaft für Soziologie. Verhandlungen des Zweiten Deutschen Soziologentages.* Frankfurt: Verlag Sauer & Auvermann, 49–52.

– ([1909–1913 + 1918–1920] 1978). *Economy and Society: An Outline of Interpretative Sociology.* Berkeley: University of California Press.

– ([1909–1913 + 1918–1920] 1980). *Wirtschaft und Gesellschaft.* Tubingen: J.C.B. Mohr.

– ([1914–1918] 1988a). 'Bismarcks Außenpolitik und die Gegenwart.' In J. Winckelmann (ed.), *Max Weber: Gesammelte politische Schriften.* Tubingen: J.C.B. Mohr, 112–29.

– ([1904] 1988b). 'Die "Objektivität" sozialwissenschaftlicher Erkenntnis.' In J. Winckelmann (ed.), *Max Weber: Gesammelte Aufsätze zur Wissenschaftslehre.* Tubingen: J.C.B. Mohr, 146–214.

– ([1905–1906] 1994). 'On the Situation of Constitutional Democracy in Russia.' In P. Lassman & R. Speirs (eds.), *Political Writings.* Cambridge: Cambridge University Press, 29–79.

Weinstock, Daniel (2000). 'La citoyenneté en mutation.' In Y. Boisvert, J. Hamel & M. Molgat (eds.), *Vivre la citoyenneté. Identité, appartenance et participation.* Montreal: Liber, 15–26.

Werbner, Pnina, & Yuval-Davis, Nira. (1999). 'Introduction: Women and the New Discourse of Citizenship.' In P. Werbner & N. Yuval-Davis (eds.), *Women, Citizenship and Difference.* London: Zed Books, 1–38.

Westin, Charles. (2008). 'European Integration: A Matter of Acknowledging Identities.' *IMISCOE Policy Brief* 14: 6.

Wherrett, Jill. (1996). *Aboriginal Peoples and the 1995 Quebec Referendum: A Survey of the Issues.* Ottawa: Library of Parliament, Background Paper BP–412E. Retrieved 6 March 2005 from http://www.parl.gc.ca/information/library/PRBpubs/bp412-e.htm.

Wieviorka, Michel. (2001). *La différence.* Paris: Éditions Balland.

Wimmer, Andreas. (2002). *Nationalist Exclusion and Ethnic Conflict: Shadows of Modernity.* Cambridge: Cambridge University Press.

– (2008). 'Elementary Strategies of Ethnic Boundary Making.' *Ethnic and Racial Studies* 31/6: 1025–55.

Wimmer, Andreas, & Glick Schiller, Nina. (2002). 'Methodological Nationalism and Beyond: Nation-State Building, Migration and the Social Sciences.' *Global Networks* 2/4: 301–34.

Winnipeg Free Press. (2006). 'Qui sont les Québécois?' Editorial, 30 Nov., A11.

Winter, Elke (2001). 'Multiculturalism versus National Unity? Rethinking the Logic of Inclusion in Germany and Canada.' *International Journal of Canadian Studies/Revue internationale d'études canadiennes* 24: 169–93.

– (2002). *Academic Research and Public Policy Impact: The Programme and Policy Relevance of CERIS Products. Final Research Report.* Toronto: Centre of Excellence for Research on Immigration and Settlement.

– (2004). *Max Weber et les relations ethniques: Du refus du biologisme racial à l'État multinational.* Quebec: Presses de l'Université Laval.

– (2007a). 'Bridging Unequal Relations, Ethnic Diversity, and the Dream of Unified Nationhood: Multiculturalism in Canada.' *Zeitschrift für Kanada-Studien* 27/1: 38–57.

– (2007b). 'De Québécois – een "natie binnen een verenigd Canada."' *Cimedart* 37/2: 35–7.

– (2009). 'Quebecs Rolle in der kanadischen Multikulturalismus-Diskussion: Vorgänger, Gegenspieler oder Gegenbild?' In U. Reutner (ed.), *400 Jahre Quebec: Zwischen Konfrontation und Kooperation.* Heidelberg: Universitätsverlag Winter, 91–108.

– (2010). 'Trajectories of Multiculturalism in Germany, the Netherlands, and Canada: In Search of Common Patterns.' *Government and Opposition* 45/2: 166–86.

– (in press). 'Territory, Descent, and Common Values: Redefining National Citizenship in Canada.' In D. Kiwan (ed.), *Naturalization Policies, Education and Citizenship: Multicultural and Multi-nation Societies in International Perspective.* London, New York: Palgrave Macmillan.

Wirth, Louis. (1945). 'The Problem of Minority Groups.' In R. Linton (ed.), *The Science of Man in the World Crisis.* New York: Columbia University Press, 347–72.

Wodak, Ruth, Rudolf de Cillia, Martin Reisigl, Karin Liebhart, Klaus Hofstätter & Maria Kargl. (1998). *Zu diskursiven Konstruktion nationaler Identität.* Frankfurt: Suhrkamp.

Wodak, Ruth, Rudolf de Cillia, Martin Reisigl & Karin Liebhart (1999). *The Discursive Construction of National Identity.* Edinburgh: Edinburgh University Press.

Woehrling, Jean-Marie. (2000). 'Le concept de citoyenneté à la lumière d'une comparaison franco-allemande.' In M. Coutu, P. Bosset, C. Gendreau & D. Villeneuve (eds.), *Droits fondamentaux et citoyenneté: Une citoyenneté fragmentée, limitée, illusoire?* Montreal: Éditions Thémis, 111–40.

Wood, Patricia K. (2003). 'Aboriginal/Indigenous Citizenship: An Introduction.' *Citizenship Studies* 7/4: 371–8.

Wotherspoon, Terry, & Satzewich, Vic. (eds.). (1993). *First Nations: Race, Class and Gender Relations*. Toronto: Nelson.

Wright, Sue. (2008). 'Citizenship Tests in Europe – Editorial Introduction.' *International Journal on Multicultural Societies* 10/1: 1–9.

Young, Iris Marion. (1989). 'Polity and Group Difference: A Critique of the Ideal of Universal Citizenship.' *Ethics* 99: 250–74.

– (1997). 'Unruly Categories: A Critique of Nancy Frazer's Dual Systems Theory.' *New Left Review* I/222: 147–60.

– (2000). *Inclusion and Democracy*. Oxford: Oxford University Press.

Yuval-Davis, Nira. (1993). 'Gender and Nation.' *Ethnic and Racial Studies* 16/4: 521–632.

Zolberg, Astride R., & Woon, Long Litt. (1999). 'Why Islam Is Like Spanish.' *Politics and Society* 27/1: 5–38.

Index

222, 245. *See also* multicultural we; pluralism model

trinationalism, 7, 101, 146–7, 157–8, 224. *See also* Aboriginal nationalism; multinationalism

Tully, James, 50, 208

United Kingdom, 34, 51, 122, 181, 223, 225, 237–8, 246–7, 249

United States, 25; diversity and diversity management in, 5–6, 9, 19, 33–4, 37, 43, 82, 86, 99, 101, 106, 117–18, 120, 122–3, 125–6, 127–8, 133, 136–9, 144, 155, 181, 204, 217, 223, 229–30, 232, 234, 237–8, 242, 244; imputed national identity, 7, 10, 19, 75, 76, 82, 98–100, 116, 118–26, 122–3, 127–9, 133–6, 138, 144, 172, 174–5, 178, 181, 220, 237, 242, 244

van Dijk, Teun A., 107, 166

Vergemeinschaftung, 58, 59, 60, 67–8, 74, 234. See also *Gemeischaft/Gesellschaft*

Vergesellschaftung. See *Vergemeinschaftung*

vertical mosaic. *See* mosaic

Vertovec, Steven, 31, 215, 227

visible minorities. *See* minorities

Voegelin, Erich, 106

Weber, Max, 9, 33, 54, 56–71, 74–5, 80–1, 197, 199–200, 234–6, 243, 245, 248–9

Wieviorka, Michel, 241

Wimmer, Andreas, 3, 56, 78, 83–4, 128, 134–5, 156, 197

Wirth, Louis, 34–5, 62, 199

Wodak, Ruth, 71, 77, 104